LAW CRAM

ESTATE & GIFT

CASENOTES PUBLISHING COMPANY, INC.

MW00967471

GIFT TAX

SCOPE OF TAX

1. Reaches any inter vivos transfer of money or property by individual (may be through a legal entity) that depletes the **gross estate**. Reaches only transfers whose aim is to increase the wealth of others (gratuitous transfers). Reg. § 2501(a)(1)

2. Not necessary to identify donees. Reaches only transfers whose aim is to increase the wealth of others (gratuitous transfers). **Smith v. Shaughnessy**

3. Gift is valued at time made; **if incomplete or open**, when completed or closed.

4. Commercial transactions, even bad bargains, are not gifts for gift tax purposes; neither are personal consumption, political contributions, support payments, or transfers pursuant to divorce.

5. Performance of services without compensation is not a gift for gift tax purposes, even though the refusal to accept compensation increases the wealth of another by relieving that person of a potential cost. It is not enough to create wealth in another; the donor must part with wealth. **Commissioner v. Hogle**

6. Taxes, fines, assessments and similar legal obligations are generally not treated as gifts. However, generation-skipping tax paid on a direct-skip transfer is treated as an addition to the gift for gift tax purposes.

7. A transfer is not a gift if made for full consideration in money or money's worth. If partial consideration is received, amount of gift is value of property transferred less value of consideration. Reg. § 2512(b)

8. Transfer to spouse in exchange for release of marital rights is not a transfer for consideration; considered an accelerated estate transfer. **Merrill v. Fahs**

9. Amounts paid directly, on behalf of another for tuition or medical care, are exempt from the gift tax. The exclusion is lost if the donee is compensated by insurance. Reg. § 2503(e)

10. If one spouse pays the other's income tax or gift tax, there is no gift.

11. Gift tax = (tentative tax on full fair market value)/(1+ tax rate)

12. Loan for consideration (such as promise to repay with interest) is a transfer to consideration if the promise to repay is bona fide.

13. Certain special rules apply to loans at interest below the prevailing rate. Reg. § 7872

14. Rent-free use of property, such as loaning jewelry, could be considered gift, but IRS generally does not enforce gift tax on such loans; loans of artwork to charities are specifically exempted. Reg. § 2503(g)

15. Jurisdiction: applies to any citizen of the United States, and to nonresident aliens making gifts of property located in the United States; jurisdiction may also be affected by treaty.

See Casenote Estate & Gift Tax Outline Chapter 2 § II

DEFINING A TRANSFER
Act or Omission that Depletes Estate and Augments Estate of Another

1. General power of appointment
2. Constructive transfer

See Casenote Estate & Gift Tax Outline Chapter 2 § IV

1. GENERAL POWER OF APPOINTMENT § 2041(b)

1. Power that enables the donee to appropriate money or property to himself or his creditors.

2. Exercise, lapse or release of a general power in favor of another is deemed a transfer. In case of lapse, transfer is exempt from tax to extent of $5,000 or 5% of property transferred, whichever is greater.

3. Where the power cannot be exercised in favor of the donee or his creditors, it is a special power of appointment, and the exercise, release or lapse of the power is not a transfer, unless donee also has a beneficial interest in the property transferred.

See Casenote Estate & Gift Tax Outline Chapter 2 § IV

COMPLETED GIFTS

1. Power is retained by transferor to revoke (take back property), alter (distribute to another) or amend (identify different beneficiaries) the gift causes it to be incomplete and not presently subject to gift tax. The power to revoke, alter or amend is deemed not retained if held jointly with a party whose interest in the transferred property would be adversely affected by exercise of the power.
   Example: Daniel creates a trust, Casenotes™ Bank as trustee, income to Emily for life, remainder to Chenin. Daniel and Emily have a joint power to revoke. Since Emily's interest would be adversely affected by any exercise of the power to revoke, and Daniel cannot exercise the joint power without the consent of Emily, the transfer is complete.

2. Trustees are presumed to be independent and adhere to their fiduciary duties; therefore, a grantor is not considered to have retained a power simply because the trustee is a friend or relative.

3. A retained power that only affects the time or manner of enjoyment, or is administrative in nature, does not render a transfer incomplete.

4. When property subject to a retained power ceases to be subject to the power, the gift is complete. If the power expires at death, it is not a gift, but property is included in the estate for estate tax purposes.

5. **When a gift is delayed, e.g. due to uncertainty over subject matter or value, where uncertainty cannot be resolved by resort to actuarial tables, gift is considered "open" and not complete. The validity of the "open gift doctrine" given recent contradictory ruling is not clear.**

6. A binding promise to make a future gift, such as a prenuptial agreement, is a gift at time of promise.

See Casenote Estate & Gift Tax Outline Chapter 2 § V

2. CONSTRUCTIVE TRANSFER

1. Where beneficiary of life insurance policy names another to receive the proceeds, a gift occurs.

2. Disclaimer of a gift, with result that it passes to another, may be treated as acceptance by the refuser and gift by refuser to the ultimate taker; some disclaimers, called qualified disclaimers, are not gifts.
   Example: Neil bequeaths Blackacre to Tim. Tim disclaims the devise under state law, and Blackacre passes to Tim's kids under the applicable "lapse" rule. If the disclaimer is made in a writing delivered within nine months of the later to occur of the creation of the interest or Tim's 21st birthday, Tim has not accepted the property or any of its benefits, and the property passes to his kids (or any other person, except Tim's spouse) without direction on Tim's part as a result of Tim's refusal; Tim will not be deemed to have made a gift, but rather his kids will have taken directly from Tim.

See Casenote Estate & Gift Tax Outline Chapter 2 § IV

THE ANNUAL EXCLUSION

1. A donor may reduce the amount of any net gifts of present interests by $10,000 per donee per year. This exclusion is indexed for inflation after 1998. The exclusion cannot be carried over to other donees or other years.

2. To qualify as a present interest, the interest must commence in possession or enjoyment immediately; the donee must be identifiable; and the value must be presently ascertainable using actuarial methods.
   Example: Nancy creates a trust of $10,000, income to Cathy for life, remainder to Diane. The income interest, valued by actuarial methods at $8,176, is a present-interest gift and is fully excluded; the remainder, valued at $1,824, is a nonexcludable gift of a future interest.

3. A trust transfer that would not otherwise qualify for the exclusion, as not a present interest, may qualify if the beneficiary is given the right to withdraw amounts shortly after the transfer. This is called a Crummey power, and is not valid if illusory, even if not expected to be exercised.

4. The exclusion is best used by transferring wealth by the maximum number of donors to the maximum number of donees over the maximum number of years. A husband or wife, in making a gift of community property, may split the gift with his or her spouse; likewise, a gift to a husband and wife as co-owners is a gift to two donees.

5. A gift to a minor subject to a guardianship, or a custodial gift, qualifies for the annual exclusion if certain conditions are met.

CONTINUED ON NEXT PAGE.

See Outline Ch 2 § VIII

THE GENERATION-SKIPPING TAX

GENERATION-SKIPPING TRANSFERS

1. Transferor is person who most recently transferred property subject to estate or gift tax where such transfer did, will, or might skip a generation. **Spouse where QTIP election is made is deemed transferor of QTIP trust**, but first transferor spouse may make "reverse QTIP election" and be treated as transferor. Spouses are deemed to be in the same generation. Reg. § 2652

2. Where transferor's child is dead, subsequent gift to or trust creation benefitting grandchild is not generation-skipping transfer (such death "moves descendants up" a generation).

3. Partial taxable termination may occur where, upon the terminating event, part of the property passes to skip persons.
   Example: Gary creates a trust for his mother for life, remainder to Gary's then living issue per stirpes, and upon death of his mother Gary is survived by a child (a nonskip person) and three children of a deceased child (skip persons).

4. Direct-skip transfer rules, such as who is to pay the tax, take priority over taxable terminations, which take priority over taxable distribution rules.

5. Certain transfers are excluded, e.g., tuition and medical care, direct-skip transfers exempt from gift tax, and taxable terminations and distributions subject to estate or gift tax.

See Casenote Estate & Gift Tax Outline Chapter 5 § II

THE GENERATION-SKIPPING TAX

Originally enacted in 1976 to impose tax on otherwise nontaxable interests and special powers held by a beneficiary in a lower generation than the settlor (e.g., income interests for life), if the succeeding interest is held by a beneficiary in a still lower generation. Current GST, enacted in 1986, does not tax expiration of special powers of appointment; does tax out-right gifts that skip a generation; tax is 55% of generation-skipping transfer to the extent that the transfer exceeds the $1 million exemption for each transferor.

1. Applies to transfers by will or under revocable trust where decedent or grantor died after 12/31/86, subject to exceptions; and to other inter vivos transfers made after 9/25/85; includes both express trusts and "trust equivalents."

2. Direct-skip transfer: transfer subject to gift or estate tax (whether or not one is due) where all transferees (called "skip persons") are at least 2 generations below transferor.

3. Taxable distributions and terminations: apply GST to trust distributions and terminations (occurring upon the death of the last beneficiary one generation below the transferor) where succeeding beneficiaries are more than one generation below transferor, when previously (not presently) subject to gift or estate tax.

4. A taxable termination occurs upon the termination of any interest in a trust, unless:
   a. Any non-skip person has an interest in the trust immediately after the termination; and
   b. After such termination distribution cannot be made to skip persons.

See Casenote Estate & Gift Tax Outline Chapter 5 § I

TAX BASE AND RATE

1. Tax base is amount of money or property included in the generation-skipping transfer.

2. GST is applied after gift and estate tax, so does not affect gift and estate tax base.

3. Estate or trust is liable for GST; charged to property constituting the generation-skipping transfer unless otherwise provided by governing instrument.

4. In direct-skip estate transfers, equal to (estate transfer (after estate taxes) x GST rate)/(1+ GST rate).

5. Because gift tax base does not include gift tax, transfer by gift tax cheaper than by estate; direct-skip transfer cheaper than by taxable termination or distribution.

6. Administrative expenses are deducted from the base.

7. Tax rate, once determined, stays with the property; thus, if trust property is within $1 million exemption, tax rate is zero, and remains zero, even if trust property thereafter increases to more than $1 million.

8. Special rules apply to charitable trusts.

9. There is a credit, not to exceed 5% of the federal GST, for any simultaneous state GST on the same transfer.

See Casenote Estate & Gift Tax Outline Chapter 5 § III

CHARITABLE DEDUCTION

IN GENERAL

1. Certain gifts to charities are fully deductible for gift tax purposes. The deduction is limited to the includable amount.
   Example: Simon and Sue create a trust with community property, income to Sue for life, remainder to charity, then upon Sue's death, half of the trust is included in Sue's estate and passes to charity. That half qualifies for the estate tax charitable deduction.

2. The deduction cannot exceed the amount of the gift. The kinds of tax-exempt donees that can receive charitable gifts are defined by statute.

3. A charitable gift of a partial interest will be wholly disallowed if the partial interest cannot be accurately valued under statutory rules.

4. A trust with a remainder interest to a charity qualifies for the deduction only if the noncharitable interest takes the form of an annuity (right to receive fixed dollar amount each year) or a unitrust (right to receive fixed percentage of the corpus annually). An income interest disqualifies the remainder.

5. If the lead interest is an annuity or unitrust for the benefit of a charity, remainder to noncharitable persons, the lead interest qualifies.

6. Estate tax charitable deduction rules are essentially the same as for gift tax marital deduction; also, after 8/97, must be more than 10% of amount transferred to qualify; and after 6/97, may not exceed more than 50% of trust value annually.

7. Contingent bequests to charities are disallowed unless likelihood of contingency is negligible.

See Casenote Estate & Gift Tax Outline Chapter 2 § IX

MARITAL DEDUCTION

IN GENERAL REG. § 2523

1. **A gift to a present spouse is deductible up to the net amount of the gift, if it is an interest that might fail on the occurrence of some event or condition; such an interest is called a terminable interest.** Reg. § 2523(a)

2. If the gift is a terminable interest that may pass to a third party pursuant to another interest created by the donor in the same property or to a retained power, or may revert to the donor, it is generally not deductible. Reg. § 2523(b)
   Example: Jenny creates a trust, income to Chloe for life, remainder to Jacky. The transfer of the income interest does not qualify for the deduction because upon its termination, the property passes to a third party under the instrument of transfer.

3. A transfer to a spouse of an income interest for life and a sole general power of appointment over trust property is deductible to the full extent of the property so appointed. Reg. § 2523(e)

4. **A qualified terminal interest property (QTIP) transfer, subjecting the donee spouse to estate or gift tax as to the property, is deductible as if fully transferred to the donee spouse**, although the donor may retain a reversion or income interest after the donee spouse's death. The transfer of an income interest in a QTIP trust by the donee spouse has complex tax consequences. Reg. § 2523(f)

5. A creation of a tenancy by the entireties by one spouse with the other spouse qualifies for the deduction even though it would not qualify under the terminable interest rule.

6. Estate tax marital deduction virtually identical to **gift tax rules**. Reduced if decedent imposes obligation on surviving spouse to transfer property to 3rd party. To qualify, property must actually pass to surviving spouse.

7. A terminable interest is nondeductible where if a condition precedent or subsequent occurs, the property would pass to a third party. Qualification is determined at date of death; if the interest may fail, there is no marital deduction, except for provision conditioning transfer on spouse surviving decedent by six months or less.

8. Under probate law, surviving spouse has rights in homestead, exempt property, and widow's allowance; may qualify for marital deduction.

9. Power of appointment to surviving spouse is deductible to extent of property subject to appointment. Disqualified if any other person can appoint the property.

10. Transfers otherwise not deductible may be so under **a QTIP election**.

11. Both power-of-appointment and QTIP terminable interest transfers require that surviving spouse have right to income, or sole possession and enjoyment, for life; full net value of qualifying transfer, not of income actually received, is deductible.

See Casenote Estate & Gift Tax Outline Chapter 2 § X

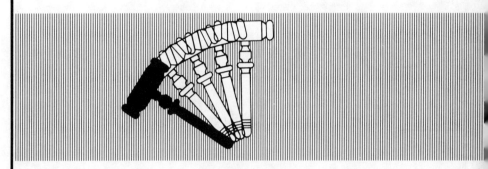

LAW OUTLINES

ESTATE AND GIFT TAX

INCLUDING THE FEDERAL GENERATION-SKIPPING TAX

Joseph M. Dodge
William H. Francis Professor of Law
The University of Texas at Austin

author: *Transfers with Retained Interests and Power*
Casenote Law Outline: Federal Income Taxation
The Logic of Tax
Wills, Trusts, and Estate Planning: Law and Taxation
Federal Income Taxation: Principles, Policy, Planning
Federal Taxation of Estates, Trusts, and Gifts

NORMAN S. GOLDENBERG
Senior Editor
PETER TENEN
Managing Editor

CASENOTES PUBLISHING CO., INC.
1640 Fifth Street, Suite 208
Santa Monica, CA 90401
(310) 395-6500

First Printing, 2000.

ISBN 0-87457-188-X

With the introduction of *Casenote Law Outlines,* Casenotes Publishing Company brings a new approach to the legal study outline. Of course, we have sought out only nationally recognized authorities in their respective fields to author the outlines. Most of the authors are editors of widely used casebooks. All have published extensively in respected legal journals, and some have written treatises cited by courts across the nation in opinions deciding important legal issues on which the authors have recommended what the "last word" on those issues should be.

What is truly novel about the *Casenote Law Outlines* concept is that each outline does not fit into a cookie-cutter mold. While each author has been given a carefully developed format as a framework for the outline, the format is purposefully flexible. The student will therefore find that all outlines are not alike. Instead, each professor has used an approach appropriate to the subject matter. An outline on Evidence cannot be written in the same manner as one on Constitutional Law or Contracts or Torts, etc. Accordingly, the student will find similar features in each *Casenote Law Outline,* but they may be handled in radically different ways by each author. We believe that in this way the law student will be rewarded with the most effective study aid possible. And because we are strongly committed to keeping our publications up to date, *Casenote Law Outlines* are the most current study aids on the market.

For added studying convenience, the *Casenote Law Outlines* series and the *Casenote Legal Briefs* are being coordinated. Many titles in the *Casenote Legal Briefs* series have already been cross-referenced to the appropriate title in the *Casenote Law Outlines* series, and more cross-referenced titles are being released on a regular basis. A tag at the end of most briefs will quickly direct the student to the section in the appropriate *Casenote Law Outline* where further discussion of the rule of law in question can be found.

We continually seek law student and law professor feedback regarding the effectiveness of our publications. As you use *Casenote Law Outlines,* please do not hesitate to write or call us if you have constructive criticism or simply would like to tell us you are pleased with the approach and design of the publication.

Best of luck in your studies.

CASENOTES PUBLISHING CO., INC.

CASENOTE LAW OUTLINES — SUPPLEMENT REQUEST FORM

Casenotes Publishing Co., Inc. prides itself on producing the most current legal study outlines available. Sometimes between major revisions, the authors of the outline series will issue supplements to update their respective outlines to reflect any recent changes in the law. Certain areas of the law change more quickly than others, and thus some outlines may be supplemented, while others may not be supplemented at all.

In order to determine whether or not you should send this supplement request form to us, first check the printing date that appears by the subject name below. If this outline is less than one year old, it is highly unlikely that there will be a supplement for it. If it is older, you may wish to write, telephone, or fax us for current information. You might also check to see whether a supplement has been included with your *Casenote Law Outline* or has been provided to your bookstore. If it is necessary to order the supplement directly from us, it will be supplied without charge, but we do insist that you send a stamped, self-addressed return envelope. If you request a supplement for an outline that does not have one, you will receive the latest *Casenotes* catalogue.

If you wish to request a supplement for this outline:

#5800, ESTATE AND GIFT TAX, FIRST EDITION   2000 (1ST PRINTING), BY Dodge

please follow the instructions below.

• **TO OBTAIN YOUR COMPLIMENTARY SUPPLEMENT(S),** *YOU MUST FOLLOW THESE INSTRUCTIONS PRECISELY IN ORDER FOR YOUR REQUEST TO BE ACKNOWLEDGED.*

1. **REMOVE AND SEND THIS ENTIRE REQUEST FORM:** You *must* send this *original* page, which acts as your proof of purchase and provides the information regarding which supplements, if any, you need. The request form is only valid for any supplement for the outline in which it appears. *No photocopied or written requests will be honored.*

2. **SEND A STAMPED, SELF-ADDRESSED, FULL-SIZE (9" x 12") ENVELOPE:** *Affix enough postage to cover at least 3 oz.* We regret that we absolutely cannot fill and/or acknowledge requests unaccompanied by a stamped, self-addressed envelope.

3. **MULTIPLE SUPPLEMENT REQUESTS:** If you are sending supplement requests for two or more different *Casenote Law Outlines,* we suggest you send a return envelope for each subject requested. If you send only one envelope, your order may not be filled immediately should any supplement you requested still be in production. In that case, your order will not be filled until it can be filled completely, *i.e.,* until all supplements you have requested are published.

4. **PLEASE GIVE US THE FOLLOWING INFORMATION:**

Name: _____ Telephone: (_____)_____-_____

Address: _____ Apt.: _____

City: _____ State: _____ Zip: _____

Name of law school you attend: _____

Name and location of bookstore where you purchased this *Casenote Law Outline:* _____

_____

Any comments regarding *Casenote Law Outlines?* _____

_____

CASENOTES PUBLISHING CO., INC., 1640 Fifth Street, Suite 208, Santa Monica, CA 90401
TELEPHONE (310) 395-6500 • FAX (310) 458-2020

LAW
OUTLINES

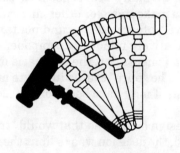

ESTATE AND
GIFT TAX

INCLUDING THE FEDERAL GENERATION-SKIPPING TAX

INTRODUCTION

The purpose of this outline is to present the rules pertaining to the federal estate, gift, and generation-skipping taxes, as well as the principal planning implications of these taxes. The federal income taxation of estates and trusts, as well as the federal income taxation of various estate planning devices is not covered in this outline, nor is the state law of wills, trusts, gifts, and related areas; most of these areas are covered in other outlines. The income taxation of gratuitous transfers, including trusts and estates, is discussed in the *Casenote Law Outline: Federal Income Taxation* at pp. 1-17 to 1-18 and 3-22 to 3-24.

Law schools display a bewildering variety of curricula in the area of gratuitous transfers (wills, trusts, future interests, estate administration, estate and gift tax, estate planning, income taxation of estates and trusts, elder law, and related areas). There is no standardized format for courses in this subject, and the various casebooks display a variety of orientations and contents. One reason for the lack of standardization is that some teachers come to this subject primarily from the property area and others from the tax area. The other is that, in recent years, there has been pressure at many law schools to compress the curriculum in the gratuitous-transfers field so as to make room for other curricular offerings. One result is that many courses in this subject have "integrated" tax and nontax components. Some courses in wills and trusts might offer a relatively minor tax component. Estate planning courses are likely to have tax and nontax components, but the emphasis might vary from school to school or even instructor to instructor. The "pure" course in estate and gift taxation is less common than formerly, and where it exists it may have been condensed.

In short, it was impractical to design an outline that would "track" with a large percentage of the courses on this topic. Instead, the decision was to limit the subject matter of this outline to the federal estate, gift, and generation-skipping taxes, with some references to, and warnings about, the federal income tax as it impacts on this topic. The student using this outline will need to be creative in two ways. First, the student may need to use this outline in conjunction with one or more other outlines in view of the contents of the particular course he or she is taking. Second, the student will probably need to be selective in using this outline, since the instructor is unlikely to pursue as much detail in his or her course as this outline does.

The student will also need to be sensitive to the instructor's pedagogical orientation with respect to the federal taxes on gratuitous transfers. One is the "system" approach which presents the federal taxes on gratuitous transfers as a coherent *corpus juris,* with underlying policies and principles, which has evolved over time in response to various pressures. Instructors following the system approach are likely to closely examine the statutes, regulations, rulings, and case law. The detail and complexity of the federal estate tax, in particular, is astounding, considering the brevity of the statute and the slight revenue yield involved. Under the system approach, the federal taxes on gratuitous transfers are capable of rivaling the Rule Against Perpetuities in being able to pose complex puzzles that demand application of a somewhat artificial but self-contained body of law.

The other main pedagogical approach might be called the "planning" or "result-oriented" approach. Here one starts with some objective, which may be either to save taxes or to simply effect a certain kind of transfer without incurring undue taxes, and then examines how the federal taxes on gratuitous transfers would impact on how one proceeds. Tax rules are not important in themselves but only in their consequences with respect to various types of transactions; the transactions may be tax- or nontax-motivated. This approach emphasizes what to do and what not to do in estates practice.

The enactment of Chapter 14 of the Code (§§ 2701-2704) in the Omnibus Budget Reconciliation Act of 1990 complicates teaching a course in the federal transfer taxes. Section 2702, in particular, adds a layer of complexity on top of traditional gift tax principles. On the one hand, this additional complexity should have the effect of simplifying practice, since certain kinds of inter vivos transfers (*i.e.,* those with retained interests) are virtually prohibited. On the one hand, it is hard to understand what Chapter 14 is all about unless one first comprehends traditional transfer-tax doctrine. Yet, once understood, Chapter 14 effectively renders much doctrine obsolete in the practical sense. This outline is systematically integrates Chapter 14 into its contents.

Ideally, the student should be exposed to both the system and planning approaches, and that is what this outline attempts to do. Chapter 1 provides an overview of the system. This chapter should be useful to students who are either taking a wills and trusts course with a modest tax component or an estate planning course which does not have an estate and gift tax course as a prerequisite. Chapters 2 and 3 methodically grind through the gift and estate taxes in a detailed and systematic manner. Chapter 4, which is new to this edition, deals with valuation under the estate and gift taxes. Valuation is where much of the "action" is in contemporary estate planning practice. Chapter 5 lays out the generation-skipping tax. Chapters 2-5 might provide more than you need to know in a wills and trusts or estate planning course, but the information is there if a particular topic needs to be pursued in some detail. Chapter 6 is tax-planning-oriented, with a discussion of the transactions most often encountered in practice. Chapter 6 is also designed to pull together and review what are the most practically important contents of Chapters 2-5.

I would emphasize to the student the importance of carefully reading and understanding the relevant Code provisions. Most of the Code provisions are relatively short, but many come with a lot of baggage. Innocuous-looking words and phrases may have heavy import. Courts take the statutory language very seriously indeed. So should you.

TC

CAPSULE OUTLINE

CO ▶

CAPSULE OUTLINE

The capsule outline is a summary of the entire outline. Where feasible, the basic rule or point is stated concisely. Caveats, exceptions, etc., are not always stated. The topic headings sometimes vary from those in the main outline, for the sake of clarity and conciseness.

OVERVIEW OF FEDERAL TAXES ON TRANSFERS OF WEALTH

CHAPTER 1: OVERVIEW OF THE FEDERAL TAXES ON THE TRANSFER OF WEALTH

CO

CO

GIFT TAX

CHAPTER 2: GIFT TAX

CO

CO

CO

CO

CO

CO

CO

CO

VALUATION

CHAPTER 4: VALUATION

CO

CO

CHAPTER 5 THE GENERATION-SKIPPING TAX

I. **OVERVIEW: The 1986 GST applies to gratuitous transfers that "skip" (are not subject to estate or gift tax at) a generation below that of the transferor.** 5-2

CO

CHAPTER 6: ESTATE PLANNING DEVICES

CO

ESTATE & GIFT TAX ◄ casenote law outlines

CO

CO

CO

CO

OVERVIEW OF THE FEDERAL TAXES ON THE TRANSFER OF WEALTH

▶ CHAPTER SUMMARY

CHAPTER 1: OVERVIEW OF THE FEDERAL TAXES ON THE TRANSFER OF WEALTH

Introduction. This chapter provides a brief history and overview of the "federal transfer taxes," consisting of the estate tax, the gift tax, and the generation-skipping tax ("GST").

The estate, gift, and generation-skipping taxes are taxes on the transfer of wealth. These taxes (the "federal transfer taxes") are distinguishable in concept from inheritance taxes, accessions taxes, wealth or property taxes, and excise taxes. The gift tax is imposed on inter vivos gifts only. The estate tax is imposed on transfers that are, or are deemed to be, testamentary. The GST is imposed on gratuitous transfers that skip one or more generations. (An example would be a bequest from a grandparent to a grandchild.)

The federal transfer taxes, found in Subtitle B (Chapters 11-14) of the Internal Revenue Code of 1986 as amended (the "IRC"), are separate and apart from the federal income tax, located in Subtitle A.

The federal estate and gift taxes have been a single "unified" or "integrated" system since January 1, 1977. Prior to 1977, they were separate taxes. The unified estate and gift tax can be described as a tax, imposed at progressive rates, on the *cumulative* taxable gratuitous transfers of a person, with the gift tax attributable to each gift being payable currently and the estate tax being due nine months after the decedent's death. The GST is a separate tax apart from the unified estate and gift tax.

In analyzing a gift tax issue, first consider whether an inter vivos transfer is a "gift" within the meaning of the gift tax. The next issue is whether the gift is a "completed" gift presently subject to tax. The third issue is to determine the net value of the gift. The fourth step is to apply any exclusions (such as the $10,000 annual exclusion). The fifth is to subtract any amounts that qualify for the marital or charitable deductions. The sixth is to compute the tax, if any, due, and to pay it.

As to the estate tax, the first issue is to constitute the "gross estate," which includes not only bequests and inheritances through the probate estate but also certain inter vivos transfers (usually in trust), certain contractual arrangements (involving life insurance and employee benefits), certain property passing by form of ownership (in-joint tenancies, etc.), and certain property over which the decedent was "constructively" the owner (because of a "general power of appointment"). The next step is to value the gross estate. The third step is to take any relevant deductions, the principal ones being the marital and charitable deductions. The gross estate less deductions is the "taxable estate." The fourth step is to compute the tax, if any, and to arrange for its payment.

The first step with regard to the GST is to identify the existence and net amount of any generation-skipping transfer, after any exclusions and deductions (which here are relatively unimportant). The second is to compute the tax, if any, and arrange for its payment.

The federal transfer taxes produce actual tax liability only for the fairly well-off. The unified gift and estate tax will reach, after 2005, wealth transfers only in excess of $1 million per taxpayer (transferor). The GST only reaches cumulative generation-skipping transfers in excess of $1 million per transferor. Husband and wife are separate transferors (taxpayers) for these purposes.

The federal gift tax is paid by the donor. The federal estate tax is paid by the executor out of the property subject to estate tax. The apportionment of the estate tax among the various bequests and other estate transfers is governed by the decedent's will, state apportionment-of-death-tax statutes, and a few provisions of the IRC. The GST is usually paid by the donor or the property subject to the GST, but in some cases it is paid by trust beneficiaries receiving trust distributions.

I.   **NATURE OF THE FEDERAL TRANSFER TAXES. Each of the federal transfer taxes is imposed on the transferor of a gratuitous transfer. A transfer tax is distinguishable from an inheritance tax, an accessions tax, an income tax, an excise tax on commercial transactions, or a property tax.**

   A. **Transfer Tax. A "transfer tax" (estate tax, gift tax, or GST) is a tax on the (net) gratuitous transfers of a person, as opposed to being a tax on the receipt of a transfer.**

      1. *Transferor tax liability.* It follows that the tax base and tax rates are constituted with respect to the transferor, not any transferee, and the transferor (or her personal representative) is (usually) liable to pay the tax.

      2. *Significance of transferor orientation.* This transferor orientation is significant because the federal transfer taxes are imposed at progressive rates on a tax base that, in general, is constituted by the cumulative (gift and estate) transfers of the transferor.

         a. *Husbands and wives as transferors.* Husband and wife are each separate transferors, as opposed to being a unitary "joint" transferor.

         b. *Transfers of property.* The tax is imposed only on transfers of money or property, not genetic endowment, love and affection, or other "intangible" benefits, nor is it imposed on "support" provided to dependents.

   B. **Other taxes distinguished:**

      1. *Inheritance Tax.* An inheritance tax is a tax on the heir or legatee with respect to amounts received from a given decedent, meaning that the tax base and rates (if not necessarily the liability for payment) are keyed to recipients.

         a. *Role.* Inheritance taxes were common in the states since the early nineteenth century, although in the present day most of these taxes have been replaced by the enactment of a state estate tax.

         b. *Nontaxable transfers.* Inheritance taxes typically do not reach (in whole or in part) certain nonprobate death-time transfers, such as by way of joint tenancy, inter vivos trust, proceeds of life insurance, annuity, and employee death benefit.

      2. *Accessions Tax.* An accessions tax is a tax, at progressive rates, on the cumulative gratuitous transfers (bequests, inheritances, nonprobate transfers, and gifts) received by an individual during life. Neither the federal government nor any state has an accessions tax.

NATURE OF THE FEDERAL TRANSFER TAXES

3. ***Commercial Excise Tax.*** Excise taxes are those taxes placed on commercial transactions, such as sales taxes, value-added taxes, customs duties, stamp taxes, stock transfer taxes, etc. They are clearly distinguishable from federal transfer taxes, which are taxes on gratuitous transfers to family and friends.

4. ***Property or Wealth Tax.*** A property tax or wealth tax is imposed periodically by reason of the ownership or possession of property. The federal transfer taxes are distinguished by their being imposed only upon the gratuitous transfer of property.

C. **Gratuitous Transfers under the Federal Income Tax. For a more detailed analysis, see part VII.,** ***infra.***

1. ***Gratuitous transfers excluded.*** While an income tax could, in theory, include gratuitous transfers received in gross income, the existing federal income tax (under § 102) and state income taxes exclude gratuitous receipts from the income tax base of the recipient.

2. ***Nondeductibility of gratuitous transfers.*** Note, however, that gratuitous transfers (other than those made to charity) are not deductible for income tax purposes.

   a. *Effect.* The effect of nondeductibility is to tax the transferor, rather than the transferee.

   b. *Transferor previously taxed.* In general, the transferred amounts have already been "subject to" the income tax on the transferor. This is not true, however, for unrealized appreciation of the transferor. Gratuitous transfers are not realization events. Under §§ 1015 and 1041, the basis to a donee is (generally) the same as the donor's basis. Under § 1014, property included in the gross estate (generally) takes on a basis equal to the estate tax value.

   c. *Transfer taxes as tax on "capital."* Since, under the income tax, gratuitous receipts are excluded by the transferee under § 102 but have (generally) been "subject to" the income tax in the hands of the transferor, it follows that the federal transfer taxes are a "second" (or third) tax on "capital" (income already subject to income tax). For example, if D earns salary of $40,000 and gives it to E, the $40,000 is subject to both income tax and gift tax in D's hands (and perhaps generation-skipping tax).

II. **PURPOSES AND EFFECTS. The federal transfer taxes serve multiple purposes and entail collateral effects.**

PURPOSES AND EFFECTS

A. **Raising Revenue.** Although enacted initially to help serve wartime revenue needs, in recent times the federal transfer taxes have raised only a small share (1%-2%) of total federal revenues.

B. **Breaking Up Undue Concentrations of Wealth.** Transferor-based taxes (like the present transfer taxes) provide some incentive for the dispersion of wealth in private hands, since progressive rates can be undermined at lower generations by transferring wealth to multiple recipients.

1. *Likely result.* The concentration of wealth in society remained relatively unchanged from the imposition of high transfer tax rates during World War II until the 1970s, but wealth has become more concentrated at the top in the 1980s and 1990s. Since the transfer taxes were weakened in 1981, it is plausible to suppose that the transfer taxes have at least some, if not a huge, impact on the concentration of wealth.

2. *Target of transfer taxes.* The taxes are designed, by way of generous exemptions, deductions, and credits, to reach only the well-off.

   a. *Actual effect.* At present, less than five percent of estates actually incur gift and estate tax, and the percentage incurring GST is much lower than that.

   b. *Greater impact.* Nevertheless, the existence and potential applicability of the transfer taxes probably impacts on the planning of a much higher percentage of estates (perhaps up to 10%).

C. **Influencing the Disposition of Wealth.** The tax scheme influences the ways in which people dispose of their property.

   1. *Marital and charitable deductions.* The marital and charitable deductions provide tax incentives (to the well-off) for transferring wealth to one's spouse and/ or to charities, and to transfer property to them in (certain kinds of) trusts.

   2. *Life insurance.* The possibility of nonliquidity in certain estates is an incentive to acquire life insurance.

   3. *Other economic arrangements.* The transfer tax system encourages devices to suppress the value of assets by means of fractional interests in property or in entities holding property, and through certain contractual arrangements.

D. **Rationalizing the Control of Economic Resources**. Although transfer taxes are imposed "on" wealth, it is a logical error to simply assume that such taxes destroy productive capital. Of course, any tax diverts resources from private hands to the government and causes economic inefficiencies.

   1. *Paid in cash.* Because the transfer taxes are paid in cash, not in assets, assets may have to be sold in order to raise cash to pay the tax.

   2. *Effect of asset sales.* Thus, the transfer taxes tend to place productive assets and investments into the hands of the highest and best users, as opposed to family members, albeit with significant transaction costs.

   3. *Farms and closely held businesses.* Political pressure from farm and closely-held business interests pushes in the opposite direction, and numerous provisions have been enacted which reduce the tendency of the transfer taxes to force the sale of farms and closely-held business interests.

E. **Inhibiting Income-Shifting Arrangements**. Progressive income tax rates can be avoided by spreading income-producing property among lower bracket taxpayers.

   1. *Limited gift tax and GST effect.* The gift tax and GST impose some cost on such arrangements, but only where large amounts are involved.

2. ***The "kiddie tax."*** Income shifting is inhibited by the "kiddie tax" (investment income of under-14 children taxed at parents' highest marginal income tax rates).

3. ***Accumulation trusts.*** Trusts that accumulate income are separate taxpayers for income tax purposes. However, the rate schedule applicable to trusts (and estates) is highly compressed (that is, the highest marginal rate bracket is quickly reached). This discourages the use of trusts to accumulate income.

III. **CONSTITUTIONALITY. In general, there is no significant constitutional problem with the federal transfer taxes.**

A. **Power to Impose the Tax:**

CONSTITUTIONA-LITY

1. ***Taxes vs. Takings.*** The federal transfer taxes, being payable in cash, are "taxes," not "takings" (of property) and, therefore, are governed by the constitutional provisions pertaining to the taxing power of Congress.

2. ***Federal transfer taxes.*** A federal gift or estate tax is constitutional because it is an "indirect" tax, *i.e.,* a tax imposed by reason of a transfer. Also, the tax is "uniform" among the states, because it does not explicitly discriminate on the basis of state or region. *Knowlton v. Moore,* 178 U.S. 41 (1900) (1896 federal inheritance tax); *New York Trust Co. v. Eisner,* 256 U.S. 345 (1921) (estate tax); *Bromley v. McCaughn,* 280 U.S. 124 (1929) (1924 gift tax). The GST is undoubtedly constitutional as an indirect tax on transfers or deemed transfers occasioned by the shifting of possession or ownership of beneficial interests. *See Chase Nat'l Bank v. U.S.,* 278 U.S. 327 (1929) (lapse of power is sufficient to constitute a transfer).

3. ***Federal wealth or property tax contrasted.*** In contrast, a federal wealth or property tax by reason of ownership would be a "direct" tax, and would (probably) be unconstitutional as an unapportioned "direct" tax that is not an "income tax" within the Sixteenth Amendment. A direct tax would be valid only if "apportioned" among the states in proportion to population, which would be impractical unless the federal government requisitioned the tax from the various states.

4. ***Progressive rate structure.*** A progressive rate structure (classification based on wealth) is not unconstitutional under the Due Process Clause of the Fifth Amendment. *See Brushaber v. Union Pacific R.R. Co.,* 240 U.S. 1 (1916) (income tax).

B. **Retroactivity.** The federal transfer taxes can reach transactions initiated prior to the date of enactment where the "transfer" occurs after the date of enactment, such as occurs with life insurance proceeds and revocable trusts. *Chase Nat'l Bank, supra*; *Reinecke v. Northern Trust Co.,* 278 U.S. 339 (1929).

1. ***Older vs. modern view.*** Although some older cases hold that completed transfers absolutely cannot be taxed retroactively (*Nichols v. Coolidge,* 274 U.S. 531 (1927); *Helvering v. Helmholz,* 296 U.S. 93 (1935)), the more modern view of due process is perhaps that they can be taxed if the transferor can take steps after enactment to remove the property from the tax base. *See U.S. v. Manufacturers Nat'l Bank of Detroit,* 363 U.S. 194 (1960).

2. *Largely moot issue.* This issue is largely moot, as Congress typically provides that transfer tax provisions are prospective only. Section 2045, which purports to provide for blanket retroactivity, is subject to these specific provisions in the Code and revenue acts limiting retroactivity.

IV. **HISTORY AND OVERVIEW. The federal estate tax, gift tax, and GST were enacted respectively in 1916, 1932, and 1986. The principal features of each tax are described below.**

A. **Gift Tax**. The gift tax is computed (and payable) for any year in which there are "taxable gifts," meaning gifts not excluded (or gifts in excess of exclusions) reduced by any available marital deduction.

1. *History.* The modern gift tax is effective for gift transfers after June 6, 1932. A gift tax enacted in 1924 had been repealed in 1926. (The estate tax entered the picture in 1916.) The gift tax comprises Chapter 12 of the Code (§§ 2501 *et seq.*). Up until 1977, the gift tax was separate from the estate tax and had its own separate rate schedule and exemption. After 1976, the gift and estate taxes were integrated in the manner described in B.6. and 7., *infra*.

2. *Purpose.* The function of the gift tax is to back up the estate tax. (The estate tax could be avoided by giving away wealth before death.) Thus, the gift tax reaches depletions of the donor's potential gross estate. Since the gross estate is constituted by material wealth (money and property), the gift tax only deals with transfers of money and property of the donor by gift. Transfers of genes, manners, culture, information, and opportunities are not covered by the gift tax.

3. *The donor.* Only individuals can be donors subject to the gift tax. Husband and wife are separate donors. Gifts of community property are treated as made half by each spouse. Gifts of noncommunity property can be treated as made one-half by each spouse if the spouses so elect on a gift tax return. *See* § 2513.

4. *Scope.* A gift for gift tax purposes is any inter vivos gratuitous transfer of money or property, or interests therein. Transfers at, or by reason of, the donor's death are not "gifts."

   a. *Consumption and waste.* To be a gift, there must be a "transfer" to another party, such as a spouse, relative, friend, or charity, to whom one might make a bequest or leave an inheritance. Thus, personal consumption spending, losses in the value of assets, theft and casualty losses, and economic waste do not entail gifts.

   b. *"Support" to legal dependents.* The provision of "support" to legal dependents is not considered to be a gift. Perhaps this category is considered to be a form of consumption or waste of the spender.

   c. *Business transaction exception.* Transactions in the ordinary course of business or investment, if at arms length, are not gifts.

   d. *Transfers for consideration.* Transfers for full and adequate consideration in money or money's worth (meaning property or reductions in liabilities) are not gifts. The rationale for this exclusion is that the money, debt relief, or property consideration (*quid pro quo*) for the transfer replenishes the transferor's potential gross estate. An example is where Mom transfers a painting worth $50,000 to Sis for $50,000 cash. If the value of the property is greater than the consideration received, the transfer is a gift, but it is "offset" by the (partial) consideration. Thus, if Sis only paid $12,000 for the painting, Mom has made a "net" gift of $38,000 ($50,000 less $12,000 monetary consideration).

e. *Exception for incomplete gifts.* To be subject to gift tax, the transfer must be "complete" (*i.e.*, not subject to a power to revoke, alter, or amend). ("Incomplete" transfers are subject to gift tax later, when the gift becomes complete, or are included in the gross estate for estate tax purposes.)

f. *Gifts involving future interests.* If the gift involves a future interest, the gift occurs when the future interest is created (or transferred), not when it vests or comes into possession. For example, if D creates an irrevocable trust with $500,000, with an annuity of $25,000/year payable to D for 15 years, remainder to R, D is deemed to make a gift of the remainder interest to R at the time the trust is created (not at the end of 15 years). (The gift is of the remainder interest only, since a transfer of an interest to oneself doesn't deplete the donor's potential gross estate and is therefore not a gift. Compare item 7. *infra*.) The gift of the remainder interest will be valued using actuarial tables.

5. ***Excluded gifts.*** Some gifts are exempt by statute, such as political contributions (§ 2501(a)(5)) and direct payments for heath-care services and tuition to educational organizations (§ 2503(e)).

6. ***Annual exclusion.*** The gift tax exempts (nonexcluded) gifts (other than gifts of "future interests") on a per-donor, per-donee, per-year basis up to $10,000 (as indexed for inflation starting in 1999).

7. ***Valuation.*** Gifts are valued at their fair market value at the time of gift. Some special valuation rules are found in Chapter 14 of the Code (§§ 2701-2704), enacted in 1990. Most importantly, under § 2702 *certain* transfers involving retained interests are treated as gifts, even though conceptually there cannot be a gift to oneself. (*See* item 4.f., *supra*.) For example, if E creates an irrevocable trust with $1 million, income to E for life, remainder to R (who is a "family member"), E is deemed to make a gift not only of the remainder interest to R but also of the retained income interest; hence, E is charged with a gift of $1 million, as opposed to merely the actuarial value of R's remainder interest.

8. ***Charitable deduction.*** Certain qualifying gifts to charity are deductible. *See* § 2522.

9. ***Marital deduction.*** A gift tax marital deduction (enacted in 1948 and liberalized in 1981) equals the value of any qualifying gift made to the donor's spouse. *See* § 2523.

10. ***When taxes imposed.*** The gross gift (after exclusions, exemptions, and offsets) minus applicable deductions with respect to the gift is a "taxable gift." Taxable gifts of a donor generate potential gift tax liability "for" the year the taxable gifts are made. Any gift tax return (with payment) is due on April 15 of the following year.

11. ***Rates.*** The gift tax rate schedule is the same as for the estate tax (*see* § 2001(c)). The progressiveness of the rate schedule over the lifetime of the donor is implemented by first imposing a *tentative* tax on the *cumulative* lifetime gifts of the donor to date (including the current-year gifts) and then subtracting (crediting) the tax on the cumulative gifts made prior to the current-year gifts ("prior taxable gifts"). § 2502.

Example: *G* makes her first taxable gift in 1995 in the amount of $100,000. The tax (before the credit, described immediately below) is $23,800. In the year 2000, *G* makes a second taxable gift of $40,000. The tax "on" this $40,000 is not the $8,200 that is shown in 2001(c) as being the tax on $40,000. Rather, one first computes a tentative tax on the cumulative tax base of $140,000, which is $35,800. Then one subtracts (credits) the § 2001(c) tax on the prior gift of $100,000, which is $23,800. The difference is $12,000. This is the tax "on" the year 2000 gift of $40,000, which happens to fall entirely in the 30% marginal rate bracket (that being the bracket that runs from $100,000 to $150,000). That is, 30% of $40,000 equals $12,000, so that the result "checks out." (There is no actual gift tax due in either 1995 or 2000 because of the unified credit described immediately below.)

12. ***Unified credit.*** The tax as computed according to the method just described is reduced (but not below zero) by any of the "unified transfer tax" credit that has not been used up with respect to prior-year gifts. The credit is a flat-amount "cumulative" per-donor credit, as opposed to being an annual credit. § 2505. The unified credit is the only credit against the gift tax. The available credit and explanation of its effect is found in the discussion of "unification" in B.6. & 7., *infra*.

Example: *C* makes her first taxable gift of $250,000 in 1988. The tentative tax of $70,800 is eliminated by the credit ($192,800 being then available), leaving an unused credit of $122,000. In 2000, *C* makes a taxable gift of $500,000. The cumulative (gift) tax base is now $750,000, the tentative tax on which is $248,300. From this is subtracted the *before*-credit gift tax on the previously-taxed 1988 gift (= $70,800), leaving a tax of $177,500 "on" the 2000 gift. The last step is to subtract the *unused* credit, which is $220,550 (the amount available in the year 2000) reduced by the $70,800 used in 1988, leaving $149,750. This produces a net tax of $27,750.

13. ***Payment.*** The donor is liable for the tax. In contrast to the estate tax, the amount used to pay the tax is not part of the gift tax base. However, an amount equal to any net gift tax paid on any taxable gift made within three years of the donor's death is added to the gross estate. § 2035(b).

B. **Estate Tax.** The estate tax is imposed on the tax base, called the "taxable estate," meaning the "gross estate" less any deductions.

1. ***Enactment.*** The modern federal estate tax was enacted in 1916 (federal inheritance taxes had existed from time to time in earlier periods), and comprises Chapter 11 of the Internal Revenue Code (§§ 2001 *et seq.*). Note that the estate tax considerably pre-dates the gift tax.

2. ***Gross Estate.*** The gross estate includes not only property owned by a decedent at death but also, roughly speaking, certain property transferred by the decedent

during life where the transfer has a testamentary flavor and property which the decedent is deemed to own.

a. *Property owned at death.* The estate tax base obviously covers property owned by a decedent at death and passing to heirs and legatees. § 2033. In the case of community property, the amount includable in the gross estate of the first spouse to die is equal to that spouse's share of the community property (*i.e.,* one half).

b. *Gift tax within three years of death.* Any (after-credit) gift tax paid on any gift made within three years of the decedent's death is included in the gross estate. § 2035(b).

c. *Inter vivos transfers of a testamentary nature.* An obvious way of avoiding an estate tax limited to property owned at death is to give property away prior to death. The 1916 estate tax was not, however, accompanied by a gift tax. In order to prevent the most obvious forms of tax-avoidance gifts, the 1916 estate tax (and its immediate successors) provided that the estate tax base included (in addition to property owned by the decedent at death) certain inter vivos transfers having a testamentary purpose or effect, namely, joint tenancies created by the decedent, revocable transfers, transfers with retained life estates, reversions, or income interests, survivorship annuities, (since 1954) employee death benefits, and (until 1981) "transfers in contemplation of death."

    (1) Doctrinal overlap with gift tax. Except for the provision covering transfers in contemplation of death, these features of the estate tax continue to the present day (in §§ 2036-2040), meaning that there is considerable doctrinal overlap between the estate tax and the gift tax, *infra.* That is, a transfer may be a gift subject to gift tax and also be included in the transferor's gross estate for estate tax purposes.

    (2) Mitigation of double taxation. Although the same transfer might be subject to both estate and gift tax, there are mechanisms in the estate tax that ultimately "undo" such double taxation. *See* item 6.b., *infra.*

d. *Constructive ownership.* After a period of development, Congress established in 1942 the rule that the gross estate included property, transferred in trust by a person other than the decedent, over which the decedent at the time of death possessed a "general" power of appointment, namely, a power (by inter vivos instrument or will) to acquire or appropriate the trust property or vest it in (or pay it to) herself or her estate. This rule (in § 2041) may be thought of as resting on a "constructive ownership" theory.

e. *Life insurance.* An ongoing issue is whether life insurance proceeds should be included in the gross estate of the person whose life is insured: (a) simply because the proceeds come into existence upon the insured's death, (b) only in cases where the insured paid the premiums, or (c) only in cases where the insured held economic rights in the policy during life and/or at death. Alternative (a) has never been followed; alternatives (b) and (c) were followed for a period. The current approach (basically, since 1954) has been to follow alternative (c) only, which is essentially an "ownership" or general power of appointment approach. *See* § 2042.

f. *Research note.* Many litigated estate tax cases arose under prior versions of §§ 2035-2042. In reading these cases, it is crucial that the reader discern the differences between the then Code provision and the current Code provision.

3. *Valuation of gross estate.* All property included in the gross estate is included at its estate tax value (not its income tax basis or gift-time value). *Estate tax value* usually means the fair market value at the date of the decedent's death, but in some cases it means the *alternate valuation date* (whichever is the earlier of the date of disposition by the estate or legatee or the date which is six months after the date of death). Special statutory valuation rules are found in §§ 2031(c), 2032A, 2703, and 2704.

4. *Deductions:*

a. *Debts, etc.* There is a deduction for estate administration expenses and estate casualty losses (not elected to be deducted for income tax purposes), funeral expenses, and claims against the decedent, assuming the expenses, etc., are actually paid from assets included in the gross estate. §§ 2053 and 2054.

b. *Charitable deduction.* There is a deduction for amounts bequeathed (etc.) to charity. § 2055.

c. *Marital deduction.* A marital deduction was enacted in 1948, under which (net) estate transfers from the decedent to his or her spouse were subtracted from the estate tax base. Originally the deduction could not exceed half of the decedent's net estate, nor did it encompass the decedent's share of community property. These limitations were removed in 1981. *See* § 2056.

Example: *H* dies owning $1 million worth of property. *H*'s estate incurs deductible debts, administration expenses (not deducted for income tax purposes), and funeral expenses, of $50,000. *H*'s will bequeaths $200,000 to his daughter and the "residue" (= $750,000) to *W*. *H*'s gross estate is $1 million, and deductions are $800,000 ($50,000 + $750,000), leaving a taxable estate of $200,000.

d. *Qualified family-owned business deduction.* Section 2057, enacted in 1998, allows a deduction (up to a limit) for the value of qualified family-owned business interests that pass to a "qualified heir."

5. *Rates.* The estate tax has always been subject to progressive rates. The current rate schedule is found in § 2001(c). The highest marginal rate is 55% (a "surtax" imposed on very large estates raises the marginal rate to 60% until the tax savings from below-55% brackets are recaptured, at which point the 55% rate is restored).

6. *Unification.* In 1976 the federal estate and gift taxes were "integrated" ("unified") meaning that the rates, *supra,* are applied against a *cumulative tax base* that is comprised by the taxable estate *and* (post-1976) "adjusted taxable gifts" subject to gift tax, but the resulting tax is reduced by the gift tax on post-1976 taxable gifts. § 2001(b).

a. *Effect of integration.* The effect of integration ("unification") is that post-1976 taxable gifts push the eventual taxable estate into higher marginal rate brackets. The intent is to create virtual "neutrality" as to whether to transfer one's wealth by gift or by bequest.

b. *Inter vivos transfers subject to both gift tax and estate tax.* The gift and estate taxes are not fully integrated in the "doctrinal" sense. That is, certain types of inter vivos transfers can be a gift for gift tax purposes and be included in the gross estate for estate tax purposes. *See* item 2.c. *supra.* In the case of an inter vivos transfer subject to both gift and estate tax, the twice-taxed transfer remains in the estate tax base but, for purposes of computing the estate tax, is removed from the total of (post-1976) "adjusted taxable gifts" in constituting the cumulative tax base. The gift tax, if any, on the prior gift is not retroactively eliminated; such tax, along with other gift taxes paid, is credited (subtracted) from the tax on the cumulative tax base, since *all* post-1976 gift taxes are pre-payments "against" the ultimate tax liability.

c. *Unified credit.* After the estate tax has been figured (*see* above), the "unified credit" is subtracted. (This credit cannot reduce the net tax below zero.) § 2010.

(1) Amount of credit. The credit is that amount which will reduce the tax (computed under § 2001(c)) on the specified cumulative tax base to zero. The specified cumulative tax base is $650,000 for decedents dying in 1999, and increases until it reaches $1 million for decedents dying in 2006 and later years. To illustrate, the credit needed to reduce the tax on a cumulative tax base of $650,000 to zero is $211,750, which is the tax (under the § 2001 rate schedule) on a cumulative tax base of $650,000. Thus, a credit of $211,750 has the effect of exempting a cumulative tax base of $650,000 (for decedents dying in 1999) from tax. But, although a credit has an "exemption equivalent," it does not operate the same way as does an exemption or a deduction, which would reduce the tax base. If there were an exemption or deduction, the marginal dollars of tax base in excess of the exemption or deduction would be subject to the lowest marginal rate bracket (which happens to be 20%). In contrast, assuming an available credit of $211,750, that portion of the cumulative tax base that exceeds the exemption equivalent of the credit ($650,000) is taxed at high marginal rates (37% and above). The unified transfer tax credit and exemption equivalents thereof are set forth in the table below:

TABLE 1-1: UNIFIED TRANSFER TAX CREDIT AND EXEMPTION EQUIVALENTS

Transfer Made In	Credit	Exemption Equivalent
1997	$192,800	$600,000
1998	$202,050	$625,000
1999	$211,750	$650,000
2000-2001	$220,550	$675,000
2002-2003	$229,800	$700,000
2004	$287,300	$850,000
2005	$326,300	$950,000
2006 and later years	$345,800	$1,000,000

(2) The credit is a "unified" lifetime credit. The transfer tax credit is a "unified" credit because it applies against the cumulative tax base amount (post-1976 taxable gifts plus the taxable estate) of a taxpayer. Thus, it is a lifetime-plus-deathtime credit, not an annual credit, and not a separate credit that exempts, say, $1 million of taxable gifts *and* a $1 million taxable estate. The credit is applied first against gift tax liability, and only what remains is available to offset estate tax liability.

7. ***The tax computational process illustrated***. The following examples illustrate the method of computing the estate tax.

Example 1: In 2000, *A* (who had made no taxable gifts during life) died leaving a taxable estate of $750,000. Under § 2001(c), the before-credit tax is $248,300. The credit that corresponds to an exemption equivalent of $675,000 is $220,550, and this is subtracted. § 2010. The net estate tax is $27,750. Note that this same result is obtained by subtracting $675,000 from $750,000 and multiplying the result of $75,000 by the marginal rate of 37%. In other words, the existing tax-credit scheme is the equivalent of an exemption scheme with marginal rates starting at 37%.

Example 2: In 1988, *B* made her one-and-only taxable gift, in the amount of $250,000, producing a before-credit gift tax of $70,800 (under the same § 2001(c) rate schedule). The then available credit was $192,800, and whatever amount is needed to reduce the gift tax to zero ($70,800) is subtracted (used up). In 2000 *B* dies with a taxable estate of $500,000. The taxable estate is added to the sum of (post-1976) adjusted taxable gifts, yielding a cumulative tax base of $750,000, and a tentative tax on such tax base of $248,300. There are two ways, arithmetically, to reach the correct end result:

Correct but complex approach. The first step is to compute the before-credit tax "on" the taxable estate: tax on cumulative tax base ($248,300) less *before*-credit tax on post-1976 taxable gift ($70,800), which is $177,500. From this subtract the *unused* credit of $149,750, which is obtained by subtracting the already used-credit of $70,800 from the now-available credit of $220,550. The remaining unused credit of $149,750 is subtracted from the tax "on" the taxable estate of $177,500, to produce a net tax of $27,750. This is the same result as in Example 1, because in both cases the cumulative tax base is $750,000 and the available credit is $220,550. This method is the one used in the gift tax. *See* § 2002. Note that the aggregate tax is the same here as when B transfers her entire $750,000 by way of gift, see the example in A.12., *supra*, or by bequest, as in Example 1 immediately above.

Short-cut method. First, figure the tax on the cumulative tax base of $750,000, which is $248,300. Next, subtract the *full available* unified transfer tax credit of $220,550. Third, subtract the *after*-credit post-1976 gift tax paid, which is zero. The result is again $27,750. This is the method used in computing the estate tax. *See* § 2001(b).

Example 3: C creates an irrevocable trust in 1988 with $500,000, income to C for life, remainder to R. Under the gift tax law in effect for 1988, this was a taxable gift of only the remainder interest to R, then worth $100,000. The before-credit gift tax on $100,000 was $23,800, which was offset by a credit of $23,800. C dies in 2000 penniless. However, the 1988 retained-interest transfer is included in C's gross estate under § 2036 at its then value of $750,000. (Assume no estate tax deductions, and a resulting taxable estate of $750,000.) Here the cumulative tax base is $750,000, as opposed to $850,000: the twice-taxed gift of the remainder interest appears in the cumulative tax base at its estate tax value of $750,000, and the gift tax value *of the same interest* ($100,000) is eliminated from the "adjusted taxable gifts" total. The tax is again $27,750.

8. ***Other credits.*** There are credits for state death taxes, foreign death taxes, pre-1977 gift taxes, and death taxes on estate accessions by the decedent (within 10 years of the decedent's death), all of which are subject to complex limitations. §§ 2011-2015.

9. ***Payment.*** The estate tax (as well as the gift tax and GST) must be paid in cash; the Treasury does not accept payment in kind. The tax is payable by the decedent's personal representative out of assets included in the gross estate.

   a. *Allocation of burden.* However, how the tax burden is allocated among the various legatees (etc.) is determined by the decedent's will and/or state (or possibly federal) law.

   b. *No estate tax deduction.* Unlike the gift tax (which is not included in the gift tax base), the estate tax is not a deduction in arriving at the taxable estate; therefore, the tax is (in effect) included in the estate tax base. Recall, however, that any gift tax paid with respect to gifts made within three years prior to death is included in the cumulative tax base: such taxes are included in the gross estate under § 2035(b). In other words, gifts (on which net gift tax is paid) made within three years of death lose the advantage that gifts generally have of the gift tax paid being treated as nontaxable economic waste rather than as a taxable transfer.

C. **Generation-Skipping Tax (GST). The GST reaches gratuitous transfers made to persons two or more generations below that of the grantor, whether outright or in trust (etc.). (Due to the complexity of the GST, its main features are described only in general terms.)**

   1. ***History.*** The first GST was enacted in 1976, but was retroactively repealed in 1986 and replaced by the present GST. The GST comprises Chapter 13 of the Internal Revenue Code (§§ 2601 *et seq.*).

   2. ***Purpose.*** The GST is a back-up to the estate tax. The underlying norm is that a transfer tax should be imposed no less than once a generation, as would occur if parents bequeathed wealth to their children, those children bequeath wealth to their children, and so on from generation to generation, with each successive transfer being subject to estate or gift tax. The at-least-one-tax-per-generation norm cannot be fulfilled by the estate tax in two common situations: (1) where a parent makes a gift or bequest directly to a grandchild, and (2) where a parent creates a trust, income to child for life, remainder to grandchild. In the first situation, the transferor's child never was an owner of the property, and so cannot make a taxable transfer of it. In the second (trust) situation, the estate tax does not apply upon the death of the child because the child's income interest has a value of zero at the child's death (and the grandchild's remainder interest was acquired at the time the trust was created from the grandparent creating the trust, not from the child who was the income beneficiary). Instead of modifying

the estate tax so as to deem a gift or estate transfer from the child to the grandchild in these situations, Congress enacted the GST as a separate tax.

3. **No integration with estate and gift tax.** The GST has its own rate schedule and exemption system, as opposed to treating generation-skipping transfers as being "additional" gift or estate transfers by individuals located in skipped generations.

4. **Taxable event.** There are three categories of generation-skipping transfers: (1) direct-skip transfers, (2) taxable terminations, and (3) taxable distributions. *See* § 2612.

   a. *Direct-skip transfers.* Direct-skip transfers include (but are not limited to) outright gifts and bequests that are "subject to" gift or estate tax, and the taxable event occurs when the transfer is made. The tax applies only if the donee is two or more generations below the donor.

   b. *Taxable terminations and taxable distributions.* In contrast, for taxable terminations and taxable distributions, which typically entail trust arrangements, the generation-skipping transfer is deemed to occur when the lower-generation transferee actually receives the transfer. The typical example of a "taxable termination" transfer is where a person creates a trust, income to child for life, remainder to grandchild: the taxable termination occurs upon the death of the child. (Recall that the trust is not included in the child's gross estate for estate tax purposes, as the child's interest has a value of zero as of the child's death.) An example of a "taxable distribution" is where, assuming the same facts, the trustee distributes income or corpus to the grandchild prior to the termination of the trust.

   c. *One tax per generation.* Suppose A creates a trust for her three children, and on the death of the last survivor of them the trust terminates and the property is distributed to the grandchildren. There is no taxable termination until the last child of A dies.

   d. *Successive taxable events.* A GST is imposed each time a new generation is skipped. Thus, if A creates a trust, income to child for life, then to grandchild for life, remainder to great-grandchild, there is a taxable termination upon the death of the child and a second taxable termination on the death of the grandchild.

   e. *No additional tax on "double"-skip transfers.* Notwithstanding the foregoing, a transfer that leaps two or more generations in one bound is subject to only one tax. For example, suppose D makes an outright gift to a great grandchild. Although this gift skips two generations at once, there is only one direct-skip transfer and only one GST.

5. **Amount of transfer:**

   a. *Direct-skip transfers.* The amount of the transfer is the same amount as the amount of the gift or estate transfer.

      (1) Direct-skip gift transfer. Here the taxable amount is the amount received by the donee. In other words, the taxable transfer excludes

both the gift tax and the GST itself. However, any GST paid with respect to a direct-skip gift is an estate depletion that is (unlike the gift tax) treated as a gift for *gift tax* purposes. § 2515.

Example: Assume the gift tax and GST rates are each 50%, and no exemptions or exclusions are available. Donor G makes a gift of $100K to grandchild X. The GST is 50% of $100K. The gift for *gift tax* purposes is the $100K gift plus the $50K GST. The gift tax is $75K. Thus, the donor has parted with $225K ($100K gift plus $50K GST plus $75K gift tax).

(2) Direct-skip estate transfer. The taxable transfer is again the amount received by the beneficiary. That is, the GST tax base excludes both the GST itself and the estate tax "on" the same transfer. However, the GST (as well as the estate tax) are included in the *estate tax* base.

Example: G bequeaths $300K to grandchild X. The estate tax is $150K. The taxable transfer under the GST is the remaining $150K less the GST itself. Using a formula, the GST taxable amount is $100K and the GST is $50K (the two add up to $150K).

b.   *Taxable termination.* The tax base is again after any estate or gift tax but "before" (*i.e.*, including) the GST itself.

Example: G creates a testamentary trust that is initially funded with $1 million (after gift or estate tax), income to child B for life, remainder to grandchild C.   This is not a direct-skip transfer, because the "lead" beneficiary, B, is in the generation immediately below the transferor. The death of B is a taxable termination. At B's death, the trust is worth $1.4 million, and the GST taxable amount is $1.4 million. The GST is (assuming no exemptions, etc., and a 50% flat rate) is $700,000. This is paid out of the trust, so that grandchild C ends up with the remaining $700,000.

c.   *Taxable distribution:*

(1) General rule. The tax-base rule here is generally the same for taxable terminations.

Example: Same facts as the previous example, except that the trust is worth $2 million; $1.4 million of corpus is distributed to grandchild C. The taxable amount under the GST is $1.4 million, so that there is again a tax of $700,000, only this time the tax is payable by C individually. C again ends up with $700K.

(2) GST paid by trust. As noted immediately above, the GST is to be paid by the distributee. If the tax is paid by the trust, the amount of tax so paid is treated as an additional taxable distribution.

Example: Same as previous example, except that the trustee distributes $700K to C. Although the operation of this provision is not completely clear, it appears that the tax of $350K would, if paid by the trust, constitute an additional taxable distribution of $350K, which would give rise to a secondary tax liability of $175K. If the trust paid this and all additional incremental taxes (on further deemed taxable distributions), the end result should be a $700K tax imposed on, and paid by, the trust, which would yield the same end result as the previous example.

d. *Valuation.* Generally speaking, the same rules apply as under the estate and gift tax. Valuation occurs at the time of the generation-skipping taxable event.

e. *Deduction for administration expenses.* In the case of a taxable termination or taxable distribution, the tax base is reduced by administration expenses, etc. *See* §§ 2621(a)(2) and 2622(b).

6. **Exclusions.** The principal exclusions are:

a. *Excluded direct-skip transfers.* The GST only applies to direct-skip transfers "subject to" estate or gift tax on the part of the donor or decedent. § 2612(c)(1). Thus, payments of support, political contributions, and business transactions, all of which are "non-gifts" cannot entail direct-skip transfers. Direct payments of medical expenses and tuition, excluded from the gift tax by § 2503(e), are excluded from the GST by § 2642(c)(3)(B).

b. *Exempt transfers.* Direct-skip gift transfers that are exempt under the gift tax annual exclusion are exempt from GST, except in certain cases involving direct-skip transfers into trust. *See* § 2642(c)(3)(A).

c. *Transferee supplies consideration.* The amount of any generation-skipping transfer is reduced (possibly to zero) by consideration in money or money's worth supplied by the transferee to the transferor. § 2624(d).

d. *Taxable termination or distribution subject to estate or gift tax.* If an event that would be taxable termination or taxable distribution also happens to be a gift or estate transfer subject to gift or estate tax, the transfer cannot to be a taxable termination or taxable distribution. The person subject to estate or gift tax is deemed to be the "new" transferor. (Conceivably, the new transfer might be a direct-skip transfer.) In short, in case of simultaneous application, the estate and gift taxes pre-empt the GST. This situation usually arises on account of trust beneficiaries possessing general powers of appointment. *See* § 2652(a)(1).

Example: A creates a trust, income to child B for life, with B having a general power of appointment by will, remainder to B's then living issue. The death of B would normally be a taxable termination, but it is prevented from being such by reason of the fact that the trust is included in B's gross estate by reason of B having a general over of appointment. If the trust assets, upon termination, are distributed to A's grandchild C, there is no GST taxable event. If the remainder distributee is A's great-grandchild D, there is a direct-skip GST from B to D.

7. **Exemption.** The transferor of a generation-skipping transfer has a cumulative (*i.e.*, lifetime plus deathtime) exemption of $1 million that can be applied to exempt all or part of a generation-skipping transfer from tax.

a. *Exemption indexed for inflation.* The $1 million exemption amount is indexed for inflation after 1998. (In contrast, the unified transfer tax credit is not indexed for inflation.) For purposes of illustration and examples, the $1 million figure will be used, because (1) it is an easy number to work with, and (2) indexed amounts for future years cannot be predicted accurately.

b. *Husband and wife are separate transferors.* Gifts of community property involve equal transfers by each spouse. Moreover, a gift-splitting election for gift tax purposes (for noncommunity property) is effective under the GST. § 2652(a)(2).

c. *Allocation of exemption.* The transferor (and her personal representative) can exercise control over how this amount is allocated among various generation-skipping trusts and transfers. *See* § 2632.

d. *Exemption operates like an exclusion ratio.* In a direct-skip transfer, the exemption operates like a deduction. In the case of taxable terminations and taxable distributions, the exclusion constitutes what is effectively an exclusion ratio *as of the transfer into trust.* This ratio is applied for all subsequent generation-skipping transfers involving the trust. *See* § 2642(a).

Example: By will, A creates a trust with $1 million in 2006, income to child B for life, income to grandchild C for life, remainder to great grandchild D. There is no estate tax charged against this transfer, and A's executor allocates $600,000 of her $1 million exemption to this trust. Thus, 60% of all generation-skipping transfers involving this trust are exempt from tax. Thus, if the trust is worth $2 million on B's death, the taxable amount is $800K ($2M - $1.2M). And, if the trust is worth $5 million on C's death, the taxable amount (with respect to this "successive" taxable termination) is $2 million ($5M - $3M).

e. *Unified credit under estate and gift tax contrasted.* The unified credit under the estate and gift taxes is not available against the GST (§ 2631), and it is used up automatically on a first-come first-served basis.

8. *Rates.* Unlike the estate and gift taxes, the GST imposes a flat rate, equal to the highest estate tax rate (currently 55%). § 2641. Because of this flat-rate feature, there is no "integration" with the estate and gift taxes. In other words, one simply applies the rate against the current-year generation-skipping transfers (after allocating all or part of the exemption to the transfer).

9. *GST as implicit deduction in direct-skip transfer.* As noted in 5.b. & c. above, the tax base for taxable terminations and taxable distributions includes the GST itself. In the case of a direct-skip transfer, the tax base is the "amount received" by the transferees. § 2623. But the tax on a direct-skip transfer is to be paid by the donor (or donor's estate) "out of" the amount transferred. § 2603(a)(3) & (b). These rules have the effects described below.

Gift transfer. The GST (as well as the gift tax) is paid out of the donor's own pocket. In this fashion, the GST amount depletes the donor's wealth (and can be said to be paid "out of" the transfer) but is not part of the GST tax base (is not received by the donee).

Example: D makes a taxable gift in 2000 to a grandchild in the amount of $1,283,710. After allocating the $1 million (nonindexed) exemption to this amount, the GST tax base is $283,710. The GST is 55% of this amount, or $156,040. At this point, D has parted with $1,439,750. The GST is a gift for gift tax purposes under § 2515. Hence, the taxable gift for gift tax purposes is also $1,439,750. The tentative gift tax on this amount is $529,893. The available unified credit is $220,550, leaving a net gift tax of $309,343. The total amount parted with by D is $1,749,093

Estate transfer. Since the transferor is dead, the tax must be paid out of the transfer itself. Since the GST tax amount is not an "amount received" by the legatee, it must be removed (deducted) from the tax base. However, that produces a situation where the tax (computed with reference to the tax base) and the tax base (computed with reference to the tax) are mutually dependent variables. Thus, there is a problem of computational circularity, which is solved by first constituting the direct-skip tax base without any deduction for the GST and then adjusting the 55% GST rate of tax downward according to the algebraic exercise, where "B" is the direct-skip tax base (unreduced by the GST) and "T" is the GST:

$$T = .55(B-T)$$

$$T = .55B - .55T$$

$$1.55T = .55B$$

$$T = .3548387B$$

Thus, where the nominal rate is 55%, the "real" rate for direct-skip estate transfers is 35.48387%.

Example: D, having made no taxable gifts, dies in 2000 with a taxable estate of $2 million, all of which is bequeathed to her grandchild. The estate tax is $560,250 ($780,800 tentative tax minus $220,550 unified credit). The direct-skip generation-skipping transfer is "after" estate tax charged to the trust, namely, $1,439,750 ($2 million minus $560,250). (Note that this figure is the same as the before-gift-tax figure in the previous example.) There being no other generation-skipping transfers, the (nonindexed) exemption of $1 million is allocated to the trust, leaving an "amount received" (tax base) of $439,750. The tax (at 55% of the tax base *reduced by the GST itself*) is $156,040 (.3548387 x $439,750). (Note that the GST here is the same as in the previous example.) The GST, when paid out of the estate along with the estate tax, leaves $1,283,710 for the grandchild. It can be observed that D had to part with more wealth ($2 million) in this hypo than in the gift hypo immediately above ($1,749,093) to "move" the same dollar amount to the grandchild. But this discrepancy merely reflects the fact that the gift tax base excludes the gift tax, so that the gift tax will be is less than the estate tax.

V. JURISDICTION TO TAX

JURISDICTION TO TAX

A. Citizens and Residents. The federal transfer taxes apply to transfers of money and property, *wherever located*, by U.S. citizens and U.S. residents (as defined in § 7701(b)).

B. Nonresident Aliens. Roughly speaking, nonresident aliens are subject to tax only with respect to property located in the U.S. *See* §§ 2101-2107, 2208-2209, 2501, 2511, and 2663(2). The transfer tax rules applicable to nonresident aliens are not discussed in any detail in this outline.

C. Foreign Death Tax Credit. The estate of a U.S. citizen or resident (and in some cases the estate of a nonresident alien) can claim a credit against the estate tax for foreign death taxes imposed upon foreign-situs assets (that are also subject to U.S. estate tax). The credit cannot exceed the U.S. estate tax attributable to such assets. § 2014. There is no similar credit under the gift tax or the GST.

D. Noncitizen Spouse. Gift and estate marital deduction rules are more restrictive where the transferee spouse is not a U.S. citizen. *See* §§ 2056(d), 2056A, and 2523(i).

VI. RELATIONSHIP TO STATE LAW. The operation of the federal transfer taxes is somewhat dependent upon property-law concepts, including the law of wills, trusts, and future interests.

RELATIONSHIP TO STATE LAW

A. Effect of State law. State law creates property rights and interests, but the federal transfer tax rules determine how such rights and interests will be taxed. Thus, federal tax law is not bound by the labels provided by state law but instead looks to the substance. *Morgan v. Com'r,* 309 U.S. 78 (1990).

Example: Section 2041 includes in the gross estate property over which the decedent possessed a general power of appointment, and § 2041 defines "general power of appointment" to include the right of a trust beneficiary to appropriate the trust property. One must look to relevant state law to determine whether any decedent who was a trust beneficiary in fact possessed such a power at the time of her death, but the result does not hinge on whether or not state law calls the power a "general power of appointment."

B. Ascertaining State law. Under the *Erie* doctrine, federal courts generally defer to state courts in defining state property rights. However, given the fact that much probate and trust litigation is not truly adversarial, there is concern that lower state courts can be manipulated to the disadvantage of the federal fisc.

1. *Effect of lower state court decisions generally.* The Supreme Court decreed that decisions of lower state courts (even in adversarial proceedings) are not binding as to federal tax controversies; instead, the federal courts are to attempt to ascertain state law on the basis of decisions of the highest courts of the state, or, if none, its divination of the law of the state. *Com'r v. Estate of Bosch,* 387 U.S. 456 (1967).

2. *Effect of final pre-gift or pre-death decrees.* On the other hand, a lower court decree that binds the parties and is "final" will be followed if the decision occurred prior to the date of gift or death.

VII. RELATIONSHIP TO INCOME TAX. As noted above at I.C., the federal transfer taxes comprise a separate tax system wholly apart from the income tax. The basic income tax rules pertaining to gratuitous transfers are set forth below.

RELATIONSHIP TO INCOME TAX

A. Nondeductibility to donor or decedent. A donor or decedent cannot deduct, for income tax purposes, the amount or value of gratuitous transfers, on the theory that they are "personal or family" expenses or losses. *See* §§ 165(c) and 263.

(Nondeductibility means that the donor or decedent is making a transfer of "after tax" dollars.)

B. Exclusion for gratuitous receipts. Gifts, bequests, inheritances, and other gratuitous transfers, are not included in gross income by the recipient. §§ 101(a) (life insurance proceeds) and 102(a) (other gratuitous receipts).

C. Income from gifts and bequests. "Income from" gratuitous receipts are included in the gross income of the donor, donee, estate, trust, or beneficiary, depending on the type of transfer. § 102(b).

1. *Outright transfers.* Unless the gift is of wages or involves a carve-out sale of an income right, the donee of a gift is taxed on the income from the gifted property. The same is true of bequests, etc., once the property has been distributed to the legatee (etc.) from the estate or a trust.

2. *Grantor trusts.* In the case of certain inter vivos trusts (including revocable trusts, trusts with reversions worth more than 5%, and trusts in which income or corpus might be paid to the grantor), the grantor is taxed on the trust income under §§ 671-677 (but for no longer a period than the grantor's lifetime). Amounts received by trust beneficiaries (other than the grantor) are treated as excludable gifts to them from the grantor under § 102(a).

3. *Beneficiary-owned trusts.* If a beneficiary can cause the income or corpus of a nongrantor trust to be paid to her, she is taxed directly on the income that can be obtained (if she can demand only the income) or on all income and gains (if she can obtain the corpus), as if the beneficiary owned the property directly. § 678. Again, amounts received by other trust beneficiaries are treated as excludable gifts to them from the beneficiary-owner.

4. *Nongrantor and testamentary trusts.* For all trusts which are not "grantor trusts" or "beneficiary-owned trusts," the income is taxed to the trust and/or beneficiaries under the rules of §§ 641-667. Basically, these rules implement a deduction-inclusion scheme, meaning that trust distributions that are deductible to the trust are includible gross income to the distributee. This scheme avoids double taxation of trust income.

   a. *Tentative trust taxable income.* Initially, trust taxable income is gross income and gains less deductions for expenses (such as trustee's fees) and losses. The basis of the trust in those of its assets received by gift or bequest are determined under § 1014 or § 1015, as the case may be.

   b. *Deductible distributions.* Basically, distributions are deductible to the extent of trust DNI (Distributable Net Income). § 651, 661. DNI is defined as tentative trust taxable income, *supra*, but (generally) excluding (except in the year the trust terminates) net capital gains that are allocated to corpus under the law of trusts. § 643(a). Distributions are gross income to the distributees to the same extent they are deductible by the trust. § 652, 662. Thus, distributions are deemed to come "first" out of the current year's (modified) taxable income (DNI).

   c. *Nondeductible distributions.* If distributions for the year exceed trust DNI, the excess distribution is neither deductible by the trust nor includible by distributees. Conceptually, such excess is deemed to come from the "corpus" in the tax sense, which is the amount received tax-free by the trust under §§ 101 and 102 and passed through to the distributees as having the same tax-free character.

d. *Conduit principle*. The "character" of income at the trust level passes through to the beneficiaries. Thus, if a distribution is deemed to consist of tax-exempt income under § 103, the tax-exempt amount is excluded by the distributee, but cannot be deducted by the trust.

e. *Trust taxable income*. Trust taxable income is tentative taxable income less the distribution deduction, *supra*, and less the specific exemption of $100 or $300. § 642(b).

f. *Trust tax*. The trust tax is figured under § 1(e), where the highest marginal rate (39.6%) is applicable to trust taxable income in excess of $7,500 (as indexed for inflation).

Example: D creates a testamentary trust with $1 million (the value for estate tax purposes), income and/or corpus to B, in the trustee's discretion, remainder to C upon B's death. The trust, not being a grantor trust or a beneficiary-owned trust, is a separate taxpayer for income tax purposes. The trust has no gross income on the receipt of the securities by reason of § 102. The trust has a basis in the securities of $1 million under § 1014. In year 1, the trust receives interest and dividends of $60,000 and incurs capital gains of $12,000, which are allocated to corpus. The trust incurs deductible expenses of $2,000. Tentative trust TI is $70,000 ($60,000 + $12,000 - $2,000). DNI is $58,000 (tentative trust TI less capital gains allocated to corpus).

First scenario. The trust distributes $20,000 to B during year 1. The trust's distribution deduction is $20,000, the lesser of the $20,000 distributed or the DNI of $58,000. B includes $20,000 in GI, none of which is deemed to be capital gains. (These results occur regardless of whether the distribution comes out of the "income" account or the "corpus" account.) The trust claims an exemption of $100. Thus, trust TI is $49,900 ($70,000 tentative TI - $20,000 - $100), which is taxed under 1(e), except for the $12,000 of capital gains, which is subject to the § 1(h) maximum marginal rate.

Second scenario. The trust distributes $60,000 to B during year 1. Here the distribution deduction is $58,000 (lesser of distribution or DNI). B has ordinary gross income of $58,000. (Essentially, B obtains the benefit of the $2,000 expense deduction). The trust has taxable income of $11,900, which is capital gains subject to the § 1(h) rate.

Third scenario. The trust distributes $84,000 to B during year 1. The results to the trust are the same as in scenario 2. B has gross income of $58,000, and the rest is tax free.

5. *Estates*. An "estate" is an income-tax entity arising on the death of a decedent and terminating upon the winding-up of estate administration. (The decedent's final taxable year ends on the day of her death.) Estates are treated for income tax purposes in the same manner as trusts, *supra*, and are also subject to the § 1(e)

"compressed" rate schedule. There is no such thing as a "grantor estate" or a "beneficiary-owned estate." Some of the important rules that mainly apply to estates (and not trusts) are described below.

a. *Certain devises ignored.* For income tax purposes, an estate is not deemed to own property (usually real estate) that, under state law, "vests" immediately in the devisee or heir and is not subject to estate administration. Such property is deemed owned by the devisee or heir immediately after the decedent's death, and any income and deductions arising from such property after the decedent's death belong to the devisee or heir, not the estate, for income tax purposes.

b. *Certain distributions ignored.* Distributions in satisfaction of specific (property) bequests or fixed monetary are not treated as "distributions" for purposes of the deduction-inclusion scheme, meaning that they are excludable by the distributee but not deductible by the estate. § 663(a)(1). Distributions in satisfaction of residuary bequests and intestate shares (and in satisfaction of "formula pecuniary" bequests) are treated as distributions that are deductible by the estate and carry income to the distributee (to the extent of estate DNI).

c. *Administration expenses.* Estate administration expenses that are deducted for estate tax purposes cannot be deducted for estate *income* tax purposes. § 642(g).

d. *Exemption.* The exemption for estates is $600. § 642(b).

D. *Basis rules.* Property received as a gratuitous transfer in kind has a basis determined as follows:

1. *Gifts of appreciated property.* For appreciated property (value at time of gift exceeds donor's basis), the donor's basis carries over. § 1015(a). Such carryover basis is adjusted upwards (but not in excess of the fair market value of the property at the time of gift) by that portion of the gift tax (if any) attributable to the unrealized appreciation at the date of gift. § 1015(d)(6).

2. *Gifts of depreciated property.* For depreciated property: (1) if the donee sells the property for less than the gift-time value, the donee's basis is equal to the gift-time value; (2) if the donee sells the property for an amount greater than the gift-time value but less than the donor's basis, the donee's basis is equal to the amount realized, producing no gain or loss; and, (3) if the donee sells the property for more than the donor's basis, the donor's basis carries over. § 1015(a).

3. *Spousal gifts.* Gifts, sales, and other inter vivos transfers between husband and wife always have a carryover basis under § 1041 (rather than § 1015).

4. *Bequests, etc.* Property included in the gross estate acquires a basis equal to its estate tax value (usually the value at the date of death). § 1014(a)

5. *Planning.* The rules of §§1014 and 1015 have the following planning implications: (1) appreciated property should be held until death, as opposed to being sold or given away; and (2) depreciated property should be sold, but if the

loss cannot be deducted it might be better to make a gift of the property than to hold onto it until death.

6. **_IRD._** Income earned before death but not received until after death (including deferred compensation, pension benefits, annuity benefits, and employee death benefits) is referred to as "income in respect of a decedent" ("IRD").

   a. _Includable by recipient, not earner._ Instead of retroactively including such income on the decedent's final income tax return, § 691(a) requires such income to be included by the actual recipient. In many cases, the recipient will be the decedent's estate as an income tax entity.

   b. _Carryover basis._ In order to "protect" such an inclusionary rule, § 1014(b) provides that the asset which is the "right to receive the IRD" (which is included in the decedent's gross estate for estate tax purposes) has a carryover basis.

      Example: Assume that the decedent earned $1,000 of salary before death which is paid to her estate after death. Although the asset (salary claim) is worth around $1,000, it has a zero basis under § 1014(b) because the decedent, on the cash method of accounting, never included the salary in gross income, so that the salary is fully includable (without offset) by the estate when received. (It is not included on the decedent's final income tax return.)

   c. _Section 691(c) deduction._ The taxpayer required to include IRD in gross income can claim a deduction, under § 691(c), equal to the net estate tax (if any) allocable to the inclusion of the "right to the IRD" in the decedent's taxable estate.

7. **_Basis to trusts and estates._** Property acquired by an estate or trust as a result of gift, bequest, etc., has a basis determined under the foregoing, or has a cost basis if purchased by the estate or trust.

8. **_Basis to distributees_**:

   a. _Pecuniary legacies._ If an estate (or trust) distributes appreciated or depreciated property to a legatee (or beneficiary) in full satisfaction (at the asset's value) of a pecuniary legacy (bequest of a fixed or formula-derived sum of money), the distribution is treated as a sale, the amount realized being the amount of the pecuniary legacy. _Kenan v. Com'r,_ 114 F.2d 217 (2d Cir. 1940). The legatee acquires a "cost basis" equal to the amount of the pecuniary legacy.

   b. _Other distributions._ Distributions in satisfaction of other (specific property and residuary) bequests or inheritances and from trusts generally are not "realization" events. Here, the trust's or estate's basis carries over to the distributee. However, the personal representative or trustee can elect to treat such distributions (except in the case of specific property bequests) as realization events, the amount realized being equal to the fair market value of the property upon distribution. In that case, the distributee obtains a basis equal to such fair market value. _See_ §§ 643(e)(3) and (4).

9. ***Basis of interests in trusts***. A trust beneficiary might sell her income interest or remainder interest, in which case it is necessary to determine the seller's basis in the interest sold.

   a. *Interests acquired by gratuitous transfer:*

      (1) Income and possessory interests. The holder of an income interest for life or a term of years, or a life estate or estate for years, has a zero basis in his or her interest as such, assuming the interest was acquired by gratuitous transfer. §§ 273 (no amortization deduction) and 1001(e) (no basis in figuring gain or loss).

      (2) Remainder interests. The holder of the remainder interest has a "floating" basis equal to the trust's or estate's initial § 1014 or § 1015 basis multiplied by the actuarial factor for the remainder interest as it rises with the passage of time. Regs. §§ 1.1014-5 & 1.1015-1(b).

   b. *Purchased interests:*

      (1) Income and possessory interests. A purchased income or possessory interest is a wasting asset the cost of which can be amortized over its actuarial life expectancy, except where a related party owns the remainder interest. *See* § 167(e).

      (2) Remainder interests. A purchased vested remainder grows in value with the passage of time (in a way similar to an original-issue-discount obligation), but such value increases are not gross income, nor does the basis of the remainder increase with the passage of time.

   c. *Trust termination.* If a trust terminates with the assets being distributed to the trust remainder, the holder of the remainder interest does not suffer a realization event on account of "exchanging" the remainder interest for the trust assets. (*A fortiori*, the vesting or failure of a remainder interest is not a realization event, except that the failure of a *purchased* contingent remainder would give rise to a loss deduction.) The remainder's basis in the assets is determined under § 643(e), *supra,* which (carryover or fair market value) basis supersedes the remainder's basis in the remainder interest prior to the termination of the trust.

CHAPTER 1 - QUESTIONS, ANSWERS, AND TIPS

EXAM TIPS:

1. Read what the question asks for. Does it call for a computation? Issue spotting and analysis (such as gift, estate, and/or GST treatment of a given transfer)? Planning advice (whether a given transfer is a sound tax-avoidance device)? A discussion of policy? Statutory exegesis (perhaps using an unfamiliar Code section)? How to act as a lawyer?

2. Determine what taxes are involved in the question. A given inter vivos transfer might conceivably be subject to all three transfer taxes. Keep in mind that, although the gift and estate taxes are "integrated" in the computational sense, that estate and gift tax doctrine

are often separate, especially with regard to what is a taxable transfer. And remember that the income tax, and its doctrine, are completely separate from the transfer taxes.

REVIEW QUESTIONS

1. **Q:** In 2000, D made a taxable gift (TG) of $500,000. In 2002, D dies with a taxable estate (TE) of $1 million. what is D's gift and estate tax liability?

   A: The year 2000 gift produces a tentative tax of $155,800 under § 2001(c). The available unified credit for that year is $220,550. One uses so much of the credit as is necessary to reduce the tax to zero. (Use of the credit is mandatory, not optional.) Although a gift tax return for 2000 must be filed in 2001, there is no net gift tax due.

   The taxable estate is stipulated to be $1 million. (Although D died within three years of making the gift, there is no inclusion under § 2035(b) of gift tax, because no gift tax was paid.) The cumulative tax base (CTB) is $1.5M ($1M TE + $0.5M TG). The tentative tax on the cumulative tax base is $555,800 under § 2001(c). There are two ways to reach the correct result:

   What's-really-going-on method: First figure the before-credit tax "on" the $1M TE by subtracting the before-credit tax on the $0.5M TG ($155,800) from the before-credit tax on the CTB ($555,800), which is $400,000. From this subtract the remaining unused credit of $74,000 ($229,800 available in 2002 less $155,800 used in 2000). The net estate tax after the unified transfer tax credit (but disregarding other possible credits) is $326,000.

   Statutory method: Follow § 2001(b). From the tentative tax on the CTB ($555,800), subtract the *after*-credit gift tax (0), and the full unified transfer credit $229,800), which yields $326,000.

2. **Q:** What taxes are the following transfers subject to (disregarding the income tax). Assume the transferor is unmarried.

   (a) A makes an outright gift of $100K to her grandchild.
   (b) B creates a revocable inter vivos trust with $1M.
   (c) C creates a trust with $1M, income to himself for life, remainder to C's child D.
   (d) Same as (c), except that D is A's grandchild.
   (e) E takes out insurance on her own life, face amount $1M, naming cousin F as sole beneficiary. Total premiums paid by E are $600K.

   A: This question asks merely what transfer taxes are implicated; it implies that exemptions, deductions, credits, and computations be disregarded. Some of these answers might be difficult to *fully* extract from the text of this chapter, but these questions are designed to highlight common and important situations and to lead forward into subsequent chapters.

   (a) A has made a gift of $100K for gift tax purposes, $10K of which is excluded (assuming no other gifts from A to this grandchild during the taxable year). The net gift of $90K is also a direct-skip generation-skipping transfer. (Yes, it may be covered by the exemption, but an "exemption" is more like a deduction than an exclusion, and the allocation of the GST exemption to a particular transfer is optional.)

(b) Although the revocable trust created by B is an inter vivos transfer, it is incomplete for gift tax purposes, and therefore not a "gift." (As will be seen later, distributions from the trust to any beneficiary other than B (or, if B is married, to B's spouse) will be treated as gifts from B to that person.) A revocable transfer ia a common type of inter vivos transfer that will be included in the gross estate. Hence, on B's death the *then* value of the trust will be included in B's gross estate.

(c) This inter vivos transfer is complete, but (conceptually) one can't make a gift to oneself. But there is a present gift of a future (remainder) interest to D. That's right, the gift to D occurs when C creates the trust, not when C dies. (A transfer that occurred only on C's death couldn't be a "gift" by C for gift tax purposes.) The gift of the future interest would be valued using actuarial tables issued under § 7520. Suppose the remainder was worth $260,000. That is a gift, and, as will be seen later, because it is a "future interest," it does not qualify for the $10K gift exclusion. Section 2702, enacted in 1990, now treats (contrary to logic) the retained income interest as a gift by A. Therefore, C is also charged with a gift of $740K. (Since this is not really a gift, it is not eligible for the $10K annual exclusion.) Hence, the taxable gift is $1 million total. When C dies, the then value of the trust is included in A's gross estate under § 2036(a)(1). This type of transfer is considered by Congress to be "testamentary," so as to justify estate inclusion, because D's *possession or enjoyment* (as opposed to the acquisition or vesting of the interest) only shifts from C to D at C's death. Since the gift tax value of the remainder is also included in the gross estate, the $260K is removed from the "adjusted taxable gifts" total. In sum, this transfer adds $740K (deemed gift of retained income interest) and the estate tax value of the *entire* trust (the value of the income interest being now worth zero) to the cumulative tax base. This is not good.

(d) Same analysis as the foregoing, with added GST exposure. The creation of the trust by C is not a direct-skip transfer, because C (a non-skip person) is a current beneficiary. The death of C constitutes this as a direct-skip transfer, because it is then subject to estate tax and goes directly to a "skip person." See § 2612(c) and 2613. (If the income beneficiary were C's child instead of C, then the trust would be a gift in full but not subject to estate tax, since C retains no interest; there would be no direct-skip transfer at the time of gift or the death of C or the child, but the child's death would cause a "taxable termination" for GST purposes. It would be C's exemption, not that of the child or of D, that could be allocated to this transfer.)

(e) The taking out of insurance on one's own life is not a completed gift, even though another person is designated beneficiary, because E still owns the policy and can change the beneficiary. On E's death the full $1M proceeds (not the cash surrender value just prior to E's death) are included in E's gross estate under § 2042(2). Presumably F is not a "skip person" (*i.e.*, two or more generations below E); hence, there is no GST exposure. If F were a skip person, there would be a direct-skip transfer as of E's death. If F dies before E, nothing is included in F's gross estate, since F has only an "expectancy," rather than a "property interest."

GIFT TAX

▶ **CHAPTER SUMMARY**

CHAPTER 2: GIFT TAX

Introduction. The gift tax is imposed on "taxable gifts," meanings "gifts" (net of exclusions and offsets) reduced by amounts qualifying for the marital and charitable deductions.

The issues, in rough analytical order, are:

Is there a gift, net of consideration in money or money's worth?
Who is the donor?
Is the transfer complete or incomplete?
Are there retained interests that can be subtracted from the amount of the gift?
What is the value of the gift?
Is the gift wholly or partially within the present-interest exclusion?
Does the gift qualify for the charitable or marital deduction?
What tax, if any, is owed?

There exist present other issues relating to jurisdiction and procedure, as well.

FEDERAL
GIFT TAX
JURISDICTION

I. FEDERAL GIFT TAX JURISDICTION:

A. Citizens and Residents. The gift tax applies in full to any individual who is either a citizen of the United States or a "resident" thereof as defined in § 7701(b). § 2501(a)(1).

B. Nonresident Aliens. Nonresident noncitizens ("nonresident aliens") are subject to federal gift tax as follows:

1. ***Real property and tangible personal property.*** Nonresident aliens are taxed on gifts of such property located in the United States. § 2511(a); Reg. § 25.2511-3(a)(1)(ii).

2. ***Intangible property.*** Intangible property "located" in the United States is subject to gift tax only if the nonresident alien is an expatriate as defined in § 2501(a)(3) & (4). § 2501(a)(2); Reg. § 25.2511-3(a)(2)(i).

3. ***Treaties.*** The foregoing (as well as the gift and estate taxation abroad of U.S. citizens and residents) can be affected by bilateral treaty between the United States and a foreign country.

SCOPE OF
GIFT TAX

II. SCOPE OF GIFT TAX. Basically, the gift tax reaches any inter vivos transfer that depletes the donor's potential gross estate.

A. Source of Doctrine. The gift tax rules as to "what is a gift" are unique to the gift tax and not imported from other areas of law. The Code doesn't say much about what is a gift, and the doctrine has mostly developed from regulations under §§ 2511 and 2512 and court decisions. State property rules (such as "donative intent") pertaining to whether a transfer is to be considered a "gift" are not controlling per se. On the other hand, property law is relevant to the issue of whether and when a transfer has occurred, what rights and interests are involved, and who is the transferor. *See* Reg. § 25.2511-1(g)(1). Income tax rules as to what is a gift under § 102 are not applicable. *Farid-es-Sultaneh v. Com'r,* 160 F.2d 812 (2d Cir. 1947).

B. **Not Necessary to Identify Donees.** Since the key to the idea of "gift" is that of estate depletion, it is not necessary that the donee(s) and their interests be identifiable or ascertainable. *Smith v. Shaughnessy,* 318 U.S. 176 (1943); Reg. 25.2511-2(a).

Example: *D* creates an irrevocable trust, naming the *X* Bank as trustee, income and/ or corpus to be paid to such of *D*'s children, and in such amounts, as the trustee determines in its sole discretion, with the trustee having the power to accumulate income, and upon the death of the last surviving child of *D*, the trust is to terminate and the assets are to be distributed to such persons (excluding the estate of such child or its creditors) as such child appoints by will, or if no such appointment is made, to the then living issue of *D*'s grandparents per stirpes. Here, it cannot be ascertained at the time of the transfer how much, if anything, will be received by any of the (possibly) large number of potential beneficiaries (including possible appointees and contingent takers in default of appointment). Nevertheless, this is a gift by *D* of the full amount transferred to the trust.

C. **Transfer Must Be Inter Vivos.** Since the estate tax has jurisdiction over transfers occasioned by a person's death, the gift tax can only reach inter vivos transfers. However, an inter vivos transfer might take the form of a gift of a future interest or a binding agreement (or promise) to make a future transfer.

Example: *D* creates an irrevocable trust, which is to pay an annuity of $X to *D* for life, remainder to *C*. Here, *D* is making a present gift of a future interest to *C*, even though *C* won't take possession of any assets until *D*'s death.

Example: *E* enters into a binding contract to transfer Blackacre to *C* as of the 10th anniversary of the contract. Assuming this transaction is otherwise in the nature of a gift (as opposed to, say, a commercial transaction), *E* is making a gift as of the contract date. *See*, e.g., Rev. Rul. 79-384, 1979-2 C.B. 344.

Example: *F* executes a will that leaves Blackacre to *C*. *F* subsequently is adjudged incompetent, so that the will (in effect) is not capable of being altered or revoked. Nevertheless, at no time has *F* made any gift, since a will only "speaks" as of the decedent's death.

D. **Transferor Must Be an Individual.** Since only individuals are subject to estate tax, only individuals can be subject to gift tax. Nevertheless, legal entities can be vehicles (or intermediaries) for gifts by individuals.

Example: A revocable trust created by *A* is to distribute income and/or corpus to any of *A* or *A*'s children as the trustee decides. The creation of a *revocable* trust is not a completed transfer (gift) by *A*, since *A* can repossess the trust property and income at any time. However, if the trust distributes income to *B*, that is considered a gift by *A*, the inter vivos donor (assuming that *A* is still living), since amounts distributed from the trust are no longer subject to the power of revocation. The donor is *A*, not the trust itself, or the trustee of the trust.

Example: A closely-held corporation voluntarily distributes $15,000 to a key employee's widow. This might be characterized as a gift by the shareholders of the corporation.

E. **Transfer Must Be of Money or Property.** Since the estate tax reaches estate transfers of only money and property, it follows from the concept of "estate depletion" that the gift tax only reaches inter vivos transfers of money and property. Section 2501(a)(1) states that a gift transfer must be of property (or interests therein).

1. *Money or property.* A transfer for gift tax purposes must be of money or property. § 2501(a)(1). This principle follows from the fact that the donor's potential gross estate consists of money and property.

2. *Services:*

   a. *Performance without compensation.* Performing services for another without compensation is not a gift under the gift tax. *Com'r v. Hogle,* 165 F.2d 352 (10th Cir. 1947). This is so even though the refusal to accept compensation increases the wealth of another by relieving the latter of a potential cost. This example illustrates the principle that creating wealth in another is not sufficient to yield a gift; the donor must part with existing wealth.

   b. *Earned salary declined.* The outcome would be different if a person earned salary under a preexisting employment contract but then declined to accept it; in that case the donor has property (a claim for money) which is relinquished for another's benefit. And clearly there would be a gift if wages earned were paid instead to a third party.

3. *Intangible benefits.* The gift tax does not reach transfers of "intangible" benefits, such as love, friendship, socialization, acculturation, exposure to potential friends, lovers, business opportunities, and so on.

F. **Money or Property Must Otherwise Be in Donor's Estate.** It is not necessary that a person part with possession of money or property already owned. A gift can be "constructive," *i.e.,* a refusal to accept a preferred increase in wealth in a way that deflects wealth to the natural objects of one's bounty. An example would be where a parent forgives a repayment obligation arising from a loan that had earlier been made to a child. This topic is explored further under the rubric of Disclaimers. See II.C., E., and F., *infra.*

G. **Aim Must Be To Increase Wealth of Others.** The gift tax does not reach every depletion of the transferor's potential gross estate; it reaches only gratuitous transfers, i.e., transfers whose aim is to increase the wealth of others.

1. *Commercial transactions.* Ordinary (arm's-length) business and investment transactions, including the settlement of disputed claims, are excluded from the concept of gift for gift tax purposes. Reg. § 25.2512-8. Both parties materially benefit from a commercial transaction. *See Estate of Anderson v. Com'r,* 8 T.C. 706 (1947) (even bad bargain in ordinary course of business is non-gift). But refer to IV.E., *infra,* dealing with non-arms-length dispute settlements.

2. *Personal consumption.* Personal consumption depletes the consumer's gross estate, but it is not a gift because consumption entails a direct material benefit, with no aim to enrich the payee (etc.) for its own sake. *See* the various opinions in *Carson v. Com'r,* 71 T.C. 252 (1978) *(reviewed) (acq.), aff'd,* 641 F.2d 864 (10th Cir. 1981).

3. ***Political contributions.*** These are similar to consumption, although there are also identifiable beneficiaries of the contributions. *See Carson, supra.*

4. ***Forced exactions:***

   a. *In general.* Taxes, fines, assessments, penalties, damage awards, and similar obligations imposed by law or legal action are generally not treated as gifts.

   b. *Section 2515: Certain GSTs treated as gifts.* Under § 2515 any GST paid with respect to a "direct skip" transfer which is also a taxable gift is treated as an addition to the gift for gift tax purposes. The application of this rule is illustrated in Chapter I, at IV.C.5.a.(1).

5. ***Support payments.*** Support transfers to spouses and dependents under legal obligations are not gifts, even where the obligations are assumed voluntarily. *See Converse v. Com'r,* 5 T.C. 1014 (1945) (IRS concession), *aff'd,* 163 F.2d 131 (2d Cir. 1947). Support can be characterized as both a forced exaction and as nonselfish consumption of the donor. Although most support is provided in-kind and is consumed by the recipient, it depletes the provider's potential gross estate and builds up that of the providee (by freeing the latter's own resources from having to be spent). Doctrinally, this exclusion is founded on the language in § 2501(a)(1) that refers to transfers of property "by gift."

6. ***Transfers pursuant to divorce.*** Section 2516 excludes transfers to spouses and ex-spouses pursuant to an agreement dealing with marital property rights. Also excluded are transfers to provide for a reasonable allowance for the support during minority of issue of the marriage. The exclusions only apply if divorce occurs during the period running from one year before to two years after the date the agreement is entered into. Even if § 2516 does not apply, divorce-related "support" transfers to ex-spouses and minor children under modifiable court decrees are exempt from gift tax. *Harris v. Com'r,* 340 U.S. 106 (1950). If the *Harris* doctrine is unavailable, the transfer may still be eligible for full or partial "consideration offset." *See* H.C.3., *infra.*

H. **Transfers for Consideration.** A transfer is not a gift if made for "adequate and full consideration in money or money's worth," since in that case there is no net depletion of the donor's potential gross estate. Similarly, if "partial" consideration in money or money's worth is received, the amount of the gift is only the excess of the amount transferred over the value of the consideration received. § 2512(b).

1. ***Money or money's worth.*** The consideration must, of course, be in money or money's worth (property or debt relief), since only money or money's worth will replenish the donor's potential gross estate. Thus, consideration for transfer tax purposes is not to be confused with consideration for contract-law purposes. Love, affection, and the promise to marry clearly don't qualify for transfer tax purposes. *Com'r v. Wemyss,* 324 U.S. 303 (1945).

2. ***Release of marital rights.*** A transfer (typically to an ex-spouse or a prospective spouse) in return for the latter releasing her inheritance, dower, and succession rights is not a transfer for consideration, since the (foregone) estate transfers would have been subject to estate tax. *Merrill v. Fahs,* 324 U.S. 308 (1945); Reg. § 25.2512-8. In other words, the transfer is an accelerated estate transfer. (Nevertheless, transfers related to divorce and separation may be exempt under

§ 2516 or the *Harris* doctrine, *see* II,H.6., *supra*.) On the other hand, the release of "support" rights and any right to receive property upon divorce does qualify as consideration, since the (foregone) support and property transfers would have been exempt from gift tax. Here the transfer is an acceleration of a non-gift transfer.

3. ***Consideration "for" what?*** Consideration exempts or offsets only those transferred interests to which the consideration pertains. Thus, if *A* creates a trust, income to *B* for life, remainder to *C*, and *C* transfers money or property to *A*, only the gift to *C* will be eliminated or reduced by the consideration. *See* Rev. Rul. 77-314, 1977-2 C.B. 349. If the consideration provided by *C* exceeds the value of the interest received by *C*, then *C* has made a gift of the excess to either *A* or (indirectly, through *A*) to *B*.

4. ***Net gifts.*** A donor can make a gift conditioned on the donee's paying the gift tax. (Legally, the liability to pay the gift tax is that of the donor.) Since the payment of the gift tax relieves the donor of a liability, it counts as a valid consideration offset in figuring the amount of the gift, but since the (net) gift and the gift tax are mutually dependent variables, a "circular" computation is involved, which can be solved by use of a simple formula:

Gift tax = $\dfrac{\text{tentative tax on full fmv}}{1 + \text{rate of tax}}$

The "rate of tax" (expressed as a decimal) is the highest marginal rate of tax (estimated by "inspection") on the net gift. Rev. Rul. 75-72, 1975-1 C.B. 310.

5. ***Loans.*** A "loan" to a related party (not in the ordinary course of business, etc.) involves a transfer for consideration, namely, the repayment obligation. However, the consideration (the promise to repay the loan with interest) must be bona fide.

   a. *Invalid consideration.* If the obligor's objective circumstances indicate an inability to repay (or, possibly, the absence of an intent to repay), the "consideration" will be treated as a sham and disregarded, meaning that the purported loan is really a gift. *Estate of Mitchell v. Com'r*, T.C. Memo. 1982-185.

   b. *Intent not to enforce loan.* In Rev. Rul. 77-299, 1977-22 C.B. 14, the Service ruled that there was a gift (of property) arising from a purported installment sale of real estate to a grandchild where the grandmother-seller intended to forgive the installment obligations as they became due. This result is questionable, because the installment obligations represented objective wealth to the grandmother until such time as they were actually forgiven. *See Haygood v. Com'r*, 42 T.C. 936 (1964), *nonacq.*, Rev. Rul. 77-299, 1977-2 C.B. 14.

   c. *Below-interest term loan.* A below-interest loan is a loan in which the interest rate is zero or below the prevailing interest in the economy (the discount rate). A "term loan" is a loan to be repaid after (or over) a specified time period. In a below-market term loan, the consideration (the repayment obligation) is less than "full and adequate" because the discounted present value of all future principal and interest payments will be less than the amount lent. See Rev. Rul. 73-61, 1973-1 C.B. 408 (prior law). This situation, which yields a gift equal to the excess of the amount lent over the present value of the repayment obligation, is now governed by § 7872, *infra*.

d. *Below-interest demand loan.* Since the lender can call the loan principal immediately, the "consideration" is worth exactly the amount lent. However, the Supreme Court in *Dickman v. Com'r,* 465 U.S. 330 (1984), eschewed a "consideration" analysis, and held that an interest-free demand loan between related parties yielded a gift, *during each calendar year,* of the interest foregone by the lender from the borrower. Thus, gifts of foregone interest occur with the passage of time. This area is now governed by § 7872, *infra*.

e. Section 7872. Below-interest loans are now governed by § 7872, which follows the outlines of prior law but fills in crucial details and also provides for corollary income tax rules (which are not discussed herein).

   (1) *Term loan.* A below-market gift term loan yields a gift, all in the year the money is lent, equal to the excess of the amount lent over the present value of all future principal and interest payments (figured by using the "applicable federal rate" compounded semi-annually). § 7872(b)(1) (triggered by § 7872(d)(2)).

   (2) *Demand loan.* A below-market gift demand loan yields an annual gift equal to the "foregone interest," meaning the excess of the interest that would have accrued during the year using the "applicable federal rate" over any interest actually payable for the year under the loan. § 7872(a) & (e)(2).

I. **Rent-Free Use of Property.** In theory, the lending of property on a rent-free basis could be treated the same as an interest-free loan.

   1. ***Loans of artworks.*** Such an approach is suggested by § 2503(g), which treats loans of artworks to museums, etc., as being specifically excluded from the concept of "gift," thereby implying that rent-free loans of property generally entail gifts. However, there is no statutory provisions, regulation, or published ruling explicitly stating that the rent-free use of property is a gift, and assumptions by Congress about "what the law is" are not themselves law.

   2. ***Possible exception for consumer assets.*** Perhaps this distinction could be drawn: a below-interest loan of cash depletes the lender's estate by being an investment that fails to yield income; a loan of personal-use property does not normally involve a depletion of the lender's estate because the lender, by purchasing the asset in the first place, has committed herself to personal consumption, not investment. Hence, the rent-free use of the property does not deplete the lender's gross estate any more than if the lender used the property herself. This theory (not expressed in any case, regulation, or ruling) might not hold up, however, in the following cases: (a) a loan of jewelry, an artwork, or a collectible, that has a strong "investment" flavor, (b) a loan, for a significant period of time, of "surplus" rentable property, such as a second residence or vacation home, and (c) a loan of nonsurplus property where the lender spends additional funds to obtain the consumption foregone by the lending transaction (e.g., a mother lends a car to her teenage daughter for a week, and the mother rents a car for herself for the same week).

3. **IRS indifference.** The IRS does not appear to be pursuing rent-free loans of property to any noticeable extent.

J. **Transfers Excluded by Statute or Regulation**:

1. **Political contributions.** Contributions to political organizations described in § 527(e)(1) are not treated as gifts under § 2501(a)(5). Political contributions not covered by § 2501(a)(5) may still be excludible. *See* G.3., *supra*.

2. **Tuition and medical care.** Amounts paid on behalf of any individual for tuition or medical care are exempt. § 2503(e).

   a. *Direct payment requirement.* The payment must be directly to the educational institution or medical care provider. Payments of cash to donee individuals are not excluded even if the donee is "required" to turn around and pay the educational institution or health care provider.

   b. *Medical insurance.* The exclusion for medical care is lost if the donee is compensated by insurance.

   c. *No legal obligation requirement.* It is not a prerequisite for the exclusion that the donor be legally obligated to support the donee. *See* Reg. § 25.2503-6.

3. **Exclusions discussed elsewhere**:

   a. *Loans of artworks to charities.* As previously mentioned, any loan of a (tangible) artwork to a qualified charity is not treated as entailing a gift. § 2503(g).

   b. *Transfers related to divorce. See* § 2516, discussed at H.6. *supra*.

   c. *Annual $10,000 exclusion for present interests.* There is an exclusion equal to $10,000 (indexed for inflation) per donor, per donee, per year. This exclusion is not available with respect to gifts of "future interests"; hence, this exclusion is commonly referred to as the "present interest exclusion." § 2503(b) & (c), discussed at VIII.A., *infra*.

   d. *Qualified disclaimers.* A disclaimer is a refusal to accept a gratuitous receipt, with the result that the cash or property passes to another. A "qualified disclaimer" under § 2518, discussed at IV.D.3.b., *infra*, is not a gift.

   e. *Waiver of spousal pension rights.* This special category of disclaimer is exempt under § 2503(f), discussed at IV.D.4., infra.

4. **Payment of joint income tax liability and gift tax resulting from gift-splitting.** If one spouse pays all of the couple's joint-return income tax liability, there is no gift. Similarly, there is no gift if one spouse pays the other spouse's gift tax liability arising from gift splitting under § 2513. Reg. § 25.2511-1(d). These rules are trivial, since any gift to the other spouse would be deductible.

III. **IDENTIFYING THE DONOR.** The donor is the individual whose potential estate is being depleted by the transfer. Obviously, only individuals (not entities) can be donors for gift tax purposes.

A. **Fiduciaries.** If an individual trustee makes a distribution to a beneficiary, the trustee is not a donor for gift tax purposes in her trustee capacity, even though the trustee is the "legal" owner of the property.

   1. *Beneficial ownership.* The estate and gift taxes reach only beneficial ownership.

      a. *Trust property excluded.* If the trustee died, the trust property would not be included in the trustee's gross estate on account of the trustee's legal ownership attendant upon trustee status.

      b. *No donor status.* Similarly, executors, administrators, agents, bailees, and other fiduciaries are not donors for gift tax purposes by reason of their office. Reg. § 25.2511-1(g)(1).

   2. *Fiduciary-beneficiary.* Of course, a fiduciary may also be a beneficial owner, but in that case the gift occurs by reason of the surrender of beneficial ownership, not the transfer of legal ownership, etc.

      Example: A creates an irrevocable inter vivos trust, naming B as sole trustee, income to B for life, with the trustee being given the power to pay corpus to C in the trustee's unfettered discretion, remainder to D upon B's death. B, as trustee, distributes the entire corpus of the trust to C. B has made a gift of her beneficial income interest to C. Reg. § 25.2514-1(b)(2). B acted in such a way as to deprive herself of future income and enrich C. If the corpus could only be payable to C pursuant to a "reasonably fixed or ascertainable standard" (such as "support"), there would be no gift by B, because now B would be acting in a fiduciary capacity rather than as beneficial owner. Reg. § 25.2511-1(g)(2). If K were the trustee (instead of B), paying the corpus to C would not entail a gift by K, since K had no beneficial interest in the trust.

B. **Co-Ownership.** If the transferred property is subject to co-ownership, each co-owner is the transferor of his or her pro-rata share of the property. Reg. § 25.2511-1(e).

   1. *Community property.* Community property, under the laws of Arizona, California, Idaho, Louisiana, Nevada, New Mexico, Texas, Washington, and Wisconsin, plus some foreign countries, is owned 50-50 by husband and wife. Thus, any gift of community property (or an interest therein) is a gift of half of it by the wife and half of it by the husband.

      a. *Role of sole management powers.* In the case of community property, this rule holds true even where one spouse, by virtue of his or her "sole management power" over the property, unilaterally makes the transfer (such person is merely the agent of the "community").

      b. *Community property with right of survivorship.* "Community property with right of survivorship" is classified as community property for purposes of identifying the transferor.

2. ***Tenacies in common.*** A gift of property subject to a tenancy in common is allocated among the tenants in common in proportion to their interests.

3. ***Joint ownership with right of survivorship.*** Gifts involving joint tenancies and tenancies by the entireties were once dealt with under regulations issued under former § 2515, repealed in 1981, dealing with the creation of joint tenancies. (Present § 2515 treats the GST on a direct-skip gift transfer as being a gift. See II.G.4.b., *supra*.) These regulations have been withdrawn and nothing has replaced them, so that there is presently somewhat of a vacuum in this area.

    a. *Result under prior law.* Under prior law, the result essentially hinged on the nature and value of the "interest" of each joint tenant at the time of gift. Thus, if the joint tenancy is "severable" under state law, then each joint tenant is the donor of his or her pro rata fraction of the property. If the tenancy is not severable, each joint tenant's interest (involving a possible right to all or a portion of the income or of possession plus a contingent survivorship right) was to be separately valued, using actuarial methods if necessary.

    b. *Possible continued validity.* This approach may still be valid, as the gift tax is imposed on the (value of) "property" transferred. As a matter of strict logic, however, the gift tax treatment of gifts of jointly-owned property should perhaps be a function of the portion that would be included in the gross estate under § 2040 of each co-tenant on the assumption that each such co-tenant died first. The amount included under the estate tax is not necessarily keyed to the value of the "interest" owned by the decedent either at death (when the value is zero) or just prior to death. *See* Chapter 3, *infra*.

C. **Elective Gift-Splitting.** Under § 2513, husband and wife can elect (by filing a gift tax return indicating the election) to treat any gift of noncommunity property as being made half by each spouse for gift tax purposes (if not for estate tax purposes).

    1. ***Purpose of rule.*** The purpose of this rule is to allow spouses under common-law regimes to be treated like their community-property counterparts.

    2. ***Advantages.*** Gift-splitting under § 2513 is usually advantageous, since;

        (a) it allocates the tax base to two different donors; and

        (b) it multiplies the available present-interest exclusions, *infra*, by two.

    3. ***Jointly held property.*** The election can be made for joint-ownership property, thereby obviating any ambiguity in the law concerning gifts of such property, *supra*.

D. **Indirect Transfers.** When one person transfers property to a second person on the condition she transfer the property to a third person, the second person is simply an agent or intermediary, and the first person is the donor for gift tax purposes. Reg. § 25.2511-1(h)(2).

Example: If *A* transfers property to *B* on condition that *B* transfer the property (or an equivalent amount) to *C*, *A* (not *B*) is the donor for gift tax purposes; *B* is simply the agent of or intermediary for *A*.

1. *Trusts.* Thus, if one creates a trust empowering the trustee (an individual) to distribute income and corpus to various beneficiaries, the grantor (not the trustee) is the donor of any gift resulting from the creation or operation of the trust. See also A.2., *supra.*

2. *Employee benefits.* The employee, not the employer, is generally the donor of any inter vivos gift resulting from an employee benefit payable to third parties. However, the employee is not the donor if the "causal chain" is broken, *i.e.,* if the benefit is not paid under an employment contract, binding resolution, or established policy. *Estate of Bogley v. U.S.,* 514 F.2d 1027 (Ct.Cl. 1975). In *Estate of DiMarco v. Com'r*, 87 T.C. 653 (1986), it was held that there was no transfer by the employee where the employee is automatically covered by the benefit plan and has no control over it. The theory is apparently that the employer, not the employee, is the transferor in such a case. The IRS has acquiesced in *Estate of DiMarco*, but only in cases where, in addition, the employer can modify the plan, and the value of any benefit payble to a third party can't be ascertained before the decedent's death.

3. *Gifts by corporations.* Any gift transfer by a corporation is attributable to the (nondonee) shareholders on a pro rata basis. Reg. § 25.2511-1(h)(1). It would appear that this rule can only come into play in the case of a closely-held corporation. In a publicly-traded corporation, the mass of shareholders would have no influence on the making of the gift, and the effect on their potential estates would be de minimis. This rule could apply in a situation where an employee benefit is not paid pursuant to an employment contract or in a case like *Estate of DiMarco* (except that the latter case involved IBM Corp.). If a controlling interest simply raided the corporate treasury without the other shareholders' consent, there would be no gift by the noncontrolling interests. *Cf. Neeley v. U.S.*, 613 F.2d 802 (Ct.Cl. 1980).

IV. **WHAT IS A TRANSFER? There can be no gift unless there is a "transfer" of wealth by the donor. In general, a transfer is an act (or omission) by a donor that causes his potential gross estate to be depleted and that of another party to be augmented. Most transfers involve gifts in the conventional sense. A gift can also take the form of avoiding certain increases in wealth. These are discussed below.**

WHAT IS A TRANSFER?

A. **Cancellation of Claim or Debt**. A transfer can occur by a person's gratuitously cancelling a debt owed to that person by a third party.

B. **Inter Vivos General Power of Appointment**. A person who possesses an inter vivos general power of appointment is deemed to be the owner of the property subject to the power for estate and gift tax purposes. It follows that acts or events that cause the property to no longer be subject to the power are potentially gifts for gift tax purposes by the person who is the holder of the power.

1. *Definition of General Power.* If *A* creates a trust, income to *B* for life, remainder to *C,* and the trust instrument gives *C* the inter vivos power to pay the corpus to any person, *including herself,* *C* holds an inter vivos "general power of appointment." In general, an inter vivos general power of appointment is a power (created by another party, who is typically the person who created the trust) that enables the holder (donee) of the power to appropriate money or property to herself or her creditors. The fine points of the gift tax definition of "general power

of appointment" (*see* § 2514(c)), are considered at Chapter 3, *infra,* since general powers are more important in the estate tax, and the definition of "general power" is the same for both taxes. The holder of a power of appointment is referred to, under the law of property, as the "donee" of the power, the creator of the power is its "donor" and the potential appointees are the "objects." Under the federal transfer taxes, the term "power of appointment" refers *only to powers created by another party,* not powers held ("retained") by the person creating the power. Reg. § 25.2514-1(b)(2) (first sentence). (Retained-power transfers raise an issue of "incompleteness," *see* V., *infra.*)

2. ***Possession of general power as constructive ownership of property.*** *Possession* of a general power is treated as the equivalent of ownership for gift and estate tax purposes. The theory is one of "constructive ownership," namely, that the donee of the power can take the property and run.

3. ***Exercise of general power as transfer.*** If an inter vivos general power of appointment is exercised so as to cause the property to be paid to a third party (or to otherwise irrevocably cease to be subject to the power), the donee of the power is deemed to have transferred the property for gift (and estate) tax purposes. § 2514(b). The theory is that the donee of the power could have taken the cash or property for herself, and therefore she is deemed to have taken it for herself and re-transferred it to the third party. This rule also backs up the estate tax: Since the mere possession of a general power of appointment at the moment just prior to death would cause the property to be included in the gross estate of the donee of the power, any act (such as exercise of the power) by which the donee of the power removes the property from being subject to the power should (and is) treated as a gift for gift tax purposes. This gift by the donee is not negated by the fact that the creation of the trust by the "donor" was previously subject to gift or estate tax. If the donee also happens to be trustee, the rule described here supersedes the rule for trustees generally (*see* III.A., *supra*), the theory being that the donee, by having the ability to pay the property to herself, essentially did so just prior to causing the corpus to be paid to the third party.

4. ***Release of general power as transfer.*** Under § 2514(b), the release (i.e., surrender, giving up) of a general power of appointment is treated as an "exercise." Thus, in the case where *A* created the trust, income to *B* for life, remainder to *C,* and *C* releases an inter vivos general power, *C* has made a gift transfer of *B*'s income interest (*C* continues to hold the remainder interest). The rationales are exactly the same as for exercising a general power.

5. ***Lapse of general power.*** A "lapse" occurs where the power expires by its own terms, by the passage of time, the happening of a contingency, or an act of a third party.

   a. *Lapse treated as "release."* Under § 2514(e), the lapse of an inter vivos general power of appointment is treated as a "release" (and hence as an "exercise"). Note that this rule applies even where the donee of the power does not take action to separate the property from the power. Thus, in the example cited in the previous item, if *C*'s power expired when she attained the age of 40, at that time she would be treated as having made a gift (to *B*) of *B*'s income interest. Another example: *A* created a trust, each year's income to be paid to *B* on *B*'s demand during *B*'s lifetime, with any income not demanded by *B* to be accumulated and added to corpus, remainder to *C*; *B* has a general power over each year's income, which lapses at the end of each year. Since the lapsed income is added to the corpus, *B* has made a transfer thereof for gift tax purposes (to *C*, but subject to a retained right to the income from such lapsed income).

    b. *"Five-and-five rule."* In the case of a lapse of a general power, § 2515(e) provides that the constructive transfer is exempt from gift tax to the extent of the greater of $5,000 or 5% of the property subject to the power. Thus, in the second example in the preceding item, if the income for the year is $7,000, *B* has made a transfer for gift tax purposes of only $2,000. *See Fish v. U.S.,* 432 F.2d 1278 (9th Cir. 1970) (estate tax).

C. **Inter Vivos Special Powers of Appointment.** An inter vivos "special" power of appointment under the estate and gift taxes is any power (held by an individual) to control the devolution or disposition of property (initially transferred by another party) that is not a "general power of appointment" as defined in § 2514(c). In other words, if the power can't be exercised by the donee of the power to benefit herself or her creditors, it is a special power. The power may be held as trustee or otherwise. Thus, if *A* creates a trust for 30 years, naming *T* as trustee, income and corpus to or among *B*, *C*, and *D* as the trustee shall determine from time to time, remainder to *E*, *T* has a special power.

    1. *Donee of special power is not the owner of the property.* The donee of a special power is not considered the owner of the property for estate and gift tax purposes on account of possessing the power. It follows that the exercise, release, or lapse thereof is not *per se* a gift transfer.

    2. *When the exercise of special power results in a gift transfer.* The donee of the power may also possess a beneficial interest in the trust. If an inter vivos special power is exercised in such a way that the donee of the power divests herself of an interest in the property, the donee has made a gift of that interest. In the example above, *T* has no interest in the trust, meaning that if *T* pays the entire trust property over to *C*, *T* has not made a gift. But take this example: *A* irrevocably in trust, income to *B* for life, remainder to *C*, giving *B* the power to pay all or any of the corpus to *C*. If *B* exercises the power and pays any of the trust corpus to *C*, *B* has made a gift of her own income interest to *C* (the amount of the gift is not the full amount of the distribution but rather the diminution in value of *B*'s income interest caused by the distribution). Reg. § 25.2514-1(b)(2); *Estate of Regester v. Com'r,* 83 T.C. 1 (1984).

    3. *Ascertainable standards exception.* Notwithstanding the rule laid out in item 2 immediately above, if the trust instrument provides that the donee's (trustee's) power is limited by a "reasonably fixed or ascertainable standard," such as "support," "maintenance," "health," "education," or "comfort" (but not "pleasure," "desire," or "happiness"), then the exercise of the power cannot result in a gift by the donee of the power. Reg. § 25.2511-1(g)(2). The rationale here is that the trustee is acting as fiduciary as opposed to acting as a transferor of a beneficial interest.

D. **Constructive Transfers.** A constructive gift transfer occurs when an individual has the right to obtain money or property that doesn't fit into the category of "general power of appointment," but declines to exercise that right in a way that results in the money or property being obtained by a third party. The most common example would be a failure to accept a gift, bequest, inheritance, right to insurance proceeds, or lottery prize, with the result being that another (related) person ends up with the bequest (etc.). The provisions of the Code and regulations pertaining to "powers of appointment" (including the "5-and-5 rule") do not apply as such to one-time refusals to accept accessions to wealth. The concept of power of appointment implies that the power continue over some period of time, as is typical of a trust.

1. ***Constructive gift of insurance proceeds.*** If B owns an insurance policy on the life of I, B could name herself as beneficiary. If B names a third party, C, as beneficiary, the death of I causes the proceeds to be paid by the insurance company directly to C. This is a constructive gift transfer of the proceeds from B to C. (The earlier naming by B of C as the beneficiary was not a gift. It was an incomplete transfer, since B, as policy owner, had the power to revoke, alter, or amend the beneficiary designation.) Another constructive transfer situation is where the insurance on H's life is community property; H dies and all of the proceeds are payable to C. Here, W has made a constructive gift of her half of the proceeds.

2. ***Constructive transfer of death benefit.*** If *H* is the employee and under community property law *W* has a one-half interest in any death benefit, the payment of the death benefit upon *H*'s death to any person other than *W* is a constructive gift by *W* of her half interest in the death benefit.

3. ***Disclaimers***. A disclaimer is a refusal to accept a gratuitous transfer, with the result that the property passes to another. In the abstract, a disclaimer could be treated as acceptance of the property followed by a gift to the ultimate taker.

   a. *Disclaimers under state law.* A disclaimer mechanism usually exists under state law. The disclaimer must usually be in writing delivered to the transferor within a certain period of the transfer. The effect of a state law disclaimer is to treat the disclaiming party as predeceasing the donor or decedent, triggering the law of "lapse" so as to determine the alternate taker(s) of the property. A valid state law disclaimer is not a "gift" by the disclaimant for purposes of state property law; rather, the ultimate taker is deemed to take directly from the transferor. However, the state law of disclaimers is not controlling for federal transfer tax purposes.

   b. *Qualified disclaimer.* Section 2518 holds that a "qualified disclaimer" of a gift, bequest, inheritance, or other accession does not constitute a (constructive-transfer) gift for gift tax purposes. The requirements of § 2518 are designed so as to be (mostly) independent of state law disclaimer rules. If a disclaimer does not "qualify" under § 2518, it is a constructive-transfer gift, even if the disclaimer is valid under state law.

      Example: T dies in the year 2000 and bequeaths Blackacre to B. B disclaims the devise under state law, with the effect that Blackacre passes to B's children in equal shares under the applicable "lapse" rule. If the disclaimer is a qualified disclaimer under § 2518, B is treated as not having made a gift of Blackacre to his children (the children are deemed to take directly from T). If the disclaimer doesn't satisfy the requirements of § 2518, B is treated as having made a gift of Blackacre to his children for gift tax purposes.

      c. *Qualifying the disclaimer.* To be a "qualified disclaimer" under § 2518 (applicable to post-1976 transfers), the following requirements must be satisfied:

(a) The person entitled to the accession must refuse it in a writing delivered to the transferor (etc.) within nine months of the later to occur of (i) the creation of the interest (not its vesting or coming into possession) or (ii) the person's twenty-first birthday;

(b) The disclaimant must not have accepted the property or any of its benefits; and,

(c) The property must pass as a result of such refusal (*i.e.,* under state law), without any direction on such person's part, to another person (unless the disclaiming person is the spouse of the transferor).

d. *When an interest is created.* The rule under § 2518 that a qualified disclaimer must (usually) be made within 9 months of the creation of an interest is significant, since state disclaimer statutes sometimes delay the time to make a disclaimer until the time the interest vests or comes into possession. Thus, if T creates a testamentary trust, income to B for life, remainder to C if living, but if not to D, C and D (who possess alternate contingent remainders) must disclaim within 9 months after T's death (not B's death). However, in the case of joint tenancies with right of survivorship, *the survivorship interest* can be disclaimed within 9 months of the death of the first joint tenant to die. Reg. § 25.2518-2(c)(4). This special rule for joint tenancy survivorship interests, promulgated in 1997, was the result of Court decisions overturning previous regulations to the contrary. *E.g., McDonald v. Com'r,* 853 F.2d 1494 (8th Cir. 1989).

e. *Transfers in lieu of a disclaimer.* There is a procedure for a written transfer of a person's entire interest in property in lieu of a disclaimer, but the transfer must generally track the requirements for a qualified disclaimer. § 2518(c)(3). This type of qualified disclaimer would be used when a state disclaimer procedure is unavailable. A common example would be where the state disclaimer period starts to run from the time an interest vests or comes into possession (as opposed to when an interest is created.) Another example would be when the state disclaimer period ends before the disclaimant reaches the age of 21.

f. *Disclaimer must be unqualified.* A disclaimer is not a "qualified" one if the purported disclaimant accepts benefits under the transfer, is offered consideration for making the disclaimer, or is promised future benefits for making the disclaimer. *See Estate of Monroe v. Com'r,* 124 then F.3d 699 (5th Cir. 1997).

g. *Partial disclaimers.* Section 2518(c)(1) permits a disclaimer of "an undivided portion" of an interest (or power), but other "partial disclaimers" do not qualify (even if valid under state law). *See* Reg. § 25.2518-3.

Example: T bequeaths Blackacre to B. B disclaims a remainder interest in Blackacre (which passes to C), in effect retaining a life estate. Assuming that this type of disclaimer is valid under state law, it is not a qualified disclaimer under § 2518, because it is not a disclaimer of an undivided interest. (An example of the latter would be if B disclaimed a one-half interest so as to end up as a tenant in common with C.) Accordingly, B is deemed to have received Blackacre followed by a gift of a remainder interest in Blackacre.

h. *Prior law*. Section 2518 only applies to interests created after 1976. The law applicable to interests created prior to 1977 still recognizes the concept of a valid disclaimer for transfer tax purposes, but the legal test for a valid disclaimer is less precise and more dependent on state law. Specifically, the disclaimer must be effective under state law and made within a reasonable time after knowledge of the transfer (and before acceptance of benefits under the transfer). *See* Reg. § 25.2511-1(c)(2).

4. *Waiver of spousal pension rights*. Section 401(a)(11) requires that death benefits under certain "qualified" retirement plans be in the form of a survivor annuity for the employee's spouse, but § 417 gives the surviving spouse the power to waive such right. Section 2503(f) treats any such waiver by an employee's spouse as a non-gift for gift tax purposes.

E. **Dispute Settlements**. An individual might attempt to disguise a gift transfer by manufacturing a dispute with a related individual and accepting a settlement, unfavorable to herself and favorable to the related individual. The principal opportunity to make such a "disguised" gift lies in the context of a settlement of a sham will contest or claim. Another situation is an "agreement" to reshuffle interests in an estate according to the supposed "real" desires of the decedent. Such devices will not succeed in disguising a gift for gift tax purposes. However, a bona fide (arms length) settlement of a genuine dispute does not entail any gift transfers, especially if it is approved by a court. *Com'r v. Estate of Vease,* 314 F.2d 79 (9th Cir. 1963); *Estate of Reed v. Com'r,* 171 F.2d 685 (8th Cir. 1948). (The cleaner way to avoid gift tax in these situations is to effect a qualified disclaimer.)

COMPLETED GIFTS (TRANSFERS SUBJECT TO RETAINED POWERS)

V. **COMPLETED GIFTS (TRANSFERS SUBJECT TO RETAINED POWERS). A transfer cannot be a gift for so long as it is incomplete. The retention by the transferor of a power to revoke, alter, or amend renders the transfer incomplete. Incomplete transfers are subject to gift (or estate) tax at a later time.** *See* **generally Reg. § 25.2511-2.**

A. **Power Must be "Retained" by Transferor.** A transfer involving a power to revoke, alter, or amend causes a transfer to be incomplete only if the power was "retained" by the transferor, as opposed to being conferred on the transferor by another party. (The "retention" idea is explored in more detail in the estate tax context.)

1. *Methods for retaining power.* A transferor can retain a power in the instrument of transfer. A power can be retained by creating a trust in which a power is conferred upon the trustee and the grantor names herself as trustee. Also, a power can be retained by a "side" agreement or understanding with the trustee or other transferee.

2. *Presumption that trustee is independent.* But a grantor is normally not considered to retain a power lodged in a trustee just because the trustee is a friend, relative, or business associate of the transferor. Trustees are presumed to adhere to their fiduciary duties.

B. **Power to Revoke.** A revocable transfer is not a completed gift so long as the power to revoke exists. *Burnet v. Guggenheim,* 288 U.S. 280 (1933); Reg. § 25.2511-2(b).

1. *Meaning of "revoke."* A retained power to revoke is a power in the transferor to draw back the property to herself at will.

2. ***Partial power of revocation.*** A power to revoke only a portion of the transfer renders only that portion incomplete. (In this Outline, any trust described in an example or hypothetical is deemed to be irrevocable unless revocability is clearly indicated.)

C. **Power to Amend or Alter. A transfer is incomplete so long as it is subject to a retained power to change the beneficiaries, even in the absence of a retained power to revoke.** *Estate of Sanford v. Com'r,* **308 U.S. 39 (1939).**

1. ***Power to amend.*** A retained power to amend the trust, or a lesser retained power to change the identity or interests of trust beneficiaries, falls within this rule.

2. ***Power to alter.*** Generally, a retained power to "alter" refers to a retained power to alter beneficial interests by effecting distributions of income and/or corpus. Reg. § 25.2511-2(c). The following examples all contain a retained power to alter:

   Example 1: *A* creates a trust, naming herself trustee, income and/or corpus to be distributed to or among *B, C,* and/or *D* in the trustee's discretion, remainder after 30 years to *R.* The entire transfer is incomplete, as *A* has retained the power to alter the beneficial enjoyment of income among *B, C,* and *D* and the power to completely defeat *R*'s remainder interest by invading corpus for *B, C,* and/or *D.*

   Example 2: Same, except the trustee's power to distribute among *B, C,* and/or *D* is limited to the trust income. Here the transfer of the income interest is incomplete and the transfer of the remainder interest is complete. (The valuation of "interests" is dealt with at Part VI, *infra.*)

   Example 3: *A* creates a trust, naming herself trustee, income to *B* or accumulated (and added to corpus) in the trustee's discretion, and upon *B*'s death remainder to *C.* Here *A* has retained the power to alter *B*'s income interest by accumulating the income for ultimate distribution to *C.* *C*'s remainder interest cannot be cut down, so the gift of *C*'s interest is complete.

   Example 4: *A* creates a trust, naming herself as trustee, income to *B* for life, remainder to *C,* with the trustee having the power to invade corpus for *B* in the trustee's discretion. Here, the gift of the remainder interest, not the income interest, is incomplete, since the ultimate enjoyment of it can be shifted from *C* to *B.* Although *B*'s "income interest" as such in the trust would disappear if all of the corpus were paid to *B, B* would then own all the property (including the income therefrom) outright. Hence, the gift of B's income interest is complete.

   Example 5: *A* creates a trust, income to *B* for life, remainder to *C,* but *A* retains a power exercisable through her will to dispose of the trust property at her death to one or more of *A*'s then living issue. *A* has made a completed gift only of an income interest for a period which ends on the earlier to occur of *A*'s death or *B*'s death (if *B* dies before *A,* the property passes to *C* outright and passes beyond the reach of *A*'s power over the trust). *See* Reg. § 25.2511-2(b).

   Note that, in all of these examples, the donor's (grantor's) retained power (typically held in her capacity as trustee) is discretionary, and without limitation by any standards (such as "support" or "maintenance"). The effect of standards is noted at E.3., *infra.*

3. *Interests subject to the power.* As noted above, only the portion of the transfer (detrimentally) affected by the power is incomplete. Thus, a transfer can be part complete and part incomplete. In that case, it is necessary to value the interests that are the subject of a completed transfer. The valuation of interests is taken up in Part VI., *infra*, and transfers subject to retained interests are dealt with in Part VII., *infra*.

D. **Power to Revoke, Alter, or Amend with Consent of an Adverse Party.** A power to revoke, alter, or amend is deemed to be held by the transferor even though the power is held jointly by a "nonadverse" party. Conversely, a power is deemed not held by a transferor if it is held jointly with an "adverse" party. Reg. § 25.2511-2(e). Thus, "adverse party" status can only negate incompleteness (impose completeness), never the other way around.

1. *Adverse party defined.* An "adverse party" is a person whose interest in the transferred property would be adversely affected by the exercise of the power. (The rule, in other words, is based upon assumptions as to how a person would act in her own self-interest.)

2. *Partial adversity.* "Adversity" may exist with respect to some interests but not others; hence, the transfer may be partly complete and partly incomplete. *Camp v. Com'r,* 195 F.2d 999 (1st Cir. 1952).

3. *Trustees.* A trustee is never an adverse party simply by being trustee.

Example 6: *A* creates a trust, naming the *X* Bank as trustee, income to *B* for life, remainder to *C*. *A* and *B* have the joint power to revoke (in which case all of the property returns to *A*). The entire transfer is complete, since *B* would be adversely affected by any exercise of the power to revoke.

Example 7: Same as 6, except that the trust is irrevocable, but *A* and the bank trustee have the joint power to invade corpus for the benefit of *D*. The transfer is incomplete: both the income and remainder interests can be altered by the grantor acting in concert with a nonadverse party. (A corporate trustee cannot be a beneficiary, and therefore cannot be an adverse party.)

Example 8: Same as 7, except the power to invade corpus is held by *A* and *C*. As *C* is an adverse party to the invasion of corpus, the entire transfer is complete.

Example 9: Same as 6, except the trustee has the power to pay income to *B* or accumulate it in its discretion. *B* no longer has an "interest" (but only an "expectancy"), and is therefore not an adverse party; hence, the transfer is wholly incomplete.

Example 10: *A* creates a trust, naming *A* and *R* as co-trustees, income and/or corpus to or among *B, C,* and *D* in the trustees' discretion, remainder after 30 years to *R,* if living, but if *R* is not then living to *S*. Although *R*'s remainder is "contingent," *R*'s contingent remainder still qualifies as an "interest." *R* is, therefore, an adverse party to the invasion of corpus, but not to the payment of income. The transfer of the corpus interest is complete, but the transfer of the income interest is incomplete.

E. Retained Powers That Do Not Render a Transfer Incomplete. Various retained powers that can affect the distribution of income and/or corpus do not necessarily render a transfer incomplete.

1. *Power to affect time or manner of enjoyment.* A retained power to affect only the timing of enjoyment, without affecting the identity of the takers, does not render the gift incomplete. Reg. § 25.2511-2(d). For purposes of this rule, the "estate" of a deceased person is considered to be the same "person" as the deceased, as is a power in the deceased person, exercisable by the latter's will, to cause the property to be paid to such deceased person's estate.

   Example 11: *A* creates a trust, naming herself and the *X* Bank as co-trustees, income and/or corpus to *B* in the trustees' discretion, with any income not paid to *B* to be added to corpus; when *B* reaches the age of 30 (or earlier dies), the trust is to terminate and the trust property is to be paid to *B* if living, or if *B* is not then living to such persons (including *B*'s estate) as *B* appoints by her will, but in default of such appointment to *C*. This transfer is complete, since *A*'s retained power (held jointly with a nonadverse party) is one that affects only the time or manner of enjoyment. This result holds true even though *B might* die without exercising her power to appoint the property to her own estate (which is called a "testamentary general powrer of appointment"). The fact that *B* could do so is sufficient to constitute the "remainder interest" as residing entirely in *B* for purposes of the "time or manner" rule.

2. *Administrative powers.* A gift can be incomplete only on account of a retained power pertaining to the "disposition" of property. Reg. § 25.2511-2(b). Thus, a retained nondispositive ("administrative") fiduciary power cannot render a transfer incomplete. Examples are: (1) powers pertaining to the acquisition, holding, and disposition of trust assets, (2) investment powers, and (3) powers pertaining to the determination of whether receipts and disbursements are to be charged to (or against) "income" or "corpus" ("fiduciary accounting powers").

3. *Dispositive powers subject to standards.* Even a dispositive power will not render a transfer incomplete if it is "limited by a fixed or ascertainable standard," such as "support," "maintenance," "health," "education," and "comfort," but not "pleasure," "desire," or "happiness." Regs. §§ 25.2511-1(g)(2) and -2(g). Thus, in any of Examples 1 through 4, *supra,* the transfer by *A* is complete if *A*'s retained power is to pay income or corpus to *B* (or *B, C,* and *D*) "for her [their] support" (etc.). This is so even (i) if the determination of the support need is to be made by the trustee (*A*), or (ii) the trustee (*A*) is to consider or disregard the other resources of any beneficiary. Where the standard is expressed as "for her [their] support in the discretion of the trustee" (the trustee being *A*), all the facts and circumstances must be consulted to ascertain whether the retained power is limited by reasonably fixed and ascertainable standards. Reg. § 25.2511-1(g)(2) (last sentence). The theory underlying this exception is that a the creation of a trust in which the retained powers are limited by ascertainable standards is the point at which the donor "lets go" of the property and assumes the role of "fiduciary" rather than "ongoing donor."

F. Completion of Previously Incomplete Transfers. An incomplete transfer of an interest becomes complete for gift or estate tax purposes when the property ceases to become subject to the power.

1. **_Gift tax._** The incomplete gift becomes complete if and when, during the lifetime of the transferor, the retained power is released or lapses, or the property is no longer subject to the power. Reg. § 25.2511-2(f). An illustration of the latter is a distribution to a beneficiary (other than the grantor) from a revocable trust, whether the distribution be of income or of corpus.

   Example: _A_ creates a joint bank account for _A_ and _B_ with $10,000, _A_ and _B_ each having a right to withdraw all the funds; _A_ has made a revocable transfer, but if _B_ withdraws $3,000 (without having to account for the same to _A_) there is a completed gift from _A_ to _B_ of the $3,000. Reg. § 25.2511-1(h)(4). The "donor" of the completed transfer is the original donor, even if the property ceases to be subject to the power because of the act of the donee or a third party (trustee, holder of special power of appointment, or joint account holder). The transfer is a gift _when_ it becomes complete, not at the earlier time that the transfer was set in motion. In the case of a trust, the subject of the completed transfer is the _then_ trust property (and/or income), even if different from the original trust property. In other words, the subject of the incomplete transfer is the trust itself (corpus and income), not the particular assets that _first_ funded the trust. Thus, a revocable trust of Blackacre does not become complete just because the trustee sells Blackacre and reinvests the proceeds in Whiteacre.

2. **_Estate tax._** If the retained power (that caused the transfer to be incomplete) expires at (or by reason of, or after) the transferor's death, the (completed) transfer is not a gift for gift tax purposes. Instead, the property will be included in the transferor's gross estate under §§ 2036-2038.

3. **_Relationship of gift and estate tax doctrine._** There is no general tax principle that holds that an incomplete gift transfer is subject to estate tax because of the incompleteness. It just happens that any inter vivos transfer of the incomplete type is included in the gross estate under the specific provisions of the estate tax. Similarly, there is no principle that holds that a completed gift transfer is excluded from the gross estate. _Smith v. Shaughnessy,_ 318 U.S. 176 (1943) (estate-included transfer was also completed gift). There are certain situations where a retained-power transfer is both a completed gift and included in the gross estate. It all depends upon the independent application of gift and estate tax law. (These cases will be pointed out in Chapter 3.)

G. **Delayed Gifts**. A "completed" gift may be treated as occurring at a time later than might be assumed due to uncertainties over the subject matter or value of the gift.

   1. **_General timing rule._** A gift is treated as being made at the earlier to occur of the time (1) the donor parts with ownership or possession or (2) the donor parts with a future ownership or possessory right (in either case assuming there is no retained power, etc.).

      a. _Mere promises._ Thus, a mere promise to make a future gift is not presently a gift, since the donor can change her mind.

      b. _Binding promises._ But if the promise is binding (supported by consideration in the contract-law sense), there is a gift when the promise becomes binding, not at such later time as the property is actually transferred. Examples of present agreements to make future transfers include prenuptial agreements, agreements to convert future community property to separate property and vice versa, and employment contracts providing for employee death benefits.

2. **"Open-gift" doctrine.** The IRS had issued several rulings indicating that a completed transfer will not be treated as having been made if the subject matter of the gift is uncertain or the valuation of the gift is uncertain in the sense of being dependent upon *non*actuarial contingencies. (Actuarial contingencies can be, and are, valued under actuarial tables.) Any such transfer was to be deemed to have been made at the time (before or at the transferor's death) that the gift can be valued. Rev. Rul. 69-346, 1969-1 C.B. 227 (future transfers of later-acquired community property); Rev. Rul. 77-359, 1977-2 C.B. 24 (agreement pertaining to after-acquired separate property); Rev. Rul. 81-31, 1981-1 C.B. 475 (unfunded employee death benefit subject to various forfeiture conditions and contingencies). In these cases the IRS preferred delayed-gift treatment to the alternative of assigning a very low (or even zero) value to the gift at the time it is made.

3. **The DiMarco case.** In *Estate of DiMarco v. Com'r,* 87 T.C. 653 (1986), a case of first impression, the Tax Court rejected the open-gift doctrine, at least insofar as the IRS attempted to delay the gift of an employee death benefit until the donor employee's death (at which time the amount of the transfer became ascertainable). Prior to death the value of the gift was unascertainable because the employer (IBM Corp.) had the power to modify the plan at will. The Tax Court emphasized that there can be no "gift" by a deceased person, but it also stated in *dictum* that the regulations only authorized a delay in the timing of a gift by reason of "incompleteness," *supra*, rather than extreme difficulty in valuation.

   a. *IRS acquiescence.* In 1990 the IRS acquiesced in *DiMarco,* 1990-2 C.B. 1, and revoked Rev.Rul. 81-31, *supra,* the facts of which closely resembled *DiMarco*. Rev.Rul. 92-68, 1992-2 C.B. 257. Although the IRS's acquiescence in *DiMarco,* as well as the actual holding in that case, had to do with the issue of whether a gift for gift tax purposes can be deemed to occur at (or after) death, *dictum* in *DiMarco* stated that the timing of a gift could be delayed only because of incompleteness, and not by difficulty in valuation.

   b. *Is the open-gift doctrine still viable?* The IRS has not given up on the open-gift doctrine except in certain cases where the value of the gift can only be ascertained at (or after) the donor's death. The Tax Court's dictum in *DiMarco* states that uncertainty in valuation is not a valid reason to postpone the time of the gift. This *dictum*, even if ultimately confirmed, may not apply to applications of the open-gift doctrine to situations where the subject matter of the future transfer is presently unascertainable.

   c. *The Dickman case.* Although not squarely on point, some support for the open-gift doctrine may lie in the Supreme Court case of *Dickman v. Com'r,* 465 U.S. 330 (1984), mentioned at II.H.5.d., *supra*. There the Court held that an interest-free "demand" loan between related individuals yielded a gift, during each calendar year, of the interest foregone by the lender from the borrower. *Dickman*, however, might be distinguished from the open-gift situation on the ground that *Dickman* involved essentially a "revocable" transfer of money, with the failure to charge interest as entailing a completed gift of the accrued but foregone interest for any given year. On the other hand, the approach the Supreme Court took in *Dickman* was necessitated by the fact that the transfer, at the date of the loan, was for full and adequate consideration, and it was only with the passage of time that the existence and amount of gift transfers became clear.

2

d. *Did the employee in DiMarco have a property interest?* The Tax Court in *DiMarco* also held that the donor-employee couldn't have made a gift because he had no property interest to transfer, because the employer had the unrestricted right to modify the plan and determine the eligibility of beneficiaries. *See also Estate of Bogley v. U.S.*, 514 F.2d 1027 (Ct.Cl.1975) (requiring a binding contract with the employer). However, the transfer by the donor should not be equated with the vested right (or lack thereof) of any beneficiary. Moreover, it is commonplace in property law to treat an interest subject to disfeasance as a property interest, as opposed to an expectancy. Economically, an employee affects a transfer insofar as his salary (which would increase his taxable estate) is reduced in order to create a survivor's benefit. *Cf. Kramer v. U.S.*, 406 F.2d 1363 (Ct.Cl.1969) (estate tax case). Thus, the employee benefit situation is really another form of constructive transfer, although the economic outcome is delayed. But it is virtually impossible to ascertain the amount by which the employee's current salary is being reduced from year to year. Thus, it would appear that there might be a series of annual gifts, but with an acute problem of valuation.

e. *How should employee benefits be taxed?* The best approach would be to use hindsight. Thus, if there is a payment by the employer to a third party (spouse or survivor), the payment should be attributable to the employee, not the employer, unless the payment was unexpected and "out of the blue." There are two factual variations:

(1) *No binding promise.* Here the open-gift doctrine never comes into play, and *DiMarco* would seem to be irrelevant. (Recall that the open-gift doctrine is a modification of the rule that a binding promise to make a future transfer is a present gift.) Thus, where there is no binding agreement, the transfer occurs when, and to the extent that, the beneficiary receives benefits (or perhaps when her rights vest). If this occurs during the employee's life, it should be treated as a gift transfer. If it occurs by reason of death, it should be (but won't necessarily be) treated as an estate transfer. The estate taxation of employee benefits is considered in Chapter 3.

(2) *Binding promise.* Here the viability of the open-gift doctrine must be squarely faced, assuming the beneficiary's interest vests or is paid while the donor-employee is still alive. There is no question that the employee is effecting a transfer by gift; the question is "when" and "how much." If the future benefit is contingent on length of employment, it can be assumed that the estate depletion occurs annually by reason of a reduced salary, but this is not determinable, nor is it feasible to assign a present value to the future benefit attributable to a year's services. Arguably, this situation (that is, the existence and amount of future payments being highly contingent) should be deemed to come within that part of the open-gift doctrine that refers to situations where the subject matter of the gift is not presently ascertainable. *See Bradford v. Com'r*, 34 T.C. 1059 (1960) (no current gift where donor didn't then own the property). But this is uncertain under current law, and legislation might be required to deal with this problem. (The estate tax angle is dealt with in Chapter 3.)

VI. **VALUATION OF GIFTS.** In general, the same valuation principles apply for gift, estate, and generation-skipping tax purposes. For that reason, the general discussion of valuation of property is assigned to a separate chapter, Chapter 4. Only rules peculiar to the gift tax, or essential to understanding the gift tax, are dealt with here.

VALUATION OF GIFTS

A. **When Valuation Occurs**. Gifts are valued at the time made, when they become complete, or when (under the open-gift doctrine, to the extent it is still valid) the gift transaction is closed, as the case may be.

B. **Willing-Buyer Willing-Seller Test.** The amount of a gift is its fair market value. The basic test for determining the fair market value of property is the "willing-buyer willing-seller" test, under which the value of property is "the price at which such property would change hands between a willing buyer and a willing seller, neither being under any compulsion to buy or sell, and both having reasonable knowledge of relevant facts." This test is based on a hypothetical situation, not the real circumstances of the donor or donee, their relationship, or their circumstances. This, and most other issues involving the valuation of property, are dealt with in Chapter 4.

C. **Life Insurance and Annuity Contracts.** An *un*matured life insurance or annuity contract is not viewed as simply a present right (or possibility) of receiving future sums of money. Under Reg. § 25.2512-6(a), the gift tax value of such a contract is its "replacement cost," *i.e.,* what a person would pay to the company for the same (or a comparable) contract. This regulation was upheld in *Guggenheim v. Rasquin,* 312 U.S. 254 (1941).

1. *Life insurance valuation*. If (as is likely to be the case) there are no such identical or comparable contracts, the value of a life insurance policy is equal to the "interpolated terminal reserve" (if any) plus the amount of any unexpired premium. The interpolated terminal reserve can be obtained only by asking the issuing company and is not identical to the "cash surrender value," although the two may be close together.

2. *Annuity valuation*. If (which is unlikely to be the case) there are no identical or comparable annuity contracts, the value can be ascertained in the same way as for a noncommercial annuity (that is, by using actuarial tables).

D. **Employee Death Benefits.** This issue rarely arises, since the employee usually has the (retained) power to change the beneficiary, and such power (to alter or amend) would render any gift transfer incomplete. But there could be a gift if the employee has no power to change the beneficiary.

1. *Incidental power to terminate, alter, or amend death benefit.* A power to terminate the death benefit, or cause it to be forfeited, altered, or amended, by such actions as quitting the job, embezzling employer funds, obtaining a divorce, acquiring children, or taking action in one's capacity as shareholder or member of the Board of Directors, is not considered such a power as would render any gift of the death benefit incomplete. *See Estate of Tully v. U.S.,* 528 F.2d 1401 (Ct.Cl.1976) (estate tax); Rev.Rul. 75-415, 1975-2 C.B. 374 (power to leave college). Powers of this sort have "independent significance" above and beyond the disposition of the death benefit. Conditions of forfeiture would, however, depress the value of any gift.

2. *Funded plans.* If the employer funds the death benefit (by paying money to a trust or purchasing an annuity or life insurance contract), the gift (if any) is the amount or value so transferred (reduced by any portion of such transfer that can be shown to be attributable to a retained interest in the donor, such as a pension). There is no discounting to present value (solely by reason of futurity of payment) in cases where income earned in the trust or on the policy inures to the beneficiary's benefit. *E.g.,* Rev. Rul. 76-490, 1976-2 C.B. 300.

3. *Unfunded plans.* An unfunded plan consists of only a promise to pay a survivor's benefit in the future. If there is a binding agreement, there is a present gift of the present discounted value of the future benefit. If the future benefit is subject to such contingencies (as to amount or possible forfeiture) as to render the future amount incapable of determination, the "open-gift" issue is raised. *See* V.G., *supra.*

E. Encumbered Gifts. If gift property is subject to a nonrecourse lien, the amount of the lien is subtracted from the amount of the gift. If the donee assumes a personal obligation of the donor, the amount of the assumed obligation is a "partial consideration offset," which likewise reduces the amount of the gift.

RETAINED-INTEREST TRANSFERS

VII. RETAINED-INTEREST TRANSFERS. Conceptually, a transfer by the donor to herself cannot be a gift, because such retained interest does not deplete the donor's potential gross estate. Therefore, transfers involving a combination of retained and transferred interests normally demand separate (actuarial) valuation of the retained and gifted interests. However, § 2702 overrides these basic principles in certain cases, resulting in a deemed gift of even the retained interests. Section 2701 provides similar rules for analagous situations involving interests in business entities.

A. Retained-Interest Transfers Not Subject to § 2702. The discussion here explores gift tax doctrine pertaining to retained-interest transfers that would apply if § 2702 were ignored. Even in cases where § 2702 does apply, it might be necessary to apply the non-§ 2702 analysis discussed herein because it affects collateral issues, such as the annual exclusion or the mitigation of double estate and gift taxation of the same interests.

1. *Present gift of future interest.* A "future interest" is defined as a present right to the future possession or enjoyment of property. It is axiomatic, then, that a gift of a future interest occurs when the donor parts with the interest (right), not when the donee actually obtains possession or enjoyment.

Example 1: If *A* creates an inter vivos trust, retaining an annuity payable to herself for life, remainder to *C, A* has presently made a gift of the remainder interest to *C*.

2. *Retained interests not taxed.* Under general gift tax principles (and disregarding § 2702), any retained interest cannot be a gift, since it fails to deplete the donor's gross estate. In the transfer with retained annuity interest, *supra,* there is a gift only of the remainder. A "possessory" interest, such a life estate in real property, is valued as if it were an income interest in a trust.

Example 2: If *A* creates a trust, income to *B* for 12 years, reversion to *A*, there is (disregarding § 2702) a gift only of the income interest to *B*. Reg. § 25.2512-1(h)(7).

Example 3: If *A* creates a joint tenancy in Blackacre with right of survivorship in *A* and *B, A* has made a gift of one-half of the property if the joint tenancy is severable (essentially *A* has retained a power to revoke as to one-half); if the tenancy is nonseverable, *A* has made a gift of the interest acquired by *B* valued according to actuarial principles (income or possessory interest in half plus "remainder" in the whole). *See* Reg. § 25.2511-1(h)(5) (disregarding references to regulations under § 2515, which no longer deals with joint tenancies).

3. ***Value of nonretained interests***. The value of nonretained interests transferred is the value of the property reduced by the value of any retained interests. If there is only one nonretained interest, its value can be determined directly.

   Example 4: Refer back to Example 1. The amount of the gift is the value of the property transferred into trust reduced by the value of *A*'s retained income interest. Alternatively, the amount of the gift is simply the value of the remainder interest given to *C*.

4. ***Actuarial tables***. Interests, whether retained or not, are generally to be valued using the actuarial tables, issued under the authority of Code § 7520, found in Notice 89-60, 1989-1 C.B. 700 and (more comprehensively) in IRS Publications 1457 and 1458. Portions of the actuarial tables are often reproduced in Appendixes to student editions of the Code and Regulations.

   a. *How constituted.* The tables are based upon assumed discount rates and rates of return equal to 120% of the "applicable federal midterm rate" for the month in which the gift occurs, and (where life expectancies are relevant) on the basis of mortality statistics. There is a separate set of tables for each discount rate (rounded to the nearest one-fifth of 1%). The tables assume no change in the value of corpus over time. All of the computations involving discounting and life expectancies are built into the tables.

      (1) *Remainder following a term of years.* For instance, the actuarial factor for a (vested) remainder following an income or possessory interest to last for a term of ten years is simply the present value, using the applicable discount rate and discounting for ten years, of the number one, and the actuarial factor for the term of years is the number one less the actuarial factor for the remainder. (The value of the remainder and term interests themselves are obtained by multiplying the value of the underlying property, as of the date of the gift, times the relevant actuarial factor.)

      Example 5: The prescribed table for the month of the gift is 7.0%. Therefore, a remainder interest following a one-year term is worth 0.9345794 times the transferred amount.

      (2) *Remainder following a life estate.* The actuarial factor for a remainder following an income interest for a person's life is computed in the same way as above, except that the number one is reduced to present value by discounting for the actuarial life expectancy of the holder of the life estate.

      (3) *Income interests and life estates.* Assuming that the property is divided into only two interests (such as life estate and remainder), the actuarial

factor for the "current interest" (income interest or life estate) is the number one reduced by the factor for the remainder. (A current income interest can be valued directly by adding together the present values of all future income receipts; each future income receipt is deemed to be equal to the initial amount transferred times the discount rate.) Note that the factors for the income interest and remainder always add up to 1.0.

Example 6: Refer back to Example 5, *supra*. The value of the one-year term interest is 0.065421 (1.0 – 0.9345794). The same number can be obtained by assuming a return at the end of one year equal to 0.07 times 1 (= 0.07) and discounting that to the present at a 7% discount rate.

(4) *Annuities.* An annuity is a right to a fixed dollar amount. The actuarial factor for a given annuity is the sum of the present values of the number one corresponding to each expected future annuity payment, and the value of the annuity is the product of the actuarial factor and the amount of the periodic payment.

Example 7: *A* creates a trust with $1 M, with an annuity of $100,000 payable annually to *A* for 2 years, remainder to *C*. Again assume that the 7% table is to be used. The first year payment is worth 0.9346 of the annuity payment, and the second year's payment is worth 0.8734 of the annuity payment. Adding the two together produces an annuity factor of 1.8080, which is multiplied by the annuity payment of $100,000. Therefore, the annuity is worth $180,800, and the remainder interest following the annuity is worth $819,200 ($1 M - $180,800).

b. *When used.* In general, the tables *must be* used in valuing present and future interests, even where "counterfacts" to the assumptions built into the actuarial tables are known to exist (such as a shorter life expectancy or a reduced rate of return). Rev. Rul. 80-80, 1980-1 C.B. 194. However, the tables will not apply to any trust interest that is not a bona fide interest protected from erosion under the law of trusts. (For example, if a trust is "locked into" unproductive property, the income interest is incapable of valuation.) Furthermore, an interest can't be valued under the tables if it is subject to disfeasance, delayed enjoyment, depletion, waste, erosion, reduction, or modification resulting from the decision of another (such as a trustee or the donee of a special power of appointment). Reg. § 1.7520-3(b)(2). And the life expectancy component will not be used where the measuring life has an incurable illness such that there is a 50% chance that she will die within one year. Reg. §1.7520-3(c)(3).

Example 8: *A* creates a trust, income to *B* for life, remainder to *C*, giving the trustee (a bank) the power to accumulate income or distribute corpus to *B*. Neither interest can be valued under the tables. The result is apparently not altered in cases where the trustee's discretion is subject to standards, such as "support" or "comfort."

c. *How used.* As indicated above, to value an interest dependent upon a period of years or the death of one person, one simply looks up the relevant actuarial factor in the tables and multiplies by the value of the underlying property. If the value of the interest is dependent on more than one event (an example would be a transfer to *B* for life, remainder to *C* if living, if not to *D,* in which the value of *C*'s and *D*'s interests depend upon both *B*'s death and the chances that *C* will outlive *B*), the factor cannot simply be looked up. More complex computations are required, which usually entails having the IRS do it.

Example 9: *A* creates a testamentary trust (subject to estate tax), income to *B* for life, remainder to *C.* Subsequently, *C* makes a gift of her remainder interest to *D.* Assume that (a) 7% tables are applicable at the time of gift, (b) *B* (the measuring life) is age 55, and (c) at the time of gift, the trust is worth $1 million. The value of *C*'s gift is $261,030.

    d. *Tables are flawed.* The Tables make no distinction between male and female measuring lives. Thus, life expectancies for males are overstated and those for females understated. As noted earlier, the tables somewhat unrealistically assume that all economic return is "income" that is not added to corpus. However, under the law of trusts, a trustee is under some duty not only to preserve corpus intact, but to cause the corpus to increase sufficiently to cope with inflation. Also, the assumption that the income yield is 120% of the applicable federal mid-term rate is wildly optimistic, because historically trust income yields have been around 3-4 percent. As of 1997, a rate equal to 120% of the applicable federal mid-term rate was about 7.2%. In short, the tables significantly overvalue income interests and undervalue remainder interests. This point has significance in tax-avoidance planning, and partially explains why "income" interests (and remainders following income interests) sometimes fail to "qualify" for certain tax benefits.

5. ***Donor must establish value of retained interest.*** Under *Robinette v. Helvering,* 318 U.S. 184 (1943), a donor can subtract the value of a retained interest only if the donor establishes the value of the retained interest *under actuarial methods. Accord* Reg. § 25.2511-1(e). This presumption is easily overcome where there are bona fide retained income and reversionary interests.

Example 10: *A* creates a trust, naming *B* as trustee, income to *A* or accumulated in the trustee's discretion, remainder to *R* on *A*'s death. Here *A* has made a gift of the entire trust, since *A*'s retained "interest" (really an "expectancy") cannot be valued using actuarial methods. (But if *A* herself was the trustee, *A* would have retained an income interest for life.) If the trustee was (instead) to pay income to *A* "for her support," it would still be too difficult to value *A*'s retained interest using actuarial methods.

Example 11: Same as Example 10, except that *A*'s creditors can reach the income of the trust. (This is the general approach under the Restatement of Trusts.) Here, *A* is deemed to have a retained interest, because *A* can indirectly obtain the income by incurring credit, which the trust income is available to satisfy. If the trustee has discretion to distribute income and corpus to the grantor, and if under state law the grantor's creditors can reach the trust income and corpus, the transfer into trust is essentially a revocable transfer, which is incomplete for gift tax purposes. *Com'r v. Vander Weele,* 254 F.2d 895 (6thCir.1958) (Michigan law); *Outwin v. Com'r,* 76 T.C. 153 (acq.) (Massachusetts law). *Compare Estate of Uhl v. Com'r,* 241 F.2d 867 (7th Cir.1957) (Indiana law).

B. Taxation of Retained-Interest Transfers Under § 2702. Notwithstanding the foregoing, § 2702, applicable to transfers after October 8, 1990, holds that the value of a retained interest is not subtracted for gift tax purposes (even if capable of actuarial valuation), unless an exception or special rule applies. § 2702(a)(2)(A). Application of this rule results in gift taxation of a retained interest!

Example 12: *A* creates a trust with $1 M, income to *A* for life, remainder to *C* (who is *A*'s son). *A* is charged with a gift of the full $1 M, notwithstanding the retained interest.

1. ***Prerequisites for § 2702 to apply.*** Section 2702 applies to most, but not all, retained-interest transfers.

    a. *Transfer into trust or trust equivalent.* Although § 2702(a)(1) only refers to transfers in trust, it also applies to any transfer with a "legal" retained interest (life estate, term of years, reversion). § 2702(c)(1).

    b. *Retained interest in the property transferred.* Section 2702 applies only where an interest is "retained" by the transferor (or "applicable family member" as defined in § 2701(e)(2)). An interest is "retained" where the same person held the same interest (or underlying property) both before and after the transfer. Moreover, the interest must be retained "in" the very property transferred. *See* § 2702(a)(1).

    c. *What is an "interest"?* The term "retained interest" includes a power to revoke, alter, or amend an interest such that the gift of that interest would be treated as being "incomplete." Reg. § 25.2702-2(a)(4).

    Example 13: *A* creates a trust, naming herself as trustee, income to *B* and/ or *C* in such amounts and proportions as the trustee determines in its discretion, remainder to *D* (a family member) upon the expiration of 20 years from the date of the creation of the trust. *A* has retained the power to alter the beneficial enjoyment of income for the lesser of 20 years or *A*'s life. This is treated as an interest retained by *A*.

    d. *Joint-purchase rule.* Notwithstanding the "retention in the same property" rule, joint purchases by members of the same family are subject to § 2702. The term "member of the family" refers to one's spouse, ancestor, descendant, descendant of one's spouse, sibling, or any spouse of any such ancestor, descendant, or sibling. §§ 2702(e) and 2704(c)(2).

    Example 14: If *A* and *B*, who are "members of the same family," with their own funds purchase a life estate and remainder respectively in Blackacre, *A* is deemed to have "transferred" the whole of Blackacre with a retained life interest in the same, thereby subjecting the transaction to § 2702. § 2702(c)(2). In this case the funds provided by *B* qualify as a "partial consideration offset" to the deemed transfer by *A*. Thus, *A* ends up making a gift equal to the full value of Blackacre reduced by the amount contributed by *B*. *See* Reg. § 25.2702-4(c) and (d).

2. ***Threshhold exceptions.*** Some retained-interest transfers fail to mount the threshhold of § 2702.

    a. *Transfer must be to a "family" member.* For § 2702 to apply, the transfer (other than the retained interest) must be to one or more "members of the [transferor's] family," referring to the transferor's spouse, any ancestor or descendant of the transferor or of the transferor's spouse, any sibling of the transferor, or any spouse of any such ancestor, descendant, or sibling. §§ 2702(a)(1) & (e) and 2704(c)(2).

b. *Exception for incomplete transfers.* Section 2702 does not apply where the gift is incomplete on account of a retained power to revoke, alter, or amend (etc.). § 2702(a)(3)(A)(i) & (B). Thus, if *A* creates a trust, income to *A* for life, remainder to such of *A*'s issue as *A* appoints by her will (but, if no appointment, to *C*), § 2702 doesn't apply, since there would be no complete gift under general gift tax principles.

c. *Exception for divorce-related trust.* Section 2702 doesn't apply to a retained-interest transfer where the nonretained interests are exempt from gift tax under § 2516, dealing with certain divorce-related transfers. Reg. § 25.2702-1(c)(7).

3. **Exception for "qualified interest."** If the retained interest is a "qualified interest" ("QI"), the actuarial value of the QI is subtracted in arriving at the amount of the net gift.

a. *Qualified Interest defined.* A QI is (1) a right to a fixed annuity payable at least annually, (2) a right to receive at least annually a unitrust interest (*i.e.*, a fixed percentage of the corpus valued annually), or (3) a vested remainder (reversion) following an interest in another party of the type described in (1) or (2). § 2702(a)(2)(B) & (b).

b. *Purpose.* The purpose of this exception is to allow subtraction of a retained interest of the type that can (aside from the mortality component) be accurately valued by actuarial methods. An "income" interest, which cannot be a QI, is susceptible to gross overvaluation, such as where, for example, the trust is expected to have a low expected income yield and a high appreciation rate.

4. **Exception for personal residence trust.** Section 2702 does not apply to the creation of a trust the (virtual) sole asset of which is property to be used as a personal residence by the holder of the life or term interest in the trust (or such person's spouse or dependents). § 2702(a)(3)(A)(ii). *See* Reg. § 25.2702-5(b). In addition, a "qualified personal residence trust" ("QPRT") as set forth in Reg. § 25.2702-5(c) also qualifies. A QPRT also has a personal residence of the grantor as the principal asset of the trust, but allows some cash to be held in the trust for mortgage payments, repairs, and improvements; if the residence is sold, destroyed, etc., any proceeds must be used to replace or repair the residence, purchase a qualified annuity, or be distributed outright to the grantor. This exception has no plausible rationale, and has to be considered to be a politically-motivated loophole in the scheme of § 2702.

5. **Special valuation rule for certain tangible property.** If the tangible property is of the type that would not increase in value if it were used by the person having possession, and if the property would not be subject to depletion or depreciation deductions if held for investment, then the donor can subtract the value of any retained term or life interest in the property. However, in this case the retained interest is to be valued by applying the willing-buyer, willing-seller

test (rather than actuarial methods). § 2702(c)(4). See Reg. § 25.2702-2(c) and (d) (Exs. (8) and (9). Examples would include retained term or life interests in art works, certain collectibles, and unimproved real estate whose value consists almost entirely of development potential (*i.e.,* with negligible recreational or agricultural value). This exception helps museums obtain (remainder) interests in art works, etc.

6. ***Subsequent gift of retained interest.*** If a donor subsequently makes a gift of a retained interest that was earlier assigned a zero value under § 2702 (and was thereby subject to tax), the amount of a subsequent gift of such interest is reduced by the lesser of (a) the prior "deemed" gift of that interest under § 2702 or (b) the current gift (after the annual exclusion). *See* Reg. § 25.2702-6. (A similar rule applies if the retained interest, as an interest, is included in the donor's gross estate.) The effect of this rule is to prevent the double gift (or estate) taxation of the same (retained) income interest.

Example 15: *A* creates a trust in year 1 with $1 M, income to *A* for life, remainder to *C* (who is *A*'s son). *A* is charged with a gift of the full $1 M, notwithstanding the retained interest, which is valued at $770,000 under the actuarial tables. In year 7, *A* makes a gift of the retained income interest, then worth $600,000, to B. After the $10,000 annual exclusion, this gift is $590,000. This year 7 gift is reduced by $590,000 to zero. The year 1 gift is unaffected.

C. **Deemed Retained-Interest Transfers Involving Business Entities**. Section 2701, which operates in a manner somewhat like § 2702, deals with situations where a donor retains certain interests in business entities while transferring others.

1. ***Basic approach of § 2701.*** Section 2701 applies to certain gifts of interests in business entities, as opposed to gifts involving interests in trusts. Under § 2701, a transfer (after October 8, 1990) of a "junior" equity interest (*e.g.,* common stock) in a corporation or partnership in which the donor (or family member) continues to hold a "senior" equity interest (*e.g.,* preferred stock) is treated as a gift by the donor of the same percentage interest in the entire enterprise as is represented by the gift of the junior equity, *with the enterprise being valued without any reduction on account of the nontransferred senior equity.* For instance, if *A* owns all of the common and (noncumulative) preferred stock of *X* Corp., and makes a gift of all of the common stock to *B, A* is deemed to have made a gift of the entire value of *X* Corp., notwithstanding the retention of the preferred stock. In short, § 2701 operates along the same lines as § 2702, *supra,,* to deem there to be a gift of a nontransferred interest! Needless to say, there are exceptions to § 2701, one of which parallels the "qualified interest" exception to § 2702.

2. ***Entity estate freezes:***

a. *Treatment under prior law.* Under prior law, if a person owned all the stock of a corporation (being one class of common stock), caused a recapitalization into (nonvoting) common stock and (voting) preferred stock, and made a gift of the common stock, the gift would be treated simply as a gift of common stock in a closely-held corporation.

(1) *Tax-avoidance potential.* This type of transaction created a transfer tax-avoidance opportunity as follows: the (fixed) dividend rate on the preferred stock would be set sufficiently high so as to absorb most of the

2

value of the corporation, and this retained (preferred) stock (which will be eventually included in the donor's gross estate) would be "frozen" in value (relatively-speaking, in the same manner as a debt obligation maintains a fairly constant value), whereas the common stock would have a very low value for gift tax purposes but would presumably appreciate over time as the value of the corporation would grow. Overall, the idea was to shift future appreciation from the donor to the donee over time, at little or no transfer tax cost, through split ownership of the entity, an opportunity that could be compounded to the extent that the dividends on the preferred stock could be waived. The same end could be accomplished through partnership interests in a partnership. This type of arrangement is similar in effect to an installment sale of appreciating property to a relative, or to a retained-interest trust funded with appreciating property.

(2) *Prior approach to the problem.* The classic estate freeze transaction bore a strong resemblance to a transfer with retained income interest, which is includible in the gross estate under § 2036(a)(1). However, § 2036(a)(1) was never held to apply here, because the income-type right (the preferred equity interest) is not retained "in" the transferred interest (the junior equity). Rather, these are separate interests in an enterprise, but the enterprise (or its assets) are not transferred. Congress at first responded in 1986 by enacting § 2036(c), which essentially treated this type of transaction as a transfer of a portion of the underlying entity (as opposed to a transfer of the residual equity interest only) with retained income interest (in the form of the preferred equity interest), causing the gifted (appreciating) equity interest to be included in the gross estate. Section 2036(c) had only weak political support, and was alleged to be too complex, and so it was repealed retroactively in 1990 simultaneously with the enactment of § 2701.

b. *Treatment under current law.* Section 2701 basically approaches this problem under the gift tax rather than the estate tax. It imposes a draconian gift tax valuation rule, but creates an exception for certain cases where the retained senior equity can be accurately valued.

3. ***Scope of § 2701.*** Section 2701 applies to situations where certain interests in an entity are transferred and certain interests are not transferred (retained).

a. *Transferred interest.* Section 2701 applies to the transfer of an interest in a corporation or partnership to a "family member" (here meaning only the donor's spouse, descendants of the donor or the donor's spouse, or any spouse of any such descendants), *unless market quotations are readily available for the transferred interest.* § 2701(a)(1) & (e)(1). Section 2701 applies even if the transferee gives full and adequate consideration for the transferred interest (at best, such consideration can be but a "partial consideration offset" against the gift).

b. *Retained interest.* Section 2701 comes to bear on nontransferred interests in the entity, referred to as "applicable retained interests."

(1) *"Applicable retained interest" defined.* This term refers to:

(a) *Distribution (dividend) rights.* The term "applicable retained interest" includes any distribution right with respect to a "senior" "equity" (as opposed to a "debt") interest, but only if the transferor and "family members" (with attribution rules) have "control" (meaning at least a 50% interest in voting rights, value, profits, or capital, or any general partnership interest in a limited partnership) immediately before the transfer.

(b) *Liquidation, etc., rights.* The term "applicable retained interest" also includes any liquidation, put, call, or conversion right. § 2701(b) & (c).

(c) *By whom held.* The applicable retained interest must be held, directly or indirectly (*i.e.,* after applying attribution rules), immediately after the transfer by the transferor or by any "applicable family member" (meaning the transferor's spouse, any ancestor of the transferor or transferor's spouse, or any spouse of any such ancestor). § 2701(a)(1) & (e)(2) and (3).

(2) *Exceptions.* Section 2701 does not apply if: (i) the retained interest is capable of being valued by market quotations on an established securities market, (ii) it is of the same class as the transferred interest, or (iii) the transfer results in a proportionate reduction of all interests held by the transferor (or applicable family members). § 2701(a)(2).

4. ***Minimum valuation of junior equity.*** The gift of the junior equity shall in no event produce a gift less than if the junior equity as a whole were worth 10% of the value of all equity *plus all debt of the entity owed to the donor or an applicable family member* (other than working-capital debt). § 2701(a)(4).

5. ***Determining the amount of the gift.*** On the basis of the following, various steps must be gone through to determine the amount of the gift. *See* Reg. § 25.2701-3.

a. *Valuing the entity.* One starts with the value of the whole entity (after allowance, if any, for fragmented ownership, *i.e.,* minority interests).

b. *Value of senior interests.* Next, one subtracts the value of all interests (held by any person) senior to the transferred interest. In determining the value of such senior interests, one applies the following rules:

(1) *Applicable retained interests.* "Applicable retained interests" held by the donor and "applicable family members" are subject to the following:

(a) *Zero-value rule.* In general, any such retained interest is deemed to be worth zero. § 2701(a)(1) & (3)(A). (This rule, which has the effect of disregarding the value of retained interests, is the heart of § 2701.)

(b) *Right to receive qualified payment.* Notwithstanding the preceding item, a right to receive a qualified payment ("QP right"), *i.e.,* a *fixed cumulative* preferred stock dividend right or its partnership equivalent, is essentially valued by discounting such dividend right to its present value and *disregarding any associated liquidation, etc., right.* § 2701(a)(3). (This rule is the counterpart to § 2702(b), the exception for "qualified interests.")

  (2) *Other senior interests.* These (mainly debt obligations) are valued at fair market value.

c. *Allocating the remaining value among junior interests.* After the subtraction described above, what remains is the (deemed) value of all junior equity. The "minimum value rule" would be applied at this point, so that the total junior equity would be deemed to be worth at least 10% of the entity's value (*see* above). After subtracting the fair market value of such equity owned by persons other than the donor and her family (taken at fair market value), what is left is the amount of the (deemed) gift under § 2701.

Example 16: Alice owns 60% of the 1,000 common shares and 60% of the 1,000 shares of 8% cumulative preferred stock of *X* Corp. The other 40% of each class is owned by Alice's sister, Bea, who is not a family member under § 2701. Alice makes a gift of all of her common stock to her child, Chris. The corporation is worth $1 million net. It owes $300,000 to Alice. Each share of the preferred stock has a liquidation value of $1,000 and a cumulative dividend value of $800; the "real" market value per share would be the greater of the two. Since the preferred stock has a FMV of $1 million, the common stock has a FMV of zero. The preferred stock in Alice's hands is a "QP right." Alice is treated as initially making a gift of the $1 million value of the corporation. From the $1 million, one subtracts the value of the preferred stock (senior equity), which is the sum of (a) $400,000, the FMV of Bea's stock, and (b) $480,000, the deemed value of Alice's QP right *disregarding the liquidation rights* (600 shares x $800). That leaves $120,000 as being the deemed value of all of the common stock. However, under the "minimum value rule," *supra,* the aggregate value of the common stock is deemed to be worth $130,000 (10% of $1 million plus $300,000). After subtracting zero (Bea's 40% of the zero fmv of the common stock), the result is that *A* has made a deemed gift of $130,000.

Example 17: Same facts as Example 1, except that the preferred stock is noncumulative. Therefore, in Alice's hands it is not a "QP right," and Alice's retained preferred stock is deemed to be worth zero, instead of $480,000. It follows that Alice has made a deemed gift of $600,000 ($1 million less $400,000, less zero). The minimum-value rule doesn't apply here, since the junior equity is deemed to be worth more ($600,000) than under the minimum-value rule ($130,000).

6. ***Deemed gift of cumulative but unpaid dividends.*** The "exception" for any "QP right" is based on the assumption that a fixed cumulative (dividend) right is capable of accurate valuation using conventional valuation methods (discounting to present value) and disregarding liquidation, etc., rights (which may never be exercised anyway). But a donor could "game" this exception by arranging for the entity to not actually make the (dividend) payments as and when due (the unpaid dividends would shift value from the retained senior interest to the gifted junior interest). Accordingly, § 2701(d) provides rules that treat any delay or permanent waiver of dividends (etc.) as involving an additional gift or estate transfer by the donor.

7. *Planning considerations.* The classic "entity estate freeze" device is alive and well so long as the applicable retained interest takes the form of a "QP right." However, liquidation, etc, rights designed to increase the value of applicable retained interests (at the expense of gifted junior interests) will be ignored. Also, the "minimum value" rule will be a factor if the noncumulative dividend rate is so high as to constitute most of the entity value in the "QP right" and/or the transferor has lent a significant amount to the entity.

VIII. THE ANNUAL EXCLUSION. The amount of any net gift is reduced by any available annual exclusions under § 2503(b) and (c). (The annual exclusion is dealt with at this point because the discussion of it presupposes being able to value interests in property.)

A. **Present-Interest Exclusion.** There is a separate exclusion equal to $10,000 per donor, per donee, per year. This exclusion is not available with respect to gifts of "future interests"; hence, this exclusion is commonly referred to as the "present interest exclusion." § 2503(b).

1. *Amount of exclusion.* The exclusion is $10,000 per donor, per donee, per year. The $10,000 amount is indexed for inflation after 1998. However, the exclusion amount increases only by $1,000 increments. Thus, the exclusion amount won't be raised to $11,000 until the CPI index reaches 110% of the CPI index for the base-line year (1997). If qualifying gifts to a donee in a year are less than the exclusion, the unused exclusion cannot be carried over to other donees or to other years. Thus, the exclusion is available on a use-it-or-lose-it basis.

2. *"Present interest" defined.* Section 2503 prescribes its own rules for defining "present interest," to wit:

   a. the interest must commence in possession or enjoyment immediately;

   b. the donee of the interest must be identifiable; and

   c. the value of the donee's interest must be presently ascertainable using actuarial methods.

   See Reg. § 25.2503-3(b). The second and third requirements are necessary because of the per-donee aspect of the exclusion. A future interest does not become a present interest just because it can be freely sold or pledged as collateral for a loan.

   Example 1: *A* creates a trust of $10,000, income to *B* for life, remainder to *C*. The applicable income interest actuarial factor is 0.81762. *A* has made a present-interest gift of $8,176 to *B*, fully excluded, and a nonexcludable future-interest gift to *C* of $1,824. If $100,000 had been transferred into the trust, it is evident that the income interest must be worth more than $10,000 (unless B is very old), so that one can simply subtract $10,000 from the $100,000 to produce a $90,000 gift.

   Example 2: *A* creates a trust of $100,000, all of the income to *B* and/or *C*, in such amounts and proportions as the trustee determines, remainder to D after 30 years. No part of this gift is excluded, as neither *B* nor *C* has any "right" to immediate possession or enjoyment, nor any "interest" capable of valuation. Similarly, a power of accumulation would negate the exclusion. Even a power defined by a standard, such as "support," does not confer a sufficiently definite value to satisfy the concept of "present interest." *Com'r v. Disston*, 325 U.S. 442 (1945).

3. ***Right to present enjoyment must have substance.*** Various cases have denied the exclusion in situations where an apparent right to present enjoyment lacked substance because the property failed to produce income. *Maryland Nat'l Bank v. U.S.*, 609 F.2d 1078 (4th Cir. 1979) (unprofitable real estate); *Calder v. Com'r*, 85 T.C. 713 (1985) (trust funded by donor's sculptures); Rev. Rul. 69-344, 1969-1 C.B. 225 (trust funded with life insurance). In other words, actuarial tables cannot be invoked to create a present interest, even though such tables must be used in valuing any present interest. *See* Rev. Rul. 70-280, 1979-2 C.B. 340.

4. ***Retained interests under § 2702***. Apparently, a deemed gift of a retained current interest under § 2702 doesn't qualify for the exclusion. *See* Reg. § 25.2702-6(c) (Ex. 1). The theory must be that there is an actual gift of only the future interest, with § 2702 being merely a valuation rule, not a deemed-gift rule.

5. ***Contract-right rule.*** Contract rights, such as (discount) bonds and notes, annuities, and life insurance policies, are not treated as future interests per se, even though no payments are to be received until the future. Reg. § 25.2503-3(a); Rev. Rul. 55-408, 1955-1 C.B. 113 (exclusion available even for insurance policy with no cash surrender value; present value consists of right to "insurance protection" for current year).

   a. *Loss of rule's benefits.* However, the benefits of this rule are lost if any such property is transferred to a trust (unless a beneficiary having a present interest in the trust can compel immediate conversion to income-producing property). The exclusion would also be lost for nontrust gifts if the donee is restricted from converting the property. Rev. Rul. 76-360, 1976-2 C.B. 298.

   b. *Treatment of premiums.* The treatment of premiums follows that of the property. Thus, if *A* pays a premium on a life insurance policy owned by *B* (with *B* not being under any restriction as to disposition), *A* has made a present-interest gift. But if *A* pays a premium on a policy owned by a trust, the gift would usually be a future-interest gift.

6. ***Crummey powers.*** A trust transfer that would not qualify for the exclusion on its face can be made to qualify by giving a person (beneficiary) the (noncumulative) right to withdraw amounts transferred into the trust shortly following such transfer. *Crummey v. Com'r*, 397 F.2d 82 (9th Cir. 1968).

   a. *How "real" must withdrawal power be?* The withdrawal right must possess substance, and not be illusory. *See* Rev. Rul. 83-108, 1983-2 C.B. 168. However, the fact that the power is expected not to be exercised (because the beneficiary is very young or under the influence of the donor) does not make the power illusory. *Estate of Cristofani v. Com'r*, 97 T.C. 74 (1991). Indeed, the whole point of the *Crummey* device is the expectation that the withdrawal power will not be exercised.

b. *Collateral consequences of not exercising the withdrawal power.* The withdrawal power is a "general power of appointment" in the beneficiary, and each lapse thereof yields a "constructive transfer" by the beneficiary for gift and estate tax purposes, subject to the "five and five rule." *See* subsections I.H.1.c. & d., *supra.*

Example 3: *A* creates a trust, income to be accumulated until *B* reaches the age of 30, after which the income is to be paid to *B* until age 50 or *B*'s earlier death, at which time the trust is to terminate and the property is to be paid over to *B* if living or if not to *A*'s then living issue. This trust does not qualify for the exclusion as described so far. However, *B* is given the power, exercisable during the month of December of each year, to withdraw from the trust an amount equal to the lesser of (a) $10,000 or (b) the amount transferred by *A* into the trust during the preceding eleven months of the year. *B* is given adequate notice of this power. In November of 1999, *A* transfers $12,000 into this trust, but *B* (who is then age 9) declines to exercise the power, resulting in its being permanently added to corpus. Under the *Crummey* rule, $10,000 of the transfer is excludible under § 2503(b), resulting in a gift of $2,000. The lapse of *B*'s power on 12/31/99 is treated, under § 2514(b) & (e), as a constructive gift transfer by *B* of $7,000 ($12,000 minus $5,000) (assuming that 5% of the then trust corpus is less than $5,000). The deemed gift is a retained-interest gift subject to § 2702, *i.e.,* a gift of $7,000 (since none of *B*'s "retained" interests can be subtracted).

7. ***Techniques for maximizing the exclusion.*** The exclusion can be best taken advantage of by spreading out a given amount of wealth so that it is transferred by the maximum number of donors to the maximum number of donees over the maximum number of years.

a. *Maximizing donors.* Gifts of community property and other co-owned property involve two or more donors. A single donor who is married can obtain an equivalent result by having her spouse consent to a gift-splitting election under § 2513. *See* III.C., *supra.* Gifts by corporations and partnerships also multiply the number of donors.

b. *Maximizing donees.* Not much need be said here, except that a gift to a husband and wife as co-owners is a gift to two donees instead of one.

Example 4: *W* gives Blackacre, worth $40,000, to her son and her son's wife as joint tenants with right of survivorship (and right of severance). *W* elects gift-splitting with *H*. The gift is absorbed by four $10,000 exclusions (each donor gives $10,000 worth to each donee).

c. *Maximizing number of years.* Here follow some common techniques for spreading a given transfer over a period of years:

(1) *Installment gifts.* The "donor" sells (hard-to-subdivide) property to a family member for full and adequate consideration in money's worth consisting of installment notes. The sale is not a gift. Subsequently, and each year, the donor cancels one or more installment obligations. Each cancellation is a present-interest gift. The viability of this technique is discussed at II.H.5.b., *supra.* (The cancellations may also trigger income-tax gain.)

(2) *Self-cancelling installment notes ("SCINs")*. A variation of the above, SCINS involve installment obligations that self-destruct by their own terms (usually) upon the donor's death, with the idea of avoiding estate tax. The self-canceling feature should reduce the value of the "consideration" represented by the notes for gift tax purposes. If the transfer involves an interest in a closely-held business, the self-cancellation of the notes might also entail a deemed (estate or gift) transfer under § 2704, discussed in Chapter 4, *infra*.

(3) *Incomplete transfers*. A trust can be set up with a retained power to revoke, alter, or amend, rendering the transfer into trust incomplete. Any subsequent distribution of income and/or corpus is a present-interest gift to the distributee from the original grantor(s). *See* V.F.l., *supra*. The distributions can be spread out over a period of years.

B. Excluded Gifts to Minors. Gifts to minors present special problems in qualifying for the annual exclusion. These problems were "solved" by the enactment of § 2503(c). A gift that qualifies for exclusion under § 2503(c) is, along with present-interest gifts under § 2503(b), subject to the same $10,000 per-donor, per-donee, per-year limitation; in other words, a § 2503(c) gift is treated as a § 2503(b) gift.

1. *Background.* An outright transfer of income-producing property to a minor might not qualify for the exclusion under § 2503(b), *supra*, if a guardian is appointed, since the guardian would have the power to deprive the minor of income by accumulating the same for future distribution upon majority. The "custodianship" device was designed to obviate any need for the appointment of a guardian of the property of a minor. A gift to a custodian under the Uniform Gift to Minors Act (or variation thereof) vests title in the minor, and the custodian (who might be the donor) has powers similar to that of a guardian, but without having to seek any approval of a court. But since the custodian has the power to accumulate, a custodianship gift would not qualify under § 2503(b).

2. *Scope of § 2503(c):*

   a. *Guardianship and custodial gifts*. Section 2503(c) was enacted so that an outright gift to a minor subject to a guardianship or a custodianship qualifies for the present interest exclusion under § 2503(b). The terms of § 2503(c) "track" guardianship and custodial arrangements under state law.

   b. *Gifts into trust*. A gift to a trust for a minor can also qualify, if the trust conforms to the requirements of § 2503(c).

3. *Requirements for qualification.* The provisions of § 2503(c) are largely self-explanatory. Thus, the minor must be the sole income and corpus beneficiary; the corpus must be paid at the age of majority (or earlier death) to the donee outright, to the donees estate, or pursuant to a general testamentary power of appointment (even though the donee may not, or may not be able to, exercise such power). A § 2503(c) gift can have only one donee. Hence, a trust for two or more minors would not qualify. Finally, the guardian, custodian, or trustee must have broad discretionary dispositive powers over income and corpus. The exclusion will be lost if the power is limited by a "substantial restriction." In other words, a

"support" trust would not qualify. Reg. § 25.2503-4(b)(1); Rev. Rul. 69-345, 1969-1 C.B. 226.

CHARITABLE DEDUCTION

4. ***Amount excludible.*** Any gift that qualifies under § 2503(c) is treated as an outright present-interest gift in full; there is no "future interest" component that must be separately valued and removed from the scope of the exclusion.

Example 5: *A* creates a trust of $10,000, income and/or corpus to *B* in the trustee's discretion, with power to accumulate, remainder to *B* when *B* reaches 21, or if *B* dies before reaching 21 to *B*'s estate. Assuming that this trust qualifies under § 2503(c), the entire $10,000 is excludible, as if *A* had made an outright gift of $10,000 to *B*.

IX. **CHARITABLE DEDUCTION. Certain (but not all) gifts to charities are fully deductible for gift tax purposes under § 2522.**

A. **Preliminary Issues:**

1. ***Deduction not to exceed amount of gift.*** Gift tax deductions (the charitable and marital deductions) are subtracted in arriving at the amount of the "taxable gift" with respect to any transfer. § 2503(a). The deductions cannot reduce the amount of a taxable gift below zero. In other words, the deduction cannot exceed that which would otherwise be a taxable gift.

2. ***Eligible charities.*** The kinds of tax-exempt donees that can receive deductible gifts are listed in § 2522(a), (b), and (c)(1), with some slight differences for nonresident alien donors. *See also* Reg. § 25.2522(d)(1) for a short list of certain kinds of tax-free gifts authorized by other provisions of federal law.

B. **Gifts of Partial Interests.** Section 2522(c)(2) provides strict rules designed to assure that gifts of partial interests (income interests and remainders) to charity are accurately valued. *If the partial-interest transfer does not qualify under these rules, the gift tax charitable deduction is wholly disallowed.*

1. ***Nontrust transfers.*** Only the following kinds of nontrust partial-interest transfers to charity qualify (*see* § 2522(c)(2), referring to § 170(f)(3)(B)):

a. *Remainder interest in personal residence or farm;*

b. *Undivided portion of donor's entire interest in property;*

c. *Qualified conservation contribution (as defined in Reg. § 1.170A-14);*

d. *Works of art and copyrights (copyrights are not treated as "partial interests in" the art work, nor visa versa). Reg. 25.2522(c)-3(c)(1)(ii);*

e. *Nonconservation perpetual easements. (See § 2522(d).)*

2. ***Charitable remainder trust.*** A trust with a remainder interest to a charity (after one or more noncharitable interests) qualifies only if the noncharitable interest takes the form of a qualified "annuity" or "unitrust" interest of the type described in § 664(d) and the regulations thereunder. (An "annuity" interest is a right to receive a fixed number of dollars per year; a "unitrust" interest is a right

to receive a fixed percentage of the corpus, the corpus to be revalued annually.) Thus, an "income" interest results in disqualification. The requirements of the regulations (which are too detailed to list here) must be strictly complied with. (Incidentally, §§ 2701 and 2702, especially the concepts of "QP right" and "qualified interest," were modelled on the charitable remainder trust rules.)

3. *Charitable lead trust.* A charitable lead trust qualifies if the charitable lead interest is an annuity- or unitrust-type interest in the charity, remainder to one or more noncharitable persons. Again an "income" interest cannot qualify. The lead interest need not be in trust. Various requirements in Reg. § 25.2522(c)-3(c)(2)(v) & (vi) must be complied with.

4. *Pooled-income funds.* A contribution to a pooled income fund, as defined in § 664(c)(5), is deductible. A pooled-income fund is basically a charitable remainder trust managed by the charity itself with multiple donors; any donor can reserve an income interest in herself and other private individuals.

5. *Amount deductible.* If the charitable lead or remainder interest qualifies, the deduction is the present value of such interest, determined under actuarial tables, but based on the actual payout rate prescribed by the trust or non-trust instrument. If a charitable lead annuity interest has a high enough pay-out rate (and has a long enough duration), the deduction may equal the entire value of the property (*i.e.,* the actuarial tables will assume that all of the corpus will be paid to the charity before the noncharitable remainder interest takes in possession). (For the same reason, a charitable remainder annuity trust might, in theory, be set up so as to provide a zero deduction.)

6. *Retained-interest charitable transfers.* The noncharitable interest may be retained by the donor in herself, and such retained interest is not a gift. Section 2702 would not come into play, as there would be no transfer to a "family member."

Example: *A* creates a trust, naming the *X* Bank as trustee, income to herself for life, remainder to charity. The charitable remainder is not deductible, because the noncharitable lead interest is an "income" interest, not an annuity or unitrust interest. Therefore, *A* has made a taxable gift of the remainder interest using conventional actuarial tables for life estates and remainders. Section 2702 does not apply because no interest was transferred to a family member.

X. **MARITAL DEDUCTION.** Certain (but not all) gifts by a donor to his or her spouse qualify for the gift tax marital deduction. § 2523.

A. **Preliminary Issues:**

MARITAL DEDUCTION

1. *Deduction not to exceed gift.* See IX.A.1., *supra.*

2. *Spouse.* The donee must be married to the donor at the time of gift. § 2523(a).

3. *Noncitizen spouse donee.* The marital deduction is not allowed unless the donee spouse is a U.S. citizen. In lieu of the marital deduction, the annual exclusion is raised to $100,000 per year for gifts to one's noncitizen spouse, to the extent that the gift would have qualified for the marital deduction if the donee

spouse had been a U.S. citizen. Also, the creation of joint tenancies with right of survivorship in the noncitizen spouse is exempted from gift tax. § 2522(i).

4. ***Gift must pass to spouse***. The donee spouse must acquire the property or the interest. This is not usually an issue, since the very idea of "gift" assumes a donee or recipient. However, if the donee spouse executes a "qualified disclaimer," see IV.D.3.c., *supra*, so that the gift passes to another, the marital deduction would be lost.

5. ***Valuation.*** The value of the interest passing from the donor spouse to the donee spouse must be ascertainable. However, interests whose value cannot be ascertained would usually be nondeductible in any event under the terminable interest rule, *infra*. If the property passing to the donee spouse and otherwise qualifying for the deduction is subject to a lien, or the donee spouse incurs a monetary obligation as a condition of the gift, the amount of the deduction is reduced by the amount of the lien or obligation. In short, the deduction is only for the "net" amount given by the donor and received by the donee.

6. ***Deduction constituted at time of gift.*** Both qualification for the marital deduction and the amount deductible must be established (prospectively) at the time of the gift. Qualification and valuation cannot be determined with the aid of hindsight.

B. **Terminable Interest Rule.** The "terminal interest" rule of § 2523(b) is designed to prevent a deduction for an interest that is in such a form (*e.g.*, a life estate) that it would avoid transfer taxation to the donee spouse as well. Not all terminable interests are nondeductible, however.

1. ***"Terminable interest" defined.*** A terminable interest is an interest in the donee spouse that *might* fail, expire, terminate, etc., on the occurrence of any event, condition, contingency, etc. Whether an interest is "terminable" is ascertained at the time of gift, and not by use of hindsight. What is critical is whether, at the time of the gift, the interest in the donee spouse *might* fail, under the worst-case scenario. Whether it in fact fails is wholly irrelevant. Examples of terminable interests are life estates, terms for years, annuities, patents, copyrights, contingent remainders, vested remainders subject to conditions subsequent (including a power of invasion for the benefit of another), conditional gifts, leases, and so on.

2. ***Nondeductible terminable interest.*** A terminable interest is *nondeductible* only if, upon the failure of the donee spouse's interest, the property (1) would pass to a third party (or would revert to the donor) pursuant to another interest in the same property created (or retained) by the donor, or (2) the property might pass to a third party pursuant to a retained power. If a person transfers to her spouse her entire interest in a patent, copyright, or single-life annuity, the value of the interest is deductible because the property simply ceases to exist in the hands of the donee (possession or enjoyment does not shift, under the terms of the transfer or by reason of the type of property interest, to a third party or the donor). Another way of looking at a gift of a single-life annuity is as a gift of a lump sum payable in installments.

Example 1: *H* creates a trust, income to *W* for life, remainder to *C*. The income interest in *W* fails to qualify because upon its termination the property passes to a third party under the instrument of transfer. (Note also that the income interest as such would not be included in *W*'s gross estate, because it expires at her death.)

Example 2: *H* creates a trust, *X* Bank as trustee, income to *W* for life or accumulated in the trustee's discretion, and on *W*'s death the remainder is to "*W*'s estate." Here, the entire transfer is deductible, since no person other than *W* receives any interest. *W*'s "estate" is merely a continuation of *W* personally. (Note that the entire trust will be included in *W*'s gross estate upon her death, since it is all payable to her estate.) This example describes what is known in estate planning lingo as an "estate trust."

Example 3: *H* creates a trust, income to *H*'s father for life, remainder to *W*. *W* has a vested remainder which cannot fail (if *W* predeceases *H*'s father, the remainder passes to and through *W*'s estate). *W*'s interest is, therefore, not a "terminable interest" at all, so the fact that a third party also has an interest in the trust is immaterial. (The deduction would be disallowed if the remainder were to "*W* if living, but if not then living to *C*.") The amount of the deduction is limited to the actuarial value of *W*'s vested remainder. This type of transfer is called a "spousal remainder trust."

C. **Statutory Exceptions to the Terminable Interest Rule.** Certain transfers that would be nondeductible under the terminable interest rule are deductible under specific Code provisions.

1. ***Creation of tenancy by the entirety with other spouse.*** If *W* buys Blackacre, causing Blackacre to be held by *W* and *H* as tenants by the entirety, the value of *H*'s interest qualifies for the marital deduction even though *H*'s interests would all fail if he predeceased *W* (and *H* did not even have a right of severance). § 2523(d).

2. ***Power-of-appointment trust.*** Section 2523(e) allows a deduction for the entire amount of a transfer, outright or in trust, that meets the following requirements:

   a. *Income interest for life.* The donee spouse must be entitled to all of the income (or sole possession) for life, payable at least annually. Under the regulations, the income interest or life estate must have substance and not be illusory.

   b. *General power of appointment.* The donee spouse must have a "general" power of appointment (*i.e.,* the power to vest the property in herself or her estate, or the creditors of either), exercisable either by will or by deed (i.e., during life), and that is held by the donee spouse "alone and in all events." (The existence of the general power causes the donee spouse to be subject to estate or gift taxation on the entire property.)

   c. *No power in another.* The transfer is disqualified if a person other than the donee spouse has the power to appoint any part of the property to any person other than the donee spouse. However, the donee spouse can be given such a "special" power of appointment, in addition to the general power of appointment referred to in the previous item.

   d. *Amount deductible.* The entire portion of the transfer that meets the above requirements is deductible, as if the transfer were an outright one. If only a "specific portion" of the transfer satisfies all of the above requirements, only the value of that portion is deductible. Thus, if the donee spouse has a right to only half the income from the property, only half of the transfer is deductible, assuming the other requirements are satisfied.

3. **QTIP transfer.** A "qualified terminal interest property" ("QTIP") transfer, in trust or otherwise, is fully deductible under § 2523(f), if the following requirements are met:

   a. *Income interest for life.* This requirement is the same as for power-of-appointment transfers, *supra.*

   b. *QTIP election.* The donor must affirmatively elect that the transfer qualify for the marital deduction. (This election causes the property to be subject to estate or gift tax to the donee spouse.) The election, once made, is irrevocable.

   c. *No powers of appointment.* No person (including the donee spouse) can be given a power to appoint any of the property to any person other than the donee spouse.

   d. *Joint and survivor annuities.* These annuities can qualify provided that there is no beneficiary other than the donor and donee spouses. Here the election is deemed to be made by the donor, who can affirmatively elect against qualification. (If the donee spouse dies first, nothing is included in her gross estate.)

   e. *Interest retained by donor.* A retained interest in the donor (*i.e.,* a reversion or income interest *after* the donee spouse's death) neither negates qualification nor results in the property being subject to gift or estate tax to the donor at the time of gift or thereafter. Nor is such a retained interest subject to tax under § 2702. *See* Reg. § 25.2523(f)-1(f) (Ex.11).

   f. *Amount deductible.* The full amount of the qualifying gift to which the election pertains (not just the value of the life estate) is deductible, as if the QTIP transfer were an outright gift to the spouse. The rationale is that the donee spouse is treated as the *full* owner of the QTIP property for estate and gift tax purposes. Hence, the entire transfer is deducted by the donor spouse, but will be in the tax base of the donee spouse. This is the same pattern as for outright deductible gifts, estate trusts, and power-of-appointment trusts.

   g. *Partial QTIP election.* A "partial" QTIP election can be made, in which case only a pro rata share of the transfer is deductible.

4. **Marital-charitable trust.** Under § 2523(g), a transfer to the spouse for life, remainder to charity, results in a marital deduction for the value of the donee spouse's interest, if the charitable remainder interest is deductible under § 2522. The donor, but no other person, can have an interest in the trust.

D. **Transfer of an Income Interest in a QTIP Trust.** Any transfer by the donee spouse of all or part of her qualifying income interest in a QTIP trust entails the following transfer tax consequences, in addition to the income-interest gift itself:

2

1. *Deemed transfer of nonincome interests.* Under § 2519, if a donee or legatee spouse transfers *any part* of her income interest in a QTIP trust, not only is there a gift of such transferred income interest but also a deemed transfer by such spouse of all other interests in the property.

2. *Right to recover gift taxes paid.* In any such case, the donee spouse making the § 2519 deemed gift is entitled to recover from the trust or other deemed transferee the amount of the gift tax attributable to application of § 2519. § 2207A(b).

3. *Deemed gift of waived right of recovery.* The failure to exercise the right of recovery described in the preceding item operates as a deemed gift of the waived tax by the donee or legatee spouse to the person obligated to bear the burden of the tax under § 2207A(b).

Example 4: *H* makes a QTIP bequest, income to *W* for life, remainder to *C,* that is fully deductible for estate tax purposes. When the trust is worth $1 million, and *W*'s income interest therein is worth $600,000, *W* makes a gift of half of her income interest to *B. W* thereby makes a present-interest gift of $300,000 to *B* under § 2511 plus a deemed future-interest transfer of $400,000 (the non-income interests) to the trust under § 2519. The deemed gift of the remainder precludes subsequent gift or estate taxation of the trust to *W* by reason of *H*'s QTIP election. The deemed corpus transfer is to a trust in which she continues to have an income interest in one-half. Thus, *W* has made a deemed gift of $200,000 in trust to *C* and a deemed retained-interest transfer of half of the entire trust. Section 2702 also applies here, so that there is no reduction for *W*'s $300,000 "retained" income interest "in" such deemed transfer. In sum, *W* will be charged with gifts of $1 million. Finally, half of the trust will be included in *W*'s gross estate under § 2036(a) on account of this deemed retained-interest transfer. (This re-inclusion supersedes the cancelled inclusion under the QTIP rules.) The gift tax attributable to § 2519 can be recovered by *W* from the trust. If she fails to recover it, she has made an additional gift transfer to the trust (with a retained income interest in one-half), and around we go again. The moral of the story: avoid involvement with §§ 2519 and 2207A(b).

E. **Tax Planning Strategy.** A marital deduction transfer can be used to shift wealth to the poorer spouse either (1) to "split" total spousal wealth (*i.e.,* remove wealth from the donor's highest transfer tax rate brackets and shift the same to the lower brackets of the donee spouse) or (2), at a minimum, shift enough wealth to the poorer spouse so as to not waste any of the poorer spouse's unified transfer tax credit (and, possibly, GST exemption).

1. *When to transfer.* These strategies only make sense if (and to the extent that) the richer spouse's potential transfer tax base exceeds the "exemption equivalent" of the unified transfer tax credit. Of course, a marital deduction gift may be "money down the drain" if a divorce occurs (but in that case the richer spouse's wealth is likely to be depleted anyway).

2. *"Hedge" against divorce.* A useful "hedge" against divorce is to make any marital-deduction tax-motivated gift in the form of a QTIP transfer, with a possible reversion to the donor after the donee spouse's death, since a QTIP transfer deprives the donee spouse of any control over corpus (unless the QTIP transfer gives the donee spouse such control).

2

XI. **GIFT TAX COMPUTATION. The gift tax is computed with respect to all taxable gifts in the calendar year.**

A. **Computational Principles.** The basic computational method is described in Chapter 1, at IV.A.11. & 12., which should be reviewed at this point. In brief, the tax, under the § 2001(c) progressive rate schedule (and before credit), is imposed on all taxable gifts through the current calendar year, and then there is subtracted the (before-credit) gift tax "on" all taxable gifts made prior to the current taxable year (the "prior taxable gifts"); finally there is subtracted any *unused* unified transfer tax credit.

B. **Refinements and Special Rules. In figuring "prior taxable gifts" and "prior credit used up," the following should be noted:**

1. *Maximum available credit.* The *maximum* available credit during the period 1977-1986 inclusive was less than $192,800 (it increased yearly from $30,000 to $155,800). From 1987 through 1997, the credit was $192,800 (the exemption equivalent being $600,000). The maximum credits after 1997 are set forth in Chapter 1, at IV.B.6.c.

2. *No credit before 1977.* Prior to 1977, there was no credit available. Instead, there was a cumulative lifetime per-donor deduction of $30,000. Although this deduction was initially $50,000 and later $40,000, before being reduced to $30,000, only $30,000 can be used in figuring "prior taxable gifts." § 2504(a).

3. *Exclusion amount.* The § 2503(b) & (c) exclusion amount was $5,000 from 1932 through 1938, $4,000 from 1939 through 1942, and $3,000 from 1943 through 1981. These amounts should still be used in figuring "prior taxable gifts." § 2504(b).

4. *Marital and charitable deductions.* The marital and charitable deductions are those in effect at the time of gift. From 1948 through 1976, gifts of interests in community property did not qualify for the marital deduction at all, and other gifts were deductible in an amount equal to half their value (before the § 2503 exclusion). From 1977 through 1981, the marital deduction computation was too complex to succinctly describe here. The charitable deduction was extensively revised in 1969.

5. *Pre-June 7, 1932 gifts.* Gifts before June 7, 1932, don't count at all.

6. *Improperly included taxable gifts.* A taxable gift that was improperly included under prior law should be removed from the "prior taxable gifts" total, even if the statute of limitations has run on the gift itself. Similarly, a gift that was improperly excluded should be added back in. Reg. § 25.2504-1(d). These rules only affect the rate to be applied to taxable gifts; they do not override the statute of limitations as such.

7. *Valuation of prior taxable gifts.* The valuation of prior taxable gifts is fixed only if the statute of limitations has run *and* a net gift tax has actually been paid (then or for a subsequent year) that was calculated with reference to such gift. § 2504(c). Again this rule does not override the statute of limitations as such; it only affects the computation of the current tax.

XII. GIFT TAX PROCEDURE

A. **Returns:**

1. *Filing date.* The return (Form 709) is due by April 15 following the year in which the donor makes any gift other than: a gift fully excludible under § 2503(b), (c), or (e) (before gift-splitting), or (2) a gift (other than a QTIP transfer) fully deductible under § 2523. § 6019.

2. *Elections.* A gift tax return must be filed to (1) elect gift splitting and (2) make any QTIP election. Gift splitting that occurs by operation of law (gift of community property or co-owned property) does not result from a § 2513 gift-splitting election.

3. *Extensions.* The filing date can be extended to the extent that the filing date for the income tax return is extended. § 6075(b)(2).

B. **Payment of Tax**. Payment must be made by April 15, even if an extension of time can be obtained for filing the return. § 6151(a).

1. *Extensions.* An extension of time for payment, up to six months, can be obtained under § 6161.

2. *Payment by donor.* The donor is required to pay the tax, § 2502(c), except with a respect to a deemed gift of non-income interests in a QTIP trust under § 2519 (§ 2207A(b)).

C. **Statute of Limitations.** The basic income tax rules apply here, meaning the basic limitations period is three years, but is six years if the taxable gifts are understated by 25%. The period never expires if the return is fraudulent or not made at all, or if a gift under § 2701 or § 2702 is not shown on the return when it was supposed to have been shown. *See* § 6501(a), (c)(1), (3) & (9), and (e)(2).

D. **Penalties.** In addition to the usual penalties for late filing and payment (§ 6651), § 6662 imposes "accuracy-related" penalties for negligence, disregard of rules and regulations, valuation understatements by 50% or more, and gross valuation understatements by 75% or more. A fraud penalty is imposed by § 6663.

CHAPTER 2 - QUESTIONS, ANSWERS, AND TIPS

EXAM TIPS:

1. In the tax area, it's crucial to take up issues in the right order. The organization of this chapter manifests a logical way to order gift tax issues. At the same time, some issues are so obvious as to not be worth mentioning at all, and others can be disposed of quickly.

2. Be sure to deal with all relevant issues. A given question may pose an issue of "completeness" and/or "retained interest," but don't forget the issues of the annual exclusion and marital deduction, for example, assuming such issues are posed.

3. Avoid common mistakes. For example, it is often assumed (incorrectly) that a gift of a future interest occurs only when the future interest vests or comes into possession, or that

a transfer must be incomplete if the donees (and their shares) can't be immediately ascertained.

4. In any question involving a retained-interest gift transfer (or perhaps even a retained-power gift transfer), be sure to consider the applicability of § 2702.

5. Be sure to distinguish between "retained" powers, which bear on the issue of incompleteness, and powers of appointment. A "general" power of appointment is a power created in property (usually in trust) by another party (almost always the grantor of the trust) that gives the holder of the power (the "donee") the equivalent of ownership for transfer tax purposes. The exercise, release, or lapse of a general power of appointment raises a "constructive gift transfer" issue as to the donee of the power. The exercise (but not the release or lapse) of even a "special" power of appointment can trigger a gift, although the donee of the power is here not treated as the owner of the property simply by reason of having the power.

REVIEW QUESTIONS:

1. *A* creates an irrevocable inter vivos trust with $1M, naming X Bank as trustee, income to *B* or accumulated in the trustee's discretion; on *B*'s death the trust is to terminate and its assets paid to *C* if living, or if *C* is not living, to *D*. What are the gift tax consequences of this transfer?

   ANSWER: A has made a gift of $1 million. The trustee is not the grantor. Hence, there is no *retained* power such as would render any part of the gift incomplete. The fact that all of the beneficial interests are contingent is immaterial. The gift does not qualify for the annual exclusion, because the income can be withheld from *B*. The remainder-interest gift is obviously a future interest.

2. Same as Question 1, except that the remainder is to "*C*, if living, but if *C* is not living then to *D* if *D* is living."

   ANSWER: *A* has retained a reversion that is "contingent" on both *C* and *D* dying before *B*. In the absence of § 2702, the value of this reversion could be subtracted from the $1 million gift transfer, since it is capable of actuarial valuation. (However, the valuation here is too complex to be derived from the published actuarial tables.) However, under § 2702 the value of this retained interest (which is not a "qualified interest" under § 2702(b)(3)) is treated as being zero, so nothing is subtracted from the $1M gift.

3. Same as Question 1, except that A designates herself as trustee.

   ANSWER: Since the grantor has a power to affect the beneficial enjoyment of income, an issue is raised of "incompleteness." The retained power to accumulate can defeat *B*'s interest, but it can only augment the value of the remainder interest. Thus, the gift of the income interest is incomplete. An incomplete interest is treated the same as a retained interest. Hence, the value of the income interest would be subtracted from the $1M gift, except that § 2702 treats retained interests as being worth zero. An "income" interest cannot be a "qualified interest" that would be subtracted. Apparently the annual exclusion does not apply to reduce the reduction (to zero) of the retained interest. The remainder interest is a future interest. Hence, *A* has made a gift of $1M.

4. *A* creates an irrevocable inter vivos trust, income to *B* for life, giving *B* the power to withdraw any and all of the corpus at any time; on *B*'s death, the remainder goes to *C*. *B* hears that possession of a power like this one might cause the trust to be included in his gross estate for estate tax purposes, which is a result to be avoided, if possible. He comes to you for advice. Is he right? Should he give up the power? Do you have any other suggestions?

    ANSWER: The question asks only about *B*, not *A*. (If it did ask about *A*, *A* would have made a completed gift. *A* retained no power.) *B* possesses a "general power of appointment," because he can withdraw the trust corpus for himself. As you will find out in Chapter 3, if *B* dies possessed of this power, the entire trust will be included in *B*'s gross estate. If *B* simply gives up the power, that constitutes a "release" of the power, and a release is treated as an exercise, and an exercise is treated as a gift transfer. But the constructive gift transfer would be to a trust in which *B* has the right to income. This is a retained-interest transfer for gift tax purposes, so that § 2702 would come into play, and there would be a gift by *B* of the entire trust. (The fact that *A* had earlier been charged with a gift of the entire property is immaterial.)

    The question doesn't say *when B* asks you for advice. If advice is sought shortly after the gift by *A*, *B* may be able to make a "qualified disclaimer" of the general power of appointment. This would simply "erase" the power, since powers are "personal" and do not "pass" from one person to another. A qualified disclaimer under § 2518 is not a "gift" transfer. If the state disclaimer statute doesn't allow *B* to make a state-law disclaimer, *B* may try a "transfer (release) in lieu of a disclaimer" under § 2518(c)(3). Since the question is unclear as to when *B* is asking for advice, the disclaimer issue should not be dealt with elaborately.

    The soundest tax savings advice may be to exercise the power (in whole or in part) so as to obtain the property directly and make multiple gifts over time that come within the annual exclusion.

5. *H* makes a gift of $1 M into an irrevocable trust, the X Bank as trustee, income to spouse *W* or accumulated in the trustee's discretion, then on *W*'s death to such of *W*'s then living issue as *W* appoints by will, or if no such appointment is made, then to *C*. How much, if any, of this gift qualifies for the marital deduction?

    ANSWER: None of it. *H* has given *W* a "terminable interest," since the interest terminates on *W*'s death. It is a nondeductible terminable interest, since on *W*'s death it will pass to one or more third parties who obtained their interests from *H*. This is an attempt at a qualified power-of-appointment trust, but it fails twice over. First, *W* wasn't given the right to all of the income payable at least annually. Second, *W*'s power of appointment by will is not a "general" one, because it cannot be exercised in favor of her estate or her creditors. No qualification, no deduction. (There is no annual exclusion either, because of the power to accumulate income.)

ESTATE TAX

▶ **CHAPTER SUMMARY**

CHAPTER 3: ESTATE TAX

Introduction. The estate tax is imposed on the taxable estate of an individual who is deceased. The "taxable estate" is the "gross estate" reduced by deductions.

The gross estate includes:

-property owned at death
-property deemed owned at death (by reason of a general power of appointment)
-certain inter vivos transfers of a testamentary nature
-life insurance over which the decedent possessed incidents of ownership (or which are
  payable to the decedent insured's estate)
-certain joint tenacies and interests therein
-property subject to a QTIP (marital deduction) election by one's predeceasing spouse
-the amount of gift tax on gifts within three years of death

Items included in the gross estate are included at their fair market values at the estate tax valuation date (usually, the date of death), unless otherwise specified in the Code. Valuation for both estate and gift tax purposes is dealt with in Chapter 4.

The available deductions include:

-the decedent's debts and funeral expenses paid by the estate
-estate administration expenses and casualty losses, assuming that they are not deducted
   for income tax purposes
-mounts qualifying for the charitable deduction
-the deduction for certain interests in family-owned businesses

The estate tax is computed under § 2001(b), using the § 2001(c) progressive rate schedule. The tax so computed is reduced (credited) by the unified transfer credit and various other credits. *See* Chapter 1, IV, B.G.C. *supra.*

ESTATE TAX JURISDICTION OF THE UNITED STATES

I. ESTATE TAX JURISDICTION OF THE UNITED STATES

A. Citizens and Residents. The estate tax applies to all U.S. citizens and residents (as defined in § 7701(b)). Under § 2209, certain U.S. citizens who are residents of U.S. possessions are not considered citizens or residents of the United States.

B. Nonresident Aliens:

1. *Gross estate:*

   a. *General rule.* Nonresident aliens are subject to the U.S. estate tax, § 2101(a), but only to the extent of property located, or deemed located, in the United States under §§ 2103-2105.

   b. *Expatriates to avoid tax.* If a decedent had renounced U.S. citizenship (and residency) within the 10-year period prior to death in order to avoid taxes, the gross estate will also include interests in controlled foreign corporations (CFCs) in proportion to the U.S. assets owned by such CFCs. *See* § 2107(b).

2. **Deductions:**

    a. *Deductions in general.* Deductions for nonresident aliens are limited as specified in § 2106.

    b. *Marital deduction:*

        (1) Spouse a U.S. citizen. The marital deduction is allowed for a *decedent* who is a nonresident alien, § 2106(a)(3), but only for property included in the nonresident alien's gross estate and only if the decedent's *spouse* is a U.S. citizen, § 2056(d)(1).

        (2) Spouse not a U.S. citizen. It follows that the deduction is disallowed if the surviving spouse is not a U.S. citizen. This rule also applies to the estate of decedents who are U.S. citizens or residents. Thus, the deduction is disallowed, even if the decedent is a U.S. resident or citizen, where the surviving spouse is a non-resident U.S. citizen (or, obviously, is a non-resident alien). However, the disallowance rule for is mitigated by the following:

            (a) *Credit by reason of first spouse's death.* If the same property is again subject to U.S. estate tax in the surviving spouse's estate, the surviving spouse's estate obtains a credit based on the U.S. estate tax on such property imposed by reason of the first spouse's death. § 2056(d)(3).

            (b) *Qualified domestic trust.* Alternatively, a transfer to a spouse who is not a U.S. citizen can qualify for the marital deduction if the transfer is to a "qualified domestic trust" as defined in § 2056A(a). § 2056(d)(2). In that case, such trust is automatically subject to U.S. estate tax on the spouse's death. § 2056A(b). Thus, either way, the property is subject to U.S. estate tax once.

            (c) *Charitable deduction.* The charitable deduction is allowable only for property included in the nonresident alien's gross estate that passes to a U.S. charity, etc. § 2106(a)(2). (For a U.S. citizen or resident, there is no requirement that the donee organization be located or organized in the U.S.)

            (d) *Family-owned business deduction.* A nonresident alien cannot claim the deduction for family-owned business interests. A U.S. citizen or resident can claim the deduction only with respect to interests in businesses located in the U.S.

3. **Credits.** The unified transfer credit is basically limited to $13,000. *See* § 2102(c). Although § 2014 generally allows a credit against U.S. estate tax for foreign death taxes attributable to property situated in the foreign country and subject to U.S. estate tax, this credit is not available to non-resident aliens, except (and only to a limited extent) for expatriates to avoid tax. *See* §§ 2102(a) and 2107(c)(2).

4. **Treaties.** Any of the rules described above pertaining to nonresident alien decedents and (nonresident alien spouses of decedents) can be modified by treaty.

II. **GROSS ESTATE. The gross estate of a decedent consists of property owned by the decedent at death, certain property transferred by the decedent during life (net of any consideration received), gift taxes on gifts made within three years of death, property over which the decedent at death possessed (or, in certain cases, during life exercised, released, or suffered to lapse) a "general power of appointment," certain insurance on the decedent's life, certain annuities and employee death benefits, certain joint tenancy property or interests therein, and property which previously qualified for the gift or estate tax marital deduction by virtue of a "QTIP election" with respect to the decedent's spouse or the estate of such spouse. Section 2031. For any item included in the gross estate, the amount includible is the fair market value as of the "estate tax valuation date," which (for the estate as a whole) is the date of the decedent's death or the "alternate valuation date." Section 2032. Valuation is the subject of Chapter 4.**

GROSS ESTATE

3

A. **Property Owned by Decedent at Death.** Section 2033 states the obvious, *i.e.*, that the gross estate includes property (tangible or intangible) owned by the decedent at the time of death, wherever situated.

1. *Beneficial ownership.* The estate tax covers only property beneficially owned by the decedent.

   a. *Express trusts and guardianships.* Property held as fiduciary under an express trust or as a guardian, custodian, or bailee is not subject to tax in the hands of the fiduciary. Reg. § 20.2033-1(a).

   b. *Resulting trusts.* In a resulting trust, the real (beneficial) owner, not the nominal owner, is deemed to own the property for purposes of § 2033. A purchase money resulting trust might be hard to prove, however. *See* Rev. Rul. 78-214, 1978-2 C.B. 285.

   c. *Constructive trusts.* A "constructive trust" is a remedial device imposed by a court to remedy fraud, unjust enrichment, etc. If a person holds property subject to a constructive trust imposed by a court prior to the person's death, the property impressed by the trust should not be included, since the personal representative would be required to transfer the property to the wronged party. Otherwise, the property would be included. On the other hand, if a court impressed a constructive trust on property after the death of the person owning or holding the property, the estate of such person should obtain a deduction under § 2053 because the constructive trust operates as a claim against the estate. *Estate of Bailey v. Com'r*, 741 F.2d 801 (5th Cir. 1984).

2. *Co-ownership.* The amount includable is only the value of the interest in the property owned by the decedent.

   a. *Community property.* Thus, in the case of community property, only half of the value of the entire property is included.

   b. *Tenancy in common.* In a tenancy in common, and in a joint tenancy (with right of survivorship) *created by a third party (i.e.,* by one who is not a joint tenant), only the decedent's pro-rata share is included.

c. *Joint tenancy.* Joint tenancies (including tenancies by the entireties) with rights of survivorship are subject to the special rules of § 2040, not § 2033. *See* II.D., *infra.*

3. ***Future interests.*** Section 2033 reaches "interests" in property which are owned by the decedent.

   a. *Interests that expire at the decedent's death.* Excluded from the gross estate are interests in property that expire at the decedent's death, such as life estates and remainders that are contingent on the decedent surviving another person. These interests might exist at the moment just prior to death, but they have a value of zero "at" the decedent's death.

   b. *Other future interests.* Interests that do not expire at the decedent's death (such as vested remainders) are includable under § 2033. Typically, the value of any such interest is figured by using the actuarial tables, and applying them "as of" the decedent's death. The actuarial tables are explained in Chapter 2, at VII.A.4.

4. ***Property created by decedent's death***

   a. *Wrongful death recoveries.* These are not includable since they do not exist "at" the decedent's death. *Connecticut Bank & Trust Co. v. U.S.,* 465 F.2d 760 (2d Cir. 1972).

   b. *Life insurance proceeds and employee death benefits.* Proceeds of insurance on the decedent's life and employee death benefits come into existence pursuant to pre-existing property (the insurance contract or employment contract). The includibility of such survivor benefits is governed by §§ 2039 and 2042, *infra,* not § 2033. However, an employee death benefit paid spontaneously by the employer not pursuant to any employment or other contract is not included in the employee's gross estate under § 2033 (or any other provision). *Estate of Bogley v. U.S.,* 514 F.2d 1027 (Ct.Cl. 1975). However, such a payment may be a gift by the shareholders or partners (other than the recipient or the decedent's estate).

5. ***Cemetery lots.*** Reg. § 20.2033-1(b) provides that the gross estate does not include the value of a cemetery lot owned by the decedent for the interment of the decedent and his or her family.

6. ***Exclusion for qualified conservation easements.*** This "exclusion," located in § 2031(c), is really a valuation discount, and is dealt with in Chapter 4.

B. **Gift Tax on Gifts Within Three Years of Death**. Under § 2035(b), the gross estate includes any gift tax paid or owed with respect to gifts made by the decedent within three years of death.

C. **Inter Vivos Transfers of a Testamentary Nature or Effect**. The obvious way to avoid § 2033 is to make gifts prior to death. Since the original 1916 Act, Congress has been alert to combat this technique of estate tax avoidance in various situations. *See* Chapter 1, at IV.B.2.c., *supra.* Although the gross estate no longer includes "transfers in contemplation of death" or transfers within a certain period of death, §§ 2036-2038 include in the gross estate property transferred by the decedent during life over which the transferor retained (or held) certain interests and/or powers. Since transfers of this type might be subject to gift tax in whole or in part, *see* Chapter 2, at V. & VII. *supra,* there is the strong possibility that they are subject to both estate and gift tax. It should be remembered especially that retained-interest and retained-power transfers that raise issues under §§ 2036-2038 may also be subject to the special gift tax rules of § 2702. *See* Chapter 1, at VII.B., *supra.* The elements of §§ 2036-2038 are laid out below.

1. ***Overview of §§ 2036–§2038.*** Sections 2036-2038 have various "elements" in common, set forth briefly here, and elaborated upon below.

    a. *Inter vivos transfer.* All three of these sections require an inter vivos transfer of property by the decedent that depletes the transferor's potential § 2033 gross estate.

    b. *For less than full and adequate consideration.* An inter vivos transfer for full and adequate consideration in money or money's worth is not subject to §§ 2036-2038, since in this case there would be no net depletion of the transferor's § 2033 gross estate.

    c. *Requisite interest or power.* It is also required that the decedent held, at the moment just prior to death, an interest or power of the type described in any of §§ 2036-2038. The decedent is deemed to have had an interest or power just prior to death if the decedent had transferred away or released such interest or power within three years of death. § 2035(c).

        (1) Section 2036. Section 2036 encompasses *interests* of the decedent-transferor to *income* (or possession or enjoyment) and *powers* to change the beneficial enjoyment of *income* (or possession or enjoyment).

        (2) Section 2037. This section mainly encompasses *interests* of the decedent-transferor in *corpus,* i.e., reversions (whether express or implied).

        (3) Section 2038. This section encompasses *powers* in the decedent-transferor to revoke, alter, amend, or terminate the possession or enjoyment of corpus and/or income.

    d. *Retention by the decedent-transferor.* Under §§ 2036 and 2037, the requisite interest or power must have been "retained" by the decedent-transferor. An interest or power is not retained if it has been conferred on the decedent-transferor by another party after the inter vivos transfer by the decedent. (Under § 2038, it is sufficient that the decedent actually possessed the power just prior to death.)

    e. *In the transferred property.* Under all three sections, the interest or power must be "in" the same property that was transferred.

    f. *Amount includable.* The amount includable is the value, at the estate tax valuation date (not the date of transfer), of the transferred property (or interest therein) "subject to" the interest or power (which is not necessarily identical to the value of the interest or power itself). The amount includable is reduced by the value, when received, of any "partial" consideration in money or money's worth received for the transfer.

2. **Section 2036.** Section 2036 encompasses the case where the transferor-decedent retained an interest in the income (or possession or enjoyment) of transferred property, retained a power over the beneficial enjoyment of income, or retained the right to vote transferred stock. (The meaning of "retained" is dealt with at II.C.5., *infra*.)

a. *Retained-income interests.* Section 2036(a)(1) refers to "the right to the income from" the transferred property.

(1) Mandatory income trusts. The typical § 2036(a)(1) situation is where A creates an irrevocable trust, income to be paid to A for life, remainder to C. The entire estate tax value of the trust is included in A's gross estate. If A has the right to only 60% of the income, only 60% of the trust is included. Reg. § 20.2036-1(a). Section 2036 would also apply in cases where the trustee was not required to pay the income to A, but A had the right under the trust to demand the income at any time. Similarly, § 2036 would apply if the trust stated that income was payable to A under a standard (such as "pleasure" or "happiness") that gave A the right, in a court of equity, to compel payment of all of the income to herself. *Estate of Boardman v. Com'r,* 20 T.C. 871 (1953), *acq.*

(2) Discretionary income trusts. Suppose A creates an irrevocable trust naming someone other than herself as trustee, income to A (perhaps under some standard like "support") or accumulated in the trustee's discretion, remainder to C upon A's death. It would appear that § 2036(a)(1) would not apply because the grantor A does not have the "right to" the income. However, the "right to" language was inserted by Congress only to cover the situation where the grantor had the right to the income under the instrument of transfer but was not actually receiving the income; if A was actually receiving the income, the income requirement of § 2036(a)(1) would perhaps be satisfied. However, a literal reading of § 2036(a)(1) would hold that the "right to income" language was not satisfied. Another way of reaching the same result is to say that the "retention" requirement has not been satisfied. Most of the cases hold that § 2036(a)(1) does not apply here unless there was a "side" agreement, express or implied, that (all of) the income is to be paid to the grantor. *See* II.C.7.c., *infra,* for more on this hypothetical.

(3) Vicarious income interests. Suppose A creates an irrevocable trust under which the trustee was required to pay income for "the support of B" during B's life, remainder to C. If A is under a legal obligation to support B, A has vicariously retained the trust income (to the extent of the support obligation) for so long as the support obligation continues. The same result occurs where income is to be used to pay A's debts or other legal obligations. Reg. § 20.2036-1(b)(2). However, if the trust states that "income is to be paid for B's support in the trustee's discretion," then the trust is not includable for the same reasons that discretionary trusts in general are not included. *Estate of Chrysler v. Com'r,* 44 T.C. 55 (1965) *acq. in result, rev'd on other issues,* 361 F.2d 508 (2d Cir. 1966).

(4) Right to an annuity. An annuity is a right to a fixed dollar amount payable periodically, whether out of income or principal. The Ninth Circuit seems to buy into the proposition that a right to annuity is not a

right to "income," and therefore that a retained annuity trust is not includible to any extent under § 2036(a)(1). *See Stern v. Com'r,* 747 F.2d 555 (9th Cir. 1984), *rev'g* 77 T.C. 614 (1981). The better view, however, is that an annuity is deemed to come first out of income to the extent thereof, and any excess is deemed to come out of principal. *Estate of Greene v. U. S.,* 237 F.2d 848 (7th Cir. 1956); Rev. Rul. 55-378, 1955-1 C.B. 447. Thus, if at the time of transfer, the value, under the actuarial tables, of the retained annuity is less than the value of an income interest in the same property for the same duration, the property should be partially includable under § 2036(a)(1), *i.e.,* in the same ratio as the annuity value bears to the income interest value using the actuarial tables. If the opposite is the case, the property should be fully includable. See Rev. Rul. 82-105, 1982-1 C.B. 133.

(5) Unitrust interest. A unitrust interest is an annual right to receive a fixed percentage of the corpus, valued as of a certain day in the year, whether out of income or corpus. A retained unitrust-interest trust is includable under § 2036(a)(1), according to the same analyses as for retained-annuity trusts. See Rev. Rul. 76-273, 1976-2 C.B. 268.

b. *Retained possession or enjoyment.* "Possession or enjoyment" is the functional equivalent of "income" where non-income-producing property is involved, such as a personal residence, automobile, or art work. A common example is where *A* deeds her personal residence to *C* but continues to occupy it *(e.g., Estate of Linderme v. Com'r,* 52 T.C. 305 (1969)). The crucial issue in this type of case is whether possession was "retained" by the donor in connection with the transfer, as opposed to *C* "giving" the possession to *A*.

c. *Retained leasehold interest.* Suppose *A* gives real estate to *C* and leases it back. If the rent is for an amount equal to the property's arms' length rental value, *A* has not kept the income or possession or enjoyment of the property. *Estate of Barlow v. Com'r,* 55 T.C. 666 (1971), *acq. Compare Maxwell's Estate v. Com'r,* 3 F.3d 591 (2d Cir.1993) (§2036(a)(1) held to apply where rent exactly offset interest obligation running to the transferor). If the rent paid by *A* is less than the fair rental, *A* has retained possession or enjoyment triggering § 2036. Establishing a fair rental value is a hazardous proposition in the case of farmland, ranchland, or recreational land, since the fair rental value is to be ascertained with reference to the land's highest and best use, not it's actual use. *See Estate of Du Pont v. Com'r,* 63 T.C. 746 (1975). (The amount includible should, perhaps, be that fraction of the property as the value of the rent-free use bears to the fair rental value.)

d. *Retained powers over beneficial enjoyment of income.* Section 2036(a)(2) is triggered if the transferor retains the right to affect the beneficial enjoyment of income, meaning the right to affect the identity of who is to receive the income. It is not necessary that the power was actually exercised. Where § 2036(a)(2) applies, the entire estate tax value of the trust is included, just as if the transferor had retained an income interest.

(1) How a power can be retained. The grantor of an irrevocable trust can retain the power in herself as grantor, but by far the most common situation is where the grantor confers the power on the trustee and then designates herself as trustee in the trust instrument. Another possibility

is that the grantor is not the trustee, but that there is a side agreement between the grantor and the trustee to the effect that the trustee will follow the grantor's directives. However, the grantor is not considered to hold the trustee's powers just because the trustee is a friend or relative of the grantor. *Estate of Sherman v. Com'r,* 9 T.C. 954 (1947). Nevertheless, if the grantor actually controls or dominates the trustee, the trustee's powers may be attributed to the grantor. *See Estate of Klauber v. Com'r,* 34 T.C. 968 (1960) *(dictum)* (reviewed), *nonacq. on other issues.* In a controversial ruling, Rev. Rul. 79-353, 1979-2 C.B. 345, the Service held that the powers of a corporate trustee would be attributed to the grantor if the grantor had the power to fire the corporate trustee without cause, but that ruling was revoked by Rev. Rul. 95-58, 1995-2 C.B. 191.

(2) Jointly held powers. Section 2036(a)(2) applies in cases where the requisite power is held by the grantor jointly with other parties, even if such parties hold an "adverse interest" and even if the other parties can act by majority vote without the transferor's consent. Reg. § 20.2036-1(b)(3); *DuCharme's Estate v. Com'r,* 164 F.2d 959 (6th Cir. 1947).

(3) Power to "affect beneficial enjoyment" of income. Not every retained power triggers § 2036(a)(2); the power must be one to affect the beneficial enjoyment of income.

   (a) Spray power. Assume that *A* creates an irrevocable trust, naming herself as trustee, income to be paid to or among such of *B, C,* and *D* in such amounts and portions as the trustee in its discretion determines for 30 years, remainder to *E. A* has retained, as trustee, the power to affect who gets the income.

   (b) Accumulation power. Now assume that *A* creates an irrevocable trust, naming herself as trustee, income to *B* or accumulated in the trustee's discretion, remainder to *C* on the death of *B.* By retaining the power to accumulate, *A* has retained the power to shift the income from *B* to *C,* since accumulated income is added to corpus and eventually goes to the remainder. *U.S. v. O'Malley,* 383 U.S. 627 (1966). Next assume the same facts, except the trust is to last for 20 years or *B's* earlier death, at which time the corpus is to be paid to *B* if living or if not to "*B's* estate." Even though *B's* estate is technically a continuation of *B, A's* retained power to accumulate has been held to run afoul of § 2036(a)(2). *Leopold v. U.S.,* 510 F.2d 617 (9th Cir. 1975).

   (c) Corpus invasion power. A power to invade corpus for the benefit of the sole income beneficiary does not cause inclusion under § 2036(a)(2), since the enjoyment of income would not be diverted or curtailed. (However, § 2038 impacts on this situation.) *See Walter v. U.S.,* 341 F.2d 182 (6th Cir. 1965).

(4) Administrative powers exception. An "administrative power" retained by the transferor, such as a power over investments or a power to decide whether receipts and disbursements are charged against "income" or "corpus" (*i.e.,* a trust accounting power), is *per se* outside of the scope of § 2036(a)(2), even if the power could be exercised in a way that would

affect the beneficial enjoyment of income. *Old Colony Trust Co. v. U.S.,* 423 F.2d 601 (1st Cir. 1970), cited with approval in *U.S. v. Byrum,* 408 U.S. 125 (1972).

    (5) Dispositive power limited by standards. A retained dispositive power over income which is limited by an ascertainable standard is also outside of the reach of § 2036(a)(2). *Jennings v. Smith,* 161 F.2d 74 (2d Cir. 1947). Although the numerous cases applying this rule are not in complete harmony on what constitutes an ascertainable standard, "support," "maintenance," "health," "education," and "comfort" are usually held to be ascertainable standards, even where they are to be applied in the grantor-trustee's discretion, *e.g., Estate of Bell v. Com'r,* 66 T.C. 729 (1976), *acq.,* whereas standards like "pleasure," "needs," or "happiness" are usually not considered to be ascertainable and therefore do not significantly limit the grantor-trustee's power to affect the enjoyment of income, *e.g., Old Colony Trust Co. v. U.S., supra.* The exceptions for administrative powers, *supra,* and dispositive powers limited by standards effectively emasculate § 2036(a)(2) in cases where the trust is properly drafted.

    (6) Incidental powers. A power which is "incidental" to some "life" decision that transcends transfer tax planning considerations is outside of the scope of § 2036(a)(2). An example would be the power to expand the class of permissible income beneficiaries by producing more children. Rev. Rul. 80-255, 1980-2 C.B. 272. *See also Estate of Tully v. U.S.,* 528 F.2d 1401 (Ct.Cl. 1976) (power to affect beneficial enjoyment by quitting one's job); Rev. Rul. 75-415, 1975-2 C.B. 374 (power to terminate one's education). (This doctrine is analagous to the doctrine of "acts of independent significance" in the law of dispositive transfers.)

    (7) Power over corporation or partnership. In *U.S v. Byrum,* 408 U.S. 125 (1972), the Court held that the grantor's power, as controlling corporate shareholder and director, to withhold dividends on the stock transferred to the corporation was not a § 2036(a)(2) power to accumulate, citing the "administrative powers" exception, since the grantor had fiduciary duties to the corporation and its other shareholders. This holding survives the 1976 enactment of § 2036(b), immediately *infra. See Estate of Tully v. U.S.,* 528 F.2d 1401 (Ct.Cl. 1976).

e. *Rights to vote transferred stock.* If a donor of stock retains the right to vote the stock, the donor is deemed under § 2036(b) to have retained possession or enjoyment of the stock for purposes of § 2036(a)(1). This rule, effective for transfers after June 22, 1976, overturns the § 2036(a)(1) result (but not the § 2036(a)(2) holding, *supra*) of *Byrum v. U.S.,* 408 U.S. 125 (1972). It only applies if the decedent at any time during the three-year period ending on her death owned (after applying the § 318 attribution rules) or had the right to vote (either alone or jointly) at least 20% of the voting power of the corporation.

f. *Period of retention.* Under § 2036, the retained interest or power must be held by the transferor for a period that falls within one of the following categories:

(1) For life. The interest is retained for the transferor's life, and expires on her death.

(2) For a period that does not in fact end before death. If *A* creates a trust, income to herself for 30 years, remainder to *B*, the trust is included in *A*'s gross estate under § 2036 only if *A* dies within the 30-year period.

(3) For a period that ends with reference to the transferor's death. If *A* creates a trust, income to herself until six months before her death, remainder to *C*, § 2036 is not avoided. The following trust is also included under this language. *A* in trust, income to *B* for life, then income to *A* for life (if living), remainder to *C*. Even if *A* predeceases *B* (so that she never came into enjoyment of her secondary income interest), the trust, reduced by then value of *B*'s outstanding income interest, is included. Reg. § 20.2036-1(b)(1).

(4) Transfer or release of retained interest or power within three years of death:

   (a) Section 2036(a) interest or power. Section 2036(a) cannot be avoided by a transfer or release by the transferor of the retained interest or power within three years of the transferor's death. § 2035(a). Nevertheless, the "lapse" of a retained interest or power within three years of death will avoid § 2036. *See* item (2) *supra*.

   (b) Transfer or release for full consideration. Section 2035(a), supra, can be negated under § 2035(d) by a transfer (or release) of the retained interest or power for full and adequate consideration. However, in *U.S. v. Allen,* 293 F.2d 916 (10th Cir. 1961), it was held that a transfer is deemed to be for full and adequate consideration for this purpose only if the consideration equals the value of the entire property that would be includable under § 2036 (as opposed to the lesser value of the transferred or released interest or power).

   (c) Relinquishment of voting rights. Section 2036(b) cannot be avoided by a transfer, relinquishment, or lapse of voting rights within three years of death, nor can it be avoided by a reduction in the decedent's voting power below the 20% threshold within three years of death. § 2036(b)(2) & (3).

g. *Contingent interests and powers.* A retained interest or power still "counts" under § 2036 even if it is merely contingent.

(1) Conditions precedent. Suppose *A* created an irrevocable trust, income to *B* for life, then income to *A* (if living) for life, remainder to *C*, and *A* dies before *B*. This situation involves a "contingent" income interest: enjoyment of *A*'s secondary income interest was contingent on *A*'s outliving *B*, but in fact *A* predeceased *B* and never came into possession of the secondary income interest. This is the same situation as is described in f.(3), *supra*. Hence, the trust (reduced by the actuarial value, as of *A*'s death, of *B*'s remaining income interest) is included in *A*'s gross estate. Thus, it would seem to follow that any contingent income or possessory interest comes under § 2036, even if the contingency never occurred.

(2) Conditions subsequent. Suppose *A* creates a trust, income to herself for life, giving the trustee discretion to pay corpus to *B*, remainder to *C* upon *A*'s death. The estate tax value of the trust is included even though the retained income interest could have been (but wasn't) defeated by the trustee paying all of the corpus to *B*. *Estate of Boardman v. Com'r*, 20 T.C. 871 (1953) *acq*. If the corpus was all paid to *B* before *A*'s death, then nothing would be included in *A*'s gross estate, of course.

(3) Contingent powers. It is settled that a transferor is deemed to hold a power, even where actual possession of the power is subject to a contingency that never occurred prior to the decedent's death. Reg. § 20.2036-1(b)(3). A common application of this doctrine occurs where a trustee other than the grantor has a power to affect the beneficial enjoyment of income, and the grantor had the power to fire the trustee and appoint herself as successor trustee (or co-trustee). (Thus, for planning purposes, if the grantor retains the right to fire the trustee, the trust instrument should prohibit appointment of the grantor as successor trustee.) The same result is likely to occur even where the grantor cannot fire the trustee but can appoint herself successor trustee should a vacancy occur. *Estate of Farrel v. U.S.*, 553 F.2d 637 (Ct.Cl. 1977). The possibility that the grantor might be designated a successor trustee (or even the fact that she was in fact designated a successor trustee) by a third party in case of a vacancy should not trigger § 2036(a)(2), since in that case the power was not "retained" by the grantor.

3. ***Section 2038.*** Section 2038 deals with situations where the transferor-decedent held a power over corpus or income at the time of death. Section 2038 can overlap with § 2036(a)(2), and it can perhaps best be grasped by comparing it with § 2036(a)(2). Under § 2038, the amount includible is the value of the interest(s) to which the power pertains. Partially for that reason, and partially because § 2038 is more commonly applied than § 2037, it will be considered prior to § 2037.

   a. *Not relevant how power acquired.* The requisite power must be held by the transferor-decedent as of the moment just prior to death. Unlike § 2036, there is no requirement that the power have been "retained" by the transferor-decedent. Thus, § 2038 applies whether the requisite power was retained by the transferor-decedent (*see* 2.d.(1), *supra*) or was acquired (by whatever means) by the transferor-decedent subsequent to the inter vivos transfer. Thus, if the grantor of a trust granted the requisite powers to the trustee and named herself as trustee, § 2038 would apply if the grantor is still the trustee at the time of her death. The same result would occur, given the same trust, even if the grantor named an independent trustee, but a vacancy occurred and the grantor was appointed by the court or third party as successor trustee, again assuming the grantor was a trustee at the time of death.

   b. *How power held.* It doesn't matter whether the requisite power is held under the terms of the instrument of transfer (such as a trust instrument) or as trustee. The fact that the trustee is a friend or relative of the trustee is not sufficient to cause the trustee's powers to be attributed to the grantor, although an actual pattern of domination or control might suffice to do so. A power in the transferor to both fire the trustee and appoint oneself as successor trustee results in the transferor being held to possess the trustee's powers. Reg. § 20.2038-1(a)(3).

c. *Capacity to exercise power.* A decedent is possessed of a power for purposes of § 2038 (and also §§ 2036(a)(2) and 2037(b)) even though the decedent lacked the legal capacity to exercise the power.

d. *Contingent powers.* Unlike § 2036(a)(2), a power subject to a condition precedent escapes § 2038, unless the condition or contingency was (1) de minimis, (2) under the decedent's control, or (3) actually occurred before death. Reg. § 20.2038-1(b). In short, the § 2038 power (normally) must be actually held by the transferor at the moment of death. That an existing power might have been (but wasn't) defeated or cut off prior to death is also of no importance, so long as the power was actually held at death.

e. *Joint powers.* As with § 2036(a)(2), § 2038 cannot be avoided by sharing the power with other parties (typically co-trustees), even in cases where the other parties can control the decisions by outvoting the transferor. Rev. Rul. 70-513, 1970-2 C.B. 194. Nor does it matter that the co-holders of the power have interests adverse to the exercise of the power. Reg. § 20.2038-1(a). However, a mere "power" to persuade the holder of the power is not a tax-triggering power. *Estate of Tully v. U.S.*, 528 F.2d 1401 (Ct.Cl. 1976).

f. *Powers described in § 2038.* Section 2038 applies where the transferor at the moment of death held a power to revoke, alter, amend, or terminate the transfer (trust).

(1) Revoke. A power to revoke means a power to terminate the transfer and cause the property to return to the transferor. If the transferor has a power to revoke only a portion of the property, only the estate tax value of that portion is included.

(2) Terminate. Literally, "terminate" means cutting short the trust but without returning the property to the transferor. However, as will be explained below under "alter," the word "terminate" in § 2038 is essentially surplusage and doesn't really add much of anything to its scope.

(3) Amend. A power to amend is a power to change the beneficial enjoyment of corpus or income by the transferor rewriting the instrument of transfer. "Amending" is only one way of "altering."

(4) Alter. A power to "alter" refers to a power to change the beneficial enjoyment of corpus or income by a means other than amendment of the instrument of transfer. Typically a power to alter occurs where the grantor is trustee (or co-trustee) and can shift the enjoyment of income and/or corpus among two or more beneficiaries.

(a) Power to affect beneficial enjoyment of income. A power to shift income among current beneficiaries or to accumulate income (resulting in the income eventually going to the remainder) comes under § 2038 as well as § 2036(a)(2). Since the amount included under § 2036(a)(2) is the entire value of the property, whereas under § 2038 only the value of the affected income interest would be included, § 2036(a)(2) controls (preempts) § 2038. Thus, there is no double inclusion.

(b) Power to alter enjoyment of corpus. If the transferor holds at death the power to change the identity of the remainder (sometimes called a retained special power of appointment), § 2038 applies. An example would be: *A* in trust, income to *B* for life, remainder to *C*, with *A* retaining the power to substitute any of *A*'s issue for *C*, assuming that *A* predeceases *B*. The amount includable, however, is only the estate tax value of the remainder interest subject to the power. Reg. § 20.2038-1(a) (last sentence).

(c) Power to invade corpus. Suppose *A* creates a trust, naming herself as trustee, income to *B* for life, remainder to *C*, with the trustee having the power to invade corpus for the benefit of *B* in the trustee's sole discretion, and *A* dies before *B*. Here, *A* has retained the power to shift enjoyment of the remainder from *C* to *B*, and it is clear that the estate tax value of the remainder is included under § 2038. Is the income interest also included under § 2038 on the theory that *A* held the power to "terminate" such interest? The IRS has conceded that the income interest is not includable: if the corpus were all paid to *B*, *B* would own the property outright and would continue to have the right to the income from such property. *Walter v. U.S.*, 341 F.2d 182 (6th Cir. 1965).

(d) Power to affect time or manner of enjoyment. Now take the case where *A* created a trust, income to *B* for 20 years or her earlier death, remainder to *B* or her estate, with *A* having the power to accumulate income or invade corpus for *B* during *B*'s life. In *Lober v. U.S.*, 346 U.S. 335 (1953), the Supreme Court held that the power was one to "alter" enjoyment, and the entire trust was includible. Accord, Reg. § 20.2038-1(a) (third sentence from end).

g. *Powers excluded from § 2038.* The exceptions described under § 2036(a)(2) pertaining to "administrative powers," "dispositive powers limited by ascertainable standards," "incidental powers," and "powers over corporations and partnerships" apply under § 2038 as well. In addition, § 2038 does not apply to the power which, under the law of trusts, any grantor possesses (together with all the beneficiaries) to terminate the trust. *Helvering v. Helmholz,* 296 U.S. 93 (1935); Reg. § 20.2038-1(a)(2).

h. *Powers released within three years of death.* Section 2035(a)(2) provides that the release by a transferor within three years of death of a § 2038 power is ineffective to avoid § 2038. There is similar language within § 2038 itself. Controversy arose over the issue of whether a distribution from a revocable trust within three years of the grantor's death to a beneficiary (other than the grantor) would be treated as a (partial) release of a § 2038 power, but that issue was resolved by the enactment of § 2035(e) in 1997, which holds that such a distribution is irrelevant under § 2038. Of course, the distribution is a deemed gift by the grantor for gift tax purposes.

4. *Section 2037.* Section 2037 is the most difficult, most obscure, and least frequently applied provision of the §§ 2036-2038 triumvirate. As an intellectual puzzle, it makes the Rule Against Perpetuities seem easy. Section 2037 applies only where the inter vivos transfer by the decedent satisfies both the "survivorship" requirement and the "more than 5% reversion" requirement. The

amount includable under § 2037 is the estate tax value of interests that are contingent on surviving the transferor (not the value of the reversionary interest, which might, or might not, be includable under § 2033 *supra*).

a. *Reversion worth more than 5%.* The transferor (including the estate of the transferor) must retain a reversionary interest in the transferred property worth more than 5% of the property as of the transferor's death (not the time of transfer).

   (1) "Reversion" defined. Section 2037(b) describes a reversion as any possibility that the *corpus* "may return to [the transferor] or his estate." A possibility of receiving future *income* does not fall under § 2037(b) by its express terms; Congress intended no overlap between §§ 2036 and 2037. The phrase "any possibility" is meant to encompass reversions that are contingent (perhaps remotely) on future events.

   (2) Reversion must be "retained." Suppose *A* creates an irrevocable trust, naming *X* as trustee, income to *B* for life, remainder to *C*, with the trustee having the power to invade corpus for the benefit of *A* in the trustee's sole discretion. Although *A* here appears to have a § 2037(b) reversion, such reversion is not "retained" and hence does not trigger § 2037. *Com'r v. Irving Trust Co.,* 147 F.2d 946 (2d Cir. 1945). If, in contrast, the trustee in the example were required under the trust instrument to pay, say, $10,000 of corpus to *A* per year, then *A* would have retained the requisite reversion. *Bankers Trust Co. v. Higgins,* 136 F.2d 477 (2d Cir. 1943).

   (3) Reversion by operation of law. The reversion can be either express or implied (*i.e.,* arising by operation of law). An implied reversion exists where the transferor has not made a complete disposition of the property. For example, assume *A* creates a trust, income to *B* for the life of *A*, then remainder to *C* if living, but if not to *D* if living. Here *A* has an implied reversion in case neither *C* nor *D* outlives *A*. Reg. § 20.2037-1(c)(2).

   (4) Contingent powers over corpus. The reversionary interest requirement is also satisfied under § 2037(b) where *A* (the grantor) retained a contingent power to affect the beneficial enjoyment of corpus. In other words, the grantor is deemed to have retained a reversionary interest (power) if, under the terms of the trust, the grantor might have acquired the power upon the occurance of future events, even though such events had not actually occurred prior to *A*'s death (*i.e., A* did not actually possess the power at death). *See Fidelity-Philadelphia Trust Co. v. Rothensies,* 324 U.S. 108 (1945).

   Example 1: *A* created an irrevocable trust, income to *B* for life, and if *A* survives *B* the remainder is to go to such of *A*'s issue as *A* appoints by a written instrument delivered by *A* to the trustee within 60 days of *B*'s death, but if no such appointment is made, or if *A* predeceases *B*, the remainder is to go to *C*. For gift tax purposes, the gift of the remainder interest is initially incomplete, and it becomes complete if *A* survives *B*, when *A* either exercises the power or fails to exercise it during the 60-day period. If *A* predeceases *B*, *A* had a contingent power over the corpus that is a "reversionary interest" under § 2037(b).

(5) Jointly held contingent powers. Unlike §§ 2036(a)(2) and 2038, a power does not come under § 2037(b) if it is held jointly by the transferor with one or more "adverse parties." *Reinecke v. Northern Trust Co.,* 278 U.S. 339 (1929).

(6) Relation to § 2038. Section 2037 cannot overlap with § 2038. Section 2037 is triggered when the transferor held a *contingent* power at death; if the power was actually possessed at death, § 2038 applies.

Example 2: If a trust grantor retained a power to, say, decide whether $10,000 of corpus per year was to be invaded for the benefit of *X*, $10,000 would be included in the grantor's gross estate under § 2038, since the grantor died holding the power over that year's $10,000, and the possibility of controlling $10,000 of corpus in future years, which was cut off by the grantor's death, would be a contingent power under § 2037(b). *Estate of Klauber v. Com'r,* 34 T.C. 968 (1960) (reviewed), *nonacq. on other issues.*

(7) Valuing the reversion. For § 2037 to apply, the reversionary interest must be worth more than 5% of the value of the corpus as of the moment just prior to the transferor's death, *disregarding the fact of such death.* Reg. § 20.2037-1(c)(3).

Example 3: Assume that *A* creates an irrevocable trust naming *X* as trustee, income to *B* for life, with the trustee required to pay $20,000 of corpus per year to *A*, remainder to *C*. Here, the value of *A*'s reversion for § 2037 purposes is the value of a $20,000 per year annuity for a person of *A*'s life expectancy at the moment just prior to *A*'s death. *Estate of Klauber v. Com'r, supra.*

Example 4: Assume that *A* creates an irrevocable trust, income to *B* for life, reversion to *A* if living, but if not remainder to *C*. If *A* outlives *B*, the property becomes part of *A*'s § 2033 gross estate and § 2037 is not a factor. If *A* predeceases *B*, *A*'s reversion is worth nothing at *A*'s death (the remainder will go to *C*) and is not included under § 2033. For purposes of § 2037, however, *A*'s reversion does have a value at the moment just prior to *A*'s death, because § 2037 mandates ignoring the actual fact of such death.

(8) How reversion is valued. Conceptually, the value of a reversion such as the one set forth in Example 4 is a function primarily of the chances that *A* would have outlived *B*, considering the actuarial life expectancies of both as of the moment just prior to *A*'s death, plus discounting the possible reversion to present value. (A contingent *power* over corpus is treated as if it were a reversionary *interest*. § 2037(b) (third sentence).) Therefore, the value of a reversion under § 2037 (usually) cannot be obtained simply by obtaining the "remainder" factor from the published actuarial tables. Since the 2037 calculation is usually too complex to be performed by a layperson, the decedent's personal representative is required to submit a request to the IRS. *See* Rev. Rul. 76-178, 1976-1 C.B. 273. The greater the number of contingencies, the less the reversion is likely to be worth.

(9) Effect of power in third party. The last sentence of § 2037(b) states that § 2037 does not apply where, at the time of the transferor's death, a person other than the transferor had an inter vivos *general* power of appointment (*i.e.,* the power to withdraw or appropriate the corpus). Although the statute does not so provide, even an inter vivos "special" power of appointment (power to distribute corpus to a person other than the power-holder) held by a person other than the transferor should bar the application of § 2037, since (as of the moment just prior to the transferor's death but disregarding the actual fact of her death) the power could be exercised to defeat any reversion in the settlor (by transferring all of the corpus to one or more appointees) and thereby would cause the reversion to have a merely speculative (*i.e.,* zero) value. *See* Rev. Rul. 79-117, 1979-1 C.B. 305.

(10) Transfer or release of reversionary interest within three years of death. If the transferor within three years of death assigns her reversionary interest (or sells it for its actuarial value) or releases her contingent power over corpus, she will be deemed under § 2035(a)(2) to possess the interest or power at death.

b. *The survivorship requirement.* Section 2037 does not apply unless possession or enjoyment of the property can be obtained "only by surviving" the transferor-decedent. § 2037(a)(1). This cryptically-phrased requirement can only be understood through examples.

(1) Transferor's death as necessary condition. Although not made explicit in the statute, the "survivorship requirement" is satisfied in any case where the decedent's death is merely a "necessary" (as opposed to "sufficient") condition for any person's obtaining possession or enjoyment of the property.

Example 5: Assume that *A* creates an irrevocable trust, income to *B* for the life of *A*, remainder to *C* if then living, otherwise remainder to *D*. The survivorship requirement is satisfied, since whether *C* or *D* will take the remainder is contingent on *A*'s death relative to that of *C*. (However, § 2037 does not apply here, as *A* has not retained any reversionary interest in corpus.) Reg. § 20.2037-1(e) (Ex.2).

Example 6: Now take the case where *A* creates an irrevocable trust, income to *B* for life, reversion to *A* if then living, but if not remainder to *C*. Reg. § 20.2037-1(e) (Ex.3). Here *C*'s remainder is dependent on *A*'s dying before *B,* and *A* has a reversionary interest (which may well be worth more than 5% as of the moment just prior to *A*'s death).

Example 7: Another case where § 2037 applies (assuming the reversion is worth more than 5%) is where an employee death benefit is payable to *B* if living at the employee's death, but if not, the benefit is payable to the employee's estate. Rev. Rul. 78-15, 1978-1 C.B. 289.

All of Examples 1-4 above also satisfy the survivorship requirement.

(2) Alternate contingencies exception. The survivorship requirement is not satisfied if possession or enjoyment by a beneficiary can be obtained upon

the *earlier* to occur of the transferor's death or some other event, since in that case possession or enjoyment cannot be obtained "only" by surviving the transferor.

Example 8: *A* creates a trust, income to *B* until the earlier to occur of *A*'s death or *B*'s death, remainder to *C* if then living, but if *C* is not living then to *A* or *A*'s estate. Here, even if *A* predeceased *B*, *C* could have taken by surviving *B* instead of surviving *A*. Hence, § 2037 does not apply, but if *A* dies before *B* the value of *A*'s reversion (which is contingent on *C*'s outliving *B*, rather than *A*'s surviving *B*) is included in *A*'s gross estate under § 2033. (If *B* dies before *A*, either the remainder will go to *C* and not appear in *A*'s gross estate or the reversion in *A* will come into possession.)

The situation described in Example 6 does not fall within the alternate contingencies exception, because in Example 6 the remainder does not come into *possession or enjoyment* upon the earlier to occur of A's death or B's death. On the other hand, one can fairly conclude that the situations described *supra* in a.(9) (effect of third-party power of appointment on value of reversion) do fall within the alternate contingencies exception. In any event, the alternate contingencies exception does not apply where the alternate contingency to A's death is "unreal." *See* Reg. § 20.2037-1(b).

    c. *Amount includable.* The amount includable under § 2037 is not the value of the reversion itself either at death or at the moment just prior to death. Rather, the amount included is the estate tax value of all interests contingent on surviving the decedent. Reg. § 20.2037-1(b) (first sentence).

Example 9: Thus, where *A* creates a trust, income to *B* for life, reversion to *A* if living but if not remainder to *C*, the amount includable if *A* dies before *B* is the value of the entire trust reduced by the then actuarial value of *B*'s outstanding income interest (*A*'s reversion at *A*'s death before that of *B* having a § 2033 value of zero). *See* Reg. § 20.2037-1(e) (Ex.3).

Example 10: In the example where *A* had the right to $20,000 of corpus per year for life, the amount includable would be the value of *A*'s annuity as of the moment just prior to *A*'s death, since such value is the measure of the value of the portion of the trust that was contingent on surviving *A*. *Estate of Klauber v. Com'r,* 34 T.C. 968 (1960) *(reviewed), nonacq. on other issues.*

    5. *Transfer requirement.* Sections 2036-2038 all require that the decedent have made an inter vivos transfer of property that depletes the decedent's potential § 2033 gross estate.

    a. *"Transfer" not synonymous with "gift."* The concept of "transfer" under §§ 2036-2038 is different from "gift" under the gift tax in certain ways.

    (1) Gift splitting. Suppose husband makes a gift of $100,000 that is complete for gift tax purposes, and husband and wife agree to split the gift for gift tax purposes under § 2013. For purposes of §§ 2036-2038, husband has made a "transfer" of the entire $100,000, since that is the amount by which his § 2033 estate is depleted, and wife has made a transfer of zero,

since her § 2033 estate has not been depleted. In contrast, if the gift is of community property worth $100,000, each of husband and wife has made a "transfer" (as well as a gift) of $50,000.

(2) Present-interest exclusion. The § 2503(b) exclusion for present-interest gifts has no application to estate tax transfers.

(3) Deductible gifts. A deductible gift is still a "transfer" under §§ 2036-2038. Nevertheless, it is very unlikely that §§ 2036-2038 will come into play in such a situation.

b. *Significance of transfer requirement.* Property transferred by persons other than the decedent cannot be included in the decedent's gross estate under §§ 2036-§2038, because any such transfer did not deplete the *decedent's* potential § 2033 gross estate. *See U.S. v. O'Malley,* 383 U.S. 627 (1986) (accumulated income in trust deemed "transferred" by trust grantor, since income was attributable to corpus transferred by grantor and was not transferred by any other party).

c. *Transferred property must have been owned by decedent.* Only property beneficially owned by the decedent can be transferred by him for estate tax purposes. Refer back to the discussion of property ownership under § 2033 in A., *supra.*

d. *Indirect transfer.* The indirect transfer concept applies for estate, as well as gift, tax purposes. If *A* gives property to *B* on condition that *B* create a trust, then *A* (not *B*) is the "real" transferor. *See* Reg. § 25.2511-1(h)(2). This doctrine is frequently applied to employee death benefits (not included under § 2039): although the death benefit is paid by the employer, the real transferor is the employee who creates value by performing services for the employer, part of which value is diverted to the death benefit. *E.g., Estate of Fried v. Com'r,* 445 F.2d 979 (2d Cir. 1979), *cert. denied.* The death benefit must be paid under an employment contract, binding resolution, or established policy in order to link the payment to the employee. *See Estate of Bogley v. United States,* 613 F.2d 802 (Ct.Cl. 1980). Compare *Estate of DiMarco v. Com'r,* 87 T.C. 653 (1986) (no indirect transfer where employee plan was involuntary and employee had no powers over the plan or its benefits), *acq.*

e. *Reciprocal transfers.* In a reciprocal transfer, two (related) parties each make transfers which, if the grantors were "switched," would be includable in the gross estate of each grantor under any of §§ 2036-2038.

(1) Illustration. The most common example is this: *A* creates a trust for *B* for life, remainder to *C,* and *B* creates a trust, income to *A* for life, remainder to *C.* In form, neither trust is includable in either grantor's gross estate, since neither grantor has retained an interest in the property transferred by him or her (and the income interest acquired from the other is not included because it has a value of zero on the owner's death). If the "reciprocal transfer doctrine" is held to apply, the trusts will be "crossed," meaning that each grantor will be deemed the grantor of the "other" trust, resulting (in the example) in inclusion of *B*'s trust in *A*'s gross estate and the inclusion of *A*'s trust in *B*'s gross estate under § 2036(a)(1).

(2) What Code sections will be applied. The doctrine will apply where each transferor has an "interest" in the other trust of the type which, if retained, would come under § 2036(a)(1) or § 2037, or would be a power of revocation. There is some question whether the doctrine will be applied where each transfer has a dispositive power (other than a power to revoke) of the type that would come under § 2036(a)(2) or § 2038. *Compare Estate of Bischoff v. Com'r*, 69 T.C. 32 (1977) (doctrine applied), *with Estate of Green v. U.S.*, 68 F.3d 151 (6th Cir.1995) (opposite result).

(3) Evidence. The doctrine will apply where there is evidence of an agreement between the parties supported by "consideration" in the contract-law sense. *Lehman v. Com'r,* 109 F.2d 99 (2d Cir. 1940), *cert. denied.* This rule is simply a variation of the indirect transfer doctrine. Moreover, under *U.S. v. Estate of Grace,* 395 U.S. 316 (1969), the doctrine will apply merely on the basis of the following "objective" facts: (1) similar ("mirror") terms in the transfers, (2) nearly contemporaneous dates of transfer, and (3) approximately equal amounts transferred. *See Estate of Bischoff, supra.*

(4) Amount includable. The amount includable on the death of a given grantor is the value of the *other* trust multiplied by a percentage. If, at the time of transfer, the decedent's amount transferred exceeded the amount transferred by the other party, the percentage is 100%. In the reverse situation, the percentage is obtained by dividing the amount transferred by the decedent by the amount transferred by the other party. Rev. Rul. 74-533, 1974-2 C.B. 293.

f. *Constructive transfers.* A constructive transfer occurs where a party refuses to accept property or an interest therein given or proffered by another, and, as a result of the refusal, the property or interest goes to (or vests) in a third party who is a natural object of the refuser's bounty.

(1) Typical situation. Assume that *A*'s will bequeaths $1 million outright to *B* and the residue of *A*'s estate in trust, income to *B* for life, remainder to *C,* and that *B* disclaims the $1 million bequest. *B* has here made a constructive transfer of the $1 million to the residuary trust, in which *B* has an income interest for life. Therefore, the estate tax value of the trust attributable to the $1 million is included in *B*'s gross estate under § 2036(a)(1).

(2) Exceptions. A constructive transfer does not occur in the following two situations:

(a) Qualified disclaimer. A "qualified disclaimer" under § 2518 is not a "transfer" for estate tax, as well as gift tax, purposes. *See* Ch. 2, at IV.D.3., *supra.*

(b) Settlement of dispute. A bona fide settlement of a genuine dispute, approved by a court, is not a transfer. Otherwise, a transfer occurs where any party ends up with less than she was originally entitled to. *See* Ch. 2, at IV.E., *supra.*

g. *Inter vivos powers of appointment:*

(1) Power of appointment defined. A power of appointment is a power granted by an owner or transferor of property (the "donor" of the power) to another person (the "donee" or holder of the power) that allows the donee to transfer all or part of the property to, or vest it in, one or more persons (the "objects"), which may or may not include the donee of the power. Powers of appointment are typically found in trusts. If a person (other than the transferor of the trust) possesses a dispositive power, such person is said to possess a power of appointment. However, only powers of appointment held by individuals can give rise to a "transfer" for estate (and gift) tax purposes. A power of appointment might be held in one's capacity as a trustee, a beneficiary, or an outside party. *See* Chapter 2, IV.B., *supra.*

(2) General power of appointment. A donee of a power has an inter vivos "general" power when the donee can appoint the property or interest to herself or her creditors.

(a) Possession of general power. If a person (donee) of a general power of appointment dies possessed of a general power of appointment, the property subject to the power is included in the donee's gross estate under § 2041(a). *See* F., *infra.*

(b) Exercise or release of general power. An individual possessing a general power may attempt to get rid of it, so as to avoid § 2041, by releasing it or exercising it. (Under state law, exercising a power of appointment may, or may not, exhaust, *i.e.*, release, the power.) A power may also lapse, *i.e.*, expire by its own terms. However, under § 2041(a)(2), the exercise, release, or lapse of an inter vivos general power is a deemed "transfer" by the donee of the power. *See* Ch. 2, IV.B.3., 4., and 5., *supra,* for the gift tax treatment, and F.5., *infra,* for the estate tax treatment.

(3) Special power of appointment. An inter vivos "special" power of appointment is a power in the donee to appoint to one or more persons other than herself or her creditors. The exercise of a special power entails the transfer of any existing interest of the donee divested by the exercise of the power. *See* Ch. 2, at IV.C.2., *supra,* for the gift tax treatment and F.6, *infra,* for the estate tax treatment. The release or lapse of a special power of appointment is not a transfer for estate or gift tax purposes.

6. ***Transfers for consideration in money or money's worth.*** A transfer for full and adequate consideration is excluded from all of §§ 2036-2038 on the theory that the potential depletion of the transferor's § 2033 gross estate was fully made up for by the consideration. Consideration that is less than full and adequate is an offset against the amount includable under § 2043(a).

a. *Consideration in "money or money's worth." See* Ch. 2, at II.H.1. & 2., *supra.*

b. *Consideration must pertain to includable interests.* The consideration must be given "for" interests that would be included in the gross estate under any of §§ 2036-§2038. For example, if *A* creates an irrevocable trust with securities worth $1 million, income to *B* for life, reversion to *A* if *A* is then living, but if *A* is not then living remainder to *C,* and if *A* dies before *B,* only the remainder to *C* would be included in *A*'s gross estate under § 2037; such inclusion can be defeated (or reduced) only if the consideration comes from (or is given on behalf of) *C,* but not if it comes from *B. Estate of Keller v. Com'r,* 45 T.C. 851 (1965). Similarly, if *A* conveys Blackacre to *B* in fee simple on condition that *B* grant *A* a life estate in Blackacre, the life estate received by *A* from *B* is not "consideration," since it supplies the very element (retained possession or enjoyment for life) that causes § 2036(a)(1) to apply in the first place. *See U.S. v. Past,* 347 F.2d 7 (8th Cir.1965).

c. *"Full and adequate."* The law is somewhat unclear on this issue. The "traditional view" is that to be "full and adequate," the amount of the consideration must equal the amount of the entire transfer, including retained interests. Thus, if *A* creates an irrevocable trust with $1 million of securities, income to herself for life, remainder to *C* (worth $360,000), *C* would have to provide consideration to *A* worth at least $1 million (as opposed to $360,000) in order to fully exempt the transfer from § 2036. E.g., *Gradow v. U.S.,* 897 F.2d 516 (Fed. Cir. 1990). This rule is questionable under economic theory, and two recent cases have taken the opposite position. *Estate of D'Ambrosio v. Com'r,* 101 F.3d 309 (3d Cir.1996), cert. denied, 520 U.S. 1230 (1997); *Wheeler v. U.S.,* 80 AFTR 2d 5075, 97-2 USTC ¶60278 (5th Cir.1997). Under these cases, inclusion in the hypothetical could be avoided if *C* purchased the remainder for $360,000.

d. *Partial consideration.* Where there is consideration for the transfer but it is not full and adequate, such "partial" consideration is an "offset" (*i.e.,* is subtracted), under § 2043(a), from the amount included in the gross estate.

e. *Valuing consideration.* Consideration is valued as of the time of the inter vivos transfer, not the estate tax valuation date. *U.S. v. Righter,* 400 F.2d 344 (8th Cir. 1968). Normal gift tax valuation rules are applied, including actuarial tables where appropriate.

7. **Retention requirement.** Under §§ 2036 and 2037, the requisite interest or power must have been "retained" by the decedent-transferor in connection with the inter vivos transfer. An interest or power is not retained if it was conferred on the transferor-decedent by another. There is no retention requirement under § 2038. Thus, under § 2038 it is sufficient that the decedent possessed the requisite power at the moment just prior to death, regardless of how such power was acquired.

a. *Express retention.* In most cases, the requisite interest or power is expressly retained under the instrument of transfer (trust, deed, etc.), which creates the interest or power in the transferor. Thus, if *A* creates an irrevocable trust under which *A* is to receive the income for life, *A* has retained the income interest.

b. *Indirect retention.* The retention can arise indirectly under a preexisting instrument created by a third party. Thus, assume that *A* creates an irrevocable trust, income to *B* for life, remainder to *C.* (This trust is not includable in *A*'s gross estate, since *A* has not retained any interest or power.) Now *B* comes along and transfers securities to the trust created by *A*; *B* has made a transfer with a retained income interest under the trust created by *A*. The amount includable in *B*'s gross estate under § 2036(a) is that portion of the estate tax value of the trust attributable to the securities transferred by *B*. *Estate of Vardell v. Com'r,* 307 F.2d 688 (5th Cir. 1962).

c. *Discretionary trusts for benefit of grantor.* A grantor creates a discretionary trust for her own benefit when she gives the trustee the absolute power to determine who will receive the income from the trust. An example would be where *A* creates an irrevocable trust, naming *X* as trustee, income to *A* or accumulated in the trustee's discretion during *A*'s life, remainder to *C*. If the trustee were required to pay the income to *A* for life, the right to income would have been retained by *A,* and § 2036(a)(1) would apply. Here, however, whether *A* will receive any income is under the absolute control of a third party, the trustee. Section 2036(a)(1) will not apply. One possible explanation for this result is that *A* does not have the "right to the income" for life. This angle is discussed at 2., a. (2), *supra.* An alternative explanation is that *A* has not "retained" the income from the trust. *Estate of Uhl v. Com'r,* 241 F.2d 867 (7th Cir. 1957).

(1) Effect of relative or friend as trustee. In the example immediately above, *A* is not deemed to have retained an income interest just because *X,* the trustee, is a relative or friend of *A,* since trustees are subject to fiduciary constraints.

(2) Effect of grantor as trustee. If, however, *A* is trustee instead of *X, A* has the right to all of the income, and § 2036(a) would apply.

d. *Implied retention.* A retention can exist by implication under a "side agreement" or understanding with the transferee (donee or trustee) not expressly set forth in the instrument of transfer. The side agreement or understanding need not be in writing, nor need it even be legally enforceable. *Estate of McNichol v. Com'r,* 265 F.2d 667 (3d Cir. 1959).

(1) The agreement or understanding might be inferred from the fact that the transferor in fact received the income from, or obtained possession or enjoyment of, the transferred property. *Estate of Skinner v. U.S.,* 316 F.2d 517 (3d Cir. 1963).

(2) An implied retention might also exist if the government can show that the transferor actually controlled and dominated the transferee (trustee), for example, in an ostensibly discretionary trust for the grantor's benefit. *See Estate of Klauber v. Com'r,* 34 T.C. 968 (1960) (reviewed), *nonacq. on other issues.*

(3) The implied retention issue comes up frequently in cases where a donor of a residence continues to live in the residence following the transfer. The courts have often found an implied retention of possession or enjoyment, resulting in inclusion of the residence in the donor's gross estate under § 2036(a)(1). *E.g., Guynn v. U.S.,* 437 F.2d 1148 (4th Cir. 1971); *Rapelje v. Com'r,* 73 T.C. 82 (1979).

3

e. *Retention by operation of law.* Here it can only be said that there can be a retention by operation of law in some situations but not others.

(1) Failure to dispose of entire interest. If a person creates an irrevocable inter vivos trust but fails to transfer away all interests in property, the nontransferred interests are deemed retained by the grantor. Thus, if *A* owns Blackacre and gives a remainder interest in it to *R*, *A* has retained a life estate that will trigger § 2036(a)(1). *Estate of Cooper v. Com'r*, 74 T.C. 1373 (1980). The most common situation involves reversions: *A* creates an irrevocable trust, income to B for the life of *A*, then to *C* if then living, but if *C* does not survive *A* then to *D* if then living. Here, *A*'s estate has a reversion based on the fact that both *C* and *D* may predecease *A*, and § 2037 could apply (even if *C* or *D* in fact outlives *A*), if *A*'s reversion (at the moment just prior to his death) is worth more than 5%.

(2) Rights of grantor's creditors. It is likely, under the law of trusts, that a trust grantor's creditors can reach any discretionary interest of the grantor, even if the terms of the trust stipulate to the contrary (in a "spendthrift" clause). If so, the grantor is deemed to have vicariously retained an income interest by operation of law. For example, if *A* has created a trust, income to *A* in the trustee's discretion, and *A*'s creditors can reach the trust income, *A* can enjoy the trust income by incurring debts which will be repaid out of the trust income, and § 2036(a)(1) should apply. *See Paolizzi v. Com'r*, 23 T.C. 182 (1954) (gift of income interest incomplete). If the trustee has discretion to pay corpus to *A*, and *A*'s creditors can reach the corpus, then *A* has retained the power to revoke under § 2038. *See, e.g., Outwin v. Com'r*, 76 T.C. 153 (1981) (no completed gift where creditors could reach both income and corpus).

(3) Marital rights. It has been held that, where *H* transfers his residence to *W* and continues to live in the residence pursuant to his marital rights, there was a retention by operation of law but that § 2036(a) was inapplicable, perhaps on the theory that such retention was unavoidable and incident to a "status" (marriage) that transcends estate tax planning considerations. *Estate of Gutchess v. Com'r*, 46 T.C. 554 (1966), *acq.*, Rev. Rul. 70-155, 1970-1 C.B. 189. Similarly, where *H* transfers separate property outright to *W*, the income from which is community property (and, hence, half that of *H*) under state law (Texas, Louisiana, or Idaho), § 2036(a) was held to be inapplicable. *Estate of Wyly*, 610 F.2d 1282 (5th Cir. 1980), *acq.*, Rev. Rul. 81-221, 1981-2 C.B. 178.

8. **Interest or power "in the transferred property."** Sections 2036-2038 do not apply unless the requisite interest or power is held by the transferor "in" the transferred property itself.

a. *Interests in entities.* If *A* owns all of the preferred and common stock of a corporation and gives the common stock to *B*, the retained preferred stock does not represent a retained interest "in" the transferred property (the common stock). *Boykin v. Com'r*, T.C. Memo. 1987-134. (A transfer of this sort raises issues under § 2701, discussed in Chapter 2, VII.,C., *supra*.)

b. *Contractual promises.* If *A* transfers Blackacre, worth $1 million, to *B* outright and *B* promises to pay $60,000 per year to *A* for life, *A* has not retained any interest in the property transferred. *See Fidelity-Philadelphia Trust Co. v. Smith,* 356 U.S. 274, 285 n. 8 (1958). (In this case *A* has made a gift equal to the excess, if any, of $1 million over the value of the $60,000 annual annuity. Rev. Rul. 69-74, 1969-1 C.B. 43.) It appears that the donor will not be deemed to have retained an interest in the transferred property just because she receives an annuity for life that is expected to reflect the income-producing capacity of the transferred property. *Cf. LaFargue v. Com'r,* 73 T.C. 40 (1979) (applying § 677 of income tax, which somewhat parallels § 2036(a)(1)), reversed on this issue, 689 F.2d 845 (9th Cir.1982)). A closer case would be presented if the donee promised to pay the donor an amount each year that exactly corresponded to the income from the transferred property. *See Estate of Schwartz v. Com'r,* 9 T.C. 229 (1947). *Cf. Lazarus v. Com'r,* 513 F.2d 824 (9th Cir.1975) (§ 677 case). And, as stated in assorted *dicta,* § 2036(a)(1) would likely apply if the donee's promise were secured by the transferred property.

D. Annuities and Employee Death Benefits. Annuities and employee death benefits (including death benefits under IRAs) are governed in the first instance by § 2039, which is closely modelled on § 2036(a)(1), and, if that section does not apply, §§ 2033, 2037, and 2038, *supra,* can be brought to bear.

1. ***Section 2039.*** Basically, § 2039 follows § 2036(a)(1), but with two exceptions: (1) the retained interest need only be a "right to payments" (like an annuity), instead of an "income" or "possessory" interest, and (2) the requirement that the transferor must retain an interest "in" the money or property transferred is replaced by a rule that the right to payments and the survivorship element (survivor or refund annuity or death benefit) must exist under a single "contract or agreement."

   a. *Transfer requirement.* Under § 2039(b), the transfer requirement is satisfied where:

      (1) the decedent paid premiums under an annuity contract;

      (2) the decedent made contributions as an employee to an employee plan (or IRA); or

      (3) the decedent's employer made contributions to any such plan (or IRA).

   b. *Effect of community property laws.* Any transfers made by a decedent out of community property are made half by the decedent's spouse. Therefore, the portion of the annuity or death benefit attributable to such spousal contributions is excludable from the decedent's gross estate. (The estate tax treatment of the non-employee spouse's interest is discussed in 3., *infra.*)

   c. *Lifetime benefits.* For § 2039 to apply, the decedent must have been either receiving an annuity or other series of payments or have had the right to receive (in the future) an annuity, series of payments, or even a single payment. The "right" idea encompasses contingent benefits and rights subject to forfeiture. Reg. § 20.2039-1(b)(1). The lifetime benefits requirement is satisfied in full even though one or more other persons is sharing in the payments, as occurs under a joint-and-survivor annuity. The annuity, etc., must be retirement-type payments. Salary or consultation fees do not satisfy this requirement. *Kramer v. U. S.*, 406 F.2d 1363 (Ct.Cl. 1969); *Estate of Fusz v. Com'r*, 46 T.C. 214 (1966), *acq.* Disability payments do not satisfy the requirement if they are merely a substitute for salary, but the opposite is true if they replace retirement-type benefits. *Compare Estate of Schelberg v. Com'r*, 612 F.2d 25 (2d Cir. 1979) (salary replacement), with *Estate of Bahen v. U.S.*, 305 F.2d 827 (Ct.Cl. 1962) (pension replacement).

d. *Period of retention.* Echoing § 2036, the annuity or right must have been possessed for the decedent's life, for any period not in fact ending before her death, or for a period ascertainable with reference to her death. If the decedent received all retirement benefits in a lump sum prior to death, § 2039 is avoided because the retirement benefit terminated before death. If, however, the decedent died before receiving the lump sum, § 2039 would apply, since the decedent retained the right to the retirement benefit until death. Reg. § 20.2039-1(b)(2) (Ex. 5). Of course, § 2039 would not apply if the decedent had in fact forfeited the retirement benefit prior to death. Unlike the situation involving §§ 2036-2038, the transfer or release (including forfeiture) of retirement-type benefits within three years of the decedent's death would not satisfy the "period" requirement under § 2039. *See* § 2035(a)(2).

e. *Survivorship benefit.* There must be one or more payments to a beneficiary or the decedent's estate following death. Survivorship or refund features of an annuity, IRA, or employee death benefit satisfy this requirement. In fact, it is the estate tax value of such benefits that are included in the gross estate under § 2039. A single-life annuity (*i.e.*, an annuity that simply expires at the annuitant's death) is not included under § 2039 (or any other section). (Of course, pre-death payments not consumed or given away will appear in the decedent's § 2033 gross estate.)

f. *Contract or agreement.* The lifetime benefit and the survivorship benefit must be combined under the same contract or agreement. A given annuity contract (other than a single-life annuity) or IRA will contain both elements. In the employee death benefit situation, the contract-or-agreement requirement has been construed expansively to refer to all contracts in the aggregate involving a given employee-employer relationship. Thus, § 2039 cannot be avoided by an employer entering into separate retirement, disability, and death benefit plans contracts with an employee. *Estate of Bahen v. U.S.*, 305 F.2d 827 (Ct.Cl. 1962).

g. *Insurance exception.* Section 2039(a) by its terms does not apply to life insurance contracts. To come under this exception, the premiums or contributions must go into an actuarial pool, and the death benefit obligor must bear an "actuarial" (as opposed to "investment") risk. *All v. McCobb*, 321 F.2d 633 (2d Cir. 1963).

h. *Annuity-insurance combinations.* Tax characterization of such combinations depends on whether the annuity and the insurance policy are contractually interdependent.

(1) Independent "package." If an insurance company offers a "package" consisting of a single-life annuity and an insurance policy (which is irrevocably assigned to a beneficiary), § 2036 does not apply, since the annuity is not retained "in" the transferred property (the insurance policy). *Fidelity-Philadelphia Trust Co. v. Smith*, 356 U.S. 274 (1958). Section 2039 does not apply, since the two investments are contractually separate, assuming that the contracts are not procured through the decedent's employer.

(2) Interdependent "package." If the annuity and insurance policy are contractually interdependent, the package as a whole avoids characterization as "life insurance." *Helvering v. Le Gierse*, 312 U.S. 531 (1941). Since the insurance exception no longer applies, § 2039 applies, *i.e.*, the annuity and insurance proceeds (death benefit) are "under" a single contract or agreement. *Estate of Montgomery v. Com'r*, 56 T.C. 489, *aff'd per curiam*, 458 F.2d 616 (5th Cir. 1972), *cert. denied*.

2. ***Employee death benefits under other provisions.*** An employee death benefit can avoid § 2039 by eschewing retirement benefits or receiving such benefits in a lump sum prior to death. Section 2039 does not pre-empt §§ 2036-2038. The "transfer" requirement is satisfied under the "indirect transfer" doctrine (*see* B.5.d., *supra*), the employment contract satisfies the "retention" requirement, and the interest or power is "in" the transferred property. But a death benefit that avoids § 2039 because it lacks the lifetime benefits element will also avoid § 2036, which requires an income or possessory interest.

a. *Section 2038.* Section 2038 will apply to an employee death benefit where the employee at death had the power to change the beneficiary. Rev. Rul. 76-304, 1976-2 C.B. 269.

b. *Section 2037.* Section 2037 will apply where, at the moment just before the employee's death, there is a greater than 5% chance that the death benefit will be payable to the employee's estate. (Since the death benefit is payable upon the transferor's death, the "survivorship" requirement is automatically satisfied.) Rev. Rul. 78-15, 1978-1 C.B. 289.

c. *Section 2035(a)(2).* If the death benefit would have been includable under any of §§ 2036-2038, except for the fact that the decedent transferred or relinquished the retained interest or power within three years of death, § 2035(a)(2) causes inclusion as if such transfer or relinquishment had not occurred. It is unclear whether § 2035(a)(2) would apply where the annuity or death benefit plan falls under both §§ 2036 and 2039, since section 2035(a)(2) refers to the former but not the latter. Reference must be had to pre-1954 case law under § 2036 dealing with the issue of whether lifetime annuities and retirement benefits were retained "in" the transferred property. *Compare Estate of Mearkle v. Com'r*, 129 F.2d 386 (3d Cir. 1942) (annuity includable under § 2036), with *Com'r v. Estate of Twogood*, 194 F.2d 627 (2d Cir. 1952) (death benefit not includable). Even if § 2036 were applicable, section 2039 (being more specific) might be treated as controlling in case of overlap, meaning that a transfer or relinquishment of a pension right within three years of death would not fall under § 2035(a)(2), since Congress must be presumed to have deliberately omitted any reference to § 2039 in § 2035(d)(2).

d. *Section 2033.* Death benefits have been included under § 2033 in cases where the employee had the right to accelerate (and obtain for herself) the "death benefit" during life. *Northern Trust Co. v. U.S.,* 389 F.2d 731 (7th Cir. 1968) (citing constructive receipt doctrine under income tax).

3. ***Community property interest of nonemployee spouse.*** If the employee's spouse dies before the employee, §§ 2036-2039 do not apply to such spouse, since the spouse did not have any retirement-type benefits for his life, etc., under the plan, nor were any benefits payable to anyone upon his death. Nevertheless, such spouse's interest is includable in his gross estate under § 2033. Inclusion under § 2033 probably occurs even if state law or ERISA prevents the deceased nonemployee spouse from bequeathing his community property interest to a person other than the employee spouse, but in that case (*i.e.,* where the nonemployee spouse's rights pass back to the employee spouse) the nonemployee spouse's estate should obtain a marital deduction for such includable amount. See § 2056(b)(7)(C).

E. **Jointly Owned Property.** Section 2040 deals with jointly owned property with right of survivorship, including tenancies by the entireties and joint bank accounts. (Tenancies in common and partnership interests are governed by § 2033.) Section 2040, where applicable, preempts all other gross estate provisions.

1. ***Interests in joint tenancies created by third party.*** If neither joint tenant created the joint tenancy, the death of a joint tenant causes a pro rata share of the estate tax value of the property to be included in his or her gross estate. § 2040(a) (2d proviso). *(The remainder of the discussion below assumes that one or more of the joint tenants created the joint tenancy or contributed to it.)*

2. ***Joint-ownership property and joint bank accounts, not between husband and wife.*** This area is governed by § 2040(a), which is similar in concept to §§ 2036-2038: the interest in the joint tenancy (which entails a right of survivorship, a right to half of the income, and possibly a right of severance) is conclusively deemed to be a sufficient retained interest or power in the property to cause inclusion, leaving the only real issue to be whether and to what extent the decedent was the "transferor."

a. *Proportionate consideration rule.* The basic operative principle is the "proportionate consideration" rule, under which the amount includable on the death of any joint tenant is the estate tax value of the property multiplied by a fraction, the numerator of which is the contributions made by the decedent, and the denominator of which is the total contributions made by all joint tenants. Since the consideration contributed by the other joint tenants bears on the "transfer" requirement, such consideration cannot also operate as a "consideration offset" under § 2043(a).

Example 11: If *A* contributes $80,000 and *B* $20,000 towards the purchase of property held as a joint tenancy, and the property appreciates to $500,000, $400,000 (80% of $500,000) is includable if *A* is the first decedent, and $100,000 (20% of $500,000) is includable if *B* is the first decedent.

b. *Improvements.* Improvements paid for by a joint tenant, regardless of when made, are treated as consideration provided by such joint tenant at cost. Reg. § 20.2040-1(a)(2).

c. *Presumption that decedent was transferor.* Section 2040(a) presumes that the decedent joint tenant supplied all of the consideration for the joint tenancy. Thus, the burden of proof is on the estate's personal representative to show the amount of consideration provided by other joint tenants. This rule constitutes a trap for the unwary and is often cited as a reason why non-spouses with potential estate tax exposure should not use joint tenancies.

d. *Consideration-tracing rule.* Not only must the personal representative of the decedent show that other parties provided consideration, but also that such consideration did not come earlier from the decedent by way of gift. The government need not show any agreement or understanding that the subject of such gift be used by the donee as consideration for acquiring the joint tenancy.

3. ***Joint tenancies between husband and wife (other than bank accounts).*** Partly in order to avoid controversy as to whether spousal "services" constituted consideration, Congress enacted § 2040(b) to govern joint tenancies between husband and wife. In any such case, half is includable in the decedent spouse's estate. Consideration is simply not relevant. In any event, the includable amount will qualify for the marital deduction, as it passes to the surviving spouse by right of survivorship.

4. ***Joint bank accounts between husband and wife.*** Such accounts are governed by § 2040(a), *supra.* Again, whatever is included in the gross estate of the first spouse to die qualifies for the marital deduction.

5. ***Community property with right of survivorship.*** Property held in this new form of property ownership is subject to § 2040(a) (bank accounts) and (b) (everything else), because of the right of survivorship in the surviving spouse. Again, the amount includable qualifies for the marital deduction. Importantly, such property qualifies as "community property" under § 1014(c)(6) of the income tax code, meaning that the entire property obtains an estate-tax-value basis. With conventional joint property, on the other hand, only the estate-included portion obtains a § 1014 basis (the remaining portion has a carry-over basis). For this reason, in states without community property with right of survivorship, the estate representative may want to establish that property (bequeathed to the surviving spouse in any event) was "really" community property (taking advantage of the usual community property presumption) rather than joint property, notwithstanding survivorship language in the deed or other instrument.

F. **General Powers of Appointment**. Under § 2041, the mere *possession* by a decedent at death of an inter vivos or testamentary general power of appointment causes the property subject to the power to be included in the decedent's gross estate. Possession of the power at death can be avoided by exercising or releasing the power or allowing the power to lapse by its terms. However, § 2041 also provides that the exercise, release, or lapse during life of a general power of appointment is treated as a "transfer" of the subject property by the decedent for purposes of §§ 2035-2038.

(Also, § 2514 provides that the exercise, release, or lapse is a transfer for gift tax purposes; *See* Ch. 2, at IV.B., *supra*.)

1. ***Scope of § 2041.*** A "power of appointment" is any power to affect the beneficial enjoyment of property. *See* C.,5.,g., *supra*.

    a. *Sections 2036-2038 distinguished.* Sections 2036-2038 deal with such powers held by a decedent *who was also the transferor of the property*. Section 2041 deals only with powers held by a person who was *not* the transferor of the property. Thus, section 2041 does not overlap with §§ 2036-2038.

    b. *Exercise, release, or lapse of general power.* An exercise, release, or lapse of a general power is treated as a *deemed* transfer under §§ 2035-2038 (as well as for gift tax purposes). However, the applicable Code section is § 2041, as the holder (donee) of the power was not the actual transferor of the property.

    c. *Section 2041 imposes second tax on same property.* The fact that the initial transfer of the property (into trust) was subject to gift or estate tax with respect to the actual (initial) transferor does not preclude application of § 2041 to subsequently tax the holder of the power. Thus, application of § 2041 entails a second tax on property that has previously been subject to estate or gift tax with respect to a different taxpayer.

    d. *Limited to general powers of appointment.* Except as noted in subsection 6., *infra,* section 2041 only applies where the decedent had a "general" power of appointment. *(The discussion below omits discussion of general powers created before October 21, 1942, which are governed by § 2041(a)(1).)*

2. **"*General power of appointment*" defined.** This crucial definition is entirely contained in § 2041(b).

    a. *General rule.* Section 2041(b)(1) defines a *general power* as a "power which is exercisable in favor of the decedent, his estate, his creditors, or the creditors of his estate." This definition encompasses both inter vivos general powers (powers exercisable during life) and testamentary general powers (powers exercisable only by will or as of death). The theory behind § 2041 is that the holder of a general power is the "constructive" owner of the property because the holder could have appointed the property to herself or her estate (or the creditors of either). (If the power had in fact been so exercised, the property would have become part of the decedent's § 2033 gross estate. As the material below indicates, the result under § 2041 can turn on the application of the law of trusts to a given trust and on slight differences in the dispositive provisions of trusts.

    b. *Acquisition of general power.* A general power can be acquired in several ways.

        (1) Conferred directly. The power can be conferred directly on the decedent under the instrument of transfer (which usually is a trust).

            Example 12: If *H*, pursuant to a contractual arrangement with *W* (perhaps under a joint-and-mutual will) leaves his estate to *W* for life, remainder to *C,* giving *W* an unlimited power to consume, *W* has a general power of appointment over *H*'s property (assuming that, under state law, *W* is not deemed to have a fee simple in *H*'s property, in which case *H*'s property will be included in *W*'s estate under § 2033).

(2) **Conferred indirectly.** A general power can be conferred (or can arise) indirectly by naming (or through the appointment of) the decedent as trustee or co-trustee of a trust under which the decedent is also a discretionary beneficiary.

Example 13: *A* creates a trust, naming *C* as trustee, income to *B* for life, remainder to *R*, with the trustee having the power to invade corpus in its discretion for the benefit of one or more of *C, D,* and *E*. *C* has an inter vivos general power causing inclusion of the trust in *C*'s gross estate (if *C* dies before *B*, at which time the trust terminates and the trust property passes outright to *R*), because *C,* as trustee, has discretion to pay corpus to herself.

(3) **Enforcing a very liberal "standard."** A general power can arise, if rarely, by virtue of the fact that a trust beneficiary (not the trustee or a co-trustee) can enforce a very liberal "standard."

Example 14: If *A* creates a trust, naming *X* as trustee, income and/or corpus to *B* for *B*'s wants, pleasure, and happiness, remainder to *C, B* has a general power of appointment because *B* can compel the trustee to pay income and corpus to *B* upon demand. However, if the trustee is given *discretion* to pay corpus to *B* for *B*'s wants, pleasure, and happiness, *B* cannot appropriate the corpus on demand and hence would not be held to possess a general power. Rev. Rul. 76-368, 1976-2 C.B. 271.

c. *"Standards" exception.* A power that meets the initial definition of general power of appointment, *supra,* is excepted if the power is limited by an ascertainable standard relating to the "health, education, support, or maintenance" of the decedent. § 2041(b)(1)(A). A standard like "comfort," although it is "ascertainable," does not fall within the exception. A standard like "maintenance in accustomed standard of living" falls within the exception, since "in accustomed standard of living" merely clarifies "maintenance." On the same grounds, "maintain in comfort" passes muster. *See* generally, Reg. § 20.2041-1(c)(2). A trust in which the trustee can pay corpus to herself for her "support, maintenance, and comfort" does not fall within the exception because "comfort" is a separate standard; it does not merely clarify "support" and "maintenance." Rev. Rul. 77-60, 1977-1 C.B. 282. State law may in some cases need to be consulted to determine whether certain standards are effectively synonymous with "health," "education," "support," and "maintenance." In estate planning practice, the "standards exception" effectively emasculates § 2041 in the context of trusts, assuming the trust is properly drafted.

d. *Jointly held powers.* Under § 2041(b)(1)(C), certain powers held by a decedent jointly with another party escape § 2041 or reduce the amount includable. These rules are based on assumptions concerning how rational persons would act.

(1) Power held together with the grantor. If the power was held by the decedent at the critical date (date of death, transfer, release, or lapse) together with the creator of the power, the power is not a general power. § 2041(b)(1)(C)(i).

(2) Power held together with an adverse party. If, at the critical date, the power is held by the decedent together with a "person having a substantial interest in the property. . .which is adverse to exercise of the power in favor of the decedent," the power is not considered a general power. § 2041(b)(1)(C)(ii).

(a) What is an "adverse interest?" To be an adverse party, a party must have an interest in the property, such as an income interest or remainder, that would be reduced or eliminated by the exercise of the power in favor of the decedent.

Example 15: If *A* creates a trust, naming *B* and *C* as co-trustees, income to *B* for life, remainder to *C,* with the trustees having the power in their discretion to pay corpus to *B*, then *B* would have a general power if she were the sole trustee, but, if the corpus were paid to *B, C*'s remainder interest would be reduced or eliminated; *C* is an adverse party, and hence *B* does not have a general power.

(b) Corporate co-trustee. A corporate trustee can never be an adverse party.

(c) Expectancy is not an interest. An *expectancy or possibility* of receiving income or corpus cannot qualify as an adverse "interest," however.

Example 16: If *A* creates a trust, naming *B* and *C* as trustees, giving the trustees the discretionary power to pay income to *B* or accumulate the same and to invade the corpus for the benefit of *C,* remainder to *C* on *B*'s death, *C* has a general power over corpus (if *C* dies before *B*), since *B* does not have an "interest" in the income. Rev. Rul. 79-63, 1979-1 C.B. 302.

(d) Potential appointee as adverse party. A co-holder of the power is not an adverse party just because the co-holder is also a permissible appointee, since (as just noted) a permissable appointee does not have an "interest" by reason of possibly receiving an appointment. On the other hand, if the co-holder who is a potential appointee might acquire the sole general power by herself, then that possibility rises to the level of an adverse interest: it is the functional equivalent of a contingent remainder.

Example 17: Assume the same facts as Example 16, except that the trustees can invade corpus for either *B* or *C.* Since the trust terminates on *B*'s death, only *B* can accede to sole possession of the power (in case *C* dies first). Hence, if *C* in fact dies before *B*, *C* does not have a general power, since *B* (who then accedes to a general power) was an adverse party by reason of possibly becoming the sole holder of the power. *See* generally, Reg. § 20.2041-3(c)(2).

(3) Power held with potential appointee not an adverse party. Look again at Example 17, but assume that the remainder was to go to *D* (and not *C*) and that *B* dies before *C*. *C* was not an adverse party to *B*, because *C* could not have acquired sole possession of the power, nor was *C* otherwise the holder of an adverse interest (*D*, rather than *C*, held the remainder). In such a case, § 2041(b)(1)(C)(iii) holds that *B* is treated as having a general power over half of the property. The rationale of this rule is that it would have been rational for *C* to have agreed to split the corpus with *B*.

3. **Consequences of possessing a general power.** Section 2041(a)(2) causes inclusion in the gross estate of property to the extent that the decedent possessed a general power of appointment over the property at the decedent's death.

a. *Power and property must exist at death.* To be included in a decedent's gross estate, both the property and the power must exist at the time of death. *Connecticut Bank & Trust Co. v. U.S.,* 465 F.2d 760 (2d Cir. 1972) (wrongful death recovery excluded because it arose after death).

b. *Incompetency disregarded.* It is only necessary that the decedent technically possess the power at death; it is not necessary that it be exercisable in the practical sense. Thus, a person is deemed to have a general power at death even though he is mentally incompetent, a minor, or under other some other legal disability (*e.g., Estate of Alperstein v. Com'r,* 613 F.2d 1213 (2d Cir. 1979), *cert. denied*).

c. *Contingent general power.* The power must exist at the moment of (really, just prior to) death. Hence, a contingent power does not exist at death where the condition precedent had not occurred prior to the decedent's death.

Example 18: Suppose *A* creates a trust, income to *B* for life, remainder to *C*, giving *B* a power to appoint the corpus, under *B*'s will, to *B*'s estate when *B* has attained the age of 50. If *B* dies before age 50, *B* does not have the general power of appointment. If *B* dies after reaching age 50, he does possess the power.

d. *Lapsing general power.* An existing power is not negated just because it might have lapsed under some contingency which had not in fact occurred by the time of the decedent's death. But, if the power did lapse before death, it is not possessed at death.

Example 19: Suppose *A* creates a trust, income to be accumulated until *B* reaches the age of 35 (or earlier dies), remainder to *B* (or, if *B* is dead, *B*'s estate), but *B* is given the right to withdraw the income for the current year. In this case, *B* has a general power of appointment over each year's income. In the year of *B*'s death (prior to reaching age 35), the income of that year which had accrued to the date of *B*'s death is included in *B*'s gross estate under § 2041, but *B* no longer possesses the power to appoint the income of prior years, since the power with respect to each year's income lapsed at the end of each prior year. (In addition, *B*'s remainder interest is included under § 2033.) The possibility that the income for prior years, subject to a succession of lapsed powers, was the subject of a deemed transfer by *B* is discussed in 5.b., *infra*.

4. ***Amount includable.*** The amount includable is the amount of the property subject to the power at the decedent's death. A general power over all of the corpus requires the inclusion of such corpus, including accumulated income added to corpus. As noted in Example 19, a general power over income only requires inclusion of only the income accrued to the time of death.

5. ***Exercise, release, or lapse of general power during the decedent's lifetime.***

   a. *Exercise or release.* The exercise or release (*i.e.*, relinquishment, surrender, or transfer) of a general power by the decedent during the lifetime of the decedent is a deemed inter vivos transfer by the decedent of property for estate tax purposes, i.e., for purposes of §§ 2035-2038. § 2041(a)(2). (Such exercise or release is also a deemed transfer for gift tax purposes. § 2514. *See* Ch. 2, at IV.B., *supra.*) In order to ascertain the gift and estate tax effect of the deemed transfer, one must consider the effect of the exercise or release and note the existence of interests and powers (retained) in the property by the decedent following the exercise or release.

      Example 20: *A* creates a trust, income to *B* for life, remainder to *C*, giving *B* a power to appoint corpus to himself. *B* appoints one-third of the corpus to *D* outright. This one-third is a present-interest gift from *B* to *D*. If, after the exercise, *B* continues to have the power over the remaining two-thirds, there is no deemed transfer of such two-thirds; *B* continues to have a general power over the two-thirds. If (under state law or the terms of the trust) *B*'s power can only be exercised once, then the exercise of it as to the one-third operates as a release by *B* of the power as to the other two-thirds. *B*, therefore, has made a deemed transfer of the two-thirds, for gift and estate tax purposes, in which *B* "retains" (has) the right to income for life, followed by a remainder to *C*. For gift tax purposes, *B* has made a (retained interest) gift of the two-thirds under § 2702, and the same two-thirds is included in *B*'s gross estate as a deemed § 2036(a)(1) transfer by way of § 2041(a)(2).

      Example 21: *A* creates a trust, income to *B* for life, then to such persons, including *B*'s estate, as *B* appoints by will, but, in default of such appointment, remainder to *C*. *B* during her life renounces her general testamentary power. Since *B* continues to have an income interest, *B* has made a deemed transfer under §§ 2702 and 2036(a)(1).

      Example 22: *A* creates a trust, naming *B* as trustee, income to or among *C, D,* and *E* as the trustee decides, corpus to *B* in the trustee's discretion, remainder to *R* after the death of the survivor of *C, D,* and *E*. *B* renounces her general inter vivos power. Since *B* continues to have a "special" power to affect the beneficial enjoyment of income, *B* has made a retained-interest deemed gift under § 2702, see Reg. § 25.2702(a)(4) (retained power can be retained interest), and a deemed § 2036(a)(2) transfer (assuming *B* dies before the trust terminates). If, instead, *B* had resigned as trustee, the resignation would have operated as a release of both the general power and the special power. In that case, *B* would have been deemed to have made an outright gift of the entire trust. (The possibility that the new trustee might distribute the corpus to B is not a retained "interest.")

b. *Lapse of general power; five-and-five exception.* A "lapse" (as opposed to a "release") occurs where the general power ceases to exist because it expires under the terms of the instrument or upon the occurrence of some condition (beyond the decedent's control). Under § 2041(b)(2), a lapse is treated as a release, and hence as an "exercise," and hence as a deemed transfer. At the same time, there is an exemption equal to the greater of (a) 5% of the appointive property or (b) $5,000.

Example 23: Suppose A creates a trust, income to be accumulated for the life of B, but giving B the annual power to withdraw the current year's income, remainder to C. Assume (unrealistically) that at all times the trust is worth $1 million, and the annual income is $60,000. If, in any given year, B fails to withdraw the income, the power over that income lapses on December 31; in that case, B has made a deemed transfer into the trust of $55,000, which is $60,000 less the greater of (1) $5,000 or (2) $3,000 (.05 x $60,000). (If B's power had been to withdraw $60,000 of corpus per year, the exemption would have been $50,000 (.05 x $1 million), and the deemed transfer would have been $10,000 per lapse year. The deemed transfer is placed back into the trust, since the lapsed income is added to the corpus; thus, the deemed transfer is with a retained right to income (since B can withdraw the annual trust income). Each year, therefore, B has made a § 2702 (retained interest) gift of $55,000 and a § 2036(a)(1) transfer of 5.5% of the trust (deemed transfer of $55,000 divided by then value of corpus, $1 million). If the lapse occurs in 10 different years, upon B's death 55% of the trust is included under § 2036(a)(1) (10 x 5.5%), and income accrued in the year of B's death is included under § 2041 (as B possessed a general power over such income at death).

6. ***Exercise of special power of appointment.*** In general, the exercise of a "special" power of appointment is outside of the scope of § 2041, which only deals with general powers. (Nevertheless, an exercise of a special power can entail a "transfer" for gift and estate tax purposes of interests held by the donee of the power before the exercise of the special power but which are given up by reason of such exercise.) There are two exceptions, however, as follows:

a. *Exercise causes release of general power.* The exercise of a special power can have the collateral effect of causing a release of a general power.

Example 24: Assume that A creates a trust, income to B for life, remainder to such persons (including B's estate) as B appoints by will), and in default of such appointment remainder to C, with B also being given an inter vivos special power to appoint the corpus to or among B's issue. If B appoints the corpus outright to G, B has made a gift to G of B's income interest. In addition, the exercise of the special power terminates the trust and thereby extinguishes B's testamentary general power over the remainder, resulting in a deemed transfer (gift) by B of such remainder. If a party other than the decedent exercised a special power so as to cause the extinguishment of the decedent's general power, the extinguishment would constitute a "lapse" (rather than a "release") of the decedent's general power, producing the same transfer tax results as a release but subject to the five-and-five rule for lapses, immediately above.

b. *The "Delaware" rule.* Under § 2041(a)(3) (and § 2514(d) of the gift tax), the exercise of a *special power* (by will or inter vivos act) so as to create another (special) power of appointment is a deemed gift, or causes inclusion of the property in the gross estate, if, under the applicable Perpetuities doctrine, the second power can be validly exercised so as to postpone the vesting of any interest (or suspend the power of alienation) for a period *not* fixed with reference to the *creation* of the first power.

(1) Relation to Perpetuities doctrine. Under the usual formulation of Perpetuities doctrine, any interest or power created by the exercise of a special power of appointment is valid only if it *must* vest or be exercised within lives in being at the *creation* of the special power (plus 21 years). Hence, section 2041(a)(3) can only apply where applicable state law has no Rule Against Perpetuities (or Against the Suspension of the Power of Alienation), or where applicable state law (such as Delaware, and perhaps Florida) provides that interests and powers created pursuant to the exercise of a special power are "tested" with reference to the date of the power's *exercise* (rather than the date the special power was created).

(2) Effect upon creation of general power. The IRS apparently does not attempt to apply § 2041(a)(3) in situations where a special power is exercised so as to create a *general* power of appointment, although § 2041(a)(3) would literally apply in many such cases, presumably because the donee of the general power will be subject to gift or estate tax with respect to the power, whereas the purpose of enacting § 2041(a)(3) was to head off a possible technique of forever avoiding transfer tax by exercising special powers so as to create future special powers *ad infinitum*.

G. **Life Insurance Proceeds.** When the insured dies, the insurance proceeds come into existence and are paid to beneficiaries, to the estate of the insured, or possibly to the creditors of the insured. However, the proceeds are not automatically included in the insured's gross estate. Under present law, the proceeds are includable in the insured's gross estate, under § 2042, only if the decedent possessed "incidents of ownership" in the policy at the time of death (or assigned such incidents of ownership within three years of death) or if the proceeds were receivable by the insured's executor (*i.e.,* estate). If a person other than the insured owns the policy (incidents of ownership) and such person dies before the insured, the policy is simply an asset in such person's § 2033 gross estate.

1. *Payment of premiums.* Under present law, the payment of premiums has *no* effect on the estate tax treatment of the policy and the proceeds. This is so even if the insured paid, within or without three years of her death, all of the premiums ever paid on a policy (*e.g., Estate of Leder v. Com'r*, 89 T.C. 235 (1987)). Nor does the payment of premiums entail the "transfer" of the policy or proceeds under §§ 2036-2038 (*Goodnow v. U.S.*, 302 F.2d 516 (Ct.Cl. 1962)). Life insurance is excluded from the scope of § 2039. Cases decided under the pre-1954 version of § 2042 and the pre-1981 version of § 2035, such as *Bel v. U.S.*, 452 F.2d 683 (5th Cir. 1971) (payment by insured of premiums on pure term insurance held to be "transfer" of proceeds under § 2035), and *Estate of Silverman v. Com'r*, 521 F.2d 574 (2d Cir. 1975) (the amount includible under § 2035 on account of the transfer by the insured of a policy within 3 years of death is reduced on account of

premiums paid by donee), which did treat the payment of premiums as being relevant, should be considered to be obsolete.

2. **Insured possesses incidents of ownership.** Under § 2042(2), the proceeds of insurance are includable in the gross estate of the insured if the insured has any of the "incidents of ownership" in the policy.

a. *"Incidents of ownership" defined.* Under Reg. § 20.2042-1(c)(2), the term "incident of ownership" includes a more than 5% reversionary interest in the proceeds and any power to change the beneficiary, to surrender, cancel, or assign the policy (or to revoke an assignment), or to pledge the policy as security for a loan. This regulation has generally been construed by the courts to include only powers which entail a potential economic benefit to the insured (or the insured's estate), *i.e.,* the equivalent of a "general power of appointment."

b. *Applications.* Thus, a power held by the insured to affect the time and manner of a beneficiary's enjoyment, being equivalent to a "special" power of appointment, does not cause inclusion. *Estate of Connelly v. U.S.,* 551 F.2d 545 (3d Cir. 1977). Also, a power over a policy exercisable by the insured only in a fiduciary capacity (*i.e.,* as trustee) that cannot benefit the insured personally is not an incident of ownership. *Estate of Skifter v. Com'r,* 468 F.2d 699 (2d Cir. 1972). The Fifth Circuit, however, disagrees on these issues. *See Rose v. U.S.,* 511 F.2d 259 (5th Cir. 1975). The IRS takes the position that the equivalent of a "special" power of appointment is an incident of ownership if it is "retained" by the insured in connection with the transfer or taking out of the policy by the insured. Rev. Rul. 84-179, 1984-2 C.B. 195. (This position would appear to be unsound, since § 2041 has no "transfer" requirement.)

c. *Jointly held powers.* An incident of ownership is deemed held by the insured even though held jointly with one or more other parties. Even a veto power over a power held by another counts as an incident of ownership. *Com'r v. Estate of Karagheusian,* 233 F.2d 197 (2d Cir. 1956).

d. *Power held indirectly.* If a corporation owns a policy on the life of a shareholder who owns more than 50% of the stock, the corporation's ownership will be attributed to the shareholder, unless the proceeds are payable to a third party for a valid business purpose. *See* Reg. § 20.2042-1(c)(6).

e. *Divesting insured of incidents of ownership.* The usual method of effecting a gift, *i.e.,* delivery plus donative intent, is not sufficient to assign ownership of an insurance policy. The assignment must conform to the procedure set forth in the policy, which usually involves notification to the insurance company. *Com'r v. Estate of Noel,* 380 U.S. 678 (1965). An insured who possesses an incident of ownership under the terms of the policy cannot avoid § 2042(2) by invoking a "side agreement" with a third party delegating the incidents of ownership to the third party. *U.S. v. Rhode Island Hosp. Trust Co.,* 355 F.2d 7 (1st Cir. 1966).

f. *Transfer within three years of death.* Under § 2035(a), the transfer by the insured within three years of death of incidents of ownership is ignored, resulting in inclusion under § 2042(2).

g. *Transfer of policy to revocable trust, etc.* If the insured transfers (all incidents of ownership over) a policy on her life prior to three years before her death, section 2035(a) does not apply. Nevertheless, if the policy was transferred to a revocable trust, the policy will be included under § 2038 or § 2042(2) (since a power to revoke gives the grantor the power to exercise incidents of ownership). If the insured has a more than a 5% reversion in the trust, the proceeds (being contingent on the insured's death) are includable under § 2037 or § 2042(2) (since a more than 5% reversion is an incident of ownership). If the policy is transferred to a trust in which the insured retains the right to income, § 2036 probably would not apply (since the policy itself does not produce income during the insured's life), unless the insured can compel the trustee to cash in the policy. In general, a transfer by the insured (or by any other party) to a trust in which the insured has a power (as trustee or otherwise) would directly pose an "incident of ownership" issue. *See* subsection a. and b., *supra.*

3. **Proceeds receivable by insured's executor.** Even if the insured has no incidents of ownership, the proceeds are includable in the gross estate to the extent they are payable to the insured's executor (*i.e.,* estate). § 2042(1).

   a. *Situations where § 2042(1) applies.* Typically, this would occur if the insured's "estate" was the designated beneficiary, or if all the named beneficiaries in fact predeceased the insured. Section 2042(1) can also apply where the insured pledged the policy as collateral for a personal debt *and* the creditor actually collects the debt out of the proceeds. *Bintliff v. U.S.,* 462 F.2d 403 (5th Cir. 1972). Similarly, if life insurance proceeds are *required* (by the insured's will, a trust, or binding contract) to be used to pay off the decedent's debts (including estate tax liability), the proceeds so committed are includable.

   b. *Situations where § 2042(1) does not apply.* On the other hand, proceeds are not included under § 2042(1) just because the estate personal representative is authorized to use such proceeds to pay debts and taxes (even if the proceeds are in fact so used), on the theory that the proceeds are not "receivable" by the estate. *See* Rev. Rul. 77-157, 1977-1 C.B. 279.

4. **Policy owned by person other than the insured.** In the event the insured has avoided inclusion in her gross estate and another individual (perhaps the insured's spouse) owns the policy, there are two possible scenarios:

   a. *Owner dies before insured.* In this case, the (unmatured) policy is simply an asset included in the owner's § 2033 gross estate at its then value.

   b. *Insured dies before owner.* If the insured dies before the owner, the proceeds (if not payable to the insured's estate, *supra*) will be either paid to the owner or to a third party. If the proceeds are paid to the owner, the owner's potential § 2033 gross estate is augmented. If the proceeds are payable to a third party (or to a trust), the owner is deemed to have made a transfer of the proceeds for gift and estate tax purposes.

(1) **Proceeds paid to third party.** Thus, if the proceeds are payable outright to the third party, the owner has made a gift of the proceeds. *Goodman v. Com'r,* 156 F.2d 218 (2d Cir. 1946).

(2) **Proceeds paid to trust.** If the proceeds are payable into a trust, the owner's interests and powers in the trust must be analyzed. *See Pyle v. Com'r,* 313 F.2d 328 (3d Cir. 1963) (that portion of a trust, created by another, funded by the proceeds was included in the policy owner's gross estate under § 2036 where the trust instrument provided that the policy owner was to receive the income for life).

5. *Community property life insurance.* State law determines what portion of a life insurance policy is community property ("CP"). *H* and *W* are deemed for tax purposes to each own 50% of the CP portion of the policy. Applying the principles described above, the following results occur:

a. *Insured spouse dies first.* Half of the CP portion of the proceeds is included in the insured's gross estate under § 2042(2). Reg. § 20.2042-1(c)(5). (If the proceeds pass to the insured's spouse, there is an offsetting marital deduction.) The non-insured spouse is deemed the owner of the other half, and the gift and estate tax treatment of that half is governed by the rules described in 4.b., immediately above.

b. *Noninsured spouse dies first.* Half of the CP portion is a § 2033 asset of the non-insured spouse's estate. If the noninsured spouse's interest passed to the insured spouse, there would be an offsetting marital deduction in the non-insured spouse's estate, and the insured spouse would then own all incidents of ownership in the policy. If the noninsured spouse's interest passed to a third party, state law must be consulted to determine the portion of the policy and proceeds deemed owned by the insured at the insured's subsequent death. *See Scott v. Com'r,* 374 F.2d 154 (9th Cir. 1967) (for states which follow proportionate-premium test, if insured spouse paid all premiums after non-insured spouse's death, amount includable is entire proceeds less half of that portion of proceeds attributable to CP premiums paid up to the death of the non-insured spouse); Rev. Rul. 75-100, 1975-1 C.B. 303 (for state following first-premium test, if policy was CP, half of proceeds are included in insured's gross estate).

H. **QTIP-Election Property**. Property included in the gross estate of the first spouse to die and which qualifies for the marital deduction under a § 2056(b)(7) "QTIP" election is included in the gross estate of the surviving spouse under § 2044 at its then estate tax value.

III. **VALUATION. Property includable in the gross estate is the fair market value of property determined at the "estate tax valuation date," which (for the estate as a whole) is the date of death, subject to a possible election in the estate personal representative to choose the "alternate valuation date." In general, valuation follows the same rules as are applicable for gift tax (and generation-skipping tax) purposes. The alternate valuation date concept, general estate and gift tax valuation rules, and valuation rules specific to the gift tax or the estate tax are all the subject of Chapter 4.**

VALUATION

DEDUCTIONS

IV. **DEDUCTIONS.** The taxable estate is the gross estate, *supra*, less the estate tax deductions, which are for (1) debts, funeral expenses, administration expenses, and casualty losses; (2) transfers to charity; (3) transfers to the surviving spouse, and (4) certain transfers of interests in closely-held businesses.

A. **Deduction for Debts, Funeral Expenses, Estate Administration Expenses, and Casualty Losses**

1. *Debts of the decedent.* Debts of the decedent incurred before death, including income and gift tax liabilities, are deductible for estate tax purposes under § 2053(a)(3), subject to the following qualifications:

   a. *Mortgages.* Mortgages are deductible if the property subject to the mortgage is included in the gross estate without any reduction in value on account of the mortgage. In other words, mortgages are deductible where the decedent was personally liable on the debt secured by the mortgage. § 2053(a)(4); Reg. § 20.2053-7. If the property is valued under § 2032A, discussed in Chapter IV, the amount of the mortgage that is deductible is the same percentage of the mortgage as the § 2032A (discounted) value bears to the "normal" value.

   b. *Consideration rule.* Debts founded on a "promise or agreement" are deductible only to the extent that the decedent obtained consideration in money or money's worth. § 2053(c)(1).

      (1) Neutralizing effect. In this situation, the deduction for the debt neutralizes the augmentation of the § 2033 gross estate attributable to the consideration.

      (2) Purpose of rule. The purpose of the consideration rule is to prevent decedents from converting what are really taxable bequests into deductible debts by "agreements," not supported by any augmentation of the gross estate, to pay sums to the natural objects of the decedent's bounty. *See Estate of Huntington v. Com'r*, 16 F.3d 462 (1st Cir.1994).

      (3) Consideration in money or money's worth. This term has the same meaning as in the gift tax context. *See* Ch. 2, at II.H., *supra. See also* §§ 2043(b)(2) & 2053(e).

      (4) Debts not founded on promise or agreement. Examples of debts not founded on a promise or agreement (which are deductible without regard to consideration) include tort claims, tax liabilities, fines, and certain payments pursuant to divorce. *See* Ch. 2, at II.G.6., *supra*.

   c. *Liability of the decedent.* Only the portion of the debt for which the decedent was liable can be deducted. Thus, if the debt is a "community" debt, only one half is deductible, even if the decedent's will mandated that the decedent's estate pay off the entire debt. *U.S. v. Stapf,* 375 U.S. 118 (1963). If the decedent was jointly and severally liable, the full amount can be deducted (if paid), but the claim for reimbursement against solvent co-obligors would be a § 2033 asset of the gross estate. *Parrott v. Com'r,* 30 F.2d 792 (9th Cir. 1929), *cert. denied.* Obviously, state law determines who is liable on debts. *See* Rev. Rul. 76-369, 1976-2 C.B. 281 (wife's estate cannot deduct expenses of last illness in certain cases where state law imposes primary liability on husband).

d. *Claims arising at or after death.* Claims arising at or after death cannot be deducted as "debts" or "claims" of the decedent. Thus, homestead rights and "widow's allowance" cannot be deducted as debts, since they arise after the decedents' death. Reg. § 20.2034-1. Funeral expenses, estate administration expenses, and estate casualty losses are separately deductible, as explained shortly.

e. *Interest on claims.* Only interest accrued to the date of death on debts of the decedent can be deducted as a debt. Reg. § 20.2053-4.

f. *Medical expenses.* Medical expenses incurred by the decedent before death, but paid within the year following death, are not deductible for estate tax purposes if they are deducted on the decedent's final income tax return pursuant to § 213(c).

g. *Relation to income tax.* Aside from medical expenses, claims and debts of the decedent are not deductible by the estate for income tax purposes unless the items are "deductions in respect of a decedent" as defined in § 691(b).

h. *Amount deductible.* The amount deductible as a debt or claim is the negative value of the debt, etc., at the decedent's death. Thus, if the decedent incurred a debt that was either contingent or did not create a payment obligation until some period following the decedent's death, normal valuation principles would come into play to possibly reduce the value of the debt below its face amount.

2. **Funeral expenses.** Funeral expenses properly paid by the estate are deductible by the estate. § 2053(a)(1).

3. **Administration expenses.** Expenses of administering the decedent's estate (*e.g.,* executor fees, legal fees, appraisal fees, etc.) are deductible under § 2053(a)(2) subject to the following:

a. *Relation to income tax.* Administration expenses are deductible (or reduce "amount realized") for income tax purposes only if they are not deducted for estate tax purposes. § 641(g). In other words, the estate representative must elect to deduct these expenses for income tax purposes or estate tax purposes, but not both. The election is not an all-or-nothing one; the estate representative can deduct some dollars of administration expense against one tax base and the rest against the other tax base.

b. *Necessity.* Outside of the 6th and 7th Circuits, administration expenses are deductible only if necessary to fulfill the functions of estate administration, but not if incurred for the convenience of estate beneficiaries. Reg. § 20.2053-3(d)(2); *Hibernia Bank v. U.S., 581 F.2d 741 (9th Cir. 1978)); Estate of Smith v. Com'r,* 510 F.2d 479 (2d Cir. 1975), *cert. denied; Contra Estate of Park v. Com'r,* 475 F.2d 673 (6th Cir. 1973). Interest (accrued after death) on debt incurred by the decedent before death would rarely be deductible for estate tax purposes as an administration expense. Rev. Rul. 77-461, 1977-2 C.B. 324. *Compare Estate of Wheless v. Com'r,* 79 T.C. 470 (1979). Interest on deferred estate tax payments, or on loans taken out to pay estate taxes, would usually be deductible. Rev. Rul. 80-250, 1980-2 C.B. 278; Rev. Rul. 84-75, 1984-1 C.B. 193. However, penalties relating to (unpaid) taxes are not deductible. Rev. Rul. 81-154, 1981-1 C.B. 470. Nor is interest on deferred estate tax under § 6166, described at VII.B.2.b.(3), *infra*, §§ 163(k) and 2053(c)(1)(D). Finally, income, property, and death taxes accrued after death are not deductible. § 2053(c)(1)(B).

c. *Nonprobate property.* The expenses (not chargeable to the probate estate) of administering nonprobate property included in the gross estate are deductible under § 2053(b), but only if actually paid before the expiration of the statute of limitations.

d. *Taxes.* Post-death income and property taxes and federal, state, and foreign death (estate, inheritance) taxes are not deductible. § 2053(c)(1)(B). (There are credits for state and foreign death taxes, described below.) *See also* § 2053(d) (election to deduct, instead of credit, certain state and foreign death taxes where result is to increase amounts passing to charity).

4. *Rules applicable to all § 2053 deductions:*

a. *Liability of estate.* The debt, expense, etc., must be "allowable" against the estate or other successor in interest under state law. Thus, if the statute of limitations has run against a claim against the estate, it is no longer deductible even if actually paid by the estate. *See* Rev. Rul. 69-193, 1969-1 C.B. 222 (no deduction if, under state law, funeral expenses are not a liability of the estate).

b. *Actual payment.* No debt, expense, etc., can be deducted unless it is actually paid by the estate (or other successor in interest).

c. *Debts, etc., allowable against probate estate.* Debts, etc., allowable against the probate estate ("property subject to claims") are deductible only to the extent of (1) the amount of the probate estate, plus (2) the amount of debts, etc., actually paid (out of nonprobate assets) by the time the estate tax return is due (nine months after death). § 2053(c)(2).

Example: If A dies with a probate estate of $200,000 and life insurance of $3 million includable in her gross estate, and items deductible under § 2053 total $500,000, necessitating payment of at least $300,000 with the life insurance proceeds, that $300,000 must be paid by the time the estate tax return is due in order to be deductible.

5. *Casualty losses.* Uncompensated casualty (etc.) losses with respect to assets included in the gross estate are deductible for estate tax purposes, but only to the extent not deducted for income tax purposes. *See* § 642(g).

B. **Charitable Deduction.** There is an estate tax deduction for qualifying amounts passing from the decedent to charity. The rules for the estate tax charitable deduction, found in § 2055, are essentially the same as those for the gift tax marital deduction. *See* Ch. 2, IX., *supra,* noting especially the rules for partial-interest transfers to charity. *Accord* § 2055(e)(2) & (f). In addition, the following should be noted:

1. ***Minimum value of charitable remainder interest.*** For gift and estate transfers into trust after August 1, 1997, a charitable remainder interest must have a present value equal to 10% of the amount transferred. § 664(d)(1)(D) & (2)(D).

2. ***Limit on annual payout.*** For transfers into trust after June 18, 1997, the annual payout under a charitable remainder unitrust (or annuity trust) cannot exceed 50% of the value of the trust. § 664(d)(1)(A) & (2)(A).

3. ***Qualified conservation easement.*** If the decedent's will carves out, from real property included in her gross estate, a qualified conservation easement (as defined in § 170(h)) in favor of a governmental unit, the estate obtains a charitable deduction equal to the decline in value of the property attributable to the easement. § 2055(f). There is also an "exclusion" with respect to qualified conservation easements found in § 2031(c) that is discussed in Chapter 4.

4. ***Deduction limited to includable amount.*** The estate tax deduction is available only for property and interests that are included in the gross estate. The deduction is available for any includable amount passing to charity, regardless of whether the transfer is through the probate estate or pursuant to a non-probate transfer.

   Example 25: Assume that *H* and *W* created an irrevocable trust with community property, income to *H* for life, remainder to charity. Upon *H*'s death, half of the trust is included in *H*'s gross estate under § 2036(a) and that half qualifies for the estate tax charitable deduction; it is not necessary for *estate tax* purposes that this transfer qualify under § 664, since upon *H*'s death the remainder passes outright to charity. § 2055(b) & (d). (Any *gift tax* deduction for the charitable remainder interest would be contingent on satisfying the requirements of § 664.)

5. ***Contingent bequests.*** A contingent bequest to charity is disallowed, unless the contingency (that would prevent the charity from taking) is so remote as to be negligible (*e.g.*, *Longue Vue Foundation v. Com'r*, 90 T.C. 150 (1988); Rev. Rul. 67-229, 1967-2 C.B. 335).

6. ***Reduction for death taxes chargeable to charitable transfer.*** If estate and other death taxes are, under the decedent's will or state law, chargeable against the amount passing to charity, the charitable deduction is reduced *pro tanto*. § 2055(c). If the *federal estate tax* is so chargeable, the tax will reduce the amount of the deduction, but the latter in turn will increase the estate tax, and so on, resulting in a "circular" computation. If a (deductible) debt of the decedent is chargeable against the charitable transfer, either it is deductible as a debt and the charitable deduction is reduced, or else the charitable deduction is simply unreduced; there is no double deduction. *See* § 2056(b)(9).

C. **Marital Deduction.** There is an estate tax marital deduction for qualifying amounts passing from the decedent to the surviving spouse. § 2056. The estate tax rules are virtually identical to the gift tax rules. *See* Ch. 2, X., with special attention to the "terminable interest rule" and the statutory exceptions thereto. *Accord* § 2056(b)(1), (5), (6), (7), & (8). In addition, or by way of elaboration, note the following:

1. ***Includable in gross estate.*** Only property and interests includable in the gross estate qualify for the marital deduction. § 2056(a). Any property passing from the decedent to the surviving spouse, within or outside of the probate estate, potentially qualifies if it is includable in the gross estate. *See* § 2056(c).

2. ***Charges against marital transfer.*** The marital deduction is reduced by any taxes, liens, or other charges or encumbrances against the marital deduction property imposed by the decedent's will or state law. § 2056(b)(4)(A). In a controversial decision, *Com'r v. Estate of Hubert*, 117 S.Ct. 1124 (1997), the Supreme Court held that estate administration expenses charged, pursuant to the exercise of the executor's discretion, against the *income* of a marital deduction QTIP trust (described below) did not reduce the marital deduction, at least under the particular facts. This decision was based on ambiguous language in Reg. § 20.2056(b)(4), which the Treasury has since reversed so as to mostly overturn *Estate of Hubert*. (It was conceded that a charge of such expenses against the *corpus* of a marital or charitable trust would reduce the deduction.)

3. ***Obligation imposed by decedent.*** The marital deduction is also reduced if the decedent imposes an obligation on the surviving spouse to transfer property to a third party. § 2056(b)(4)(B).

   a. *Spousal election wills.* Section 2056(b)(4)(B) comes into play under a "spousal election will," under which the decedent makes a bequest to a surviving spouse on condition that the surviving spouse (in effect) immediately convey (all or a portion of) her own property to a third party or a trust with beneficiaries who are third parties. See *U.S. v. Stapf*, 375 U.S. 118 (1963).

   b. *Reciprocal wills.* Reciprocal wills (sometimes referred to as joint and mutual wills) involve a contractual arrangement under which each spouse is to leave his or her (entire) estate to the other spouse on condition that the surviving spouse bequeath any property remaining at her death to designated third parties. Although this situation appears to fall under § 2056(b)(4)(B), the government has not attempted to reduce the marital deduction under this provision. Instead, the government is likely to advance the theory that this arrangement amounts to a life estate in the surviving spouse followed by a remainder to the designated third parties, which is subject to total disqualification as a nondeductible terminable interest (*see* 5., *infra*), unless it can be salvaged under a QTIP election or as a power-of-appointment trust equivalent (discussed in 6. And 7., *infra*).

4. ***"Passing" requirement.*** To qualify for the marital deduction, the property or interest included in the gross estate must actually pass to the surviving spouse. Such "passing" can occur by will or non-probate mechanism, such as a trust, a right of survivorship, a beneficiary designation, the exercise (or nonexercise) of a power of appointment, the exercise (by the surviving spouse) of an elective right under state law (such as dower or elective share), or pursuant to the bona fide settlement of a will contest. *See* § 2056(d).

5. ***Issues under the "terminable interest" rule:***

   a. *"Terminable interest" defined.* Recall from Chapter 2, X.B.1., that a "terminable interest" is any interest that *might*, as of the decedent spouse's death, be defeated, now or in the future, under *any* condition precedent or subsequent, *regardless of whether or not the interest is ever actually defeated*. There is a crucial but subtle interplay between the terminable interest rule and the passing requirement: the occurence (or nonoccurence) of a condition or event that *actually* prevents the surviving spouse from acceding to the property (or interest therein) will cause a violation of the passing requirement, but the mere *possibility* that a condition or event might occur to defeat such an interest is sufficient to cause the interest to be a terminable interest.

b. *Deductible vs. nondeductible terminable interests.* A terminable interest is non-deductible only where, if the condition were to occur, the property *would* pass to a third party "from" the decedent.

(1) Deductible terminable interests. Examples of deductible terminable interests are bonds, patent rights, copyrights, and similar contract rights that don't pass to, or vest in, a third party when the owner's rights expire. Similarly, annuities that expire at the surviving spouse's death are deductible.

(2) Non-deductible terminable interests. Examples of non-deductible terminable interests include a life estate followed by a remainder in a third party, a survivor or refund survivor annuity, any conditional bequest, or any contingent interest in a trust. The deduction is nevertheless "saved" if the transfer comes under a statutory exception, the main ones being for "QTIP elections" and power-of-appointment trusts, discussed in 6. and 7. below.

(3) Estate trust. If the decedent creates a testamentary trust, income to the surviving spouse for life or accumulated in the trustee's discretion, remainder to the surviving spouse's estate, the trust (in its entirety) is a deductible terminable interest, because the "estate" of the surviving spouse is not a person "other than the surviving spouse (or the estate of such spouse)" within § 2056(b)(1)(A). This arrangement is called an "estate trust." Note that, unlike a QTIP trust or a power-of-appointment trust, an estate trust can provide that income be accumulated, since any accumulated income must eventually pass to the surviving spouse or her estate. Of course, if current income, accumulated income, or corpus can be distributed to any person other than the surviving spouse or her estate, the trust will be a nondeductible terminable interest. The entire value of an estate trust qualifies for the marital deduction.

c. *Qualification (and value) must be determinable at date of death.* Qualification for the marital deduction is "tested" as of the date of the decedent spouse's death. *See Jackson v. U.S.,* 376 U.S. 503 (1964). Thus, if *H* bequeaths $1 million to *W* on condition that she be alive when estate administration is concluded, the deduction fails, even if *W* does survive the period of administration. The crucial point is that, as of the date of death, there was a *possibility* that the interest would fail. The rule that qualification for the marital deduction must be determined at the date of death seemingly implies a parallel principle that the amount (value) of the marital deduction also be determinable at the date of death (or alternate valuation date). Reg. § 20.2056(b)-4(a).

d. *"Six months" exception to terminable interest rule.* Notwithstanding the above, a provision *in the governing instrument* that conditions a transfer to the surviving spouse on her (a) surviving the decedent by six months (or less) or (b) surviving a common disaster which resulted in the decedent spouse's death does not disqualify the marital deduction, if the spouse in fact "takes" under the transfer by satisfying the condition. § 2056(b)(3). Thus, a bequest under *H*'s will "to *W* if she survives me by nine months" is disqualified, even if in fact *W* survives *H* by nine months and takes the bequest. *H* should have changed the "nine" to a "six."

e. *Elective rights.* If a conditional bequest is a nondeductible terminable interest, it would seem that any interest that can be obtained by the surviving spouse only by way of an election or application to a court must also be disqualified, on the ground that the election or application might not be made. However, the correct view is that a right, arising at the decedent's death under state law or the terms of the will (or other instrument), to take or claim money or property is not treated as a conditional interest. The election or application is merely a ministerial act that causes the right to be converted into possession or enjoyment, but the right itself is property that exists as of the decedent's death, and the exercise of such right is under the control of the surviving spouse (or her representative). E.g., *Estate of Neugass v. Com'r*, 555 F.2d 322 (2d Cir.1977) (elective bequest under will), *acq.*, Rev. Rul. 82-184, 1982-2 C.B. 215; *First National Exchange Bank of Roanoke v. U.S.*, 335 F.2d 91 (4th Cir.1964) (commutation of dower), *acq.*; Rev. Rul. 72-7, 1972-1 C.B. 308. The right must be exercisable within a reasonable period of time following the decedent's death. If the right is not exercised, then the marital deduction is lost because the "passing" requirement is not satisfied.

f. *Elections of the personal representative.* The deduction will not be lost under the terminable interest rule just because, as of the decedent's death, various elections and choices might be made by the estate personal representative pertaining to (1) valuing assets included in the gross estate, and (2) deducting estate administration expenses for estate tax purposes or for income tax purposes, even if these choices might affect what the surviving spouse ultimately receives. These choices are analagous to spousal elections in that they help to constitute the interest that passes to the surviving spouse. *See Estate of Smith v. Com'r*, 66 T.C. 415 (1976) (reviewed), *aff'd per curiam*, 565 F.2d 455 (7th Cir. 1977). Once the qualified interest passing to the surviving spouse is determined, it is valued at estate tax values (rather than distribution date values). *See 9.a., infra.*

g. *Spousal rights under probate law.* A surviving spouse might be able to claim widow's allowance, homestead, and exempt property, by making application to the probate court.

(1) Homestead. Homestead is a right to occupy the personal residence indefinitely. It is a nondeductible terminable interest, because it terminates on death or abandonment, and possession reverts to the legatee or heir of the decedent. *See Estate of Kyle v. Com'r*, 94 T.C. 829 (1990) (Texas).

(2) Exempt property. "Exempt property" refers to certain tangible personal property that can be claimed by the surviving spouse (or possibly children). State law should be examined to see if exempt property is a vested or contingent right. *See* Rev. Rul. 76-166, 1976-1 C.B. 287 (Arizona exempt property, and a cash allowance in lieu of homestead, was vested and qualified for the marital deduction).

(3) Widow's allowance. A widow's allowance is a right to cash, whether in a lump sum or installments, during the pendency of probate, payable out of the residue. (It is not deductible under § 2053 as a claim or administration expense.) Whether widow's allowance qualifies for the marital deduction is an issue that has been much litigated, if with more heat than light. Basically, widow's allowance does not qualify under the marital deduction if, under state law, and viewed as of the moment of the husband's death, the allowance *might* be cut off or defeated if the widow dies, remarries, or has sufficient resources. *Jackson v. U.S., supra* (California). However, if it is not subject to these kinds of contingencies, it is not disqualified just because she (or her representative) has to appear in court to claim it. (Of course, if she does not in fact claim it, it never would have "passed" to her.) *See Estate of Green v. U.S.*, 441 F.2d 303 (6th Cir. 1971) (Michigan). In addition, it can be argued that a widow's allowance, being essentially a sum of money payable in one or more installments, should not be viewed as being disqualified solely because the right to it will eventually terminate or expire, since no interest in "the same property" was acquired by another person from the decedent. This point is somewhat debatable, since a widow's allowance might be called an interest in underlying property, namely, the residue. *Jackson v. U.S.*, 317 F.2d 821 (9th Cir.1963), *aff'd on other grounds*, 376 U.S. 503 (1964). *See* Reg. § 20.2056(b)-1(e)(2) (defining "property"). Cf. *Meyer v. U.S.*, 364 U.S. 410 (1960) (insurance fund payable in installments). However, the residue is a portion of an "estate," which is an aggregation of "property" items rather than being itself property. Nevertheless, if the allowance, once granted, can be cut off or reduced according to subsequent events or contingencies, the deduction should be disallowed on the ground that it cannot be valued as of the estate tax valuation date. Finally, if the residue also passes to the surviving spouse, the deduction will not be disallowed under either a "condition subsequent" theory or an "incapable-of-valuation" theory. Reg. § 20.2056(b)-1(g) (Ex. 8).

h. *Interest in unidentified assets.* If a (pecuniary or residual) bequest *might* be satisfied out of an asset that would be a nondeductible terminal interest if left directly to the surviving spouse (such as a term interest retained in connection with an inter vivos gift of a remainder interest in the property), the marital deduction will be reduced by the value of such nonqualifying interest, *even though such interest is not in fact used to satisfy the bequest.* § 2056(b)(2); Reg. § 20.2056(b)-2. This rule seldom applies, since it would be rare that a *nondeductible* terminable interest would be an asset "already in" a decedent's estate (as opposed to being created by the decedent's will, etc.).

i. *Terminable interest purchased by executor or trustee.* A bequest of an annuity to and for the life of the surviving spouse is a "deductible" terminable interest (since no interest passes to a third party from the decedent upon the surviving spouse's death). However, if the decedent's will directs the executor or trustee to purchase an annuity, etc., for the surviving spouse, the bequest is disqualified. § 2056(b)(1)(C).

j. *Converting terminable interest to cash.* A nondeductible terminable interest cannot be saved by an action of the surviving spouse or executor, etc., such as by selling a contingent interest for cash. Reg. § 20.2056(b)-1(e)(3).

6. ***Power-of-appointment trust.*** A trust (or equivalent) that gives the surviving spouse the right to all the income for life plus a general power of appointment qualifies under § 2056(b)(5). The "income" requirement is discussed separately in subsection 8 below. The general-power-of-appointment requirement assures that the consumed property will appear in the surviving spouse's gross estate.

   a. *Alone and in all events.* The power can be an inter vivos general power or a testamentary general power. It must be exercisable by the surviving spouse alone and in all events, *i.e.,* there must be no co-holders or conditions attached to the power.

   b. *Legal life estate coupled with power to consume or dispose of property.* State law must be applied to determine the quality of the interests created. If the life estate combined with power in the surviving spouse to consume or dispose of the property is determined to confer a fee simple absolute in the surviving spouse, the surviving spouse receives the equivalent of an outright transfer that clearly qualifies for the marital deduction. Otherwise, the issue is whether the power to consume or dispose of the property is a general power or a special power and, if a general power, whether it is exercisable by the surviving spouse "in all events." A power to dispose may be only a special power, and a power to consume will probably fall short of being a power to "vest" the property in the surviving spouse at any time. *See Estate of Carpenter v. Com'r,* 52 F.3d 1266 (4th Cir.1995) (power must be such as would, if exercised, be able to convert the property to a fee simple).

   c. *Joint and mutual wills.* Essentially, a joint and mutual (*i.e.,* contractual or reciprocal) will creates a life estate in the surviving spouse coupled with a power to consume, but not to freely dispose of the property at death. Again state law and the terms of the "contract" must be consulted to determine exactly what interests the surviving spouse has received. If, as is common, the surviving spouse is treated as having a life estate coupled with a power to consume, the latter usually fails to qualify as a general power of appointment exercisable in all events. *Estate of Opal v. Com'r,* 450 F.2d 1085 (2d Cir. 1971).

   d. *Specific portion.* If the power qualifies but pertains to a "specific portion" of the trust, only that portion is deductible. Section 2056(b)(10) states that specific portion means only a fractional or percentage portion. This provision, enacted in 1992, overturned the results *of Northeastern Pennsylvania Nat'l Bank & Trust Co. v. U.S.,* 387 U.S. 213 (1967), and *Estate of Alexander v. Com'r,* 82 T.C. 34 (1984) (reviewed), *aff'd unpublished opinion* (4th Cir. 1985).

e. *No power to appoint to third party*. The trust is disqualified if any person (other than the surviving spouse) can appoint or distribute the property to any person other than the surviving spouse. Reg. § 20.2056(b)-5(j).

f. *Life insurance equivalent*. Section 2056(b)(6) provides a parallel set of rules to § 2056(b)(5) for life insurance, endowment, and annuity contracts.

g. *Possibility of double taxation*. As noted above, the power-of-appointment requirement under § 2056(b)(5) is "stricter" than it is under § 2041, leading to the possibility that the power might be such as to cause inclusion in the surviving spouse's gross estate under § 2041 while failing to obtain qualification for the marital deduction under § 2056. That would be an estate planning disaster. However, a trust that satisfies the "income" requirement (discussed in 8., *infra*) while flunking the power-of-appointment requirement can probably be salvaged by making a QTIP election, discussed next.

7. **QTIP transfers.** Certain transfers that would otherwise not be deductible can be rendered deductible, in full, under a QTIP election. *See* § 2056(b)(7). *See also* Ch. 2, at X.C.3., *supra,* for a discussion of its gift tax counterpart, § 2523.

a. *Income requirement*. As with a power-of-appointment trust, the surviving spouse must be given the right to all of the income, payable at least annually. The "income" requirement is discussed in 8., *infra*.

b. *Income equivalents*. Possessory life estates can satisfy the income requirement. Reg. § 20.2056(b)-7(h) (Exs. 1 and 5). Thus, the QTIP election can be made to "save" an election to take dower in kind, an elective share that consists of a life estate (or an income interest in trust), or a "defective" power-of-appointment trust.

c. *No power to appoint or distribute to third party*. In order to qualify, no person (even including the surviving spouse) can have a power to appoint, prior to to the surviving spouse's death, any part of the property to any person (other than the surviving spouse). § 2056(b)(7)(B)(ii)(II); *Estate of Manscill v. Com'r*, 98 T.C. 413 (1992). The trustee can be given the power to distribute corpus to the surviving spouse. Reg. § 20.2056(b)-7(d)(6). Also, the surviving spouse can be given a testamentary power of appointment.

d. *Homestead*. "Homestead" in kind would not qualify where, under state law, it would terminate upon abandonment prior to death, and therefore does not satisfy the "income for life" and "no power of disposition to third persons" requirements for QTIP transfers.

e. *Legal life estates coupled with powers*. A legal life estate, including one created under a joint and mutual will, followed by a remainder, cannot be the subject of a valid QTIP election if the surviving spouse has the power to give any of the property away during life. The surviving spouse would usually be able to make gifts to their minor children or persons who hold the remainder interests. However, precise drafting of the instrument of transfer or contract could overcome this difficulty. *See Estate of Pyle v. U.S.*, 766 F.2d 1141 (7th Cir.1985) (surviving spouse had, under contractual will, power only to consume for her own benefit).

f.   *The election.* The estate representative makes the election on the estate tax
     return. The election, once made, is irrevocable. Reg. § 20.2056(b)-7(b)(4).
     The election can be "partial," so long as it relates to a fractional or percentage
     share of the property. § 2056(b)(10).

8.   ***Income requirement.***   Both the QTIP and power-of-appointment types of
     "qualified" terminable-interest transfers require that the surviving spouse have
     the right to income for life payable at least annually or, in a nontrust situation,
     sole possession and enjoyment for life. Some details:

     a.   *Accumulation power.* A power in a trustee to accumulate income disqualifies
          the trust unless the surviving spouse has the power to demand the income at
          least annually. Reg. § 20.2056(b)-5(f)(7) & (8).

     b.   *Unproductive property.* Funding the trust with unproductive property will
          disqualify the transfer unless the surviving spouse has the right to demand
          that the trust property be converted to productive use. Reg. § 20.2056(b)-
          5(f)(4) & (5). The same principles would apply to a legal life estate in
          unproductive property.

     c.   *Administrative powers.* The trustee must not be given powers, such as the
          power to retain or invest in unproductive assets, or the unfettered power to
          allocate receipts to corpus and expenses to income, that would operate as the
          equivalent of a power to accumulate income or invest in unproductive assets.
          See Reg. § 20.2056(b)-5(f)(1)-(4).

     d.   *Inception income of trust.* If a trust is a testamentary trust or an inter vivos
          trust that receives a "pour-over" from the decedent's will or under a
          beneficiary designation, the trust will not be funded as of death.
          Nevertheless, the trust will not be disqualified just because receipt of the
          income by the surviving spouse is delayed for a reasonable period of estate
          administration. Of course, the surviving spouse must eventually receive all
          the income (including estate income allocable to the trust) that accrues after
          the decedent's death.

     e.   *Termination of trust.* A QTIP trust is not disqualified just because income
          accrued in the QTIP trust before the surviving spouse's death and after the
          last payment to her ("stub income") is not payable to her estate. (Such income
          is includable in her gross estate under § 2044.) Reg. § 20.2056(b)-(7)(d)(4).)
          In a power-of-appointment trust, this rule only holds if the stub income is
          subject to the surviving spouse's power of appointment. Reg. § 20.2056(b)-(5)
          & (8).

     f.   *Trust providing that surviving spouse receive income from only the elective
          portion of the trust.* The government has been forced to concede that a trust
          is not disqualified solely because it provides that the surviving spouse is
          entitled to the income only from that portion of the trust for which the
          executor makes a partial QTIP election. Reg. § 20.2056(b)-7(d)(3). Cf. *Estate
          of Robertson v. Com'r,* 15 F.3d779 (8th Cir.1994) (no disqualification where
          executor could choose between funding a trust that met QTIP requirements
          and one that did not).

3

g. *Unitrust interests.* A unitrust interest is a right of a beneficiary to receive a fixed percentage of corpus (or the trust) valued annually. Standing alone, a unitrust interest in the surviving spouse would not satisfy the income requirement, even if the unitrust percentage is set high. Nevertheless, a provision that required the trustee to distribute to the surviving spouse the *greater* of the "income" *or* the unitrust amount would not cause disqualification.

h. *Annuities.* An annuity is a right to receive a fixed dollar amount annually. There are three possible situations:

(1) Annuity contract or IRA bequeathed to surviving spouse. Section 2056(b)(7)(C) states that an annuity contract (including an IRA) is to be treated as a qualifying income interest for life. Moreover, the QTIP election is assumed to be made for the annuity unless the executor otherwise elects. The theory is that an annuity payment is necessarily greater than the current "income" accrued inside the annuity contract.

(2) Annuity or IRA payable to "income" trust. What if an annuity contract or IRA is owned by a trust that is to pay all of the income to the surviving spouse? State law might treat all, or an arbitrary percentage, of an annuity payment to a trust as "corpus" rather than "income." As a matter of economics, on the other hand, an annuity payment consists "first" of (all) accrued income on the principal balance and "last" of principal. The IRS has ruled that the annuity or IRA includible in the decedent's gross estate and payable to the trust can qualify as QTIP property where (assuming that the annuity payment is greater than the annuity income) the trust treats the annuity income as *trust income* distributable to the surviving spouse and where the surviving spouse is entitled also to the income from the corpus that includes the "principal" portion of annuity payments). Rev. Rul. 89-89, 1989-2 C.B. 231. Compliance with this rule would usually require careful drafting of the trust instrument.

(3) Annuity payout from trust to surviving spouse. Here, the position of the IRS appears to be that the annuity payment will be treated as the "income" obtainable by multiplying a hypothetical corpus amount by the interest rate used in valuing annuities under the applicable actuarial tables. *See* Reg. § 20.2056(b)-7(e) and (h) (exs. 10-12) (pre-10/24/1992 wills and trusts).

Example 26: The trust is funded with an initial corpus of $1 million (at estate tax values), and provides that the surviving spouse shall be paid $60,000 annually. Assume the applicable interest rate under the tables is 5%. Five percent of $1.2 million equals the $60,000 annual payment. Since the hypothetical corpus needed to produce $60,000 of "income" is greater than the initial corpus of the trust, all of the trust ($1 million) is deductible. If the rate under the tables were 8%, the hypothetical corpus would be $750,000, and this lesser amount is what would be deductible. Presumably, if the trustee were required to distribute the *greater* of $60,000 *or* the actual trust income, the entire $1 million would be deductible.

i. *Marital-charitable trust.* Under § 2056(b)(8), a qualifying charitable remainder trust, with the surviving spouse having a qualified unitrust or annuity interest for life (rather than an income interest), is fully deductible.

j. *Estate trust compared.* An "estate trust" is a trust for the benefit of the surviving spouse for her life, remainder to such surviving spouse's estate. This type of trust qualifies as a deductible terminable interest, since no interest passes to a third party upon the surviving spouse's death. Therefore, an estate trust is not subject to the "income" requirement described herein, which pertains only to QTIP trusts and power-of-appointment trusts. In other words, income can be accumulated in an estate trust (such income will eventually pass to the estate of the surviving spouse). However, an estate trust would be disqualified if any income or corpus could be distributed to a third party. See 5.b.(3), *supra.*

9. **Valuing the marital deduction:**

a. *Amount deductible.* It needs to be reiterated that the full net value of the qualifying transfer is deductible.

(1) Power-of-appointment, QTIP, and estate trusts. The amount deductible is the full net value of the qualifying transfer, not the value of any income interest, power of appointment, remainder interest, etc., actually received by the surviving spouse. The concept of "net " value is discussed in 2. and 3., *supra.*

(2) Spousal remainder trust. Suppose Frankie dies leaving a trust, all of the income to Frankie's mother for life, remainder to spouse Johnny. This is not a QTIP trust, since the surviving spouse does not receive the income interest. However, the remainder interest qualifies, because it cannot be defeated by any contingency. Here, the amount deductible is the actuarial value, as of Frankie's death, of Johnny's remainder interest.

b. *What values are used.* The amount of the marital deduction is keyed to facts in existence on the date of death (or alternate valuation date), namely, the *estate tax value* of the property (or interest therein) that ultimately passes to (or for the benefit of) the surviving spouse from the decedent. This rule follows from the fact that the marital deduction is taken from the gross estate, which is also valued at the estate tax valuation date. It should be noted that, in the case of specific property bequests and bequests from the residue, the estate tax value (the deduction) will likely differ from the value of the property on the date the estate or trust distributes the property to the surviving spouse or qualifying trust (the "distribution date value"). The rule about constituting the marital deduction at estate tax values appears to potentially conflict with the "passing" requirement, which would seem to limit the amount of the deduction to the amount actually received by the surviving spouse. However, the passing requirement (as well as qualification under the terminable interest rule) pertains to the *interest* received by the surviving spouse, at estate tax values, not the distribution-date value of such interest. It is not practical to use distribution date values, since the distribution date will normally occur after the estate tax return is due and perhaps after the statute of limitations has run.

c. *Effect of executor elections, etc.:*

(1) Elections constituting the deductible interest. In certain cases the amount of the marital deduction may not be ascertainable at the estate tax valuation date due to various elections (such as to take dower in kind, to deduct administration expenses for income or estate tax purposes, to elect special use valuation under § 2032A, and so on). Nevertheless, the deduction is not disallowed for that reason alone. Once the property passing to the surviving spouse from the decedent is ascertained, it can be valued as of the estate tax valuation date. *Estate of Smith v. Com'r,* 66 T.C. 415 (1976) (reviewed), *aff'd per curiam,* 565 F.2d 455 (7th Cir. 1977). *See* Rev. Rul. 82-23, 1982-1 C.B. 139 (IRS concedes this point where amount passing to surviving spouse is ascertainable by the estate tax return date).

Example 27: Jack's will leaves "to my wife Jill that fraction of my residue (at distribution date values) as (1) half of my adjusted gross estate bears to (2) the residue as valued for estate tax purposes." (This is a "formula" "fraction of the residue" marital bequest.) The "adjusted gross estate" is the gross estate less estate tax deductions under §§ 2053 and 2054. Assume that: (1) the value of Jack's gross estate is $12 million at Jack's death and $10 million on the alternate valuation date, (2) there are no potential deductions under §§ 2053 and 2054 except for estate administration expenses, which are $2 million, (3) the value of the gross estate assets are $8 million at the date bequests are distributed to the legatees, including Jill, and (4) the administration expenses are not chargeable against Jill's share of the residue. Jill is entitled, *as of Jack's death*, to half of the adjusted gross estate. Assume that Jack's executor elects (1) to use the alternate valuation date and (2) to deduct estate administration expenses for estate tax purposes (rather than income tax purposes). Jack's gross estate is $10 million, the § 2053 deduction for estate administration expenses is $2 million, and the marital deduction is $4 million (half of the adjusted gross estate at estate tax values). However, Jill actually receives $3.2 million ($8 million residue at distribution date multiplied by $4 million estate tax value of marital bequest/$10 million estate tax value of residue). It just happened that the 4/10ths share of the residue that Jill owned shrank by 20% between the estate tax valuation date and the distribution date, but this could have occurred if the bequest had been distributed to Jill on the estate tax valuation date. Now suppose, in the alternative, that estate administration expenses had been deducted for income tax purposes. In that case, Jill would have been entitled, under the formula, to 50% of the residue, since the adjusted gross estate would be the same as the gross estate. Therefore, the marital deduction would be $5 million, but Jill would actually receive $4 million. Note that the decision to deduct estate administration expenses for income tax purposes or estate tax purposes gives the executor, under the formula, the power to alter the marital bequest. Indeed, if the gross estate were 2 million or less, the marital bequest could be eliminated completely. Why doesn't this scenario violate the terminable interest rule? Because the problem of manipulating the marital deduction is dealt with by the passing requirement: if the expenses are deducted for income tax purposes, the interest passing to

3

Jill is 50% of the residue; if the expenses are deducted for estate tax purposes, the interest passing to Jill is 40% of the residue. (The analysis is the same as where Jill takes an elective share under state law instead of the bequest.) Whatever interest passes to Jill is valued at the estate tax valuation date.

(2) Excessive discretion in constituting the interest. The IRS will disallow the marital deduction where the estate representative has such discretion that renders the value of the qualifying transfer as being unascertainable.

(i) Rev. Proc. 64-19. The classic illustration is found in Rev. Proc. 64-19, 1964-1 C.B. 682, where the governing instrument containing a pecuniary (fixed dollar) marital bequest stated that the executor could satisfy it in kind "at" income tax basis (instead of at fair market value). In other words, if the bequest amount was $1 million, the executor could satisfy this bequest by distributing assets which had an *income tax basis* of $1 million, but the *fair market value* would depend on what assets the executor would select having aggregate income tax bases of $1 million.

(ii) Abuse potential. The typical pecuniary bequest (that can be satisfied in kind) must be satisfied by assets with aggregate *fair market values* equal to the pecuniary amount. In such a case, the estate tax value of the bequest is identical to what the legatee ultimately receives: the amount of the bequest is truly "frozen." In contrast, the type of pecuniary bequest described in Rev.Proc. 64-19 allows the executor to select property that has fallen in value (relative to income tax basis) to satisfy the bequest, thereby resulting in "underfunding" (overstating) the marital bequest (and allowing appreciating assets to fund the nonmarital residual trust, which is normally not includible in the surviving spouse's gross estate). This funding of the bequest can take place long after the federal estate tax return is filed and perhaps even after the statute of limitations has run. (In contrast, the elections described in (1) above "register" on the federal estate tax return.) This systematic abuse potential, of shifting value from the deductible interest to the nondeductible interest, does not exist in the case of specific property bequests (where the executor has no options) or residuary bequests (where the executor must distribute the residue or a fractional portion of the then value of the residue). *See also* Rev. Rul. 90-3, 1990-1 C.B. 174.

(iii) Theory of disallowance. The theory of disallowance under Rev.Proc. 64-19 is presumably that on the estate tax valuation date there is, on account of the executor's discretion, no ascertainable "interest" passing to the surviving spouse that can then be reasonably valued. An analogy might be to a bequest to a surviving spouse "of assets, selected by my executor, with an aggregate weight of 100 lbs."

(iv) Curing the defect. Rev. Proc. 64-19 goes on to hold that the marital deduction is "saved" in this situation if the governing instrument (or state law) provides *either* that the amount distributed must have a distribution date value *at least* equal to the fixed dollar amount *or* that the value of the amount distributed be fairly representative of appreciation or depreciation in the estate as a whole subsequent to the estate tax valuation date.

d. *Valuation discounts and premiums.* In *Estate of Chenoweth v. Com'r,* 88 T.C. 1587 (1987), *H* owned all of the stock of a closely-held corporation and bequeathed 51% of it to *W* and the rest to his daughter. Although the stock was included in *H*'s gross estate without discount or premium, the amount of the marital deduction was greater than 51% of the whole to reflect a "control premium" with respect to her majority interest. This rule cuts both ways. In Ltr. Ruling 9050004, the marital deduction bequest was discounted on account of the fact that *W* received a minority interest (49% of the stock), the other 51% going to a son.

10. **Surviving the decedent.** The surviving spouse must survive the decedent for the marital transfer to qualify for the deduction. If the order of deaths cannot be proved, one looks to state law and the terms of the governing instrument to determine which spouse is "deemed" to have survived the other.

11. **Surviving spouse is not a U.S. citizen.** *See* I.B.2.b., *supra.*

D. **Deduction for Closely Held Business Interests**. Section 2057 allows a "deduction" with respect to Qualified Family-Owned Business Interests (QFOBIs) in the gross estate. This provision first entered the Code in § 2033A (now repealed) as an exclusion from the gross estate, but was changed to a deduction in 1998. Section 2057 is too complex to describe in exhaustive detail in an outline of this scope.

1. **Amount of deduction.** The deduction is the *lesser* of (a) the adjusted value of QFOBIs includable in the gross estate, or (b) $675,000.

a. *"Second" limitation.* The § 2057 deduction is limited not only by the "first" limitation of $675,000 but also, implicitly, by the excess of $1.3 million over the "applicable exclusion amount" that defines the unified transfer tax credit under § 2010. This is accomplished under § 2057(a)(3), where the sum of the § 2057 deduction and the "applicable exclusion amount" cannot exceed $1.3 million. In effect the § 2057 deduction (up to a maximum of $675,000) is taken first, with the applicable exclusion amount being $625,000. However, if the § 2057 deduction (the adjusted value of QFOBIs) is less than $675,000, the applicable exclusion amount is raised above $625,000 by the excess of $675,000 over the adjusted value of the QFOBIs, but not to exceed the amount specified in § 2010 for the year of the decedent's death.

Example 28: The decedent dies in the year 2006 with, among other assets, a QFOBI having an adjusted value of $750,000. The applicable exclusion amount for that year is $1 million. In the absence of the QFOBI, the estate would obtain a § 2010 credit that would exclude the first $1 million of the (unreduced) taxable estate from tax. Under § 2057, the deduction for the QFOBI is $675,000 and the § 2010 credit would exclude only the first $625,000 of (reduced) taxable estate from tax. The total tax base amount exempt from tax is $1.3 million. Thus, the maximum deduction here is "really" $300,000, despite the appearance of its being $675,000.

Example 29: Same facts as above, except that the value of the QFOBI is $225,000. The § 2057 deduction is $225,000 and the applicable exclusion amount is $1 million [$625,000 + ($675,000 - $225,000), but not to exceed $1 million]. The total tax base amount removed from tax is $1,225,000.

b. *Adjusted value of QFOBI*. The "adjusted" value of a QFOBI is the value of the QFOBI for purposes of inclusion in the gross estate reduced by the excess of the § 2053 deduction for claims and mortgages over qualified residence (and certain other) debt. § 2057(d).

c. *No double deduction*. A QFOBI cannot be deducted under § 2057 if it also qualifies for a marital or charitable deduction. § 2056(b)(9) (no double estate tax deductions).

2. **QFOBI defined**. A QFOBI is an interest in a proprietorship or in a family-controlled (nonpublicly traded) entity as defined in § 2057(e). The proprietorship must carry on a U.S. trade or business that does not have substantial passive investment income. Even if the interest otherwise passes muster, any portion thereof which consists of excess passive investments is not eligible for the deduction.

3. **QFOBI passing to qualified heirs**. The § 2057 deduction is only available for QFOBIs that are includible in the gross estate and pass to qualified heirs (close family members) as defined in § 2057(i)(1) (with reference to § 2032A). § 2057(a)(1) and (b)(2).

4. **Eligible estates**. The § 2057 deduction is only available if various requirements found in § 2057(b) are satisfied:

a. U.S. citizen or resident. The decedent must have been a U.S. citizen or resident.

b. Relative size of QFOBIs. The estate-included (and gift-tax included) adjusted value of QFOBIs must exceed 50% of the "adjusted gross estate" as defined in § 2057(c) (gross estate plus certain gifts and minus deductible claims and mortgages).

c. Bona fide family business. Any QFOBI must have been held by the decedent or a family member (who materially participated in the business) for 5 out of the 8 years before death.

d. The executor must elect the deduction and file the agreement referred to in § 2057(h), described immediately below.

5. **Agreement to pay recapture estate tax**. The agreement described in § 2057(h) is signed by parties interested in the QFOB (the qualified heirs), and promises to pay a recapture estate tax if various contingencies occur, such as that the qualified heir disposes of, or ceases to be involved in, the QFOBI within 10 years following the decedent's death. *See* § 2057(f).

TAX COMPUTATION AND CREDITS

V. **TAX COMPUTATION AND CREDITS. The tax on the taxable estate (the "gross" estate tax) is figured, under § 2001, as if the taxable estate were the decedent's** last taxable gift. The "net" estate tax is arrived at by subtracting the unified transfer tax credit and certain other credits whose function is, roughly, to avoid or mitigate various kinds of "double" taxation. The credits are nonrefundable, *i.e.*, they cannot reduce the net estate tax below zero.

A. **The "Gross" Estate Tax**. The estate tax before credits is computed under § 2001(b). The following steps are involved:

1. *Figure tax on cumulative tax base.* One applies the § 2001(c) rate schedule against the cumulative tax base, which is the sum of (a) the taxable estate and (b) adjusted taxable gifts. § 2001(b)(1).

   a. *Adjusted taxable gifts.* "Adjusted taxable gifts" refers to all taxable gifts of the decedent after 1976. Under § 2001(f), added in 1997, the IRS cannot revalue (upward) adjusted taxable gifts made after August 5, 1997, if (1) the value of the gift was adequately disclosed to the IRS and (2) the gift tax statute of limitations has expired. Otherwise, adjusted taxable gifts might be revalued upwards by the IRS solely for estate tax purposes even though the statute of limitations has run on the gift for gift tax purposes and such revaluation would have been barred for gift tax purposes under § 2504(c) (requiring payment of gift tax). *Estate of Smith v. Com'r,* 94 T.C. 872 (1990), *acq.*

   b. *Post-1976 taxable gifts excluded.* Nevertheless, the term "adjusted taxable gifts" excludes post-1976 taxable gifts of interests which are also included in the gross estate by reason of the form of transfer (*i.e.*, are includable under §§ 2035-2042). § 2001(b) (second sentence).

   c. *Prevents double transfer taxation.* In other words, the *gift tax value* of any interests subject to both estate and gift tax is eliminated from the cumulative tax base, leaving only the estate tax value (constituting a portion of the gross estate). This device prevents double transfer taxation of the same interests. However, taxable gifts of interests that are includable under § 2033 because the donee has re-transferred the interest to the donor are not removed from the total of adjusted taxable gifts.

   d. *Rates: surtax.* The progressive rate schedule is found in § 2001(c)(1). The top marginal rate is 55%. Section 2001(c)(2) imposes a "surtax" of 5% on so much of the cumulative tax base as exceeds $10 million. The surtax stops when the average tax rate is 55%. In other words, the purpose of the surtax is to "recapture," in very large estates, the benefits of the below-55% marginal tax rates. Although the caption to § 2001(c)(2) refers to the phase-out of the unified credit as well, the text of that section only appears to phase out the graduated rates, not the credit.

2. *Subtract the after-credit gift tax ("tax ... payable under Chapter 12") on all post-1976 taxable gifts (not just "adjusted taxable gifts") of the decedent.* One first figures what the *before*-credit gift tax would have been on all post-1976 taxable gifts if the § 2001(c) rate schedule in existence at the time of the decedent's death had been in effect at the time of the gifts. One then reduces this tax by the amount of the unified transfer credit *actually* used against such gifts. *See* § 2001(b)(2). (In virtually all cases, the after-credit gift tax on

post-1976 taxable gifts is simply the sum of the actual net gift taxes shown on the post-1976 gift tax returns.) The net gift taxes on post-1976 taxable gifts are subtracted because such taxes were "down payments" against the ultimate unified transfer tax liability.

3. **_Effect of gift splitting._** Recall that § 2513 allows a donor to "split" a gift with his or her spouse under § 2513 for gift tax purposes. (This election does not apply to gifts of community property, which are already "split.") Gift splitting affects the foregoing as follows:

   a. _Result to transferor spouse with respect to estate-included transfers._ Recall from II.C.5.a.(1), _supra_, that gift-splitting has no effect on (does not reduce) the amount included in the decedent's gross estate where the decedent made an inter vivos transfer included in his gross estate under §§ 2035-2042. If the entire estate-included transfer is taxed to the transferor's estate, so should the transferor's estate obtain credit for any gift tax paid by the transferor's spouse on the same transfer due to gift splitting, and § 2001(d) does precisely that. (Thus, the tax borne by the _spouse_ on the decedent's estate-included transfer is treated as a down payment towards the decedent's estate tax.)

   b. _Result to consenting spouse._ The term "adjusted taxable gifts" includes the taxable gifts attributed to the consenting spouse as a result of gift-splitting, even though the other spouse actually made the "transfer" which was of a type that is fully includible in the other spouse's gross estate under §§ 2036-2041. Likewise, any gift tax paid by the decedent pursuant to a gift-splitting election is subtracted under § 2001(b)(2), even if (again) the other spouse was the one who actually made the transfer. Note that these rules operate to push the consenting spouse's taxable estate into higher marginal rate brackets, even though the consenting spouse made no actual estate-included transfer of her own and even though the transfer is fully accounted for in the other spouse's gross estate. However, an opposite set of results occurs under § 2001(e) where the other spouse's transfer is includible in the other spouse's gross estate under § 2035(a): here the taxable gift of the consenting spouse is excluded from her adjusted taxable gifts total and any gift tax she paid is not creditable under § 2001(b)(2) (it being creditable by the estate of the transferor spouse under § 2001(d)).

B. **Unified Transfer Tax Credit.** Next, one subtracts the full amount of the unified transfer tax credit, which is that amount which equals the § 2001(c) tax on the "applicable exclusion amount."

   1. **_Amount of credit._** Starting in 2006, the applicable exclusion amount is $1 million, which translates into a credit of $345,800. The credit amounts corresponding to other exemption equivalent amounts are set forth in Table 1-1 in Chapter 1, IV.B.6.c.(1). The credit amounts (and applicable exclusion amounts) are not indexed for inflation. (Contrary to first impression, subtracting the full credit for estate tax purposes does not entail using the same credit dollars twice for both estate and gift tax purposes, because the amount of the unified transfer tax credit actually taken for gift tax purposes reduces the § 2001(b)(2) "credit" for post-1976 gift taxes described immediately above. _See_ Chapter 1, IV.B.7. Example 2.)

2. ***Effect of late-1976 gifts.*** The credit is reduced by 20% of any of the $30,000 gift tax specific exemption (repealed as of Jan. 1, 1977) that was applied against gifts made after Sept. 8, 1976 and before 1977. § 2010(c).

3. ***Credit cannot exceed the tax.*** The unified transfer tax credit, which is taken "before" any of the other credits described below, cannot exceed the tax calculated under § 2001.

C. **Credit for State Death Taxes.** State death taxes are creditable up to the limitation prescribed by § 2011(b). Note that the limitation is calculated with reference to the "adjusted taxable estate," meaning the taxable estate reduced by $60,000. This credit is available only "after" the unified transfer tax credit, § 2011(f), meaning that it is not available where the cumulative tax base is at or below the applicable exclusion amount.

D. **Credit for Pre-1977 Gift Tax on Gifts Included in the Gross Estate.** Section 2012 allows a credit with respect to gift taxes on pre-1977 taxable gifts, but only for gifts that were also included in the gross estate (under §§ 2035-2042). (This credit serves the same purpose as the "adjusted taxable gifts exclusion" does for post-1976 gifts, namely, to mitigate double estate and gift taxation of the same transfer; however, gift taxes on pre-1977 gifts not included in the gross estate are not credited because pre-1977 gifts are not included in the cumulative tax base.) The credit is the lesser of the gift tax or the net estate tax (if any) attributable to the gift transfer.

E. **Credit for Estate Tax on Prior Decedent.** The purpose of this credit, found in § 2013, is to mitigate the tax impact of deaths that occur in close succession. The calculation of the credit is rather complex, since it involves four steps:

1. ***Identifying the previously-taxed transfer.*** The first step is to identify and value any estate transfer from the prior decedent (the "transferor") to the current decedent (the "decedent") whose estate is subject to estate tax after the credits discussed above. The value of such interest is the net value to the transferor's estate, reduced by any portion thereof which qualified for the marital deduction. It is not necessary to trace this value into the decedent's gross estate as such, since the transfer augmented the decedent's potential § 2033 gross estate.

2. ***Tentative credit.*** The second step is to figure that portion of the transferor's net estate tax attributable, on an average marginal rate basis, to the value of the transferred interest. Note that the credit is only available for *estate*-included transfers made by the transferor, not gift transfers.

3. ***First limitation.*** The third step is to figure the current decedent's estate tax attributable, on a highest marginal rate basis, to inclusion in the decedent's gross estate of the value of the transferred interest, whether or not such interest is actually included in the decedent's gross estate and regardless of the value (if any) of such interest at the decedent's death. As mentioned in 1., *supra,* it is simply postulated that the transferred interest augments the decedent's gross estate at its net estate tax value reduced by any marital deduction attributable thereto. The purpose of this first limitation is to assure that the credit will not exceed the current decedent's estate tax attributable to having received the estate transfer of the prior decedent.

4. *Second limitation.* The tentative credit, as reduced (if at all) by the first limitation, is taken in full if the transferor died within two years before (or after) the death of the decedent. The credit is eliminated entirely if the decedent outlived the transferor by ten years. The credit is phased out by allowing a diminished credit where the decedent outlives the transferor by: more than two years, but less than four years (80% of the credit is allowed); four to six years (60%); six to eight years (40%); and eight to ten years (20%).

F. **Credit for Foreign Death Taxes.** Section 2014 provides a credit for foreign death taxes on property "situated" in such foreign country (*see* §§ 2104-2107) and included in the decedent's gross estate. Roughly, the credit is the lesser of the net foreign death tax or the net U.S. estate tax attributable to the foreign-situs property. Thus, if the item is fully deductible under the U.S. marital or charitable deduction, the credit will be lost. The credit is not available to the estates of nonresident alien decedents. § 2102(a). The United States has entered into death tax conventions with various countries, which may have the effect of avoiding double taxation in the first place, thereby obviating the need for the credit.

3

VI. **PROCEDURE AND PRACTICE**

A. **Returns**

PROCEDURE AND PRACTICE

1. *When required.* An estate tax return (Form 706) must be filed where the date-of-death value of the gross estate exceeds the applicable exclusion amount referred to in § 2010(c) reduced by "adjusted taxable gifts" (and also by the amount in reduction of the unified transfer credit attributable to late-1976 gifts). § 6018(a)(1) & (3).

2. *When due.* The return is due nine months after the decedent's death. § 6075(a). The deadline can be extended for up to six months under § 6081(a).

3. *Contents.* The return must list all property in the gross estate. In addition, it must list virtually all gifts made by the decedent during life. *See* Reg. § 20.6018-3 & 4.

B. **Payment**

1. *Medium of payment.* Payment must be in cash or in "flower bonds" (low-interest U.S. bonds designated to be redeemable at par in satisfaction of estate tax liability). The requirement of payment in cash raises a potential liquidity problem for estates. Planning for liquidity is discussed at Ch. 6.

2. *Time:*

   a. *In general.* Payment is due within nine months of death. § 6151(a). The § 6081 six-month extension for returns is not available for payment.

   b. *Extensions of time are provided in certain cases.* Generally, interest runs against the estate for taxes paid nine months after death.

   (1) Twelve months. The estate can obtain up to 12 months under § 6161(a)(1).

(2) Ten years. An extension of up to ten years can be obtained under § 6161(a)(2) for "reasonable cause" pertaining to illiquidity. *See* Reg. § 20.6161-1(a)(1).

(3) Closely held business deferral with installment payments. Under § 6166, an estate can defer payment for five years, followed by ten years of installment payments, at only 2% interest, for the estate tax attributable to a qualified small business (or farm) interest. The 2% interest rate pertains to a maximum of $1 million of value (as indexed for inflation) plus the applicable exclusion amount (but reduced by the applicable § 2010 credit amount, etc.). The interest rate on the excess is 45% of the general underpayment rate. *See* § 6601(j). To qualify, the value of the closely-held business interests must exceed 35% of the "adjusted gross estate" (gross estate less deductions for debts, etc., under §§ 2053-2054). Transfers within three years of death are to be disregarded for purposes of applying the 35% test. § 2035(c)(2). The interest on deferred estate tax is not deductible for either estate or income tax purposes. §§ 163(k) and 2053(c)(1)(D).

c.   *Remainder interests.* Payment of tax attributable to a remainder interest can be postponed for up to six months after the remainder interest comes into possession. § 6163(a). *See also* §§ 2015 and 2016 (interplay of § 6013(a) with credits under §§ 2011 and 2014).

3.   **Source of payment.** The tax is to be paid by the estate personal representative. §§ 2002 and 2203. The payment is to be made out of assets included in the gross estate. If the property is not collected out of the estate assets prior to distribution, the IRS may proceed against the executor personally, until the latter is discharged pursuant to § 2204. The IRS can also proceed against the transferees of the estate under § 6324(a)(2).

4.   **Liens.** To aid in collecting against the estate and the transferees, a lien arises against the estate assets, which can be levied and executed upon in due course. *See* §§ 6323 and 6324(a)(1) & (3).

5.   **Right of reimbursement.** The means whereby the IRS actually collects the tax does not affect the issue of who, legally, is *ultimately* to bear the burden of the tax. *See* § 2205. How the payments are to be allocated among the various legacies and other estate-included transfers is determined under the decedent's will (and possibly other instruments of transfer). If the will is silent on this point, the estate tax is to be allocated according to the applicable state death tax apportionment rule in combination with Code § 2206 (estate tax attributable to included life insurance), § 2207 (estate tax attributable to included power-of-appointment property), § 2207A (estate tax on surviving spouse attributable to inclusion of QTIP property), and § 2207B (estate tax attributable to retained-interest transfer included under § 2036). Thus, if the IRS collects the entire estate tax by executing upon an estate tax lien on Blackacre, which was specifically bequeathed to X, but the decedent's will allocated the burden of estate taxes to the residue, X can proceed against the residuary legatees (and/or the executor) for reimbursement.

CHAPTER 3 - QUESTIONS, ANSWERS, AND TIPS

EXAM TIPS:

1. Keep inclusion and deduction issues separate. Don't treat deductible items as exclusions from the gross estate. A deduction can only be taken for an item includible in the gross estate.

2. Don't confuse estate tax and gift tax doctrine. Inclusion in the gross estate under §§ 2035-2042 on account of an inter vivos transfer is keyed to the concept of "economic transfer" as distinct from "gift" for gift tax purposes. Thus, for example, the gift tax exclusions under § 2503, gift splitting under § 2513, the gift tax deduction provisions, and the concept of "incomplete transfer," have no impact on the "transfer" issue for estate and gift tax purposes. Also, the fact that an inter vivos transfer is a gift for gift tax purposes does not, in itself, prevent it from being included in the gross estate. Similarly, there is no rule that a non-gift transfer is per se included in the gross estate, although the operation of estate tax doctrine will usually cause such an item to be included in the gross estate.

3. In problems involving §§ 2036-2038, consider the following issues in the following order: (1) whether the decedent made an inter vivos transfer (and, if so, of what or of how much); (2) whether it was made for full and adequate consideration in money or money's worth; (3) if not, whether the decedent held the requisite interest or power under any one or more of §§ 2036-2038; (4) if so, whether (in the case of § 2036 or 2037) such interest or power was "retained"; (5) whether the interest or power was held "in" the (same) property that was transferred; (6) assuming one or more of §§ 2036-2038 apply, what is the amount includible; and (7) if there is an includible amount, whether theres is any "partial consideration offset" in money or money's worth. The problem might also ask you to describe the extent, if any, to which the transfer is subject to both estate and gift tax, which involves applying the "adjusted taxable gifts exclusion" of § 2001(b) (last sentence).

4. Another point of potential confusion is the sometimes overlap among the gross estate inclusion sections. First, the following provisions presuppose an inter vivos transfer by the decedent: §§ 2035-2039, 2040(a), and so much of § 2041 that refers to the exercise, release, or lapse (during life) of a general power of appointment. Sections 2040(b), 2041 (referring to the "possession" of a general power of appointment), and 2042, being based on a "power of appointment" concept, do not presuppose an inter vivos transfer by the decedent. Indeed, § 2041 presupposes no inter vivos transfer of the property by the decedent. Section 2033 stands apart. There is no overlap between §§ 2036-2039 as a group, 2040-2042 as a group, and 2033. Thus, a revocable transfer is subject only to § 2038, not § 2041. A joint tenancy subject to § 2040 cannot be reached by any of §§ 2036-2039. Property (not transferred inter vivos by the decedent) over which a decedent possesses a general power of appointment is subject to § 2041, not § 2033 and not § 2038. There is also no overlap among §§ 2040, 2041, and 2042, nor between §§ 2036(a)(1) and 2037 with respect to retained interests, nor between §§ 2037 and 2038 with respect to powers, but there is some overlap between §§ 2036(a)(2) and 2038 with respect to powers, and § 2039 can overlap all three of § 2036-2038 in the case of annuities and employee survivor benefits. In case of overlap, the section including the largest amount prevails. There is no double inclusion.

5. The terminable interest rule in the marital deduction is complex and artificial, and its relation to the "passing" requirement is potentially confusing. Consider these steps in the following order, *all (except item (4)) from the vantage point of the decedent spouse's death looking forward*: (1) whether or not the interest is a "terminable" interest, (2) if yes,

whether it is a nondeductible terminable interest, (3) if yes, whether it falls within a statutory exception, (4) if potentially deductible after (1)-(3), whether it in fact failed to satisfy the "passing" requirement, (5) if still potentially deductible, whether the interest is reasonably capable of valuation (usually not a problem), and (6), if deductible, the amount of the deduction. Don't belabor the obvious, and if the interest obviously flunked the passing requirement, the other steps in the analysis become irrelevant.

REVIEW QUESTIONS:

1. In the following, state what *interests* in property (if any) are includible in X's gross estate upon X's death and under what Code section(s). Assume that, unless stated otherwise, community property is not involved.

   (a) B creates a testamentary trust, income to C for life, remainder to X if living at B's death, but if not to D. Assume that X dies before B.

   (b) X creates an irrevocable trust, naming the X Bank as trustee, income to X or accumulated in the trustee's discretion; on X's death the trust terminates and the remainder is payable to C. Assume, in the alternative, that X's creditors under state law (a) can and (b) cannot reach the trust income while X is alive.

   (c) X takes out a life insurance policy on her own life in 2001, naming B as beneficiary, and irrevocably assigns all of the incidents of ownership to B in 2005. Assume that X dies, in the alternative, in (a) the year 2006 and (b) the year 2010.

   (d) X creates an irrevocable trust, naming the X Bank as trustee, income to X for 25 years (or earlier death), remainder to C. Assume, in the alternative, that X dies (a) 21 years, (b) 30 years, and (3) 26 years after creating this trust.

   (e) A creates a trust, naming X and the Z Bank as co-trustees, income and/or corpus to X for X's support and welfare as determined by the trustee, for X's life, remainder to C.

   (f) X is employed by Z Corp., which has a nonqualified pension plan in which X's pension rights become vested if X is still employed by X Corp. at age 50. X dies at age 49 while employed by Z Corp., and Z Corp., pursuant to its death benefit plan, pays a death benefit of $60,000 to X's spouse Y.

   (g) X, as community property manager, creates a trust revocable by X during X's lifetime; on X's death, if X is survived by X's spouse S, the income is to be paid to S for life; on the death of the later to die X and S, the trust is to terminate and the corpus be paid to R.

   (h) X creates an irrevocable inter vivos trust, naming X and the Z Bank as trustees, income to B or accumulated in the trustee's discretion; at B's death the trust is to terminate and the corpus, together with any accumulated income, is to be paid over to C. X dies before B.

   (i) X buys real estate with $100,000 and puts it in the name of X and Y (X's bother) as joint tenants with right of survivorsip. X dies before Y. At X's death, the property is worth $100,000.

   (j) X creates an irrevocable trust, income to B for 15 years, reversion to X if then living, but if not to K. X dies 13 years after creating this trust.

2. State whether the following items are deductible in whole or in part:

(a) In the year 2000, H and W become divorced, and H is obligated to pay child support until their young child reaches 18. Three years later, H discovers that he has hepatitis C, which could cause his death in the relatively near future. H enters into an agreement with W to the effect that H, in consideration for W's raising their child, owes W the sum of $100,000. Shortly thereafter H dies, and H's executor pays W the $100,000.

(b) H dies, leaving half of the $1 million residue to W if she survives H by one year. W dies 5 months after H, but W's executor validly elects under state law to take against H's will, resulting in the sum of $700,000 being paid from H's estate to W's estate.

(c) X dies and bequeaths the residue of estate to B for life, remainder to the Z Charity.

(d) W dies and leaves $1 million in trust, income to H for life payable at least annually, giving H a power to appoint all or so much of the corpus to or among the issue of W and H as H from time to time decides, and on H's death the corpus is to be paid over to C.

(e) H and W agree that each of them will leave their property to the other, provided that the survivor will bequeath the property received from the first decedent to their surviving issue per stirpes. Under state law, this contractual arrangement is legally enforceable, and its effect is to give the surviving spouse a life estate (not in trust) plus the power to consume the property, followed by a remainder to the surviving issue.

ANSWERS:

These questions are relatively straightforward.

1. Gross estate inclusion:

(a) X has a contingent remainder that is worth zero at X's death prior to B's death. § 2033. No transfer by X with retained reversion under § 2037.

(b) If the creditors of X can reach the income, then X has retained the right to the income, causing inclusion under § 2036(a)(1) of the entire trust. If not, no inclusion, since X has not "retained" the "right to" any income.

(c) X has divested herself of incidents of ownership, so § 2042 would not apply directly. However, if X dies in 2006 (within three years of the transfer), she is treated as not having made the transfer, resulting in inclusion of the proceeds under § 2035(a). Sections 2036-2038 are not implicated: no transfer with retained interest or power. Section 2039 does not apply to life insuransce.

(d) X has made a retained-income-interest transfer, but the trust is includible only if X dies within the 25-year retained-income period. ("... retained for a period ... that did not in fact end before his death") The *lapse* of the income interest after 25 years is not a "transfer" that would trigger § 2035(a) if X were to die within three years after such lapse.

(e) This does not involve a power held or retained by X following a transfer by X, so that §§ 2036-2038 are not relevant. X, along with the Z Bank, has a power to pay corpus and/

or income to X. This is a § 2041 general power of appointment, unless the "standards" exception of § 2041(b)(1)(A) applies. It does not, since "welfare" is a standard looser than (not defined in terms of) "support," "maintenance," "health," or "education." Also, none of the "co-holder" exceptions apply, since the co-holder (Z Bank) is neither the grantor nor an adverse party. (A corporate trustee cannot ever be an adverse party.) Hence, the entire trust (corpus and undistributed income) is includible in X's gross estate under § 2041(a)(2).)

(f) The death benefit is includible in X's gross estate under § 2039: (1) X possessed a contingent right to a payment or payments during life (the pension right); (2) the death benefit was a payment by reason of X's death; and (3) the employment relationship satisfies the "contract or agreement" requirement. The employee is deemed under § 2039(b) to be the "transferor." Death benefits of this type are not "life insurance" subject to § 2042 (instead of § 2039), since there is no actuarial risk pool. Since § 2039 applies, there is no need to consider §§ 2036-2038.

(g) Only half of the trust is includible in X's gross estate under § 2038, since X is the "transferor" of only half. The other half (of which S was the transferor) is includible in X's gross estate under § 2041(a)(2), but only if all of the property would be X's separate property upon a revocation. Assuming that, under state law, the property would be community property following a revocation, X would not have a general power of appointment over S's half. (Whatever portion of this trust is includible in X's gross estate can probably qualify for the marital deduction as a QTIP, because the surviving spouse S has the right to income for life, etc.)

(h) X, along with the co-trustee, has retained a power (for life) to "designate the person(s) who will possess or enjoy the income" under § 2036(a)(2): a power to accumulate is a power to shift enjoyment from the income beneficiary to the remainder. The co-trustee (even if an adverse party) cannot "block" the application of § 2036(a)(2) (or § 2038). Since the entire trust is includible under § 2036(a)(2), there is no need to apply § 2038 to include the value of the income interest only.

(i) The entire property is includible in X's gross estate under § 2040(a). X was the transferor (provider of all consideration). Y is not X's spouse.

(j) As in (a), the reversion is not included under § 2033, since it has a value of zero at X's death. Nevertheless, this is a retained reversion transfer under § 2037: (1) K can take only by surviving X (that is, X's death before that of B is a prerequisite for K's taking anything); (2) X's reversion, at the moment just prior to X's death (and disregarding the fact that such death actually occurred when it did) is undoubtedly worth more than 5%. The amount includible in X's gross estate is the value of the trust at X's death less the then actuarial value of B's outstanding term interest.

2. Deduction questions.

(a) The payment of $100,000 to W does not qualify for the marital deduction, because W is not H's spouse when H dies. H's estate can't deduct the payment as a claim under § 2053, because this claim was founded on a promise or agreement but was not supported by consideration *in money or money's worth* from W to H (as would be the case in a loan). This is a disguised bequest (probably meant to benefit the child) masquerading as a claim. (H's obligation to pay child support, which is founded on a court decree rather than a promise or agreement, would support a deduction under § 2053.)

(b) The bequest to W flunks the terminable interest rule, since it is conditioned on W's surviving X by more than the 6 months permitted by § 2056(b)(3). The bequest also doesn't pass to W, since she in fact failed to survive long enough to take. But the elective share amount ($700,000) does qualify: (1) it in fact passes to W, and (2) it's not a terminable interest. This right vested in W at H's death, and the fact that someone had to go to court to apply for it did not render it a terminable interest.

(c) There is no charitable deduction for a remainder in trust following an income interest. The noncharitable lead interest must be a qualified unitrust interest or a qualified remainder interest.

(d) This fails to qualify for the marital deduction, despite the income interest for H. It is not a power-of-appointment trust because H's power of appointment is only a "special" one. It doesn't qualify for the QTIP election because H can appoint to a third party.

(e) The analysis here is similar to that in the previous item. Possession of property in kind would satisfy the "income" requirement. However, a power to consume is not a power to "vest" the property, free of the obligation, in the surviving spouse. Hence, it is not a general power of appointment exerciseable alone and in all events, although it is sufficient to cause inclusion in the survivor's gross estate under § 2041. The deduction might be salvaged by a QTIP election, but it won't qualify if, under state law, the surviving spouse has the power during life to make gifts of the deceased's spouse's property, which is the equivalent of a special power of appointment. (Such a power can be negated under the terms of the contract, but here the contract is silent.)

VALUATION

▶ ## CHAPTER SUMMARY

CHAPTER 4: VALUATION

Introduction. The tax base under the estate, gift, and generation-skipping taxes is constituted by the fair market value of included assets at the relevant valuation date. Generally, fair market value is determined according to the willing-buyer, willing-seller test, but there are the usual statutory exceptions.

The fact that valuation has become increasingly prominent as an arena for transfer tax litigation and planning justifies placing this topic in a separate chapter. This chapter is placed immediately after the estate tax chapter, because valuation issues are most prominent in the estate tax context, and estate tax valuation doctrine is mostly "transferable" to the gift tax and generation-skipping tax contexts. However, differences in valuation doctrine among the several taxes are duly noted.

This chapter first discusses the willing-buyer, willing-seller test and its most common applications, including the imposition of various kinds of valuation discounts. Succeeding parts deal with with special estate tax valuation rules, special gift tax valuation rules, and (the few) special generation-skipping tax valuation rules.

I. **THE WILLING-BUYER, WILLING-SELLER TEST.** **In the absence of some special statutory rule to the contrary (outlined in II.-IV., *infra*), the valuation of assets under the transfer taxes follows the willing-buyer, willing-seller test. This test is applied at the date of gift, the estate tax valuation date, or the generation-skipping tax valuation date.**

THE WILLING-BUYER, WILLING-SELLER TEST

    A. Valuation Generally. The value of an asset at the relevant valuation date is "the price at which the property would change hands between a willing buyer and a willing seller, neither being under any compulsion to buy or sell, and both having reasonable knowledge of relevant facts." Regs. §§ 20.2031-1(b) and 25.2512-1. *Facts idiosyncratic to the transferor (or a likely buyer from the transferor), such as family relations, age, gender, and tastes, are irrelevant.* A "forced sale" price is not determinative. Nor are assessed values for property tax purposes. The relevant market is usually the retail market (as opposed to what the donor or donee could have obtained by selling the item to a dealer). If the item is actually sold shortly after the transfer, the sales price may be a relevant fact, but it is not controlling *per se*.

    B. Securities Traded on an Exchange. One looks to the (mean) market price on the date of the transfer, or if there are no transactions on that date, one uses a weighted average of market prices on the nearest dates when sales occurred, or if there are no such proximate sales, one takes the mean between the "bid" and the "asked" prices. *See* Regs. §§ 20.2031-2(b)-(g) and 25.2512-2(b)-(d).

    C. Blockage Rule. If the securities (which are the subject of the gift) constitute a large proportion of the issued and outstanding securities of the same class, or are a large proportion of those normally traded, the donor can claim a "blockage" discount to reflect the likelihood that dumping the securities on the market all at once would somewhat depress the price. Regs. §§ 20.2031-2(e) and 25.2412-2(e). A similar kind of discount can be obtained any time a large quantity of unique property is involved, such as the works of a particular artist, collectibles, or real estate. *E.g., Estate of Smith v. Com'r,* 57 T.C.650 (1972)*(acq.), aff'd on other issue,* 510 P.2d 479 (2d Cir. 1975). The blockage rule illustrates the point that *the particular quality of the transferor's interest is a relevant fact.* At the same time, it raises the larger issue of whether value as of the valuation date should be figured with reference to events that may or may not occur in the future (in this case, the possible sale of the property as one unit).

D. Mutual Funds. Certain mutual fund shares can only be purchased from the fund itself, and the purchase price (based on net asset value plus a "load") will exceed the price at which the same shares could be sold back to (redeemed by) the fund. After losing the case of *U.S. v. Cartwright*, 411 U.S. 546 (1973), the Treasury now concedes that the lower redemption price controls. Regs. §§ 20.2031-8(b) and 25.2512-6(b).

E. Interests in a (Closely Held) Business for Which There is No Market. This area is perhaps the most difficult and imprecise "factual" area in the transfer taxes. Valuing an interest in a closely-held business is basically a three-step process: one first values the underlying enterprise, then makes adjustments appropriate for the quality of the interest involved, and last applies any relevant statutory rules (discussed in II.-IV., *infra*).

1. **Valuation of underlying business.** Here one considers all the facts and circumstances, including: the value of the constituent assets, the earning capacity of the enterprise, its dividend-paying capacity, the prospects for the industry, the firm's place in the industry, and so on. *See* Reg. §§ 20.2031-3 and 25.2512-2(f) and -3; Rev. Rul. 59-60, 1959-1 C.B. 237 (and subsequent rulings amplifying and modifying the same). This is strictly a factual issue, which typically calls for the opinions of valuation experts. Most controversies of this type are resolved at audit or internal appeal within the IRS. Trial court decisions, which often adopt a compromise between the IRS and donor positions, are rarely appealed (or overturned on appeal).

2. **Valuing the interest in the enterprise.** Logically, the next step would be to multiply the value of the enterprise by the percentage that corresponds to the interest in the enterprise represented by the transfer, and this may be sufficient where a partnership interest is involved (and the owner of the partnership can cause a liquidation of her interest). But matters are usually not so simple, because the ultimate test is what a willing buyer would pay to a willing seller for the particular interest that is the subject of the gift.

   a. *Lack-of-marketability discount.* An interest in a closely-held business may be worth less than its pro rata share of the underlying enterprise value simply because the enterprise (and the interest therein) is unique and does not command a ready market (and cannot be liquidated). This downward adjustment is referred to as the "lack of marketability discount." *E.g., Estate of Hall v. Com'r*, 92 T.C. 312 (1989) (35% discount). However, this discount should be allowed only where the value of the enterprise was initially based on comparisons with publicly traded enterprises. *See Estate of Jung v. Com'r*, 101 T.C. 412 (1993). (There is a actually a liquidity "premium" that derives from being publicly traded, but this premium is built into market prices quoted on exchanges.) The lack-of-marketability discount is now affected by §§ 2703 and 2704, discussed in II.C., *infra*.

   b. *Underwriters' and other selling expenses.* As a general rule, anticipated extraordinary expenses of selling stock cannot reduce the includible value, since such expenses (even if likely to be incurred) would be potentially deductible under § 2053 as estate administration expenses. *See Estate of Smith v. Com'r*, cited at C., *supra. Cf.* Reg. § 20.2031-1(b) (retail price in "normal" market). (This rule might also be based on the broader principle that possible post-transfer events should be disregarded, in which case this rule and the blockage rule, *supra*, seem out of sync with each other.)

c. *Future taxes:*

(1) Capital gains taxes on stock itself. A buyer of the stock (or of any asset) would be indifferent to any built-in gain (and taxes payable) by a seller. These facts (basis, character, and marginal rate bracket) are idiosyncratic to particular sellers, and hence must be disregarded. Future capital gains taxes on buyers are universal, and are implicitly factored into the market value of all assets, and hence should not give rise to a separate discount. E.g., *Estate of Robinson v. Com'r*, 69 T.C. 222 (1977).

(2) Capital gains taxes on corporate assets. It has been held that future capital gains taxes on inside corporate assets can be taken into account in figuring (reducing) the value of the underlying stock, especially if the corporate assets are of the type that do not usually depreciate in value, on the theory that such taxes can't be avoided. *Eisenberg v. Com'r*, 155 F.3d 50 (2d Cir.1998); *Estate of Davis v. Com'r*, 110 T.C. 530 (1998).

(3) Excise taxes on particular types of assets. It has been held, controversially, that special excise taxes on particular kinds of assets (as opposed to retail sales taxes generally) should *increase* the value of assets within the taxed category, since the seller will demand a higher price. *Estate of Gould v. Com'r*, 14 T.C. 414(1950) (reviewed); Rev. Rul. 55-71, 1955-1 C.B. 110.

d. *SEC restrictions.* Restrictions on the sale of stock resulting from SEC requirements reduce the value of stock, just as governmental regulation can depress the value of any class of asset. Rev. Rul. 77-287, 1977-2 C.B. 319. However, restrictions that are idiosyncratic to particular owners are not taken into account. *Kolom v. Com'r*, 644 F.2d 1282 (9th Cir.1981), *cert. denied*, 454 U.S. 1011 (restriction under § 16(b) of the Securities Act of 1934).

e. *Restrictions imposed by contract.* Under prior law, restrictions imposed on property by contract (such as a buy-sell agreement) often resulting in a reduction in value. This area is now governed by §§ 2703 and 2704, dealt with in II.C. *infra*.

f. *Control premium.* The best that can be said is that, if the interest is a controlling interest, it will be worth more (per share or per other unit of ownership) than minority interests, discussed in g., *infra*. (It does not follow that the sum of all interests must equal 100% of the enterprise value, since there may be no controlling interest. *See Estate of Newhouse v. Com'r*, 94 T.C. 193 (1990).) Whether a controlling-interest premium (or a minority-interest discount) is factored in depends on the valuation of the underlying enterprise. Thus, if the underlying enterprise is valued as a noncontrolled enterprise, it would be proper to add a control premium to the pro-rated value of the controlling interest. *Estate of Jung v. Com'r*, 101 T.C. 412 (1993). *Compare U.S. v. Parker*, 376 F.2d 402 (5th Cir.1967) (control premium dubiously added on to pro-rated value even where enterprise was valued as a controlled enterprise).

g. *Minority interest discount.* The opposite of a control premium is a minority interest discount. In *Estate of Bright v. U.S.*, 658 F.2d 999 (5th Cir.1981) *(en banc)*, it was held that when one spouse transferred (bequeathed) her community property (one-half) interest in a controlling (but less than 100%) interest in a corporation, the transfer was of a minority interest (at least where the other spouse was not the transferee).

(1) No family attribution. *Estate of Bright* and other cases have rejected a "family attribution" rule advanced by the IRS in attempting to negate minority interest discounts on a "family harmony" theory. Rev.Rul. 81-253, 1981-1 C.B. 187, *revoked by* Rev. Rul. 93-12, 1993-1 C.B. 202

(2) Minority interests created by gift. If X owns 100% of the stock of X corporation, and makes a gift of 25% of it to each of A, B, C, and D, each 25% gift is treated as a gift of a discountable minority interest. Rev. Rul. 93-12, 1993-1 C.B. 202. The theory is that the gift is of *each* minority interest, which is to be valued separately.

(3) Minority interests created by bequest:

(a) Amount includible. If X owns 100% of the stock of X corporation, and *bequeaths* 25% of it to each of A, B, C, and D, each bequest is *not* treated as a gift of a discountable minority interest, because the tax base is constituted with reference to the property owned by the decedent at death, a controlling interest (subject to a control premium). *Ahmanson Foundation v. U.S.*, 674 F.2d 761 (9th Cir. 1981). Accord *Cullman v. Com'r*, T.C. Memo. 1981-666 (same result for fractional bequest of real estate).

(b) Amount allowed as marital or charitable deduction. In contrast, the amount of the estate tax marital or charitable deduction is determined with reference to what passes to the qualified transferee. Thus, in *Ahmanson Foundation, supra*, the decedent (owning a controlling interest) made a bequest of a minority interest to a charity. Although the amount included in the gross estate did not obtain a minority-interest discount, the deductible bequest to charity was saddled with a minority interest discount. Accord, Ltr. Ruling 9050004 (marital deduction). In *Chenoweth v. Com'r*, 88 T.C. 1587 (1987), the marital bequest, being of a controlling interest, obtained the control premium.

(4) Minority interests transferred by series of gifts or of gifts and bequests. Suppose X owns 55% of Z corporation, and makes an inter vivos gift of a 28% interest to K, and thereafter makes another gift of a 27% interest to K. Here, each of the gifts is of a minority interest. The fact that they coalesce into a majority interest in the donee is an irrelevant "extrinsic" fact. However, if the gifts are made so closely together so as to appear to be part of a single transaction, they might be combined, so as to negate minority-interest discounts. *Driver v. U.S.*, 76-2 U.S.T.C. (CCH) ¶13155 (W.D.Wisc.1976). Cf. *Estate of Murphy v. Com'r*, T.C. Memo. 1990-472 (gift shortly before death combined with bequest to same person).

(5) Minority discount affected by § 2704(b). *See* II.C.3., *infra.*

4

3. **Statutory valuation rules**. Statutory valuation rules affecting the value of stock and other closely held business interests are discussed in Parts II and III, infra.

4. **Valuation discounts are cumulative**. The blockage, lack-of-marketability, and minority-interest discounts are taken one after the other on a decreasing value. For example, if all three discount percentages are applicable in a particular case, the initial value is $100x, the blockage discount (x) is 20%, the lack-of-marketability discount (y) is 15%, and the minority-interest discount (z) is 25%, the discounted value of the asset is $51x, obtained as follows: $(1 - x)(1 - y)(1 - z)\$100x$. (The discounted value is *not* $40x, which would be obtained by simply adding the discount rates together.)

F. **Debt Obligations.** The value of a debt obligation (not traded on an exchange) is merely presumed to be the unstated principal plus accrued but unpaid interest. The donor can attempt to show a lower value on account of (1) the present value of future principal and interest payments, (2) the poor condition of the debtor, and/or (3) the absence of sufficient security or collateral. Reg. § 25.2512-4.

G. **Future Interests**. The value of future interests (life estates, terms for years, remainders, etc.) is obtained by using the prescribed actuarial tables. *See* Chapter 2, VII.A.4., *supra*.

H. **Life Insurance, Annuities, and Employee Death Benefits**. *See* Chapter 2, VI.C. and D., *supra*.

I. **Real Estate**. What has been stated above in connection with property in general and closely-held business interests also applies to real estate. There are a few wrinkles:

1. **Highest and best use.** Except where § 2032A applies (for estate tax and generation-skipping tax purposes only), real estate is to be valued at its highest and best use, not at its actual use. Of course, the highest and best use is affected by zoning and land use restrictions. *Symington v. Com'r*, 87 T.C. 892 (1986). Section 2032A is discussed in Part II., *infra*, as is § 2031(c), dealing with reductions in value on account of conservation easements.

2. **Fractional ownership**. An undivided interest in real estate is usually worth less than a pro rata share of the value of the property due to (1) being subject to the rights of other co-owners and (2) the built-in transaction costs of obtaining a partition. *E.g., Estate of Pillsbury v. Com'r*, T.C. Memo 1992-425.

3. **Encumbrances.** Property might be subject to future claims or encumbrances that might possibly reduce value, assuming that the claims or encumbrances have not already been factored in during the initial valuation.

   a. *Mortgages.* Mortgages, etc., reduce value, but only where they are a lien on the property for which the decedent had no personal liability. (Only half of mortgages, etc., on community property are attributable to the transferor spouse, however). Mortgages for which the decedent was personally liable are potentially-deductible debts under § 2053, *infra*.

   b. *Homestead.* By analogy with § 2034 (concerning dower rights), homestead rights are treated as passing from the decedent to whomever might exercise such rights, and therefore do not reduce the value of real property. *Estate of Johnson v. Com'r*, 718 F.2d 1305 (5th Cir.1983).

    c. *Environmental cleanup costs.* In theory, a liability to pay such costs might reduce the value of the property if: (1) the liability existed at the time of transfer, (2) was not in fact then known (so as to not have been factored into the initial valuation), and (3) would probably have been been discovered by a reasonable buyer. *See Estate of Necastro v. Com'r*, T.C. Memo. 1994-352.

II. **SPECIAL ESTATE TAX VALUATION RULES. There are certain (mostly) statutory rules that are specific to the estate tax, including the concept of the estate tax valuation date.**

4

SPECIAL ESTATE TAX VALUATION RULES

  A. **Estate Tax Valuation Date.** *All* of the items in the gross estate are valued at the "estate tax valuation date," which is the date of death (*see* § 2031(a)) or, if the estate representative so elects under § 2032 with respect to the *entire* gross estate, the alternate valuation date.

    1. *Alternate valuation date.* If the alternate valuation election is made, the alternate valuation date for *any given asset* in the gross estate is whichever is the earlier of (a) the date which is six months after the date of death or (b) the date on which the asset is sold, exchanged, distributed, or otherwise disposed of by the estate, heir, or legatee. § 2032(a)(1) & (2). *See* Reg. § 20.2032-1(c); Rev. Rul. 71-396, 1971-2 C.B. 328 (funding of testamentary trust).

    2. *Eligibility.* The alternate valuation election can be made only if it will decrease both the gross estate *and* the net (after credit) estate and generation-skipping taxes. § 2032(c). This rule is intended to prevent an alternate valuation election for the purpose of *increasing* the aggregate § 1014 basis for income tax purposes.

    3. *Procedure.* The election, which pertains to the entire estate, is made on the estate tax return, is irrevocable, and is foreclosed if the return is filed later than one year after the return date (plus extensions). § 2032(d).

    4. *Effect of election.* Essentially, the election has no effect other than on the valuation of assets.

      a. *Actuarial valuation.* Election of the alternate valuation date has no effect on the use of actuarial tables. Thus, if *A* dies owning a vested remainder in Blackacre following the life of *B* and the alternate valuation election is made, *A*'s remainder is valued by taking the value of Blackacre at the alternate valuation date and multiplying it by the remainder factor for a person of *B*'s age as of *A*'s death. § 2032(a)(3).

      b. *Assets in gross estate.* The alternate valuation election does not enlarge the gross estate. Thus, although the alternate valuation election might affect the value of the includable item, it does not affect whether it is includable in the gross estate in the first place. *Maass v. Higgins*, 312 U.S. 443 (1941). *See* Reg. § 20.2032-1(d) & (e).

        (1) Items accrued after death. Thus, *income* items accrued after death and received or acquired by the estate, heirs, or legatees before the alternate valuation date are not thereby included in the gross estate.

(2) Items accrued before death. However, if the item accrued before death (such as interest, or dividends declared to persons of record before the date of death), or if the item embodies, in a new form, the "principal" of property that existed at death (such as a pro-rata stock dividend), the item is included in the gross estate regardless of whether an alternate valuation election is made. *See Estate of Johnston v. U.S.*, 779 F.2d 1123 (5th Cir.1986) (proceeds from sale of oil and gas in place at time of decedent's death are includible in gross estate).

c. Deductions. The value of assets qualifying for the marital and charitable deductions shall be determined under the same rules that apply to the valuation of assets included in the gross estate. § 2032(b).

B. Special Statutory Valuation Rules Affecting Real Property:

1. *Special use valuation real property.* Section 2032A, the longest provision in that part of the Code dealing with the transfer taxes, allows the estate representative to elect to value qualifying real property on the basis of its current use (as agricultural or small business real property), as opposed to the willing-buyer, willing-seller test (which, recall, would yield a "highest and best use" value).

   a. *Definitions.* Certain recurring terms are defined as follows:

      (1) Qualified use. "Qualified use" means use of the property for "farming" or in a trade or business. § 2032A(b)(2).

      (2) Farming. "Farming" includes virtually any agricultural or grazing use, including tree farming. *See* § 2032A(e)(4) & (5).

      (3) Family member. With respect to any individual, a "family member" is such person's spouse, ancestor, lineal descendant, or a lineal descendant of such person's spouse or parent. § 2032A(e)(2).

      (4) Qualified heir. A "qualified heir" is a family member (as defined immediately above) who acquired the property from the decedent (or to whom the property passed from the decedent). In addition, if a person to whom a qualified heir transfers property is a family member of that qualified heir, that person is also termed a "qualified heir." § 2032A(e)(1).

      (5) Material participation. This term is defined in Reg. § 20.2032A-3(e)(1) to mean direct and personal physical labor and/or management of the farm or business on a day-to-day basis. Material participation by the decedent is also deemed to include any period that the decedent was disabled or receiving Social Security retirement benefits.

   b. *Eligibility.* The election can be made only if *all* of the following eligibility requirements are met:

      (1) Citizenship/residency: The decedent was a citizen or resident of the United States. § 2032A(a)(1)(A).

(2) Qualified real property. The property is qualified real property, being such by satisfying *all* of the following conditions under § 2032A(b):

    (a) Property requirements. The property must be *real* property located in the United States, and must be designated in the "agreement" made in connection with the "election," *infra*. § 2032A(b)(1)(D).

    (b) Pre-death use. During at least 5 years during the 8-year period prior to the decedent's death, the decedent or a family member must have (i) owned the property, (ii) used the property for a "qualified use," *and* (iii) "materially participated" in the operation of the "farm" or other business. § 2032A(b)(1)(C).

    (c) Use at death. At death, the property must have been used for a "qualifying use" by the decedent or a "family member." § 2032A(b)(1) & (2). As to post-death use, *see* f., *infra*.

    (d) Disposition at death. The property must pass from the decedent to a "qualified heir" such that the basis of the property would be determined under § 1014 (i.e., included in the gross estate). § 2032A(b)(1) & (e)(9).

(3) Relation of property to adjusted gross estate. Fifty percent or more of the adjusted gross estate (gross estate less mortgages) must be comprised by the value of real and personal property (net of mortgages) used for a qualified use by the decedent or a family member and passing to a qualified heir. In addition, 25% of the adjusted gross estate must be comprised by the value of the real property used as a qualified use and which meets the 5-out-of-8 rule referred to in b.(2)(b), *supra*. § 2032A(b)(1)(A) & (B). Any transfers by the decedent of (nonqualifying) property within three years of death shall be ignored for purposes of applying these rules. § 2035(c)(1)(B).

c. *Election requirements.* An election can only be made on the estate tax return and is irrevocable. It covers all real property that qualifies (in other words, it cannot be made on a property-by-property basis), and it must be accompanied by an agreement, signed by each living person who has an interest in the property, which operates as a consent to application of the cessation-of-use rules (*see* f., *infra*). § 2032A(a)(1)(B) & (d).

d. *Effect of election on valuation:*

(1) Method of valuation. If the election is valid, etc., the "special use value" of "farm" real property is the present value thereof determined by dividing the cash rental for comparable land (reduced by property taxes) by the average interest rate for new Federal Land Bank loans. If there is no comparable land, value is based on net crop income or, if the estate representative elects, under the rule for (non-farm) business real property. For the latter, a facts-and-circumstances test is used, which is again keyed to actual use. *See* § 2032A(e)(7) & (8).

(2) Limit on valuation reduction. Application of § 2032A shall not result in a value reduction of more than $750,000, as indexed for inflation. This limitation is per estate, not per each item of property. § 2032A(a)(2).

(3) Income tax effect. The estate tax value under § 2032A fixes the basis for income tax purposes as well. § 1014(a)(3).

e. *Special rules:*

(1) Real property. If property meets the 5-out-of-8 rule, *supra,* residential buildings and related structures occupied regularly by the owner or manager, as well as other improvements related to the qualified use, qualify as real property. § 2032A(e)(3). Real property does not include the crops and animals themselves, except that timber sometimes qualifies as real property. *See* § 2032A(e)(13).

(2) Community property. If qualified real property was held as community property, the valuation result should be consistent with the outcome that would have occurred if the property had not been community property. § 2032A(e)(10). Presumably this rule bears mainly on the eligibility requirements.

f. *Cessation of qualified use by qualified heir.* All, or a pro rata portion, of the net estate tax savings resulting from special use valuation are recaptured (in the form of an "additional estate tax") if the "qualified heir," within 10 years of the decedent's death, either disposes of any qualified real property, or an interest therein, to any person (other than a "family member") or ceases "qualified use." § 2032A(c)(1) & (2).

(1) Instances of cessation of qualified use. Cessation of qualified use includes certain cases where the qualified heir (or family member) and/or the decedent (or family member) has failed to "materially participate" in the operation of the farm or business for periods aggregating more than three years out of any eight-year period (ending after the decedent's death, but before the death of the qualified heir). *See* § 2032A(c)(6). However, the material participation requirement is reduced to an "active management" requirement where the qualified heir is the decedent's spouse, a student, a minor, a disabled person, or a fiduciary of a minor or disabled person. *See* § 2032A(c)(7)(B)-(D).

(2) Grace period. There is a two-year "grace period" for a qualified heir to commence use after the death of the decedent. *See* § 2032A(c)(7)(A).

(3) Tax liability. The additional estate tax, if any, is personally owed by the qualified heir, unless the qualified heir arranged with the IRS to post a bond covering the maximum additional estate tax liability. § 2032A(c)(5) & (e)(11).

g. *Special rules for surviving spouse.* If property was "qualified real property" with respect to the first spouse to die (or would have been such except for a failure to file an election and agreement), the surviving spouse is deemed to "materially participate" in the operation of the farm or business even though only participating in major management decisions. Also, a surviving spouse is not deemed to "cease qualified use" just by renting to a family member on a net cash basis. Finally, the surviving spouse can claim the advantage of the "disability or Social Security retirement benefits" rule (*see* D.1.a.(5), *supra*). *See* § 2032A(b)(5) & (e)(12).

2. ***Qualified conservation easements.*** Recall from Chapter 3, IV.B.3., *supra*, that a deduction is allowable under § 2055(f) for certain estate transfers of conservation easements. Section 2031(c), enacted in 1997, provides for an "exclusion" (value reduction) of a portion of real property subject to "qualified conservation easements."

 a. *Qualified conservation easement.* A qualified conservation easement is basically a surrender of development rights to a governmental or quasi-governmental body. Commercial recreation activity (in excess of a de minimis level) must be prohibited. *See* § 2031(c)(8)(B).

 b. *Election.* The § 2031(c) exclusion is obtained by an irrevocable election made on the estate tax return. The "price" to be paid for making the election is that any portion of the property "excluded" from the gross estate under § 2031(c) obtains a carryover basis (rather than a § 1014 basis) for income tax purposes.

 c. *Creation of easement.* The easement can be created by the decedent (by instrument taking effect at death or perhaps by inter vivos instrument) or, *following the decedent's death*, by the personal representative of the decedent's estate, or a party acceding to the property ("family member" devisee or trustee). *See* § 2031(c)(8)(A)(iii), (C), and (D).

 d. *Eligible property.* The property must be within (a) 25 miles of a "metropolitan area." (b) 25 miles of a national park or national wilderness area (unless such area is not under significant development pressure, or (c) within 10 miles of an Urban National Forest. In addition, the property must have been owned by the decedent (or a "family member") for the continuous three-year period ending on the decedent's death. § 2031(c)(8)(A)(i) & (ii).

 e. *Calculating the exclusion.* The statutory language is not a model of clarity. The statute states that the exclusion is equal to the value of the "applicable percentage of the value of the land subject to a qualified conservation easement, reduced by the amount of any deduction under § 2055(f)." § 2031(c)(1)(A). Thus, the exclusion is not equal to the actual value of the conservation easement.

 (1) Applicable percentage:

 (a) Conservation easement worth 30% or more of value of the land. In this case, the percentage is 40%.

 (b) Conservation easement worth less than 30% of the value of the land. Here, the percentage is 40% reduced by 2% for each percentage point (or fraction thereof) that the conservation easement is worth less than 30% of the land. § 2031(c)(2). Thus, if the value of the conservation easement is worth 10% (or less) of the value of the land, the applicable percentage is zero.

(2) Value of the land. It is not clear from the statute whether the "value of the land" is before or after reduction by the actual value of the qualified conservation easement, but the Senate Report suggests that it is "after" being so reduced.

(3) Reduction for § 2055(f) deduction. It is also not clear, assuming "value of the land" is after being reduced by the value of the qualified conservation easement, whether the product of the applicable percentage and the value of the land is (again) reduced by the § 2055(f) deduction. There is no stated rationale or inherent logic to § 2031(c) that would suggest an answer. (If there is no "second" reduction, then the same dollars of conservation easement would generate both a deduction and an exclusion.) If "value of the land" is before taking the qualified conservation easement into account, then the amount of the exclusion would be reduced by the § 2055(f) deduction.

f. *Limitation.* The "exclusion" cannot exceed $500,000 for decedents dying in 2002 and later years. The exclusion started at $100,000 for decedents dying in 1998 and is to increase by $100,000 in each year of 1999, 2000, and 2001. The dollar figures are not indexed.

C. ***Property whose value is affected by the decedent's death.*** Rights (augmenting value) or restrictions (depressing value) with respect to property may either arise or lapse at the decedent's death. Such rights or restrictions raise the issue of whether value is: (a) the value of what the decedent had, (b) the value of what the decedent's successor obtains, (c) the greater of the two, or (d) the lesser of the two. There is no categorical solution to this issue, and, in fact, the answer may be "none of the above." *See Ithaca Trust Co. v. U.S.*, 279 U.S. 151 (1959) (value is of property transferred at death, not what decedent had or what legatee received).

1. ***The "common law" pertaining to the effect of rights and restrictions affected by death.*** Although valuation of property affected by restrictions and rights that are keyed to the decedent's death are now controlled, in part, by §§ 2703 and 2704, these provisions can only be understood with reference to the "common law" background. Moreover common law rules still control where §§ 2703 and 2704 don't apply.

a. *Time of valuation.* In general, value is determined at death, not the moment just prior to it. *U.S. v. Land,* 303 F.2d 170 (5th Cir. 1962) (stating that valuation necessarily looks forward).

b. *Lapse at death.* If a restriction or right lapses at death, the lapsed restriction or right is ignored, meaning that the asset is valued without regard to the restriction or right. *U.S. v. Land, supra; Goodman v. Granger,* 243 F.2d 264 (3d Cir. 1957), *cert. denied,* 355 U.S. 264 (in both cases, result was higher value); *Estate of Harrison v. Com'r,* T.C. Memo. 1987-8 (lapse of liquidation right at death depressed value). *Compare Estate of McClatchy v. Com'r,* 147 F.3d 1089 (9th Cir.1998) (SEC restriction lapsing "after" death by reason of provision in decedent's will is not to be ignored).

c. *Imposed at death.* Similarly, if a right or restriction is imposed by reason of the decedent's death, it would add to, or subtract from, value, as the case may be. Thus, the value of a closely-held business interest would be reduced by reason of the fact that the decedent no longer can guide the business. On the other side, insurance policies (proceeds) and employee death benefits are valued at death, rather than their lower value at the moment just prior to death.

d. *Imposed by mode of transfer.* In contrast, a restriction imposed by the way property is disposed of (or the identity of the successor in interest) does not affect value for estate-inclusion purposes. Thus, if a controlling interest is made the subject of fractional bequests, the estate will not obtain a minority interest discount. *Estate of Curry v. Com'r*, 706 F.2d 1424 (7th Cir.1983); *Ahmanson Foundation v. U.S.*, 674 F.2d 761 (9th Cir.1981). Similarly, a minority interest discount would not be lost just because the legatee ended up with a controlling interest. *Estate of Pillsbury v. Com'r*, T.C. Memo 1992-425. However, the distinction between restrictions impacted by death (where value *is* affected) and those impacted by the form of bequest (where value is *not* affected) is sometimes hard to draw. *See Estate of McClatchy, supra* (SEC restrictions) (2-1 decision); *Ahmanson Foundation, supra* (*dictum* that direction in will to destroy papers would result in zero value). *But cf.* TAM 9207004 (illegal drugs included in gross estate despite being consfiscated by government authorities immediately following decedent's death in a plane crash).

e. *Included in gross estate under different provisions.* In seeming contrast to the previous item, it has been held that stock includible in a surviving spouse's gross estate under § 2044 would not be aggregated with stock (of the same corporation) included in her gross estate under § 2033, with the result that both items obtained minority interest discounts. *Estate of Bonner v. U.S.*, 84 F.3d 196 (5th Cir.1996). The IRS doesn't agree. TAM 9550002. Query if the IRS would prevail if inclusion were obtained under §§ 2036-2038 or 2040, where the amount includible derived from an inter vivos transfer of the decedent (rather than a transfer from another person).

f. *Restrictions resulting from contracts entered into by decedent.* Restrictions, often created by buy-sell agreements, would also appear to depress value, since such restrictions affect what the estate can obtain for the property. *See* generally, Rev. Rul. 59-60, 1959-1 C.B. 237 (restrictions binding after death *may* be taken into account in appropriate circumstances).

    (1) Need to scrutinize situations involving self-imposed restrictions. A restriction that depresses value after death would, by itself, entail economic waste to the estate, which would not normally be intended (absent taxes) except possibly in a pure business context, in which case the decedent likely received consideration augmenting her potential § 2033 gross estate. Since restrictions depressing value may be tax motivated and may be self-imposed, restrictions resulting from voluntary agreements by the decedent must be scrutinized to determine if they do not in fact create an (offsetting) benefit in a natural object of the decedent's bounty. This issue commonly arises in the context of buy-sell agreements, where the contract provides (or allows) a related party to purchase a closely-held business interest at a price that is lower than fair market value. Such a right or option is called a bargain-purchase right.

(2) Is there a separate transfer gift of a bargain purchase right? As a matter of economics, a bargain-purchase right has value. If a decedent enters into a contract giving a related party a bargain purchase right, there would seem to be a transfer of value from the decedent to the related party, at least as a general matter. Rev. Rul. 80-186, 1980-2 C.B. 280 (grant to a related person of a currently-exercisable option to buy property at a bargain price is a gift equal to the value of the option). An issue might be whether the decedent transferred the bargain purchase right during life by gift or at death by bequest. If the decedent is bound by the restriction during life, it would seem that the decedent would have made an inter vivos transfer when the contract was entered into, and the estate tax value of the stock would be correspondingly reduced. However, the IRS has never attempted to impose a gift tax when the contract is entered into and the party benefiting from the restriction is a natural object of the decedent's bounty. Two possible reasons: (1) the valuation of any such gift would be problematic, since the bargain purchase, if any, would occur only after the decedent's death and the purchase, the purchase price, and the then value of the property would be subject to contingencies, and (2) there would be an issue of whether the decedent received full and adequate consideration in money or money's worth for any transfer.

(3) Restriction disregarded in certain cases. Instead of finding an inter vivos gift, the IRS has taken the position, which some courts accepted, that the restriction will be ignored for estate tax purposes if the contract was a device to pass value to a natural object of the decedent's bounty free of tax, even if there was also a business purpose (*i.e.,* to keep the business in the family). *St. Louis County Bank v. U.S.,* 674 F.2d 1207 (8th Cir. 1982). But *see Estate of Bischoff v. Com'r,* 69 T.C. 32 (1977) (restriction binding on decedent until death depresses value so long as there was a business purpose, even if economic benefit flowed to decedent's kin).

(4) Restriction not binding during decedent's life. If the contract did not prevent the decedent during life from selling the property for its full fair market value, there would have been no inter vivos gift, and the restriction would be properly ignored for estate tax purposes, at least if the restriction favors a natural object of the decedent's bounty, since the depressing effect of the restriction would be "offset" by the benefit "bequeathed" to the person who benefits from the restriction. *See U.S. v. Land, supra; Giannini v. Com'r,* 148 F.2d 285 (9th Cir.1945), *cert.denied, 326 U.S. 730.* The IRS did, nevertheless, allow such a restriction to have some effect on value if there is a business purpose for the restriction and the latter does not involve a concealed bequest to a natural object of the decedent's bounty. *See* Rev. Rul. 59-60, *supra.*

2. ***Buy-sell agreements under § 2703.*** Section 2703 now controls the estate tax valuation of property subject to buy-sell (etc.) agreements.

a. *Applicability of § 2703.* Section 2703 is applicable only to agreements, etc., entered into (or significantly modified) after October 8, 1990. Agreements entered into before then are subject to the somewhat-murky common-law rules, *supra.*

b. *Restrictions on sale or use disregarded.* Under § 2703, any buy-sell or other agreement (etc.), or any restriction on the right to sell or use the property, shall be totally disregarded *unless:*

(1) the agreement is pursuant to a bona fide business arrangement;

(2) it is not a device to effect a gratuitous transfer to (bargain purchase by) any family member; *and*

(3) its terms are comparable to similar arrangements entered into by persons in an arms' length transaction.

The legislative history indicates that § 2703 was intended to adopt the position taken in *St. Louis County Bank v. U.S., supra,* namely, that the fact of a bona fide business arrangement (including the retention of family control) does not by itself give estate tax effect to the agreement. The third requirement is new. (Nevertheless, it was applied in a case arising under prior law, *Estate of Lauder v. Com'r,* T.C. Memo. 1994-527.)

c. *Restrictions binding before and after death.* The common-law rule that a restriction cannot be given effect unless binding on the decedent up to death (and binding on the estate or successor after death) is retained.

d. *Possible application to interests in entities.* The IRS appears to be developing the position that restrictions built into an interest in an entity (such as restrictions on sale of a limited partnership interest) can be disregarded under § 2703. If successful, application of § 2703 would defeat the lack-of-marketability discount. *See* TAM 9842003.

3. **Restrictions on liquidation under § 2704(b).** In the absence of statute, a lack-of-marketability discount is available where the owner of the interest could neither sell nor liquidate the interest for a specified period of time. Section 2703, supra, has potential application to restrictions on sale. Section 2704(b) deals with restrictions on liquidation, and impacts not only on lack-of-marketability discounts but also minority-interest discounts, which exist, in part, due to an inability to liquidate.

a. *Interests affected.* Section § 2704(b) applies to restrictions (created after October 8, 1990) on liquidation of an entity (or interest therein) that, after an estate (or gift) transfer, either lapses (in whole or in part) or can be removed by the transferor or any member of the transferor's family (as defined in § 2704(c)(2)).

b. *Restrictions on liquidation disregarded.* Such a restriction is disregarded where (a) the transfer of the interest is to a "members of the family" (meaning the donor's spouse, any ancestor or descendant of the donor or the donor's spouse, a brother or sister of the donor, or any spouse of any such ancestor, descendant, or sibling), and (b) immediately after the transfer the donor and family members are in "control" (meaning at least 50% by vote, value, capital, or profits interest, or any general partnership interest in a limited partnership).

c. *Other restrictions*. The same rule also can be extended by regulations to other restrictions that would depress value for transfer tax purposes. However, no such regulations have been proposed or issued.

d. *Exception for restrictions imposed by law*. Section 2704(b) does not apply to restrictions imposed by state or federal law. § 2704(b)(3)(B). This exception is important, because limited partnership or LLC law may itself impose the restriction on liquidation.

e. *Financing exception*. Commercially reasonable restrictions imposed by non-family-member lenders are also unaffected by § 2704(b). § 2704(b)(3)(A).

4. ***Lapse of voting or liquidation rights under § 2704(a).*** Suppose a decedent owns (preferred) stock in a corporation that has liquidation rights that lapse at death. The lapse of the decedent's liquidation rights is the equivalent of imposing a restriction (barring liquidation) that takes effect immediately after death, and this would normally produce a reduction in the value of such interest. *Estate of Harrison v. Com'r*, T.C. Memo. 1987-8. Under § 2704(a), however, the lapse of any voting or liquidation right is a deemed transfer if the person holding such right, together with "members of the family" (*supra*) "control" the corporation or partnership. The amount of the (gift or estate) transfer is the excess of the value of all of such holder's interests in the entity before such lapse over such value after such lapse. In effect, the amount subject to transfer tax is the pre-lapse value of the property. The Treasury can issue regulations applying § 2704(a) to rights similar to voting and liquidation rights, but so far it has not done so.

III. **SPECIAL GIFT TAX VALUATION RULES. There are a few rules that impact primarily on gift tax valuation. These are basically covered in Chapter 2, *supra*.**

A. **Annuities, Employee Death Benefits, and Unmatured Life Insurance Policies.** *See* Chapter 2, at VI., *supra*.

SPECIAL GIFT TAX VALUATION RULES

B. **Partial-Interest Gifts**. The basis and use of actuarial tables is discussed in Chapter 2, VII.A. Partial-interest gifts are subject to § 2702, discussed in Chapter 2, at VII.B., *supra*.

C. **Gifts of senior interests in entities.** Gifts of preferred stock and other senior equity interests in entities are subject to the special valuation rules of § 2701, discussed in Chapter 2, at VII.C., *supra*.

IV. **SPECIAL GENERATION-SKIPPING TAX VALUATION RULES. General valuation rules applicable to estate and gift tax transfers also apply for purposes of the GST.**

SPECIAL GENERATION-SKIPPING TAX VALUATION RULES

A. **Direct-Skip Transfers**. A direct-skip transfer, by definition, is a transfer simultaneously subject to estate or gift tax. It follows that these valuations (including use of the alternate valuation date for estate-included transfers) generally control. It is clear that special valuation under § 2032A is applicable in this situation. § 2624(b). It is unclear if the § 2031(c) "exclusion" with respect to qualified conservation easements applies. The § 2057 deduction for closely-held business interests does not apply.

B. Alternate Valuation Date for Certain Taxable Terminations. If a taxable termination occurs as the result of a person's death, an alternate valuation date election can be made for purposes of valuing the property involved in the taxable termination. § 2624(c).

CHAPTER 4 - QUESTIONS, ANSWERS, AND TIPS

EXAM TIPS:

1. Although valuation is often "where the action is" in estate planning and litigation, valuation questions are not likely to feature prominently in an exam in a basic estate and gift tax course (much less a course in Wills and Estates) due to the fact that valuation is so highly fact dependent. Indeed, valuation topics may be de-emphasized in an estate and gift tax course because: (1) valuation is not given much attention in the text, (2) there are many other topics that have higher priority or are more intellectually challenging, and (3) the student learns about valuation in practice and at CLE programs.

2. In dealing with valuation issues, be sure to consider statutory provisions, such as §§ 2032A, 2703, and 2704 and their relation to the underlying "tax common law" of valuation.

3. Do not lose sight of the fact that the willing-buyer, willing-seller test is an artificial construct that requires that certain facts, especially those involving intra-family relations, are to be disregarded.

REVIEW QUESTION:

Harry initially owns 100% of the voting preferred stock of X Corporation. An owner of the preferred stock in a corporation generally has no right to "put" the stock back to the Corporation (cause his interest to be liquidated), and no such right exists under X Corporation's by-laws. Harry created X Corporation, and has been its CEO and driving force. All the stock of X Corporation has greatly appreciated in value. The preferred stock as a class elects 4 out of 7 members of the Board of Directors. The X Corporation by-laws stipulate that the voting rights attached to preferred stock terminate on the owner's death. The common stock elects the other three Board Members. The voting common stock is owned 50% by each of Harry's daughters (by an previous wife). The corporate by-laws stipulate that the corporation cannot be liquidated until the year 2015, at which time a vote of 60% of the common stock is needed to liquidate. In the absence of this provision in the by-laws, State law would provide that 80% of the voting interests are needed to liquidate X Corporation. Finally, all shareholders are prohibited from making any gift, sale, or pledge of the stock to any outsider during life.

Harry makes an inter vivos gift of 40% of his voting preferred to his wife Harriet in the year 2000.

Harry dies in 2002, leaving 1/3 of his preferred stock to each of Harriet (in a marital deduction QTIP trust) and his two daughters.

In 2003, Harriet proposes to X Corporation that they enter into an agreement to the effect that the Corporation will purchase the stock that Harriet owns personally for a price equal to 60% of what the stock would otherwise be valued for estate tax purposes. Harriet dies in 2009.

Sort out and discuss the valuation issues raised by the foregoing.

ANSWER:

The first issue has to do with Harry's gift of 40% of the preferred to his wife Harriet. If the gift were to any other person, Harry might try to claim discounts for lack of marketability, restrictions on sale, and restrictions on liquidation, and Harry would succeed in claiming a minority interest discount, because what Harriet receives is a minority interest (even though Harry had a majority interest and even though it may be expected that Harry and Harriet will act in concert). However, since the gift qualifies for the gift tax marital deduction, and since basis of appreciated property is not affected by the value at the time of gift (see § 1015), the valuation issues are moot. In fact, Harry does not even have to file a gift tax return here. See § 6019(2).

On Harry's death, the normal procedure would be to value X Corporation as an entity without regard to the quality of any interests therein. This would be a fact question. The value of the entity as a going concern would undoubtedly by reduced by reason of the fact that its driving force, Harry, is no longer there to guide it. This may be referred to as the "loss of key person" discount.

Turning to the value of the interest included in H's gross estate (60% of the voting preferred), all of it (even the marital deduction portion) has to be valued, because the income tax basis depends on estate tax valuation. § 1014.

The stock would be valued at the date of death, unless the alternate valuation date is elected for Harry's entire estate, but this is only possible in the event that Harry's taxable estate (as a whole) and net estate tax would be reduced by such an election. Any valuation discounts, including the "key person" discount, would be deemed to exist as of the date of Harry's death. Thus, any valuation discounts would not *by themselves* create a decrease in the value of Harry's stock *after* his death such as would render conceivable an alternate-valuation-date election.

Since Harry owns preferred stock, which normally carries a fixed (and perhaps) guaranteed rate of return, Harry's preferred stock may be valued in a way similar to a bond, that is, by discounting the future cash flow back to Harry's death, rather than by applying some percentage against the X Corporation entity value. In other words, entity valuation (and a "key person" discount) may help Harry's estate very little under these facts (unless X Corporation can avoid, or has avoided, paying dividends).

Harry's interest would initially obtain a lack-of-marketability discount (apart from the restrictions on sale and liquidation), since X Corporation is a closely-held family corporation.

Harry has 60% of the voting power to elect a majority of the Board of Directors. Therefore Harry has a controlling interest, which creates the possibility of a "control premium." Harry's executor can argue that the control premium was not worth very much to Harry in dollar terms, since Harry had only fixed-return preferred stock and no common stock. (This depends on the terms of the preferred stock.)

The executor can argue that there is no control premium because the voting rights on Harry's preferred lapse at Harry's death. This argument is technically correct, but at this point § 2704(a) steps in to deem an estate transfer (estate inclusion) equal to the difference between the value of the stock (but disregarding the lapse feature) and the (lower) value of the same property because of the lapse of voting rights. All the pre-conditions for applying §

2704(a) are in place. For the operation of this provision, see Reg. § 25.2704-1(f) (Example 1), which involves a similar fact situation. In effect, section 2704(a) restores whatever value to the property would otherwise be lost by reason of the lapse at death of voting rights.

In any event, Harry's estate cannot claim a minority interest discount on account of the fractionalized bequests, under the *Ahmanson Foundation* case. (That case might be criticized as being inconsistent with the *Land* case, which states that valuation "looks forward," which implies that one values what the respective legatees get, which are minority interests, at least in the daughters' case. On the other hand, what is valued is the interest of the decedent, rather than the individual legacies.)

As a result of the bequest of 20% of the stock into a QTIP trust, Harriet (arguably) ends up with a controlling interest by reason of the fact that she alone can elect a majority of the Board, so that under *Chenoweth* there would be a "control premium" on the marital deduction. However, the bequest itself was of a minority interest, without any voting rights, so that the marital deduction would be burdened by a minority interest discount under *Ahmanson Foundation*. Moreover, it seems that one cannot aggregate pre-existing outright ownership together with the quasi-ownership obtained under the QTIP trust bequest. *Estate of Pillsbury*; *Estate of Bonner*. (It is unclear if there is a deemed bequest of voting rights or value under § 2704(a) that would alter this result, but it would appear not, since neither § 2704(a) nor the regulations say that there is a deemed bequest to any particular person.)

The next issue has to do with the restriction on sale, which would normally depress value further. Restrictions on sale are, however, disregarded under § 2703(a)(2), unless the restriction satisfies all three of the requirements of § 2703(b). It is debatable if the restriction on sale satisfies any business purpose other than that of maintaining family control. The *Estate of Bischoff* case (dubiously) held that maintaining family control was a business purpose. Query if that holding survives the subsequent enactment of § 2703 in 1990. Another issue is whether this restriction satisfies the arm's-length-equivalence test. On the one hand, it appears that nobody gave any dollar's-worth consideration for these restrictions, but it is conceivable that unrelated parties might agree (or have agreed) to such a restriction in the same or similar business. See Reg. § 25.2703-1(b)(4). The "disguised transfer" test does not seem to be implicated here, because there is no bargain-purchase opportunity. All things considered, the sale restriction may well be disregarded, but it is not an open-and-shut case.

The restriction on liquidation of the entity will be disregarded, since all of the requirements of § 2704(b) are satisfied. These facts fall under neither of the "state law" or "financing" exceptions found in § 2704(b)(3). See Reg. § 25.2704-2(d) (Example 3).

After Harry's death, Harriet enters into a buy-sell agreement with X Corporation. The IRS does not usually assert an inter vivos gift in this situation, even though she is creating, for no consideration in money's worth, a bargain purchase opportunity that will benefit the daughters.

On Harriet's death, there are all of the same valuation issues that existed on Harry's death. Harriet has voting control on account of her 40% preferred stock acquired by gift and included in her gross estate under § 2033. The QTIP interest that is separately included under § 2044 obtains a minority interest discount, because it is not aggregated with the stock she already owns. The only additional issue is whether the buy-sell agreement will be given affect so as to reduce value. Again, it will, unless § 2703(b) applies, but this appears to be a disguised transfer to the natural objects of her bounty. Her executor might claim that stepdaughters are not the natural objects of her bounty, but that claim seems disingenuous in light of the fact that she entered into this agreement without receiving any money's worth consideration.

THE GENERATION-SKIPPING TAX

▶ **CHAPTER SUMMARY**

5

CHAPTER 5: THE GENERATION-SKIPPING TAX

Introduction. A dynastic trust can avoid gift and estate tax at succeeding generations by conferring nontaxable interests and powers (income interests for life and special powers of appointment) upon its beneficiaries. To plug this perceived gap in the transfer taxes, a generation-skipping tax (GST) was enacted in 1976, which, roughly-speaking, imposed a tax upon the expiration of the interest (or powers) of beneficiaries in a lower generation than the settlor, if the succeeding beneficial interest was held by beneficiaries in a still lower generation. The prototype situation is where mother creates a trust, income to children for life, remainder (upon the death of the last child) to the settlor's then living issue. The death of any child of the settlor does not result in estate inclusion, since the expired interest of any child is then worth zero, but the death of the last child gave rise to generation-skipping tax. The 1976 GST was considered to be unsatisfactory for various reasons, such as the treatment of special powers of appointment and the concept of the "deemed transferor." A given generation-skipping transfer of a deemed transferor (a person located in an intermediate generation) was treated as a gift or estate transfer of the deemed transferor. Thus, the 1976 GST was integrated with the federal gift and estate tax. The 1976 GST was retroactively repealed in 1986, and was replaced by the current GST.

The current GST is similar to the 1976 GST insofar as it imposes a tax when the interest of intermediate-generation beneficiaries expires. However, the expiration of a special power of appointment is not a taxable event. The current GST is broader than the 1976 GST insofar as it subjects to tax outright transfers that skip a generation, such as outright gifts to grandchildren. Finally, the concept of "deemed transferor" was abolished. The current GST is a separate tax apart from the estate and gift tax, with a flat (55%) rate and a lifetime (*i.e.*, cumulative) exemption for each transferor. The transferor is the most recent person who is subject to estate or gift tax with respect to the trust, meaning (in the typical case) the creator of the trust. Thus, and stated crudely, cumulative generation-skipping transfers "of" a transferor are subject to an additional 55% tax to the extent that they exceed the exemption ($1 million, as indexed for inflation).

Since the current GST is relatively young, and it will take some time for taxable events under it to unfold, the "law" of the GST is found mostly in the Code and regulations, rather than in cases and rulings.

OVERVIEW   **I.   OVERVIEW. The 1986 generation-skipping tax applies to gratuitous transfers that "skip" (are not subject to estate or gift tax at) a generation below that of the transferor.**

   A.   Effective Dates. The current generation-skipping tax applies only to "generation-skipping transfers" (*see* below) that occur *with respect to*:

   1.   *Testamentary transfers.* Transfers by will or under a revocable trust are potentially subject to the GST, where the decedent or grantor died after December 31, 1986 (or where the decedent or grantor died before such date but the will or trust was executed after October 21, 1986), but not in cases where the decedent or grantor was incompetent at all times after September 25, 1985 and to the time of death.

   2.   *Inter vivos transfers*. Inter vivos transfers (other than revocable trusts) made after September 25, 1985, are potentially subject to the current GST.

3. ***Additions to pre-1986 trusts.*** If an addition is made to a trust that would otherwise not be subject to the GST, the portion of the trust attributable to the addition shall be potentially subject to the GST. *See* Reg. § 26.2601-1(b)(1)(iv).

4. ***Modification of pre-1986 trusts.*** The significant modification of the terms of a pre-1986 trust may cause it to be subject to the current GST. *See* Lt Ruling 8851017.

B. **Relation to Estate and Gift Tax.** The generation-skipping tax is an additional tax separate from the federal estate and gift tax. A rough outline of the tax, and its relation to the gift and estate taxes, follows. A generation-skipping transfer must take one of three possible forms: (1) a "direct skip transfer," (2) a "taxable distribution," or (3) a "taxable termination."

1. ***Direct-skip transfer.*** A direct-skip transfer occurs upon the making of a gift or estate transfer that is "subject to" federal gift or estate tax (whether or not a gift or estate tax is actually due), where (roughly speaking) *all* of the donees or legatees are at least *two* generations *below* the transferor.

    a. *Tax effect.* If a direct-skip transfer occurs, the generation-skipping tax will be imposed, in addition to the gift or estate tax, on the occasion of the transfer (*i.e.*, simultaneously with any estate or gift tax).

    b. *Common direct-skip transfers.* Common types of direct-skip transfers are:

        (1) an outright gift or bequest to a grandchild (assuming the grandchild's parent is alive).

        (2) proceeds of life insurance, includible in the decedent's gross estate, are payable to a grandchild (again assuming that the grandchild's parent is alive).

        (3) a bequest into testamentary trust for the exclusive benefit of the grantor's grandchildren (again assuming that the grandchildren's parent is alive).

2. ***Taxable distributions and terminations.*** A "taxable distribution" or "taxable termination" is a transfer that occurs with respect to a "generation-skipping trust" or "trust equivalent," namely, a trust (or similar arrangement involving annuities, life insurance, employee death benefits, etc.), where at least some beneficiaries occupy two (or more) generations below that of the transferor.

    a. *Tax effect.* The creation of the trust (or trust equivalent) is subject to estate or gift tax, but not generation-skipping tax.

    b. *When tax liability arises.* The taxable distribution or taxable termination occurs later, namely, when all beneficial interests in the money or property subject to the transfer held by a generation below that of the transferor expire in favor of a still lower generation.

    Example 1: To illustrate, assume a testamentary trust, income to the testator's child for life, remainder to a grandchild, with the trustee having discretion to invade corpus for the benefit of the grandchild.

5

(a) *Trust creation.* The *creation* of trust is subject to estate or gift tax but not generation-skipping tax (this is not a direct-skip transfer since the first generation below the transferor is represented);

(b) *Distributions to child.* Distributions of income (or corpus) to the testator's *child* are not generation-skipping transfers (since the distribution stays within the *first* generation below the grantor).

(c) *Distributions to grandchild.* A distribution of corpus (or income) to the testator's *grandchild* is a "taxable distribution" (since the child's interest in the trust represented by such distribution expires in favor of the grandchild). The distribution to the grandchild "skips" the child's generation.

(d) *Death of the child.* The death of the testator's child constitutes a "taxable termination" (since the child's interest in the trust expires in favor of the grandchild).

3. ***Exception for taxable terminations and distributions subject to estate and gift tax.*** If a taxable termination or distribution is also subject to estate or gift tax (usually due to the possession or exercise by a lower-generation beneficiary of a general power of appointment), the generation-skipping tax is "ousted." Thus, in Example 1, part (d), immediately above, if the testator's child died possessed of a general power of appointment, the trust would be included in such child's gross estate, and there would not be a taxable termination or distribution.

4. ***Rates.*** The generation-skipping tax rate is a flat rate equal to the highest marginal gift or estate tax rate, which is 55%. (Since the rate is a flat rate, the tax base is not cumulative, as it is under the estate and gift tax.)

5. ***Exemptions, deductions, and credits.*** The GST has its own limited system of tax-free allowances. The unified transfer tax credit of the estate and gift tax is not applicable here.

   a. *Exemption equivalent.* There is the functional equivalent of an exemption, factored into the tax rate, that has the effect of exempting the first $1 million (as indexed for inflation) of generation-skipping transfers, per transferor, from tax. The "transferor" is, basically, the last person who was subject to estate or gift tax with respect to the trust property.

   b. *Marriage.* There is no marital deduction as such, but transfers between spouses are considered intra-generational transfers which are generally not subject to tax.

   c. *Charitable transfers.* Transfers to charity are usually not taxed for essentially the same reason as intra-generational transfers.

   d. *Present-interest exclusion.* There is a narrower version of the gift tax present-interest exclusion.

   e. *Administration expenses.* There is a deduction for GST administration expenses.

6. *Computation of tax.* The generation-skipping tax is imposed with respect to any generation-skipping transfer, as described above.

a. *Tax base.* The tax base is the amount (value) subject to the current generation-skipping transfer, after any deductions or exclusions (other than the "exemption equivalent" referred to in 5.a., *supra*).

b. *Inclusion ratio.* The tax base is, in effect, multiplied first by the 55% rate and then by the "inclusion ratio." The inclusion ratio is 1.0 minus the "exclusion ratio" (basically, the exemption equivalent allocated to the transfer divided by the value of the *initial* transfer). If the *exclusion* ratio is 1.0 (because the transferor's exemption equivalent allocated to the transfer is equal to the value of the transfer), the tax is zero, because the "inclusion ratio" is zero (1.0 minus 1.0).

7. *Payment.* The tax return and payment are due shortly after the generation-skipping transfer occurs. The tax is generally payable: (1) by the transferor (or transferor's estate), in the case of a direct skip; (2) by the distributee, in the case of a taxable distribution; and, (3) by the trust, in the case of a taxable termination.

II. GENERATION-SKIPPING TRANSFERS DEFINED. Moving to specifics, this section outlines the technical definitions pertaining to generation-skipping transfers, namely, direct-skip transfers, taxable distributions, and taxable terminations.

GENERATION-SKIPPING TRANSFERS DEFINED

A. Preliminary Definitions. The crucial statutory terms, such as "direct-skip transfer," are in turn dependent on other statutory definitions.

1. *Transferor.* The term "transferor" refers to the person who most recently transferred the property by inter vivos transfer or at death such that (a) such transfer was then "subject to" estate or gift tax and (b) a generation-skipping transfer either occurs at the time of transfer (as in a direct-skip transfer) or will (or might) occur later (as in a taxable distribution or termination). § 2652(a)(1).

a. *"Subject to" estate or gift tax.* A transfer is "subject to" estate or gift tax if it is included in the gross estate or is treated as a gross gift, even though there is no net gift or estate tax attributable to the transfer on account of an estate or gift tax exclusion, deduction, or credit.

b. *General power of appointment.* A person who possesses, exercises, releases, or suffers a lapse of a *general* power of appointment is deemed to be a transferor.

c. *Transferee spouse.* Similarly a transferee spouse is the deemed transferor of a QTIP trust created by her spouse where a QTIP election was made, and the trust is subject to gift or estate tax with respect to such surviving spouse under § 2044 or § 2519.

d. *Reverse QTIP election.* However, in this situation the first transferor spouse can make a "reverse QTIP election," effective for generation-skipping tax purposes only, which has the effect of treating such first transferor spouse as the "transferor" for generation-skipping tax purposes. § 2652(a)(3).

e. *Gifts by spouses.* In a gift of community property, or a gift subject to a § 2513 gift-splitting election, each spouse is the transferor of one half. § 2652(a)(2).

2. *Generation assignment.* The donees, legatees, and beneficiaries are assigned to various generations above or below the transferor or in the same generation as the transferor. Any former or current spouse of the transferor spouse and charities are deemed to occupy the same generation as the transferor. Relatives of the transferor are assigned generations according to the nature of the relationship, not age. Spouses of relatives are deemed to be in the same generation as the relative to whom they are married. Nonrelatives are assigned to generations according to age differential. *See* § 2651.

3. *Predeceased-parent rule.* Basically, if the parent of a beneficiary is dead on the date of initial transfer (the date the transfer is subject to estate or gift tax), such parent's descendants all move up a generation. *See* § 2651(e). Thus, if a person makes an outright gift to a grandchild, and the intervening link (the parent of the grandchild who is the child of the transferor) is dead when the gift is made, then the grandchild is considered to be the transferor's child, so that the gift is not a direct-skip transfer.

4. *Trust.* The term "trust" includes not only an express trust but also arrangements involving property interests and contract rights which, alone or in combination, have an effect similar to trusts in that successive (or deferred) interests and rights are created. These include (a) life estates (or terms for years) and remainders and (b) annuity-insurance combinations. *See* § 2652(b). These are sometimes referred to as "trust equivalents."

5. *Interest.* A person (other than a charity) has an interest in a trust (or trust equivalent) if she has a *current* right to receive income or corpus or is a *current* permissible recipient of income or corpus. Thus, neither holders of a special power of appointment nor remainders (vested or contingent) have "interests," but potential appointees under a currently-exercisable special inter vivos power of appointment do have interests. Charities possess (remainder) "interests" where the trust interest qualifies for the gift or estate tax charitable deduction (the trust is a charitable remainder unitrust or annuity trust or a pooled income fund). A person does not have an interest solely by reason of having a support obligation towards a beneficiary of a discretionary trust or of a custodial account (or similar type of trust). *See* § 2652(c).

6. *Skip person.* A skip person is any individual who is two or more generations below the "transferor," taking into account the predeceased-parent rule. Thus, a grandchild of the transferor is a skip person, unless the grandchild's parent (who is the transferor's child) was dead at the time the transfer was subject to estate or gift tax. The definition of skip person also includes a *trust* in which *all* of the beneficial "interests" are held by skip persons. Finally, a trust is a skip person if (a) no person has an "interest" in the trust (at the time the determination is to be made) and (b) no distribution can ever be made to a "nonskip person," *infra.* § 2613(a). Neither a charity nor a qualified charitable remainder trust can be a skip person.

7. *Nonskip person.* A nonskip person is any person who is not a "skip person," after taking into account the predeceased-parent rule § 2613(b).

5

B. **Definitions Pertaining to "Generation-Skipping Transfer."** The generation-skipping tax is imposed on a "generation-skipping transfer." § 2601. The latter term refers to any of a "direct-skip transfer," "taxable termination," or "taxable distribution." § 2611(a).

1. ***Direct-skip transfer.*** Generally, a direct-skip transfer is any transfer of an interest by the "transferor" to a "skip person" that is also "subject to" estate or gift tax. § 2612(c)(1).

2. ***Taxable termination:***

   a. *Basic definition.* A taxable termination occurs upon the termination of any "interest" *(see supra)* in a trust (or trust equivalent), *unless* (1) any non-skip person has an "interest" in the trust immediately after the termination and (2) after such termination distributions *cannot* be made to skip persons. § 2612(b)(1).

   b. *One taxable termination per generation.* The definition of taxable termination generally assures that there will be only one taxable termination per generation.

      Example 2: Assume *T* creates a trust, income and/or corpus to or among *T*'s children in the trustee's discretion, and upon the death of the last surviving child remainder to *T*'s then-surviving issue per stirpes. Here all of *T*'s children have "interests," since they are current permissible recipients of income or corpus. A taxable termination occurs only upon the death of the last survivor of *T*'s children, assuming that the remainder passes to one or more grandchildren, etc. Before such time, nonskip persons (children of *T*) continue to have interests in the trust.

   c. *Partial taxable termination.* A trust may suffer a "partial" taxable termination.

      Example 3: Assume Y creates a trust for her mother for life, remainder to Y's then living issue per stirpes, and upon the death of her mother Y is survived by a child and the three children of a deceased child. Here, upon the mother's death, half of the property passes to nonskip persons (the surviving child) and half to skip persons (the three grandchildren).

   d. *Taxable termination of separate share, etc.* A partial taxable termination can occur under a "separate share" rule even where nonskip persons continue to have interests, but only where the interest of a lineal descendant of the transferor is involved.

      Example 4: If *A* creates a trust for her children, and on the death of any child that child's share is to be set aside in a separate share or trust for the benefit of such deceased child's issue, the death of a child (leaving surviving issue) triggers a taxable termination as to that share, even though other children of the transferor are then living. § 2612(a)(2).

3. ***Taxable distribution.*** A taxable distribution occurs when property (income or corpus) is distributed from a trust to a skip person. § 2612(c).

5

4. *Priority-ordering rules.* Certain rules, such as who is liable to pay the tax, vary according to which category of "generation-skipping transfer" a given transfer falls under.

a. *Taxable termination ousts taxable distribution.* The taxable distribution rule cedes priority to both taxable-termination and direct-skip-transfer rules. § 2612(b). Thus, in Example 2, *supra*, the taxable event occurring upon the termination of the trust is characterized as a taxable termination, not a taxable distribution, even though the distribution of all or part of the trust to the remainder (one or more skip persons) literally satisfies the definition of "taxable distribution."

b. *Direct skip takes precedence.* Direct-skip rules implicitly take priority over taxable termination rules.

Example 5: Assume that *S* creates a trust, income to *B* for life, giving *B* a general power of appointment by will, and *B* exercises this power in favor of her grandchildren. There is a direct-skip transfer at *B*'s death, since the property is currently included in *B*'s gross estate and goes immediately to skip persons (*B* being the "transferor"). Although the expiration of *B*'s life estate also satisfies the definition of "taxable termination" (*S* being the transferor), the fact that the property is subject to estate tax at *B*'s death effectively precludes *B*'s death from being a taxable termination (but such inclusion partially satisfies the direct-skip transfer definition). In addition, under § 2653(a) the "transferor" (*B*) is deemed to be dropped down into the generation of the grandchild's parents immediately after the direct-skip generation-skipping transfer, so that the termination distribution to the grandchildren, who are now no longer "skip persons," cannot be a taxable termination (although it is a direct-skip transfer).

C. **Complex Situations.** Certain special rules exist for complex situations.

1. *Successive skips.* A given trust may suffer generation-skipping transfers at successive generations. The most common situation involves two or more taxable terminations.

Example 6: If *X* creates a trust, income to child *C* for life, then to grandchild *G* for life, remainder to great-grandchildren, the deaths of both *C* and *G* result in taxable terminations.

2. *Direct-skip transfer followed by taxable termination.* Notwithstanding the rule that the direct-skip idea has priority, a direct-skip transfer can *subsequently* be the subject of a taxable termination or distribution.

Example 7: If *A* (having living children) creates a trust for the exclusive benefit of her grandchildren, remainder to great-grandchildren, the creation of the trust is a direct-skip transfer, and the death of the last surviving grandchild constitutes a taxable termination.

3. *Multiple skips.* A generation-skipping transfer that involves a skip "over" two or more generations at once is only treated as a single taxable event. Thus, an outright gift to a great-grandchild involves only one generation-skipping transfer, not two.

D. Effect of Qualified Disclaimers. If a person makes a "qualified disclaimer" under § 2518, such person cannot be a "transferor" for GST purposes. § 2654(c). However, the disclaimer could produce a generation-skipping transfer from the original transferor.

Example 8: If A bequeathed Blackacre to child B, who files a timely disclaimer such that grandchild G takes, A ends up making a direct-skip estate transfer to G.

E. Exclusions. There are rules that exclude certain generation-skipping transfers from tax.

    1. *Tuition and medical care.* A gift or distribution that is a direct payment of tuition or medical care within the meaning of § 2503(e) is not a generation-skipping transfer. § 2611(b)(1).

    2. *Direct-skip transfers exempt from gift tax.* If all or a portion of a *direct-skip* transfer is exempt from gift tax under the $10,000 exclusion of § 2503(b) or (c), it is not a generation-skipping transfer. § 2642(c).

        a. *Outright gifts.* This exclusion is mostly available for outright gifts.

        b. *Gifts in trust.* In the case of gifts in trust (etc.) which qualify under § 2503(b) or (c), the exclusion is lost unless:

            (1) only the beneficiary can receive income or corpus during the beneficiary's life; and

            (2) any amount remaining at the beneficiary's death is includable in the beneficiary's gross estate (*i.e.,* under § 2033 or § 2041).

    3. *Prior tax at same or lower generation.* A generation-skipping transfer is exempt if (and to the extent that) the transferees in a prior generation-skipping transfer (with respect to the same property) were in the same or lower generation as the transferees of the current (but for the exemption) generation-skipping transfer, so long as the effect of the exemption is not to avoid generation-skipping tax. § 2611(b).

Example 9: Assume that A creates a trust for her child B for life, then for her grandchild G for life (if living), then for her child C for life, remainder to then living issue. The death of B is a taxable termination, since C, a non-skip person, does not then have an "interest," and since distributions will then be made to a skip person, G. The death of G is not a taxable termination because a non-skip person, C, does then have an interest. The later death of C would be a second taxable termination (if there were no more surviving children), but this taxable termination is exempted to the extent of the dollar amount treated as a prior taxable termination, since the transferee is in the same or lower generation as G, the transferee of the first taxable termination.

    4. *Taxable terminations and distributions subject to estate or gift tax.* See I.B.3., *supra.* The person subject to estate or gift tax becomes a "transferor." See II.A.1.b., *supra.*

Example 10: Assume that *A* creates a trust for child *B* for life, giving *B* a general power of appointment, remainder to grandchild *C*. The death of *B*, which would otherwise be a taxable termination, is not a taxable termination because it is subject to estate tax under § 2041. Also, *B* becomes the transferor, but *C* is not a "skip person" with respect to such superseding transferor. However, if *C* were *A*'s great-grandchild, *B*'s death would entail a direct-skip transfer, since *C* would then be a skip person in relation to *B*.

5. ***Predeceased-parent rule.*** This rule, described at II.A.3., *supra,* sometimes has the effect of exempting transfers from tax, because persons who would otherwise be skip persons become non-skip persons.

6. ***Per-transferor exclusion.*** The $1 million per-transferor exclusion is factored into the rate, as described in IV.B., *infra.*

III. **THE TAX BASE. For each type of generation-skipping transfer, the tax base rules vary.**

THE TAX BASE

A. **Property Transferred.** Initially, the generation-skipping tax base is the amount of money or property that satisfies the definition of generation-skipping transfer, *supra.*

Example 11: If *A* creates a trust, income to child *B* for life, remainder to be divided between child *C* and grandchild *G,* the death of *B* involves a generation-skipping transfer of half of the trust in existence at *B*'s death (assuming *B* is survived by *C*).

B. **Valuation.** Normal valuation rules are applied as of the date of the generation-skipping transfer. Special valuation rules are described in Chapter IV, at IV. A separate alternate-valuation date election can be made for taxable terminations occurring at a person's death, even if said election is not made for estate tax purposes. § 2624(a)-(c).

C. **Consideration Offsets.** The amount subject to tax is reduced by any consideration in money's worth received by the transferor from a transferee. § 2624(d). The consideration is valued as of the time the transferor receives the right to it.

D. **Possible Reduction by Estate, Gift, and Generation-Skipping Taxes.** The basic issue here is whether the tax base includes the gift, estate, and generation-skipping taxes themselves. Although the discussion below is complex, it is important for obtaining an understanding of the actual impact of the taxes on various forms of transfer, and is therefore crucial for planning purposes.

1. ***Incidence of gift and estate taxes.*** A taxable termination or taxable distribution is made out of property that was *previously* subject to estate or gift tax. A direct-skip transfer by definition is one that is *simultaneously* subject to gift or estate tax.

   a. *Estate taxes.* Estate taxes, recall, are payable out of property constituting the gross estate. The estate taxes are not themselves deductible for estate tax purposes, *i.e.,* they are included in the estate tax base. The ultimate burden of estate taxes is a function of the governing instrument(s), state law, and federal law. *See* Ch. 3.

5

b. *Gift taxes.* In general, gift taxes are payable by the donor out of her own pocket. Also, they are excluded from the gift and estate tax bases, except that gift taxes on gifts made within three years of death are included in the gross estate of the donor. *See* § 2035(b).

c. *Effect on generation-skipping tax base.* The generation-skipping tax base is "after" any estate and gift taxes "on" the property transferred. (Otherwise, at maximum rates of 55% under both taxes, the transfer might be wholly confiscated.) It is not that the estate and gift taxes are "deductible" as such under the generation-skipping tax. Rather, it is the generation-skipping tax that is applied to generation-skipping transfers "after" the estate and gift taxes have been applied.

2. ***Effect of generation-skipping taxes on gift or estate taxes.*** Since the GST, conceptually, is imposed "after" the estate and gift taxes, the GST does not reduce the estate or gift tax base.

a. *Taxable terminations and distributions.* Taxable terminations and distributions occur after the initial gift or estate transfer. Hence, it would be impossible for the generation-skipping taxes to be deductible for estate or gift tax purposes.

b. *Direct-skip transfers.* Since the GST is imposed on direct-skip transfers "at the same time as" the estate or gift tax, it is necessary to deal with the issue of whether the generation-skipping tax is deductible for estate or gift tax purposes.

(1) Direct-skip estate transfers. The generation-skipping tax is not deductible for estate tax purposes, since said tax is *deemed* to occur "after" the estate transfer.

(2) Direct-skip gift transfers. Essentially the same result occurs here as with estate transfers. Under § 2515, any generation-skipping tax paid on an *inter vivos direct-skip* transfer is a gift for *gift tax* purposes. This rule simply prevents the gift tax base (which is already exclusive of the gift tax itself) from being further reduced by generation-skipping taxes. (Without this rule, the gift tax base would be reduced by the generation-skipping tax, since the initial gift tax base is the amount received by the donee.)

3. ***Liability for generation-skipping taxes.*** The generation-skipping tax base rules presuppose knowledge of the rules for payment of the GST itself.

a. *Direct skip.* The transferor or transferor's estate is liable for the generation-skipping tax on a direct-skip transfer. § 2603(a)(3). In case a direct-skip transfer is made *from* a trust, the tax is paid out of the trust by the trustee, as with a taxable termination. § 2603(a)(2).

b. *Taxable termination.* The trustee pays the tax out of the trust assets. § 2603(a)(2).

c. *Taxable distribution.* The distributee pays the tax. § 2603(a)(1).

d. *Source of payment.* In each case, the tax is to be charged to the property constituting the generation-skipping transfer, unless the governing instrument *specifically* states otherwise with respect to the generation-skipping tax. § 2603(b).

4. ***Generation-skipping taxes and the generation-skipping tax base:***

   a. *Direct-skip transfers.* The generation-skipping tax, payable by the transferor or the trust, is *excluded* from the generation-skipping tax base. § 2623.

      (1) Direct-skip gift transfers. The initial tax base is simply the amount received by the transferees.

      (2) Direct-skip estate transfers. Since the GST is payable out of the estate transfer, and since the GST base is "after" the GST (is what the transferee receives), it follows that here the GST is, in effect, deducted from the GST base, which has already been reduced by any estate tax charged to the transfer. But since GST and the GST base are here mutually interdependent, a formula is required to figure out the tax:

$$GST = \frac{\text{estate transfer (after estate taxes charged thereto) x GST rate}}{1 + GST\ rate}$$

      This formula is used in Example 13, *infra*.

   b. *Taxable terminations.* The initial tax base is the before-GST amount with respect to which the taxable termination has occurred. § 2622(a)(1). In other words, the tax base includes the GST, and there is no implicit deduction for the GST.

   c. *Taxable distributions:*

      (1) Distributee pays tax. The initial taxable amount is the value of the property received by the distributee, before taxes. § 2621(a)(1). Thus, given that the distributee is liable for the tax, the tax base includes the tax.

      (2) Trust pays tax. If (contrary to the default rules for payment) the trustee pays the generation-skipping taxes on a taxable distribution, such taxes constitute an additional generation-skipping transfer (taxable distribution). § 2621(b).

5. ***Practical effect of liability and source-of-payment rules.*** Unless the governing instrument specifically mandates otherwise, the rules described above have the following tax-base effects:

   a. *Direct-skip transfers (not from a trust).* The effect differs between gift and estate transfers.

      (1) Gift transfer. The gift and generation-skipping taxes are paid by the transferor out of her own pocket in the case of a gift transfer.

Example 12: If *A* makes an outright gift of $1 million to a grandson, the grandson gets $1 million, and the donor pays any gift and generation-skipping tax out of her own pocket. The generation-skipping tax base is $1 million. At the same time, the generation-skipping tax is treated as a gift for gift tax purposes under § 2515.

(2) Estate transfer. The GST base is reduced both by GST on the transfer and any estate taxes charged thereto.

Example 13: Suppose *A*'s will makes a $2 million bequest to a grandchild, which is required to be the source of a $1 million estate tax. The GST base is $1 million less the GST itself. Assuming a GST rate of 55% (0.55), and applying the formula set forth above, the GST is obtained as follows:

$$\text{GST} = \frac{\$1{,}000{,}000 \times .55}{1.55}$$

$$= \$354{,}838.71$$

Therefore, the GST tax base must be $645,161.29, which is what the grandchild ends up with.

b. *Taxable terminations (and direct-skip transfers from a trust).* The transferees receive the termination distribution net of any GST, which is not implicitly deducted in arriving at the GST tax base.

Example 14: A trust, created by X and now worth $1 million (net of initial estate or gift tax) is the subject of a taxable termination. The GST tax base is $1 million, and the GST is paid out of the trust. Thus, if the GST rate is 55%, the successors receive $450,000 after all taxes.

c. *Taxable distributions.* The distributee is to pay the tax, and can do so from any source, but the IRS has a lien on the distributed amount for collection purposes.

Example 15: Assume that a trust distributes $1 million to a grandchild. The tax on the $1 million is payable by the distributee from any source, including the distribution itself. In effect, the distributee has a *net* accession equal to the distribution minus the tax. If the GST rate is 55%, the grandchild receives $450,000 net.

6. **Alternatives compared.** In light of the foregoing, is any category of generation-skipping transfer to be preferred over the others as far as the tax base is concerned? Analysis of this question involves consideration of the effect of gift, estate, and generation-skipping taxes on the tax base, as described *supra*. The issue can best be described as, "How much must a transferor part with (including taxes) to affect a net receipt of $100 by a transferee?" *The following assumes that: (1) no exemptions or exceptions apply, (2) the gift, estate, and generation-skipping tax rates are 55% at all times, (3) estate taxes are borne by bequests on a pro-rata basis* (i.e., *the estate tax on any transfer is charged against the transfer), and (4) the property maintains a constant value over time.*

5

a. *Direct-skip transfers.* In this instance, recall, the generation-skipping tax base is "tax exclusive."

(1) By gift. The donor must part with $240.25 for the donee (grandchild) to receive $100 free and clear. Since the generation-skipping tax (payable by the donee) is 55% of the amount received by the donee, the donor must part with $155 not counting the gift tax. Since (1) the $55 GST is treated as a taxable gift under § 2515 and (2) the *gift* tax is excluded from the *gift* tax base, the gift tax must be $85.25 (55% of the "gift," which is the sum of the donee receipt plus the GST). Thus: $100 (net receipt) + $55 (GST) + $85.25 (gift tax) = $240.25.

(2) Estate transfer. Here the decedent must part with $344.44 to get $100 in the hands of the legatee. Again, (*i.e.,* since the GST base is tax exclusive), the GST (payable out of the estate) is $55. Since the estate tax is included in the estate tax base (i.e., not deducted), the estate tax must have been $189.44. (The estate tax base is $155/(1 - .55) = $344.44.) The total is $344.44: $100 (net receipt) + $55 (GST) + $189.44 (estate tax).

b. *Taxable terminations.* Here, the generation-skipping tax base includes the generation-skipping tax itself.

(1) With respect to gift transfer. The transferor must (again) part with $344.44 so that the transferee may receive $100. Since the GST is included in the GST base, the GST base is $222.22 [$100/(1 - .55)]. The GST, which is 55% of $222.22, is $122.22. Since the gift tax is *not* included in the GST base (although the GST is included), the gift tax base is also $222.22, and the gift tax is $122.22. The foregoing adds up to $344.44: $100 (net receipt) + $122.22 (GST) + $122.22 (gift tax).

(2) With respect to estate transfer. Here, the transferor must have parted with $493.82 for the transferee to have received $100, since the estate tax is included in the estate tax base. Thus, $493.82 minus an estate tax of $271.60 leaves a GST base of $222.22, which in turn yields a GST (payable out of the trust) of $122.22, leaving $100 for the successor in interest.

c. *Taxable distributions.* Since the generation-skipping tax is again included in the generation-skipping tax base, the results are the same as with taxable terminations.

d. *Summary of results:*

(1) Gift route cheaper than estate route. Within each category of generation-skipping transfer, the gift route is substantially cheaper than the estate route, but this difference is attributable to the fact that the gift tax base does not include the gift tax itself, whereas the estate tax base includes the estate tax. In other words, the difference is not attributable to any feature of the GST as such.

(2) Direct-skip transfers cheaper than other forms. Direct-skip transfers by gift or at death have a significant advantage over transfers by way of taxable termination or taxable distribution by gift or at death for an

analogous reason: the GST is excluded from the generation-skipping tax base in the case of direct-skip transfers.

e. *Caveats.* Refer back to the assumptions, set forth at the beginning of this section 6.

(1) Tax rates. The basic points (if not the absolute numbers) made above would not be affected by differences in the various tax rates.

(2) Burden of taxes. If the burden of the estate taxes were shifted to other legatees, the difference between the gift and estate tax results within any category would be altered. Nevertheless, it is still "cheaper" for tax purposes to dispose of *all* of one's wealth by gift than by estate transfer. Also, the burden of generation-skipping taxes can be shifted by specific mandate under the instrument of transfer, § 2603(b), but note in this connection § 2621(b), which states that any GST paid by the trust (instead of the distributee) with respect to a taxable distribution is treated as an additional generation-skipping transfer.

(3) Per-transferor exemption. It turns out that gift transfers are not more favorably treated than estate transfers as far as the $1 million (as indexed) per-transferor exemption is concerned. *See* IV.D.7., *infra.*

(4) Time value of money. Although the GST on a direct-skip transfer is smaller than the equivalent tax on a taxable termination or distribution, the tax on direct-skip transfers is paid up front, whereas that on taxable terminations and distributions is deferred. In other words, the time-value-of money benefit of deferral *might* make the taxable termination (or distribution) route cheaper. On the other hand, appreciation or accumulations in the trust would expand the tax base with respect to taxable terminations and distributions, and this would tend to cancel out the advantage of deferral. Another factor to consider is the role of the exemption, discussed in IV.B., especially as it shelters appreciation from the tax base. Thus, one cannot generalize as to whether direct-skip transfers are cheaper than taxable terminations and distributions. Computer programs are available to analyze the economics of alternative scenarios involving generation-skipping transfers under alternative assumptions.

E. **Deduction for Administrative Expenses**. Administration expenses pertaining to figuring the generation-skipping tax are removed from the tax base one way or another.

1. *Direct-skip transfers.* No deduction as such is allowed for administration expenses. However, since the tax base is what the transferees receive, any such expenses incurred by the transferor will simply not appear in the tax base to begin with.

2. *Taxable terminations.* Administration expenses incurred by the trustee (including those relating to the GST itself) are a deduction from the tax base. § 2622(b).

THE TAX RATE

3. ***Taxable distributions.*** Expenses of the distributee relating to the GST tax are deductible. § 2621(a)(2).

IV. **THE TAX RATE. The rate is the maximum federal estate tax rate (55%) times the "exclusion ratio." § 2641.**

A. **Flat Rate.** The flat rate is the maximum federal estate tax rate at the date of the taxable event, which is curently 55%. § 2641(b).

B. **Inclusion Ratio.** The flat (55%) rate is multiplied by the "inclusion ratio."

1. ***Basic idea.*** The "inclusion ratio" is the number "one" *minus* an "exclusion ratio" (the "applicable fraction"). § 2642(a)(1). The exclusion ratio is, basically, the per-transferor lifetime exemption allocated to the transfer in question *divided by* the value of the transfer. The per-transferor lifetime exemption is $1 million, as indexed for inflation (in $10,000 increments). *See* § 2631(c). Thus, if the *exclusion* ratio is 100% (= 1.0), *i.e.*, the transfer is fully covered by the exclusion allocated thereto, the *inclusion* ratio is zero, and hence the rate is zero, resulting in a zero tax. Thus, the per transferor "exemption" ultimately *acts* like an exclusion by reducing the *rate* applicable to a particular transfer from 55% downwards, possibly to zero, in a given case.

2. ***Exclusion ratio.*** The exclusion ratio, which is called the "applicable fraction," is constituted according to § 2642(a)(2) as follows:

a. *The numerator.* As mentioned just above, the numerator of the exclusion ratio is the amount of the exemption allocated to the transfer. The amount so allocated cannot exceed the denominator of the fraction, immediately below. The mechanics of the allocation are described *infra* at C.

b. *The denominator.* The denominator is the value of the property initially transferred to the trust or involved in the direct-skip transfer *reduced by*:

(1) any federal and state death taxes recovered from the property; and

(2) the amount of any gift or estate tax charitable deduction with respect to the property.

3. ***Comparing transfers by gift and bequest.*** As just noted, the denominator of the fraction is reduced by death taxes (but not gift taxes) charged to the transfer. This rule has the effect of somewhat equalizing gift and estate transfers with respect to the amountf the exemption needed to fully shelter them from tax.

Example 16: Assume that *X* desires to transfer $1 million to her grandchildren in direct-skip transfers, and that gift, estate, and generation-skipping tax rates are all 55%. If the transfer is by gift, *X* owes $550,000 in gift tax out of her own pocket, but must allocate $1 million to the transfer (disregarding gift-tax exclusions) to fully shelter the gift from generation-skipping tax. If *X* makes a bequest of $2,222,222 to her grandchildren and the $1,222,222 estate tax is charged to the property, the transfer can be fully sheltered from GST by an exemption allocation of $1 million.

5

4. *Why an inclusion ratio?* One might well ask why the exclusion is factored into the rate, rather than simply having a progressive rate schedule coupled with a "straight" exemption or credit. The answer is that the 1976 generation-skipping tax (retroactively repealed) unsuccessfully attempted to add particular generation-skipping transfers to the estate and gift tax bases of "deemed transferors," who were persons between the initial transferor and the transferees of the transfer.

   a. *Complex and arbitrary:* It was felt that this system was complex, difficult to apply, and produced arbitrary results.

   b. *Benefit of flat rate.* A flat rate (coupled with an exemption "for" the *initial* transferor) avoids any need to identify (subsequent) deemed transferors.

   c. *Why a ratio approach?* However, an exemption that derives from the initial transferor creates problems for taxable distributions and terminations, which occur after the initial transfer and perhaps long after the transferor is dead. One problem with a flat amount exemption would be how to parcel it out during the duration of the trust. For example, would taxable distributions and terminations occurring first in time "use up" the exemption "first," leaving later taxable events without the benefit of an exemption? A second problem is that a flat amount exemption would be swallowed up by subsequent appreciation, so that a transferor would obtain more "bang" for her exemption dollar by making direct-skip transfers, where subsequent inflation would not be a problem. These problems are "solved" by the ratio approach, which operates so that *each taxable transfer obtains the same benefit from the exemption* through the exclusion ratio.

   d. *Effect of exclusion ratio.* The inclusion ratio is constituted at the time the transfer is made by the (initial) "transferor," *supra, i.e.,* at the time the gift or bequest is made or the trust (etc.) is created. (If an inter vivos trust, etc., and the transfer is subject to both gift and estate tax, the trust is deemed created at the transferor's death. § 2642(f).) The allocation of all or part of the exemption to particular transfers is somewhat under the control of the transferor and her personal representative; the allocation issue is discussed shortly. For now it is important to note that the allocation is usually made at the time of the initial transfer. *Once constituted, the tax rate (i.e., with the inclusion ratio factored in) applies to all generation-skipping transfers, whenever made, with respect to the initial transfer.*

5. *Leveraging of exemption.* The fact that the rate, once constituted, "stays with" the property forever has two very important ramifications.

   a. *Subsequent appreciation.* In the case of taxable terminations and taxable distributions, the rate is constituted when the trust (etc.) is created (*see* above) and applied to subsequent taxable events. *The effect is that the exemption "grows" at the same rate as the property appreciates.*

   Example 17: Assume that *X* creates a testamentary trust with $1 million (after death taxes), income to children for life, remainder to then-living issue, and that *X*'s personal representative allocates *X*'s entire $1 million exemption to this trust. Since the exclusion ratio is 1.0 ($1 million exemption/$1 million value of transfer), the inclusion ratio, and the tax rate, are zero. At the death of the last child, when there is a taxable termination, the trust is worth $5 million. There is no generation-skipping tax, since the rate is (still) zero. Once zero, always zero. The $1 million exemption wholly sheltered a generation-skipping transfer of $5 million!

b. *Successive skips.* The same rate applies to all generation-skipping transfers with respect to the trust (etc.), *whenever made.* Thus, the exemption allocated to the transfer is used over and over again at each generation in the event of successive taxable events. § 2653(b)(1). *In effect, the transferor's exemption is "renewed" at each generation.*

6. ***Per-transferor nature of exclusion.*** Each transferor has a lifetime (indexed) $1 million exclusion for generation-skipping tax purposes. Husbands and wives are separate transferors. There are three basic strategies for maximizing the use of exemptions:

   a. *Joint funding of generation-skipping trust with community property or co-owned property; gift splitting.* Each transferor can use up one's $1 million exemption as one deems appropriate. The § 2513 gift-splitting election is also effective for generation-skipping-tax purposes. § 2652(a)(2).

   b. *Which spouse is the transferor of a QTIP trust?* If *H* creates a trust, income to *W* for life, remainder to their grandchildren, and a QTIP election is made, *H*'s status as "transferor" is superseded by *W* (being subject to estate tax at her death under § 2044 or prior gift tax), who will be the transferor of a direct-skip transfer to the grandchildren. *H*'s exemption could be wasted (unless there are other generation-skipping transfers of which he is the transferor). However, under § 2652(a)(3), *H* (or his personal representative) can make a "reverse QTIP election" for generation-skipping tax purpose, which has the effect of making *H* the transferor, so that at *W*'s death there would be a taxable termination in favor of the grandchildren. The reverse QTIP election can be made for generation-skipping-tax purposes even where a "straight" QTIP election is made for gift or estate tax purposes with respect to the same property. *See* II.A.1.b.(1), *supra.* However, it is not possible to make a "partial" reverse QTIP election. Therefore, in order to use up both *H* and *W*'s exemptions (and assuming that *W* has negligible wealth of her own), *H* can create two marital-deduction trusts, both with QTIP elections for gift or estate tax purposes, but with a reverse QTIP election being made for only one of them. (*H* might also create a third generation-skipping trust that fails to qualify for the marital deduction, which trust, when combined with the reverse-QTIP-election trust, will exhaust *H*'s indexed $1 million exemption.)

   c. *Creating general powers of appointment.* If a person possesses a general power of appointment, that person becomes a potential transferor for generation-skipping tax purposes, and that person's exemption becomes available. Since the general power will subject the person to gift or estate tax, this strategy makes sense if the person has little wealth of her own, so that gift or estate tax can be avoided under that person's unified transfer tax credit.

   Example 18: *X* creates two trusts, one with $1 million and one with $500,000; each trust provides that the income is to be paid to child *C* for life, remainder to great-grandchild *G,* with *C* (who has negligible wealth of her own) being given a general testamentary power of appointment over the second trust. *X* is the transferor of the first trust, but (if all of *X*'s $1 million exemption is allocated to such trust) the trust is exempt from generation-skipping tax at *C*'s death. As to the second trust, none of *X*'s exemption is allocated thereto, but *C* becomes the superseding transferor in a direct-skip transfer to *G,* but *C* can allocate *her* exemption to this trust to escape generation-skipping tax. Yes, the trust is included in *C*'s gross estate, but, assuming that *C* has negligible wealth of her own, the estate tax is wiped out by the unified transfer tax credit available to her estate.

7. ***Split-interest charitable transfers:*** Recall that charities are assigned to the same generation as the transferor, and hence are "nonskip persons." Thus, transfers "to" charities are exempt from generation-skipping tax, but split-interest charitable transfers may involve generation-skipping transfers.

   a. *Charitable remainder trusts and charitable lead unitrusts.* A charitable remainder trust provides for a remainder to charity following a qualified annuity or unitrust interest.

      Example 19: Assume that *X* creates a trust with $1 million, qualified annuity to *A* for life, remainder to charity, and that the value of the charitable remainder (= $400,000) is deductible for gift or estate tax purposes. If *A* is a nonskip person, there is never a generation-skipping transfer. If *A* is a skip person, all payments to *A* are taxable distributions, but *A*'s death is not a taxable event. Recall that amounts qualifying for the charitable deduction reduce the denominator of the fraction of the exclusion ratio. In this example, generation-skipping tax can be avoided by allocating $600,000 (instead of $1 million) of *X*'s exemption to the trust. In short, the gift or estate tax charitable deduction reduces the amount of exemption needed to fully shelter the trust from generation-skipping tax, thereby increasing the effect of any exemption allocated to the trust. The same principle applies with respect to a charitable lead unitrust (*i.e.,* 8% of the corpus, valued annually, to the *Y* charity, remainder to grandchild *Z*).

   b. *Charitable lead annuity trusts.* Contrary to the general rule, when a trust grants a qualified *annuity* to a charity and the value of the charitable lead interest is deductible by the grantor for gift or estate tax purposes, the "exclusion ratio" is simply the exemption initially allocated to the trust (increased by compound interest using the same interest rate as used in figuring the charitable deduction, compounded over the actual period of the lead annuity) *divided by* the value of the property in the trust at the end of the annuity (without reduction for the amount of the charitable deduction). § 2642(e).

      Example 20: Assume that *X* creates a trust, qualified annuity to the *Y* charity for 15 years, remainder to *Z,* and that the value of the charitable lead interest is deductible for gift or estate tax purposes. The creation of the trust is not a direct-skip transfer, even if *Z* is a skip person, but in that case the termination of the charity's annuity would be a taxable termination. The exclusion ratio is determined at the end of the annuity period, with the numerator of the exclusion ratio having grown by compound interest rather than in proportion to changes in the value of the property.

C. **Allocating the Exemption.** The allocation of the exemption to generation-skipping transfers is not purely automatic. Decisions are called for.

1. *Mechanics:*

   a. *Direct-skip gifts.* The exemption is allocated automatically to direct-skip gifts on a first-come, first-serve basis, unless the transferor elects otherwise on the return. § 2632(b).

   b. *Other gift transfers.* The transferor can choose to allocate all or part of the exemption to such transfers. In fact, the transferor can subsequently "add" to such allocation, but prior allocations cannot be reduced. *See* § 2632(a). If the gift is of the type that will be included in the gross estate, the allocation must await the transferor's death. § 2642(f).

   c. *Death of transferor.* Any unused exemption remaining at the transferor's death must be allocated as provided by the transferor's will, or, if the will is silent, by the personal representative. § 2632(a). If the latter fails to act, statutory "default" rules kick in. *See* § 2632(c) (allocation made first to estate-included, direct-skip transfers).

   d. *Value of the property.* The "value of the property" for purposes of the "exclusion ratio," *supra,* is generally the value of the property as of the time of the allocation. *See* § 2642(b) & (f).

2. *Planning.* The exemption should be allocated to transfers so as to take maximum advantage of the leveraging phenomenon. *See* B.5., *supra.* Thus, it may not be desirable to allocate the exemption to direct-skip transfers. The optimal allocation would be to a highly appreciating trust subject to multiple taxable events.

CREDITS AND MISCELLANY

V. **CREDITS AND MISCELLANY.**

A. **Credit for State Generation-Skipping Tax**. There is a credit, not to exceed 5% of the federal GST, for any state generation-skipping tax with respect to a generation-skipping transfer, other than a direct-skip transfer, that occurs at the same time (and by reason of) a person's death. § 2604.

B. **Returns.** The person required to pay the tax is required to file the return. The gift tax return has a section devoted to direct-skip gift transfers. For non-direct-skip gift transfers, an exemption allocation can be made by filing a "Notice of Allocation" with the gift tax return. Information returns can be required by the IRS. *See* § 2662.

C. **Payment**

1. *Liability.* *See* III.D.3., *supra.*

2. *Time for payment.* Except as provided in § 2662 with respect to returns, the procedural rules (including those for payment) applicable to gifts and estates apply. § 2661.

D. **Basis Adjustments.** *See* § 2654(a).

1. ***Taxable termination at death.*** If a taxable termination occurs at the same time as (and as the result of) a person's death, the property's basis for income tax purposes is its value at the time of such transfer. However, no step-up in basis can exceed an amount equal to the tentative step-up multiplied by the inclusion ratio.

2. ***Other cases.*** The income tax basis is adjusted upwards in an amount equal to the generation-skipping tax attributable to the excess, if any, of the property's value over its basis (after adjustment under § 1015 in the case of a direct-skip gift transfer) as of the moment just prior to the transfer. In the case of a direct-skip estate transfer, any § 1014 step-up would fully absorb (pre-empt) the adjustment described herein.

E. **Regulations.** The Treasury is given a broad grant of authority under § 2663 to issue regulations under the generation-skipping tax.

CHAPTER 5 - QUESTIONS, ANSWERS, AND TIPS

EXAM TIPS:

1. The GST, remember, is a separate tax on property that is, or was, also subject to estate and gift tax.

2. The GST applies not only to trusts, but also to outright transfers, that skip one or more generations.

3. Direct-skip transfers are (initially) favored in the sense that the GST base excludes the GST tax itself.

4. The GST per-transferor exemption is "leveraged" by being factored into an "exclusion ratio," which ratio "sticks" with the property and applies to all generation-skipping transfers derived from such property, until the property is entirely distributed or until there is a new "transferor" of the property.

REVIEW QUESTIONS:

State whether the following are generation-skipping transfers and, if so, the tax due. Assume that the maximum per-transferor exemption is $1 million.

1. X and Y make a $100,000 gift to grandson Charles, electing gift splitting under § 2513, and each of X and Y allocates $40,000 of his or her GST exemption to the transfer.

2. J dies, resulting in the inclusion in his gross estate of an employee death benefit worth $100,000, payable to grandson James. J's daughter Mary, the mother of James, predeceased J. J's executor allocates none of the exemption to this transfer, and no estate tax is charged against the death benefit.

3. K creates an inter vivos irrevocable trust with $100,000, income to herself for life, then income to K's children until the death of the survivor, then income to K's grandchildren until the death of the survivor, remainder to K's then living issue. The trust is worth $1.4 million at K's death, but $400,000 of estate tax is charged against this trust under § 2207B. The maximum allocation of the exemption is made to this trust. At the death of the survivor

of K's children, the trust is worth $10 million. At the death of the last surviving grandchild, it is worth $100 million.

4. H dies, bequeathing a trust of $1 million to W for life, remainder to such of H's issue as are then surviving per stirpes. An estate tax QTIP election is made. The trust is worth $3.6 million at W's death, at which time half passes to H's daughter Pat and half to H's granddaughter Jill. An estate tax of $800,000 is charged to this trust at W's death. (What options are available here?)

5. Phil's will creates a trust, initially worth $2 million (after payment of estate tax), income to son Mark for life, giving Mark a general testamentary power of appointment, but in default of such appointment the trust is to pass to Phil's grandchildren. Mark, by will, appoints the corpus, then worth $2.4 million, to his companion Harry, who was born 14 years later than Mark, and 29 years later than Phil. An estate tax of $800,000 is charged against the trust at Mark's death. Any necessary exemption allocation is made.

6. Jorge creates a trust with $4 million (after estate taxes), income to daughter Pilar for life, giving Pilar a power to appoint corpus, from time to time, to such of Jorge's extended family members as Pilar decides; on Pilar's death, the income is payable to Jorge's mother Maria, if then living, and on Maria's death the remainder is to go to Jorge's then living issue per stirpes. Pilar appoints $100,000 of corpus to her first cousin Lourdes and $200,000 to her nephew Juan. On Pilar's death survived by Maria, the trust is worth $5 million. On Maria's death, the trust is worth $6 million, and passes to Pilar's grandchildren. The maximum exemption allocation is made.

ANSWERS:

1. Each of X and Y is a transferor of $50,000 to Charles in a direct-skip gift transfer, since Charles is a skip person and the gift is subject to gift tax. Each transfer is exempt from GST to the extent of $10,000. § 2642(c)(1). The remaining $40,000 is exempted under the GST exemption allocation. Neither X nor Y owes GST.

2. Here the predeceased-parent rule applies, so that James, who would otherwise be a skip person, is not a skip person. § 2651(e). Hence, there is no generation-skipping transfer.

3. This trust is included in K's gross estate under § 2036, as well as being subject to gift tax (partly under § 2702) at the time the trust is created. This is not a direct-skip transfer, since both K and her children are non-skip persons who have interests in the trust at relevant times. There is a taxable termination on the death of the survivor of K's children, and another one on the death of the survivor of her grandchildren. In each case, the tax base is the amount then in the trust. The tax rate however, is zero, because the "exclusion ratio" is 100%: $1 million exemption divided by $1.4 million value at transfer reduced by $400,000 estate tax charged against same. The exemption allocation must be made at K's death, rather than the date of gift. § 2542(f). This example illustrates the power of "leveraging the exemption."

4. This trust is not a direct-skip transfer by H, since W (who has an "interest") is a non-skip person. On W's death, there would be a taxable termination as to the half that passes to Jill, assuming that H is the transferor. However, the transferor would be W, not H, since the trust is includible in W's gross estate under § 2044 subsequent to its being "subject to" estate tax in H's estate (although qualifying for the marital deduction). If W is the transferor (and assuming that the estate tax is charged half to each remainder share), there is a direct-skip

estate transfer to Jill of $1.8 million. The exclusion ratio would be $1 million divided by $1.4 million ($1.8 million less $400,000 estate tax). The resulting GST rate is 15.71% [0.55 x (1 – 1.0/1.4)]. Since this is a direct-skip estate transfer, the GST is implicitly deducted from the GST base, which requries applying the formula set forth in II.D.4.a.(2), *supra*:

$$GST = \frac{\$1,400,000 \text{ (after estate tax) x } 0.1571}{1.1571}$$

$$= \$190,078.60$$

If H's executor makes a reverse QTIP election, H would be the transferor and the exclusion ratio would be 100%: $1 million exemption/$ 1 million transfer. (No estate tax would be charged to the marital deduction transfer.) Thus, there would be no GST due on W's death (which is a taxable termination for the amount passing to Jill).

5. Phil's trust is not a direct-skip transfer, because Mark is a non-skip person. On Mark's death, the property is included in Mark's gross estate under § 2041, and therefore Mark supersedes Phil as the transferor for GST purposes. Harry is a non-skip person in relation to Mark. See §§ 2513(a)(1) and 2651(d)(2) (although he would be a skip person in relation to Phil). There is no generation-skipping transfer, and hence there is no exemption allocation.

6. Jorge's trust is not a direct-skip transfer, since Pilar is a non-skip person. Pilar has a special power of appointment. Since special powers are not subject to estate or gift tax, Jorge (rather than Pilar) is the transferor. The $100,000 to Lourdes is not a taxable distribution, since Lourdes (being in the same degree of descent from a common ancestor as Pilar) is a non-skip person in relation to Jorge. § 2651(b)(1). The $200,000 to Juan is a taxable distribution, since Juan is a skip person. The exclusion ratio is $1 million/$4 million, or 25%. Hence the tax rate is 41.25% [55% x (1 – 0.25)]. The tax is $82,500, payable by Juan. On Pilar's death, there is not a taxable termination, since Maria is a non-skip person then having an interest. On Maria's death there is a taxable termination of $6 million, subject to the same 41.25% tax rate, producing a tax of $2,475,000, payable by the trust just prior to distribution to Phil's greatgrandchildren. There is no further tax on account of the fact that the termination distribution skips Pilar's children's generation.

ESTATE PLANNING DEVICES

▶ **CHAPTER SUMMARY**

CHAPTER 6: ESTATE PLANNING DEVICES

Introduction. The term "estate planning" is broad enough to encompass such matters as investment planning, medical care decisions, asset protection, and planning for incompetency. Since this outline is devoted to the federal transfer taxes, this chapter will be limited to techniques that implicate such taxes. Thus, a better title for this chapter might be "transfer tax planning for gratuitous transfers." It should be kept in mind that most persons do not have sufficient wealth accumulation to worry about tax planning. But real estate and stock appreciation, employee benefits, life insurance, and receipts of gratuitous transfers can raise a person's wealth to the point where transfer tax planning is advisable. Even for the wealthy, the goal of tax savings should be kept in perspective; the likelihood of substantial tax savings should be weighed against possible distortions of the "natural" dispositive plan and the risks of incurring (and losing) disputes with the IRS.

This chapter cannot comprehensively deal with every transaction that implicates the federal transfer taxes. The estate planner should be well versed in federal income taxes and the law of donative transfers; unfortunately, the scope of this outline precludes more than cursory mention of state law and income tax issues. In a few states, state and local income taxes and death taxes must also be taken into account.

The focus of this chapter is on common, useful, and/or well publicized techniques for saving federal transfer taxes, as well as on the avoidance of transfer-tax traps. Topics covered include: funded revocable trusts, advantages of inter vivos gifts, maximizing the gift tax exclusion, providing liquidity to pay debts and taxes, irrevocable insurance trusts, marital deduction planning, charitable deduction planning, use of disclaimers, value reduction techniques, and estate freeze devices. Since virtually all of the transfer tax rules covered in this chapter have been discussed previously in this outline, this chapter can be said "to review and highlight" that material in this outline which possesses significant practical importance. This chapter is the culmination of this outline, for it answers the "So what?" implicit in all of the detailed rules that have gone before.

INTER VIVOS TRANSFERS

I. INTER VIVOS TRANSFERS. This part reviews transfer tax opportunities (other than value reduction and estate freeze techniques) and transfer tax traps with respect to inter vivos transfers.

    A. Trusts Created for Reasons Other than Avoiding Federal Transfer Taxes:

        1. *Trusts for the present or future benefit of the grantor.* Inter vivos transfers may be made for such "selfish" nontax reasons as avoiding estate administration, evading the grantor's creditors, disinheriting a spouse, qualifying for state welfare benefits (such as Medicaid), and providing for the grantor's future needs in case of disability. The effectiveness of such transfers in achieving the various nontax goals is beyond the scope of this outline. These types of trusts often involve retained interests and powers in the grantor. Some typical transfer tax issues will be discussed here.

            a. *Retained power to revoke.* When a grantor retains the power to revoke a gift, the transfer will not be a completed gift (nor will § 2702 apply), though it will be included in the gross estate under § 2038. Distributions from the trust to third parties during the grantor's lifetime will be present-interest gifts qualifying for the annual gift tax exclusion. Such distributions made within three years of the donor's death will not be included in the donor's gross estate under § 2035(a), because of § 2035(e).

b. *Retained right to, or power over, income or corpus.* A retained interest in income or corpus is, under § 2702, *not* subtracted from the value of a completed gift. (A retained power over income or corpus that would cause the gift of income or corpus to be incomplete is treated as a retained interest for purposes of § 2702.) Yet such an interest or power causes gross estate inclusion under §§ 2036-2038. The resulting double taxation is usually not mitigated. (For the various exceptions to § 2702, *see* Ch.2, VII.B., *supra.*) Section 2702 can also be avoided if the transfer of nonretained interests is incomplete due to a retained power to revoke, alter, or amend *all* of such non-retained interests. In short, irrevocable transfers with retained rights to income or corpus are to be approached with extreme caution.

c. *Grantor as permissible recipient of income or corpus.* A trustee (other than the grantor) may be given, in the context of an irrevocable trust, the power to pay income or corpus to the grantor in its discretion or under "standards."

(1) Retained interest. In general, the *possibility* of receiving income or corpus would not be an "interest" that would be subtracted from the amount of the gift, nor would it be an interest that would trigger § 2036(a)(1), § 2037, or § 2702.

(2) Exceptions. Notwithstanding the foregoing, the grantor will be treated as retaining an interest in the following situations:

(a) Standards enforceable by the grantor. If the grantor can compel the trustee to make distributions under enforceable standards, the grantor has retained an "interest" to the extent that distributions can be compelled by the grantor for her own benefit or for the benefit of persons the grantor is legally obligated to support. This exception can be effectively negated by language in the trust instrument giving the trustee discretion in applying the standards.

(b) Grantor's creditors can reach trust. If (and to the extent that) under state law the grantor's creditors can reach the income or corpus (which is often the case under the *Restatement of Trusts* with respect to trusts of this type), the grantor has retained an interest in the trust.

(c) Grantor controls trustee. Estate inclusion occurs if the grantor is both trustee and a permissible recipient of income or corpus. It follows, in theory, that the grantor may be deemed to have "retained" an interest or power by actual domination over a third-party trustee. However, the courts are very reluctant to look at informal relations between the grantor and the trustee. The courts are likely to take the position that a trustee, being a fiduciary, cannot be viewed as the alter ego of the grantor.

d. *Contingent interests and powers.* The grantor is deemed to have retained a contingent interest or power under § 2036 or § 2037, even if the contingency never occurred before the grantor's death. The opposite is true under § 2038. Contingent retained interests are subject to § 2702 (i.e., they are disregarded for gift tax purposes). Interests subject to contingent powers are usually not subtracted from the amount of any gift.

2. ***Trusts created to avoid income tax.*** A "Clifford trust" designed to save income tax (by shifting income to taxpayers in lower tax brackets) must comply with income tax §§ 671-677, which effectively prohibit the grantor (or in some cases, either a "related or subordinate party" or a "nonadverse party") from retaining (1) a power to revoke, (2) a reversion worth more than 5% of the corpus, (3) a possibility of obtaining income or corpus in the future, or (4) certain powers over income or corpus. In general, the grantor would like the transfer to be a completed gift and not included in the gross estate. However, the income tax rules are not identical to the gift and estate tax rules, so that a trust transfer that is complete for income tax purposes may be incomplete for federal transfer tax purposes (or one that is incomplete for income tax purposes may be complete for federal transfer tax purposes).

3. ***Trusts for the support of relatives.*** An inter vivos trust may be created to support a spouse or relative, sometimes on account of long-term disability and sometimes as the result of a divorce or separation. (One nontax issue in the case of a disabled or handicapped beneficiary is to assure that the trust assets or income cannot be reached by a government welfare authority or its assets and income taken into account in reducing welfare benefits.)

   a. *Support trusts.* A trust in which the income or corpus is required to be distributed to a person whom the grantor is obligated to support may be characterized as a retained-interest trust, subject to § 2702 and (if the support obligation is still outstanding at the date of the grantor's death) § 2036(a)(1) or § 2037. *See* Ch.3, at II.C., *supra.*

   b. *Divorce or separation.* Transfers to a spouse, ex-spouse, or minor children connected with divorce or separation may be excluded from the category of "gift" (and the reach of § 2702) or may be deemed to be made for full or partial consideration. *See* Ch.2, at II.G.6., *supra.*

B. **Transfer Tax Advantages of Completed Gifts Not Included in the Gross Estate.** Turning to pure transfer tax planning, inter vivos gifts have certain inherent advantages compared to assets included in the gross estate. (Keep in mind, however, that avoiding inclusion in the gross estate is also a waiver of obtaining an income-tax basis step-up under § 1014; however, the value of this basis step-up can be overrated, given the low income tax rates applicable to net capital gains.)

   1. ***No grossing up:***

      a. *Advantage.* The gift tax paid or owed is excluded from the transfer tax base, since the amount of the gift is the amount transferred to the donee, not the amount (including the tax) parted with by the donor. Any unpaid gift tax would, when paid, be a deduction against the gross estate under § 2053. In contrast, the estate tax base includes amounts used to pay the estate tax. Thus, gifts are more efficient means to transfer wealth, other things being equal.

         Example 1: If *D* has total wealth of $1 million subject in full to an estate or gift tax rate of 50%, his legatees would receive $500,000 net of estate tax, but donees would receive $666,666.67 net of gift tax (of $333,333.33) on gifts to donees of $666,666.67.

b. *Exceptions.* There are two "exceptions" to the no-grossing-up principle:

(1) Gifts within three years of death. Any net gift tax on gifts made within three years of the donor's death is included in the gross estate under § 2035(b). This result directly cancels the potential no-grossing-up advantage of the gift.

(2) Net gifts. If the donor makes a gift conditioned on the donee paying any net gift tax, the gift tax is a consideration offset, necessitating recomputation of the amount of the gift, and so on without end. However, the conundrum can be solved by the formula:

$$\text{Actual Gift Tax} = \frac{\text{Tentative Net Tax}}{1 + \text{marginal tax rate}}$$

Example 2: If *D* makes a gift of $1 million on condition that the donee pay the gift tax (at a 50% rate), the tax turns out to be $333,333.33, leaving $666,666.67 for the donee net of tax, the same result as in Example 1. Thus, there is really no gift tax advantage in a net gift transaction, other than to avoid the possible application of § 2035(b).

2. ***Bracket effect.*** Making gifts saves taxes in "real" terms by undermining the effect of the progressive rate schedule and making more efficient use of exemptions and the unified transfer tax credit.

a. *Basic assumption.* The bracket effect can be understood starting with the proposition that, the gift tax on a given amount of wealth *would* equal the present value of the estate tax on the same wealth, *assuming* that:

(1) the initial wealth grew at the same (compounded) rate as the rate used for discounting;

(2) there is a flat tax rate; *and*

(3) there are no exemptions.

Example 3: Thus, given a rate of return and a discount rate that are the same, and a flat tax rate of 40% with no exemption, suppose that $1 million of net wealth quadruples in 20 years to $4 million, at which time the owner dies; although the estate tax on $4 million will be four times as large as the gift tax on $1 million, the present value of the taxes would be the same. Thus, aside from the no-grossing-up phenomenon, *supra,* there would be no advantage in making inter vivos gifts. However, this neutrality gives way when the various assumptions are violated, as will now be explained, using the same basic example.

b. *Augmentation in excess of discount rate.* Assuming a flat rate and no exemption, gifts save taxes in present value terms where the property augments until death at a rate faster than the discount rate (*e.g.,* to $5 million in Example 3).

c. *Progressive rates.* Under a progressive rate structure, the increase in the tax base up to death (in Example 3, the increase is $3 million) may be subject to higher marginal rates. In that case, other things being equal, the present value of the estate tax on $4 million will be greater than the gift tax on $1 million. In addition, the taxpayer's remaining wealth may be pushed into still higher marginal rate brackets. Therefore, a gift of the $1 million is preferable to an estate of $4 million.

   d. *Exemption.* The exemption represented by the unified transfer tax credit has a two-fold effect that encourages gift transfers rather than estate transfers.

      (1) Zero rate bracket. An exemption amounts to a zero rate bracket, that exaggerates the effect described in previous paragraph. Thus, if the exemption is $1 million (but assuming a flat rate of 40%), a gift of $1 million produces zero tax, whereas the estate tax on $4 million (reduced by the $1 million exemption) would be $1.2 million.

      (2) Deferral effect. The exemption allows current gifts to be made free of any up-front tax. Any current payment of gift tax on taxable gifts would result not only in the loss of the tax (which would be paid eventually, in the absence of economic waste) but also amounts that could have been earned "on" the amount of the tax. If one assumed no exemption, no wealth augmentation, and a (reduced) flat rate, a gift transfer would be disadvantaged by reason of the fact that the tax would be paid earlier than later.

3. ***Leveraging of generation-skipping tax exclusion.*** The GST per-transferor exclusion ($1 million as indexed) effectively increases at the same rate as the property increases in value. Suppose A creates an inter vivos irrevocable trust of $1 million which is assigned the exemption of $1 million. The GST rate is zero. Hence, assuming that after 20 years (at A's death) the trust, then worth $4 million, is subject to a taxable termination, the GST rate is still zero. (And it will continue to be zero through subsequent taxable terminations and taxable distributions.) If, instead, the same trust were included in A's gross estate at $4 million, and other things being equal (including a $1 milion exemption), the tax rate would be 75% of the flat GST rate, which in this example would be the same as if the (unreduced) flat rate were applied against a tax base of $3 million. Thus, in this scenario the gift route produces a better GST result than the estate result. (Recall that the GST exemption cannot be assigned to an inter vivos transfer at the time of transfer if such transfer will be included in the gross estate; the exemption will be assigned to the transfer at death, or such earlier time as the transfer is no longer subject to estate inclusion. § 2642(f).)

4. ***Qualification for certain tax benefits.*** Inter vivos gifts of property (farms, ranches, and small business interests) can help qualify such farms (etc.) for special use valuation (*see* Ch.4, at 4. II.B.1., *supra*) or such business interests for (a) the § 2057 exclusion, (b) a § 303 redemption (*see* IV.B.2., *infra*), or (c) a § 6166 deferral of tax payments (*see* Ch.3, at VI.B.2.(3), *supra*). Gifts within three years of death will, however, be disregarded for these purposes. §§ 2035(c)(1) & (2) and 2057(c)(2).

5. ***A disadvantage: loss of the § 2013 credit.*** The gift tax is not eligible for the § 2013 credit, which might otherwise apply against the estate tax of the donee if the donee instead had received an estate-included transfer and dies within ten years of the transferor's death.

C. **Maximizing the Gift Tax Exclusions.** The exclusions under § 2503 of the gift tax are not available for estate tax purposes. Of particular tax-saving utility is the annual exclusion. *See* Ch.2, at VII., *supra.*

1. *Lifetime gift program.* The exclusion ($10,000, as indexed, per donee per year) can be maximized by a program of lifetime gifts involving several donees over a period of many years. The number of exclusions can be doubled if the donor is married and the gifts are of community property or co-owned property or if a gift-splitting election is made under § 2513.

2. *Spread-out completion of incomplete transfers.* If the (unmarried) donor creates an irrevocable trust with $100,000, the taxable gift is $90,000. If the transfer is to a revocable trust (not a completed gift), and the trust distributes $10,000 to *X* each year, the trust grantor makes a present-interest gift each year of $10,000 which is cancelled out by the exclusion.

3. *Gifts to minors.* The goal is to obtain the maximum use of $10,000 exclusions without giving the (minor) donee premature control over substantial sums.

    a. *Problems.* Donors are reluctant to make substantial outright gifts to minors. A trust or custodial account can be created for a minor that qualifies for the § 2503(b) exclusion by way of § 2503(c), but a transfer qualifying under § 2503(c) must be distributable to the donee upon reaching the age of majority (or age 21), which still may not be desired by the donor. A minor donee can be given a present interest (life estate, annuity, or term of years) in a trust that continues until the donee reaches a specified age beyond 21, but only the actuarial value of the present interest qualifies for the exclusion, which is obtained under § 2503(b) rather than § 2503(c).

    b. *Crummey powers.* The accepted solution to the late-maturing donee problem is to create an irrevocable trust and then each year make transfers into the trust of $10,000 (or less) which the (minor) beneficiary has the right to withdraw only during the same year (or a shorter period). The year's contribution qualifies for the § 2503(b) exclusion in full because the beneficiary has the immediate right to withdraw an equal amount from the trust; actual withdrawal is not necessary. This device was sanctioned by *Crummey v. Com'r,* 526 F.2d 717 (9th Cir. 1979). (The beneficiaries are informally made to understand that they are not normally to exercise the withdrawal power.)

        (1) IRS acquiescence. The IRS has acquiesced in the *Crummey* device provided that the beneficiary has a meaningful opportunity to withdraw the amount contributed (*i.e.,* the beneficiary must be given notice and a reasonable period of time, about a month). *See* Rev. Rul. 83-108, 1983-2 C.B. 168.

        (2) Multiple beneficiaries. The trust may be set up so as to have more than one beneficiary with withdrawal powers; the excluded amount would be a function of the amount contributed and the number of *Crummey* type beneficiaries. *See Estate of Cristofani v. Com'r,* 97 T.C. 74 (1991) (acq. in result).

6

(3) Lapsing powers. Each *Crummey* beneficiary has what is called in estate planning jargon as a lapsing general power of appointment by deed.

(a) Lapse treated as a "transfer." Each lapse of a withdrawal power entails a "transfer" of the lapsed amount back to the trust for estate and gift tax purposes. §§ 2041(b)(2) and 2514(e). The estate and gift tax consequences to the beneficiary of such deemed transfer are determined by treating the beneficiary as the transferor of the lapsed amount to the trust (and considering the terms of the trust).

(b) Lapse exemption. However, the gift and estate tax transfer is equal to the lapsed amount minus the greater of $5,000 or 5% of the amount that can be withdrawn per year. (If the amount that can be withdrawn in any year is only $10,000, the "lapse exemption" is going to be $5,000, since 5% of $10,000 is only $500.) This "lapse exclusion" (commonly referred to as the "five-and-five" exclusion) is separate from (and prior to) the present-interest exclusion. (Keep in mind that the lapse exclusion pertains to the deemed transfer by the donee-beneficiary, not to the transfer into trust by the donor.) The five-and-five exemption applies against cumulative lapse transfers of the beneficiary in the aggregate for the year, rather than to each lapse transfer or to all lapse transfers with respect to a given trust. Thus, the grantor cannot "multiply" available lapse exemptions for a given beneficiary by creating multiple trusts or by providing that several lapses of powers are to occur annually within each trust.

Example 4: Grantor A creates a trust, with the trustee having discretion over all distributions, until B obtains the age of 40, at which time the trust is to terminate and the assets are to be distributed to B's then living issue, etc. B is given the power to withdraw $10,000 each year during the month of December. Assume that there are no other trusts under which B has withdrawal powers. Each year A contributes $10,000 to the trust. Each such gift comes within the annual exclusion of A under the *Crummey* doctrine. At the end of December each year, B has made a deemed gift for gift tax purposes of $5,000 ($10,000 over which B's withdrawal power lapsed less $5,000 annual lapse exclusion). The $5,000 is a completed gift by B because B has no "retained" interests or powers in the trust. The $5,000 gift does not qualify for the § 2503 exclusion (as to B) because no benefiary has any present interest (aside from B's withdrawal power, but to the extent that would be a retained interest it would be disregarded under § 2702).

(c) Hanging power. In order to avoid lapse transfers by the beneficiary, the trust may provide that the annual *lapse* of the withdrawal power shall be limited to the available lapse exemption. Thus, the beneficiary's withdrawal power continues to "hang" over contributed amounts to the extent that the contributed amounts withdrawable by the beneficiary during the year exceed the lapsed amount. The effect of a hanging power is to preclude the beneficiary from being charged with "transfers" for estate and gift tax purposes. The only tax downside is that, if the beneficiary dies (or releases the hanging power), the beneficiary will be charged with an estate (or gift) transfer over the cumulative amount subject to the hanging power. Such amount will increase so long as the trust grantor makes withdrawable contributions in excess of the lapse amount. However, once the donor ceases making contributions, the hanging power can be made to lapse each year in an amount equal to the available lapse exemptions of beneficiaries.

Example 5: Same as Example 4, except that the trust states that B's withdrawal power, each year, lapses only to the extent of the 5-and-5 exclusion available to B. A's annual contributions continue to be exempt under the *Crummey* doctrine, but now B's deemed transfer is fully exempted under the 5-and-5 rule. However, B's withdrawal power (general power of appointment) extends beyond the current $10,000 contributions by A to include prior contributions of A reduced by prior lapsed amounts. (If the aggregate withdrawable amount is greater than $100,000, the available lapse exemption, based on 5% of the aggregate withdrawable amount, will rise above $5,000.) So long as A's annual contributions exceed B's lapse exemption, the amount subject to B's general power of appointment will increase. If A ceases to make contributions, and it the power continues to lapse on an annual basis, the amount subject to B's general power of appointment will decrease.

4. *Generation-skipping tax.* The § 2503(b) exclusion also exempts inter vivos direct-skip generation-skipping transfers from the generation-skipping tax.

5. *Payments of tuition and medical care.* Direct payments by a person of tuition or medical bills owed by another person are exempt from gift tax and generation-skipping tax without limit and without any requirement of a "present interest." Such payments are in the nature of consumption, and do not directly increase the wealth of the beneficiaries of the payments, but by reducing the beneficiaries' expenses such payments may indirectly allow the beneficiaries to accumulate wealth on their own.

D. **Hybrid Transfer Pitfalls.** The term "hybrid transfer" refers to a transfer with retained interest or power, or other feature, that will (or might) cause all or a part of the transferred property to be brought back into the transferor's gross estate. Although the "adjusted taxable gifts exclusion" operates so as to generally prevent double taxation of the same property, several traps for the unwary lurk in this area.

1. *Retained-interest transfers.* A transfer under which the grantor retains an "interest" in income or corpus is deemed to be a taxable gift in full, without reduction for the value of the retained interest, under § 2702, with certain important exceptions. *See* Ch.2, at V. & VII., *supra.* The transfer is also likely to be included in the gross estate in whole or in part. *See* Ch.3, at II.C., *supra.* There is mitigation of double gift and estate tax only with respect to gift-taxed *interests* in property that are also included in the gross estate *by reason of the form of transfer. See* Ch.3, at II.C.5., *supra.* Thus, a retained-interest transfer is might incur unmitigated double gift and estate taxation. The "optimal" retained-interest transfer is one that is undervalued for gift tax purposes but not included in the gross estate. (As a matter of doctrine, there is no hybrid transfer that completely avoids both gift tax and estate tax.)

2. *Retained-power transfers:*

    a. *Subject to § 2702.* A transfer wherein the grantor retains a power over an (income or corpus) interest sufficient to render the transfer of that interest "incomplete" for gift tax purposes is deemed to be a retained-interest transfer potentially subject to § 2702, *supra.* Reg. § 25.2702-2(a)(4).

    Example 6: Suppose A creates an irrevocable trust, naming herself as trustee, income to B or accumulated in the trustee's discretion until B's death, remainder to C. Here A has a retained a power over income such as would render the transfer of such interest incomplete. Section 2702 applies, so that A is deemed to make a completed gift of the income interest, as well as of the remainder. (The trust will also be included in A's gross estate under § 2036(a)(2) if A predeaceases B.)

    b. *Retained power can avoid § 2702.* A retained-interest transfer will avoid § 2702 if the grantor retains a sufficient power over *all* of the nonretained interests so as to render the transfer of such interests "incomplete" for gift tax purposes. Reg. § 25.2702-1(c)(1).

    Example 7: If A creates a revocable trust, the entire transfer is incomplete, and § 2702 is avoided. Similarly, if A creates an irrevocable trust, income to A for life, remainder to such persons as A may determine during A's lifetime, the transfer of the nonretained interest (the remainder) is incomplete, and section 2702 is avoided. The transfer will be subject to estate (or gift) tax at a later date.

    c. *Retained powers that avoid §§ 2036-2038.* A retained power does not fall within §§ 2036-2038 if the power is (i) an "administrative" power or (ii) a dispositive power limited by reasonably definite and ascertainable standards. *See* Ch.3, at II.C.1.c., *supra.* The transfer will be fully subject to gift tax (and § 2702 will not apply) because retained powers of this type would not cause the transfer of any interest to be incomplete.

3. *Discretionary trusts for the grantor.* A grantor might attempt to avoid § 2702 and/or §§ 2036-2038 by creating an irrevocable trust in which the trustee (other than the grantor) has discretion (or is subject to standards) to pay income or corpus to the grantor. This transfer may be deemed to be a retained-interest transfer under various theories. *See* I.A.1.c., *supra.*

4. *Split gifts.* If a gift by one-spouse is split with the other spouse for gift-tax purposes under § 2513, and the transfer is included in the first spouse's gross estate under any of §§ 2036-2038 (since only the first spouse is the "transferor" for *estate tax* purposes), the deemed gift by the second spouse is not erased and will push the second spouse's subsequent taxable gift and estate transfers into higher marginal rate brackets. Thus, gift-splitting in this situation is a bad idea. There is a possible exception where the split-gift transfer was made within three years of the first spouse's death. *See* the discussion of 2001(d) & (e) at Ch.3, at V.A.3., *supra.*

5. *Premature exposure to gift tax.* Taxable gifts will use up the exemption equivalent of the unified transfer tax credit, possibly leading to actual gift tax exposure (and loss of earnings on amounts used to pay gift tax) prior to death. If

the gift transfers are of the type that will also be included in the gross estate, this premature exposure to gift tax turns out to have been unnecessary.

6. ***Exclusion ratio under generation-skipping tax.*** A transfer subject to both gift and estate tax shall be deemed to have been made at death for purposes of the generation-skipping tax. § 2642(f). If the property has appreciated between transfer and death, more of the generation-skipping-tax exemption will be needed to shield the transfer from tax.

7. ***Qualification for the § 2013 credit.*** If the transfer is included in the gross estate of the transferor and creates an interest in a transferee who dies within ten years of the death of the transferor, the latter's estate may obtain an estate tax credit for the transferor's estate tax (if any) attributable to the transfer. The § 2013 credit is not available for gift taxes paid by a transferor.

II. **TECHNIQUES AIMED TO FREEZE OR DEPRESS VALUE.** The term "estate freeze" refers to a situation where a transaction is undertaken so that future appreciation in property is removed from the gross estate of a person in an older generation and inures for the benefit of a natural object of such person's bounty, leaving the person in the older generation with assets whose (estate tax) value is "frozen." Certain estate freeze transactions involve business entities (corporations, partnerships, and LLCs) and interests therein. Interests in entities (or undivided interests in property) are also able to obtain significant valuation discounts in certain situations.

A. **Gifts.** The simplest form of estate freeze is the inter vivos transfer that will *not* be included in the donor's gross estate: the (gift tax) value is fixed for transfer tax purposes, and all post-gift appreciation inures to the benefit of the donee without being taxed to the donor. The donor can retain some control over the transferred property without subjecting the property to inclusion in the gross estate. *See* I.D.2.c., *supra.*

B. **Statutory Valuation Discounts.** Certain Code provisions provide for a value reduction for certain kinds of property interests.

1. ***Special valuation real property.*** Under § 2032A, certain farm, ranch, and small-business real property is valued (up to a limit) according to its actual use in farming, etc., as opposed to its highest and best use (*e.g.,* as a housing development). To qualify, the interest must comprise a certain percentage of the net estate, meaning that gifts of nonqualifying property before death may aid in qualification. *See* Ch.4, at II.B.1., *supra.*

2. ***Family-owned business interests.*** Under § 2057, a deduction is allowed (up to a limit) for estate-included family business interests. Again, to qualify the interest must comprise a certain percentage of the net estate. *See* Ch. 3, at IV.D., *supra.*

3. ***Qualified conservation easements.*** The estate tax value of real property can be reduced on account of a qualified conservation easement. See § 2031(c), discussed at Ch. 4, at II.B.2., supra.

6

TECHNIQUES AIMED TO FREEZE OR DEPRESS VALUE

C. **Transactions Involving Equity Interests in Entities.** One or more items of property can be placed in commercial entities (general partnerships, limited partnerships, limited liability companies, corporations, or business trusts), ownership of which is evidenced by various debt and equity interests. The estate planner should be familiar with the income tax aspects of entities. The issues discussed below revolve around equity interests in entities.

1. *Nontax reasons for using entities.* Entities may provide certain nontax advantages relative to ownership of the underlying assets. Such advantages may include: centralized management (including the ability to retain, rather than distribute, earnings), limited personal liability, the facilitation of (or restrictions on) the transferability of interests (including by way of gift), adaptability to divorce and other dispute settlements, and state law treatment of the interest as personal (rather than real) property.

2. *Family-limited partnerships.* Family limited partnerships offer the foregoing advantages plus the ability to protect partnership assets against limited partner creditors, since an assignee of a limited partnership interest (such as a judgment creditor) may possess only the right to share in partnership distributions as and when they occur (while being subject to income taxation of profits on a current basis). The holder of a limited partnership interest (or an assignee) typically has no right to require current distributions or to liquidate the interest (or to indirectly do so by controlling management). Finally, there well may be restrictions on the sale of a limited partnership interest. Restrictions on sale, liquidation, and the obtaining of distributions, combined with the lack of control over management (the general partners), greatly help in obtaining significant valuation discounts. (General partners are usually not subject to such restrictions, but the general partner can be a corporation, the interests in which might themselves be subject to restrictions.) Restrictions on sale, liquidation, or voting powers (but not restrictions on obtaining nonliquidating distributions) raise issues under §§ 2703 and 2704, discussed at d.2., *infra*.

3. *Obtaining valuation discounts.* An equity interest in an enterprise may, depending on the circumstances, qualify for various kinds of valuation discounts. For valuation of interests in closely-held enterprises, *see* Ch.4, at I.E., *supra*. Here is a quick run-down of types of valuation discounts available to equity interests in business entities:

   a. *Blockage discount.* An equity interest may qualify for a discount under the "blockage rule," which refers to a situation in which disposing of a large number of shares all at once would depress the price thereof. This type of discount generally comes into play for corporate stock that is traded "over the counter" or for an unusually large equity holding in a publicly traded enterprise, but not for equity holdings in closely controlled enterprises.

   b. *Lack-of-marketability discount.* An equity interest in a closely held enterprise may be discounted due to the fact that there is no ready market for the type of interest in question.

   c. *Minority interest discounts.* A minority interest in a closely held enterprise usually entails a substantial discount. (On the other hand, a controlling interest may entail a valuation premium.) The fact of being a minority interest also reinforces lack of marketability: few would want to buy a minority interest in a closely-held enterprise, especially if the holder of the minority interest cannot enter into coalitions with other shareholders (*i.e.*, where one or more persons have clear control). Community property interests held by husband and wife will not be aggregated for purposes of testing control premiums and minority-interest discounts, nor will other kinds of family relationships be taken into account. Two caveats must be kept in mind, however:

(1) Minority interests created by act of estate transfer. The courts have been holding that minority interest discounts are not obtainable where a majority interest is divided into minority interests by the act of *estate* transfer (bequest or intestate succession). However, minority interests created by gift (out of a controlling interest) will obtain a minority interest discount.

(2) Creation of minority interest in contemplation of an estate transfer. If a controlling interest is whittled down to a (barely) minority interest by one or more gifts shortly before and in contemplation of the estate transfer, the courts may disregard the prior gifts so as to treat the later transfer as of a controlling interest.

d. *Restrictions on sale and liquidation.* A restriction on sale or liquidation may exist under state law, the organizational charter (articles of incorporation, partnership agreement, etc.), the organizational by-laws, or by private contract. State law is particularly important in the case of (family limited) partnerships. For example, the right of a limited partner to liquidate (redeem) her interest may depend on whether the limited partnership is for a specified term of years.

(1) How restrictions depress value. Restrictions on sale, liquidation, and management rights are what create and "deepen" the lack-of-marketability and minority-interest discounts. The most potent type of restriction is perhaps a prohibition on liquidating the interest.

(a) Outright prohibition on sale. An outright (and permanent) prohibition on sale would mean that the value could not be higher than the greater of (a) the liquidation value (if there is a right to liquidation) or (b) the present value of future non-liquidating distributions.

(b) Outright prohibition on liquidation. The term "liquidation" can refer either to the liquidation of the underlying enterprise or the liquidation (redemption) of the interest in the enterprise. A prohibition on either type of liquidation, combined with an inability to control or influence management, should produce deep lack-of-marketability and minority-interest discounts.

(i) Redemption of interest in enterprise. The liquidation of an interest in an enterprise involves the redemption of the interest, *i.e.*, the sale of the interest back to the enterprise for cash or assets of the enterprise. An outright prohibition on the redemption of an interest in an enterprise would prevent the holder of the interest from obtaining the underlying assets.

6

Thus, a person subject to such a restriction, *and any potential buyer* (assuming the restriction does not disappear), could expect nothing more than future nonliquidating distributions. Since nonliquidating distributions are normally discretionary with management, the holder of a minority interest that is subject to a prohibition on redemption can expect very little, and the value of such an interest would be very low under the willing buyer, willing seller test. Corporate stock generally cannot be redeemed at will, unless the stockholder controls management or has entered into a stock purchase agreement with the corporation. General partnership interests, and sometimes limited partnership interests, can be redeemed at the will of the equityholder unless the partnership agreement provides otherwise.

(ii) Liquidation of enterprise. A liquidation of the entire enterprise would result in the redemption of the interests of all the shareholders. Normally, a liquidation of the enterprise, if permitted at all, requires the vote of a supermajority.

(c) Restrictions permanently affecting price. An interest may be subject to a restriction falling short of a prohibition on sale or liquidation, such as an obligation of the holder to offer, or an option in another party (perhaps the entity iteself) to purchase, the property at a fixed price or a price set by a formula, which price may well be below the current fair market value of the interest. *See* also 5., *infra*.

(d) Restrictions affecting voting (management) rights. An equity interest without voting or management rights cannot compel distributions (liquidating or nonliquidating) and cannot select management, and therefore cannot influence distribution policy. Preferred stock and limited partnership interests typically lack voting rights with respect to most types of management decisions. An interest without voting rights cannot even influence management (cannot enter coalitions with others having voting rights), and this creates a "deeper" minority-interest discount than would attach to a minority voting interest as such.

(2) Statutory disregard of certain restrictions. Sections 2703(a)(2) and 2704(b), effective for arrangements entered into after October 8, 1990, negate certain of the foregoing techniques, but not others.

(a) Restrictions on sale. Section 2703(a)(2) states that a restriction on "sale" shall be disregarded in valuing the property.

(i) Exception where nonfamily members are a majority. Treas.Reg. §25.2703-1(b)(3) states that a restriction is not subject to § 2703(a)(2) if nonfamily members own 51% or more of the equity interests and the nonfamily members are subject to the same restrictions as the transferor.

(ii) Exception for certain bona fide business arrangements. Section § 2703(b) provides an exception where the restriction meets all of the following: (1) the restriction is a bona fide business

6

arrangement; (2) the restriction is not a device to transfer the property to family members for less than full and adequate consideration; and (3) the restriction is comparable to those entered into by unrelated persons in an arms length transaction. Keeping the management within the family group by prohibiting sale to outsiders was considered to be a bona fide business arrangement under prior law. The second requirement is easily satisfied, since a prohibition on sale is not a device to allow family members to acquire the property at a bargain price. The third requirement, which has no antecedent in pre-1990 law, is the most indeterminate. The IRS may take the position that no rational businessperson would agree to being locked into an investment. *See* TAM 9723009 (Feb.24, 1997). However, a rational businessperson might accept being locked in if other equity holders also are locked in, so as to preserve the continuity of the enterprise and of management.

(iii) Applicability to restrictions on redemptions. A prohibition on redemption should not be considered to be a restriction on "sale," since Congress has used the term "redemption" elsewhere in the Code, and restrictions on liquidation are commonplace for certain equity interests. If this is correct, then § 2703(a)(2) can be finessed (avoided) by prohibiting only a redemption and allowing a sale. However, a restriction on sale may be desired for non-tax reasons.

(b) Restrictions on liquidation. Section 2704(b) states that certain restrictions on liquidation shall be disregarded in valuing an interest in a corporation or partnership.

(i) Applicable restriction. A restriction on liquidation is subject to § 2704(b) only if it limits the ability of the "corporation or partnership" to "liquidate." (An LLC is either a corporation or partnership under the "check the box" regulations.) A restriction that prohibits a particular equity interest from being liquidated (*i.e.*, redeemed by the entity) should not be subject to § 2704(b). Thus, a restriction on redemption would appear to avoid both § 2703(a)(2) and § 2704(b).

(ii) Restriction must lapse or be removable. To be an "applicable restriction," the restriction must either lapse, in whole or in part, following the transfer or be removable after the transfer by the transferor or any "member of the transferor's family," acting alone or collectively. § 2704(b)(2)(B). Such action can be in any form, such as amending the organizational document or by-laws. The rationale of this rule is that a restriction that will lapse or is removable is "illusory" and probably tax motivated.

(iii) Transfer must be to a family member. Section 2704(b) only applies if the transfer is to a "member of the transferor's family," which term refers to the transferor's spouse or siblings, any ancestor or descendant of the transferor or transferor's spouse, or any spouse of such sibling, ancestor, or descendant. § 2704(b)(1)(A) and (c)(2).

(iv) Family control. Section 2704(b) only applies if the transferor and "members of the transferor's family" control the entity immediately before the transfer. § 2704(b)(1)(B). The term "control" means at least 50% of the equity, or a general partnership interest in a limited partnership. §§ 2701(b)(2) and 2704(c)(1). Interests held by a family member include interests held indirectly through other entities. §§ 2701(e)(3) and 2704(c)(3).

(v) Exception for restrictions imposed by state law. A restriction on liquidation imposed by state law is not within the scope of § 2704(b). § 2704(b)(3)(B). Restrictions contained in the entity's charter or by-laws, or under a contract, are not imposed "by state law." This exception is quite important, since state partnership law may prohibit a redemption (withdrawal of a limited partner) or liquidation where (1) the partnership is for a term of years or (2), in other cases, where the partnership agreement does not expressly allow a redemption.

(vi) Financing restrictions. Restrictions on liquidation imposed in connection with unrelated-party financing of the entity are not subject to § 2704(b).

(c) Restrictions on voting rights or management. *Permanent* restrictions on voting rights or management are not subject to either § 2703(a)(2) or § 2704(b). Certain types of equity interests inherently lack such rights or provide voting rights only in connection with certain structural changes.

(3) Possible loss of present interest exclusion. In TAM 9751003, the IRS held that a gift of a limited partnership interest did not qualify for the annual exclusion where: (1) the general partners could withhold nonliquidating distributions at will, (2) the donee could not redeem his interest until a date far in the future, and (3) the donee was, as a practical matter, barred from selling or assigning his interest. This effect of this ruling can presumably be avoided by allowing the general partners to withhold distributions only for reasons germane to the business.

4. *Lapsing rights.* A technique related to value-reducing restrictions that permanently attach to equity interests is that of a valuable right (such as a liquidation or management right) that lapses, so that such lapse depress the value of the holder's interest for transfer tax tax purposes. (Recall that valuation looks forward from the time of transfer, so that the absence of a valuable right at the time of transfer, or the disappearance of a valuable right attendant upon the transfer itself, will depress the property's value.) The lapse of a valuable right of the property owner (whether or not the lapse occurs simultaneously with a transfer) may indirectly enhance the rights of others. For example, if the voting rights attached to a person's equity interests lapse when the person attains the age of 70, the voting power of other equity holders (who are likely family members) would be increased, and so would the value of such equity interests.

a. *Tax-avoidance potential.* This technique attempts to take advantage of the fact that, under estate and gift tax principles, the termination or expiration of an interest or right does not (usually) involve a transfer of wealth. Any transfer in such a situation would have occurred earlier, namely, when the arrangement was entered into (unilaterally or by contract) whereby value "vanishes" at some future time or event but an equivalent value would "spring up" in the hands of a natural object of one's bounty. In theory, the act of gratuitously entering into such an arrangement would be a present gift of a future interest, but no gift for gift tax purposes has ever been established on this theory, since the amount of and timing of the future value shift may be speculative or hidden. Nor has the government been able to bring these situations within § 2036(a)(1), even though there is a clear analogy between the lapsing restriction situation and that of an expiring retained life estate followed by a remainder. Section 2036(a)(1) is limited to situations involving retained life estates and income interests, and does not cover the expiration of retained rights with respect to entities. *U.S. v. Byrum,* 408 U.S. 125 (1972) (retained voting rights in corporation and attendant right to control dividend policy).

b. *Retained voting rights in transferred stock.* Under § 2036(b), added in 1976 in response to the *Byrum* case, *supra,* a retained right to vote transferred stock is deemed to be a right to possession or enjoyment of the transferred stock within § 2036(a)(1), thereby overturning the result of *Byrum. See* Ch.3, II.C.2.e., *supra.* If the transferor retains the voting rights until her death (or for a period not ending before her death, or for a period determined with reference to her death), the full value of the transferred stock is pulled back into the transferor's gross estate. Section 2036(b) applies only to corporate stock, not partnership interests.

c. *Section 2704(a): lapsing liquidation and voting rights.* Under § 2704(a), the lapse of certain voting and liquidation rights shall constitute a gift or estate transfer in an amount equal to the decrease (if any) in the value of all of the individual's equity interests in the entity. The effect of § 2704(a) is to negate the valuation discount attributable to the lapsing voting and liquidation rights.

(1) Broad applicability. This section is potentially applicable to lapses with respect to any kind of business entity. The lapse may occur "on its own" or in conjunction with a transfer of the property. The term "liquidation" in this context includes any right to have the interest redeemed by the entity. Also, a liquidation right may exist by reason of voting control. Reg. § 25.2704-1(a)(2)(v).

Example 8: Mom owns voting preferred stock in X corporation, and her daughter owns nonvoting common stock in the same corporation. Under the applicable corporate documents, the voting rights in the preferred stock lapse at the owner's death, at which time they attach to the common stock. The lapse of voting rights results in a valuation discount in the stock owned by Mom included in her § 2033 gross estate at her death. Section 2704(a) causes there to be a deemed estate inclusion in Mom's gross estate equal to such discount. The end result is negation of the discount that would otherwise be caused by the lapsing voting rights.

(2) Lapse by operation of state law. A valuable right incident to an equity interest (particularly a partnership interest) may disappear or be suspended pursuant to state law as the result of a transfer. For example, if a partner dies or makes a gift of a partnership interest, or the interest is seized by a creditor, the partner's estate or other successor may not acquire the management rights the partner had. However, § 2704(a) is implicated only if the lapse itself reduces the value of the individual's interests in the entity. Thus, if a liquidation right technically lapses as the result of a transfer, but the same right is automatically reacquired by the transferee, there is no loss of value due to a lapse.

(3) Lapse by imposing a restriction. The act of imposing a restriction on a valuable right constitutes a "lapse" under Reg. § 25.2704-1(a)(4) and (b).

(4) Lapse by change in state law. A lapse caused solely by a change in state law does not trigger § 2704(a). Reg. § 25.2704-1(c)(2)(iii).

(5) Transfer resulting in loss of voting control or liquidation power not a lapse. If a person holding 60% of the equity in an enterprise makes a gift of 15%, the resulting loss of control is not considered a lapse so long as the donee succeeds to the donor's voting rights in the transferred stock. Similarly, if a person has a right to liquidate his interest solely by virtue of possessing supermajority voting power, and loses such power by reason of making a gift of some of her equity, section 2704(a) will not apply so long as the transferee acquired whatever voting rights in the transferred equity that the donor had. Reg. § 25.2704-1(c)(1) and (f) (Example 4).

(6) Family-control requirement. Section 2704(a) only applies if the individual and "members of her family" (supra) "control" (supra) the entity both before and after the lapse. § 2704(a)(1)(B).

(7) Liquidation right can't be exercised by family members. If, immediately after the lapse of a liquidation right, the interest can't be liquidated by the holder, her estate, and/or members of her family, section 2704(a) shall not apply. Reg. § 25.2704-1(c)(2)(i). In this scenario, no value "springs up" to the holder or the natural objects of her bounty.

(8) Potential application to lapses of other kinds of rights. The Treasury is authorized, by § 2704(a)(3), to "extend" § 2704(a) to rights "similar to" voting and liquidation rights. The Treasury has not yet issued any such regulations. *See* Reg. § 25.2704-1(e) (reserving this issue).

d. *Nonlapsing voting rights in nontransferred stock.* Sections 2036(b) and 2704(a) can be avoided where the grantor's (non-lapsing) voting rights in *non*transferred stock are sufficient to control dividend policy of the corporation.

5. ***Buy-sell agreements.*** A common example of a lapsing restriction is the buy-sell agreement involving family members. The younger generation person is given the right (or is obligated) to buy the equity interest from the estate of the deceased older generation member at a fixed or formula price that is likely to be less than the then fair market value of the interest. (A mandatory buy-sell agreement also

assures liquidity to the estate.) The price restriction reduces value under the willing-buyer willing-seller test. Since the purchaser of the equity interest is not bound by any restriction involving future sale, the price restriction (on the transferor) in effect lapses upon the purchase. Although this situation might be described as a lapse of a liquidation right (at least if the entity is the potential buyer), section 2704(a) would not help the government, since any lapse of any liquidation right would here increase, rather than decrease, the value of the equity. Also, to the extent that the buy-sell agreement can be said to involve a lapse of a *restriction* on redemption of an interest, section 2704(b) does not apply because the term "liquidation" there refers to the liquidation of the whole enterprise. To fill this gap, section 2703(a)(1) was enacted to deal with buy-sell agreements.

(1) Prior law. Aside from assisting an estate to achieve liquidity, the purpose of a buy-sell agreement is to depress the value of the property subject to the agreement. Such agreements were used not only for equity interests but also for real estate and other assets. The IRS allowed these agreements to fix (depress) the value of the stock if certain conditions were satisfied, such as that the agreement be mandatory and binding on both parties. Watered-down versions of the buy-sell agreement, such as giving the younger-generation a right of first refusal or a "call option" or giving the estate a "put" option, were often taken into account in fixing value.

(2) Section 2703(a)(1). For agreements, etc., entered into after October 8, 1990, among family members, buy-sell agreements (etc.) shall be disregarded for valuation purposes. Section 2703(a)(1) is not limited to equity interests, but potentially encompasses all property.

(3) Exception for arms-length business arrangements. Section 2703(b) states that a buy-sell agreement, etc., shall not be disregarded in fixing value if all of the following requirements are met:

(a) the agreement, etc., is a bona fide business arrangement;

(b) it is not a device to transfer the property to members of the decedent's family for less than full and adequate consideration in money or money's worth; and

(c) its terms are comparable to similar arrangements entered into by persons in an arms' length transaction.

(4) Relation to prior law:

(a) Bona fide business arrangement. Case law prior to 1990 had posited the first requirement, but it was easy to satisfy. Thus, perpetuation of control within the family was seen as a "business" purpose. This interpretation presumably continues under § 2703(b)(1).

(b) Not a disguised gratuitous transfer. Normally, a sale to a family member at a price below fair market value is a gratuitous transfer. However, in the buy-sell agreement situation, it was held to be not a gratuitous transfer because the property was "worth" the price under

6

the buy-sell agreement. If there was any gratuitous transfer, it must have occurred when the agreement was entered into, not at the transferor's death. Nevertheless, the effect of a buy-sell agreement as a whole is to effect a gratuitous transfer if the purchaser is (directly or indirectly) a family member. Some courts required that the buy-sell agreement must not only be a bona fide business arrangement but must also not be a device to effect a gratuitous transfer, but other courts held that a bona fide business motive was sufficient to allow the agreement to determine estate tax value. The text and legislative history to § 2703(b) clearly indicate that the "no device" test must be satisfied in addition to the other two tests.

(c) Arms'-length equivalent test. This test was added by the enactment of § 2703(b). Satisfaction of this test necessarily involves the resolution of a question of fact that can be quite burdensome to carry off, since a rational businessperson would normally not agree to sell property for less than what it is worth.

6. **Hidden value transfers through employee death benefits.** An employee death benefit can be a vehicle for transferring wealth through the medium of an entity in a way that avoids or minimizes transfer tax.

a. *Gifts of employee death benefit rights.* Normally, an employee death benefit is included in the employee's gross estate under § 2039, or possibly § 2037, or § 2038. However, the death benefit can avoid estate inclusion if the employee has no right to payments for life (etc.), the employee's estate is not a contingent beneficiary, *and* the beneficiary designation is irrevocable.

(1) Minimal gift tax value. In cases described in the preceding paragraph, the making of an irrevocable beneficiary designation in theory constitutes the completion of a gift transfer, but the then value of the gift may be zero or *de minimis* due to various future contingencies, especially risks of forfeiture.

(2) Lapsing contingencies. For a while, the IRS treated the lapse of the contingencies (at death) as the completion of an earlier incomplete transfer, but the only case on point held that the completion of the gift occurred when the death benefit beneficiary became irrevocable, and any value shifting that occurred at death could not be subject to the gift tax. The IRS has acquiesced. *See* Ch.2, at VI.D., *supra.* Section 2704(a) does not cover this situation, because that section only refers to lapsing "voting or liquidation rights" in business entities, and a death benefit is a contract right apart from a voting or liquidation right. Although § 2704(a)(3) authorizes the Treasury to issue regulations extending § 2704(a) to "rights similar to voting and liquidation rights," it is not clear that this authority extends beyond rights that pertain to equity interests in business entities. In any event, the Treasury has not yet issued any regulations under § 2704(a)(3).

(3) Inapplicability of §§ 2036-2038. The fact that the employee might be able to destroy the death benefit or control the beneficiary designation through her control of the entity is usually not treated as a retained power to alter the death benefit. *See* Ch.3, at II.C.1.c., *supra.*

6

b. *Family member loots the entity.* The person who controls the business entity can allow the entity to accumulate earnings. After such person's death, the family member who accedes to control of the entity may be able to loot the entity by causing the entity to pay a large "death benefit" to herself. If the death benefit is not paid pursuant to a preexisting contract with the deceased employee-equity holder, it will avoid inclusion in the latter's gross estate. The "death benefit" may allow the successor in control to extract more from the entity than is represented by the liquidation value of his or her equity interest. (In some cases, a transaction of this type might entail present-interest "gifts" by the other equity holders, but the gift-tax consequences thereof may be minimal due to, *inter alia,* the § 2503(b) exclusion.)

7. ***Classic entity freezes.*** In the typical entity freeze, a controlling (or sole) stockholder will have the corporation undergo a recapitalization in which the sole equity (*e.g.*, common stock) is exchanged for nonvoting "junior" equity (common stock) and voting "senior" equity (*e.g.*, preferred stock) of the same entity. The senior equity will typically have a fixed annual distribution (*e.g.*, dividend) rate sufficiently high so that the senior equity constitutes most of the value of the original pre-recapitalization equity, so that the new junior equity constitutes very little of the value of the original pre-recapitalization equity. The non-voting junior equity interests are given to children and the senior equity is retained.

a. *Desired result.* The retained voting senior equity, which will be included in the donor's § 2033 gross estate, will retain a relatively constant (frozen) value, because it is similar to a bond or debt obligation. The nonvoting junior equity, which represents the future appreciation potential of the enterprise, will have a low value for gift tax purposes but will grow in value in the hands of the donees. Section 2036(a) does not apply because no interest was retained by the donor until death "in" the transferred junior equity, and § 2036(b) does not apply because the donor did not retain the right to vote the transferred junior equity.

b. *Section 2701.* Section 2701 applies in this situation to *deem* a gift of the value of the retained senior equity, provided that the transaction was entered into after October 8, 1990 and involves family members. (Retained debt instruments and employment contracts would not, alone, usually be sufficient to trigger § 2701.) Even if § 2701 applies, future appreciation may be removed from the gross estate.

Example 9: *D* owns 100% of *X* Corp., which has a value of $2 million, and causes a recapitalization into 8% voting preferred stock, with a future-dividend and liquidation value of $1.9 million, and nonvoting common stock worth $0.1 million, which *D* gives to her daughter *E*. Under § 2701, *D*'s retained preferred is deemed to be worth zero, resulting a total gift of $2 million, consisting of an actual gift of $0.1 million and a (deemed) gift of $1.9 million. *D* dies ten years later, at which time the preferred stock is worth $2.3 million and the common stock is now worth $7.7 million in *E*'s hands. The preferred stock worth $2.3 million is included in *D*'s gross estate under § 2033, but "adjustment" is made for the fact that there was the earlier deemed gift of the same preferred stock having a then value of $1.9 million; hence, only $0.4 million is actually included in *D*'s gross estate; the appreciation in the common stock has been removed from *D*'s transfer tax base.

6

(1) Exception for Qualified Payment Right. There is an exception where the retained interest is a "qualified payment right" which is essentially a preferred distribution right that cannot be manipulated so as to withhold or waive preferred distributions (with the aim of building up the value of the transferred junior equity).

(2) De minimis gift value. If the exception cited immediately above applies, in no event shall the transferred junior equity be worth less than 10% of the enterprise value multiplied by the percentage of all of the common represented thereby. *See* Ch.2, at II.C.4., *supra*.

> **Example 10:** Assuming that the preferred stock in the above example represents a Qualified Payment Right, the following results occur: (1) there is no deemed gift of the preferred, (2) there is a gift of the common in the deemed (minimum) amount of $0.2 million (10% of the total), and (3) $2.2 million is included in *D*'s gross estate under § 2033 ($2.3 million adjusted downward for the $0.1 million added to the gift of the common stock).

c. *Section 2704(a)*. If the voting rights appurtenant to the senior equity lapse at death (and re-surface in the junior equity), the value of the senior equity (included in the gross estate under § 2033) will be discounted under the willing-buyer, willing-seller test, but death will cause a deemed estate transfer equal to such discount under § 2704(a). *See* Example 8, *supra*. This deemed transfer has the effect of negating the valuation discount.

D. **Transactions Involving Debt Obligations.** The following transactions involve debt obligations (whether or not the obligor is a business entity), as opposed to equity interests in business entities.

1. ***Applicability of § 2703.*** Section 2703, which mandates that certain restrictions, etc., on the sale (or use) of property be disregarded for valuation purposes, applies to "property" (including debt obligations), not just equity interests in entities.

2. ***Straight installment sale to related party.*** The older person sells property (usually real estate or securities) to a natural object of her bounty; the latter agrees to pay the purchase price in installments, which is typically represented by a series of interest-bearing notes. Planning in this area involves thorough knowledge of the income tax rules, which are beyond the scope of this outline.

   a. *Intended results:*

      (1) Simple estate freeze. In a straight installment sale, the seller ends up with a debt obligation whose value is essentially "frozen" for purposes of her § 2033 gross estate, and the related buyer ends up with the "equity" in the property, whose value (hopefully) will appreciate.

      (2) No present gift. The sale does not involve a gift, assuming that the notes have a value equal to the property sold.

   b. *When present gift might occur:*

(1) Inadequate interest. A zero or below-market interest rate will usually cause the value of the notes to be less than the value of the property transferred; the shortfall is a gift from the seller to the buyer. § 7872(a)(1) & (d).

(2) Sham notes. If the buyer really has no wherewithal to make the note payments, the notes may be treated as a sham, meaning that the sale was in substance a gift.

3. **Installment gifts.** This transaction is the same as an installment sale, except that the seller intends to forgive the notes as they become due, hopefully at a rate equal to the applicable present interest exclusion(s) available to the seller.

   a. *Intended results.* In addition to the results aimed at in a straight installment sale, the idea is that the retained debt interest is gradually transferred to the buyers at little or no gift tax cost thanks to the § 2503(b) exclusions. The same problems of inadequate interest and sham notes as discussed immediately above would also apply here.

   b. *Is there a present gift?* The IRS may claim that the present intent to forgive future installments entails a present gift of the entire property. *See* Rev. Rul. 77-299, 1977-2 C.B. 14. The better view is that there is no such present gift (assuming adequate interest, etc.), since the installment obligation taken back is objectively an asset that (to the extent of any unforgiven installments) will be included in the seller's § 2033 gross estate (*e.g., Haygood v. Com'r,* 42 T.C. 936 (1964), *nonacq.*).

4. **Self-cancelling installment notes ("SCINs").** This transaction is structured like an installment sale or gift transaction, except the installment notes self-cancel at the date of the seller's death.

   a. *Intended result.* The aim is the same as with an installment sale and/or installment gift, with the additional aim of creating a value of zero for the retained notes if the seller should die prematurely.

   b. *Obligation not includible under other Code sections.* Section 2704(a) (lapsing voting and liquidation rights) currently applies only to equity interests in entities. Section 2704(a)(3) possibly authorizes extension of § 2704(a) beyond equity interests by regulation, but no regulations have been issued under this authority. Sections 2036(a)(1) and 2702, which deal with property transfers with retained interests, do not apply, because installment notes are not retained interests "in" transferred property.

   c. *Possible inter vivos gift.* In theory, there is a gift at the time of sale equal to the excess of the value of the property sold over the value, if any, of the notes as discounted by the self-cancelling feature. This gift element, which may be quite small to begin with, can be avoided if the buyer pays an appropriate premium for the self-cancelling feature. Maximum tax avoidance would occur if the discount was small due to the seller's relatively young age but the seller in fact dies shortly after the sale.

5. **Sale to defective grantor trust.** The term "defective grantor trust" refers to an inter vivos trust that will not be included in the transferor's gross estate under §§

2036-2038 but which is treated as still the grantor's property for income tax purposes under §§ 671-677. The aim of an installment sale of property by a grantor to a defective grantor trust is to obtain current liquidity without incurring capital gains tax, on the theory that a sale to oneself is not a sale for income tax purposes. See Rev.Rul. 85-13, 1985-1 C.B. 184. Otherwise, the aim is the same as a straight installment sale, the installment gift, or the SCIN, as the case may be.

E. **Leasebacks.** Here the owner of property makes a sale or a gift of property to the natural object of one's bounty and continues to use or occupy the property pursuant to a lease. (The sale may be an installment sale, with or without the intent to forgive installment notes as they become due, or with or without a self-cancelling feature.)

1. *Aims.* Again, the chief transfer tax goal is to remove future appreciation from the gross estate of the transferor. In addition, the lease payments deplete the transferor's gross estate without being gifts that use up the transferor's annual exclusion.

2. *Excessive rent payments.* Rent payments by the transferor in excess of the fair rental value will be present-interest gifts to the owner-lessor.

3. *Inadequate rent payments:*

   a. *In sale-leaseback.* If the sale was for full and adequate consideration in money or money's worth, no transfer tax issue is posed by the making of inadequate rent payments by the seller-lessee, since the IRS is not currently asserting that gifts occur by reason of the below-market rent of property to a related person.

   b. *In gift-leaseback.* If the transfer of property was by gift (including a sale for less than full and adequate consideration in money or money's worth), the use by the transferor of the property at a below-market rental is considered to be the retention of a possessory interest that will trigger § 2036(a)(1) and, presumably, § 2702. *See* Chapter 2, at VII.B., *supra.* In addition, if the property is used at times by the transferee as a personal residence, the transferee's income tax deductions may be limited under § 280A.

F. **Taking Advantage of Actuarial Errors.** The valuation of interests and property for gift and estate tax purposes often depends upon actuarial tables. The tables are usually required to be used, even where the facts of a particular case indicate that they are not appropriate. Reg. § 20.7520-3(b)(3). The tables are based on assumptions pertaining to life expectancies, discount rates, and rates of return, and they also assume that the underlying property will neither appreciate nor depreciate in the future. *See* Ch.2, IV.G., *supra.* There are opportunities to save transfer taxes where actual facts do not conform to the actuarial tables. *See* the discussion of SCINs, *supra.* There are others:

1. *Transactions involving life insurance.* Economic gain occurs with respect to life insurance where the insured dies prior to his actuarial life expectancy. Normally, such gain is included in the insured's gross estate under § 2042(2) (insured has one or more incidents of ownership). The actuarial gain is greatest in the case of pure term (or accidental death) insurance, as opposed to ordinary (cash surrender value) life insurance. (There is no actuarial gain at all if the ordinary life policy is fully paid up, *i.e.*, the cash surrender value equals the face

amount.) *See* Ch.3, at II.G., *supra,* for estate tax issues pertaining to life insurance. Transfer taxes on this gain are avoided by:

a. *Gifts of life insurance.* The insured should make a gift of the policy before death. The gift tax value of the insurance will be significantly less than the amount of the proceeds payable to the beneficiary, especially in the case of term insurance. *See* Ch.2, at VI.C., *supra.* To be effective in avoiding tax on the actuarial gain, the gift must be more than three years before death. *See* § 2035(a)(2).

   (1) Gift to beneficiary. If the gift is to be made to an individual, the donee should be the beneficiary, since if a third party is the beneficiary, the donee will be charged with a gift of the proceeds to the third-party beneficiary upon the insured's death. Gifts of the policy, as well as subsequent gifts of premiums, will qualify for the § 2503(b) exclusion. Gifts (or even direct payments) of premiums by the insured within three years of death will not trigger estate inclusion under § 2035(a)(2).

   (2) Irrevocable insurance trust. A trust offers more flexibility than a lump-sum payment to a beneficiary or periodic-payment settlement options under the policy. The gift of the policy and of premiums to the trust will not usually qualify for the § 2503(b) exclusion, unless *Crummey* powers are built into the trust. *See* I.C.3.b., *supra.* The grantor-insured can make a supplementary gift of income-producing property to the trust to fund the future premium obligations.

b. *Non-insured takes out policy on life of another.* Instead of the insured buying the policy and then making a gift of it to the putative beneficiary or to a trust, consider having the latter take out the policy on the life of the insured, naming herself (or itself) as beneficiary. This technique avoids the risk of § 2035(a)(2), should the insured die within three years, since the insured never transferred incidents of ownership over the policy. This conclusion holds even if the insured was involved in the procurement of the policy.

c. *Other general considerations:*

   (1) Spousal involvement. There is no particular point for tax purposes in having one spouse own insurance on the life of the other. (Neither is there anything disadvantageous about such an arrangement.)

   Example 11: If, say, *H* owns the policy on his own life and names *W* as beneficiary, the proceeds are includable in *H*'s gross estate, but there is an offsetting marital deduction. This result is really no different than if *W* owned the policy on *H*'s life naming herself as beneficiary. Getting the proceeds down to the next generation will involve an additional gift or estate transfer.

   (2) Generation-skipping tax. If the donee of a policy is two or more generations below that of the donor, or if the beneficiary is two or more generations below that of the policy owner, generation-skipping tax issues are raised, but that does not necessarily produce a worse overall transfer tax result than if the proceeds were to pass through the intermediate generation.

d. *Annuity-insurance combinations.* A gift of life insurance combined with the retention of a single-life annuity resembles a § 2036(a)(1) transfer, yet it is possible that §§ 2033, 2036, 2039, 2042, 2702, and 2704 are all avoided.

Example 12: Suppose *B,* having $10 million, purchases for $6 million a paid-up ordinary life insurance policy having a face amount of $10 million and for $4 million a single-life nonrefund annuity providing for annual payments to *B* of $600,000 per year until death. Note that the $600,000 is a reasonable "income" return of the total investment of $10 million. The insurance policy is given to an individual or irrevocable insurance trust.

(1) Objectives. *If properly structured,* the following results occur: (1) there is a gift of the insurance policy in the amount of $6 million, and (2) the annuity is not included in *B*'s gross estate because it lapses at *B*'s death. The life insurance beneficiary will receive $10 million on *B*'s death; $4 million will have been removed from *B*'s transfer tax base. The maximum tax savings will occur if *B* dies shortly after the gift of the insurance policy: the actuarial gain on the insurance policy will have been maximized and very little in the way of annuity payments will have been received to augment *B*'s potential § 2033 gross estate. Note that the actuarial gain potential in the insurance policy offsets the actuarial loss potential in the annuity (assuming that *B* dies shortly after this transaction is entered into), but $10 million is nevertheless transferred to the next generation with only $6 million appearing in *B*'s transfer tax base.

(2) Is this a retained-interest transfer? The government might argue that this transaction is a retained-interest transfer subject to one or more of §§ 2036, 2039, 2042, and 2702. If the government prevails, the $10 million insurance proceeds will be included in *B*'s gross estate.

(a) Section 2036. The Supreme Court has held that § 2036(a) does not apply to this transaction, even if the annuity and insurance policy are purchased from the same company in an "integrated" transaction. *Fidelity-Philadelphia Trust Co. v. Smith,* 356 U.S. 274 (1958) (holding that the annuity was not a retained "income" interest "in" the insurance policy, each being economically self-sufficient).

(b) Section 2042. If the annuity and life insurance policy are acquired in an integrated transaction, the package as a whole is not "life insurance," since the actuarial risk factors cancel each other out, and hence § 2042 simply cannot apply. *Helvering v. LeGierse,* 312 U.S. 531 (1941). Even if § 2042 were to apply, the proceeds would not be includible because the insured has not retained incidents of ownership and the proceeds are not payable to the insured's estate.

(c) Section 2039. If the annuity and insurance are acquired in an integrated transaction, section 2039 will apply because that section only requires that an annuity and the death benefit (here, the insurance proceeds) be payable under the same "contract or agreement." *Estate of Montgomery v. Com'r,* 56 T.C. 489 (1971), *aff'd per curiam,* 458 F.2d 616 (5th Cir. 1972), cert. denied. This result can be avoided if the annuity and insurance are acquired from different companies or perhaps even from the same company in a nonintegrated transaction.

(d) Section 2702. This section appears not to apply for the same reason that § 2036 does not apply, namely, that the annuity and life insurance are not successive interests in the same property. *See* Reg. § 25.2702-4(a).

(3) Is the annuity a lapsing right under § 2704(a)? The annuity-insurance situation bears a certain resemblance not only to the income-remainder situation governed by § 2036(a)(1) but also to that where valuable rights lapse with respect to equity interests in business entities at a person's death but equivalent value "springs up" in equity interests owned by the natural object of the decedent's bounty. Section 2704(a), however, currently only covers lapsing "voting and liquidation rights" with respect to equity interests in business entities. It seems unlikely that any possible regulations that might be issued under § 2704(a)(3) would, or validly could, cover the annuity-insurance situation, especially if the two contract rights are acquired separately.

2. *Two-step transfers.* Along the same general lines as the annuity-insurance combination, a two-step transfer occurs where a single-life annuity is purchased and the remaining cash or property is transferred into an irrevocable mandatory accumulation trust during the donor's lifetime. However, despite the fact that §§ 2036, 2039, 2702, and 2704(a) will be avoided, no real transfer tax savings occur here, since premature death only produces actuarial loss in the annuity with no offsetting actuarial gain. If the annuitant lives out her actuarial life expectancy (or more), she will have received the "principal" back (plus the income), restoring her potential § 2033 gross estate to the *status quo ante*.

3. *Joint purchase of income and remainder interests.* Here the older generation person (*A*) purchases a life estate or term interest in property and the younger-generation person (*B*) purchases the remainder interest, possibly with funds provided by *A*.

a. *Prior law.* This arrangement resembles the annuity-insurance combination. On *A*'s death *A*'s interest terminates and is not included in *A*'s gross estate, and *B* has instant actuarial gain that is free from transfer tax. Only the amount of cash, if any, transferred from *A* to *B* (so that the latter can purchase the remainder interest) is subject to gift tax. The gift of the remainder (if any) would have a low actuarial value if the discount rate used in the applicable actuarial tables is high. At the same time, the actual income yield (augmenting *A*'s potential gross estate) may be lower than the income yield assumed by the same actuarial tables. Again maximum transfer tax avoidance occurs if *A* dies prematurely. The IRS attempted (with sporadic success) to bring some of these transactions within § 2036(a)(1) under a step-transaction theory in cases where *A* supplied the consideration with which *B* purchased the remainder, the idea being that *A* "transferred" the property in which *A* "retained" an income interest, etc.

6

b. *Section 2702.* Under § 2702, applicable to transactions of this type entered into after October 8, 1990, *A* is deemed to have made a gift of the entire property (including the retained interest), less any consideration supplied by the other party out of her own funds, assuming both are family members. This rule applies even if the purchaser of the remainder supplies her own funds.

Example 12: If Dad buys a life estate in Blackacre for $750,000 and Son buys the remainder interest for $250,000 out of Son's own funds, and these amounts accurately reflect the actuarial values of their respective interests, Dad is charged with a deemed gift of the $750,000 life estate. The same result occurs if Son simply "purchases" the remainder interest in property already owned by Dad. Reg.§ 25.2702-4(c). (Again, one must be aware of the income tax consequences of this kind of transaction.)

4. ***Private annuities.*** In a private annuity transaction, the older-generation person (*A*) transfers property to a younger-generation person (*B*) in exchange for *B*'s promise to pay an annuity to *A* for *A*'s life. This transaction is very similar to the SCIN, *supra.*

   a. *Objectives.* If structured properly, the following results occur: (1) there is no gift by *A* if the actuarial value of *B*'s annuity promise equals or exceeds the value of the property transferred by *A*; (2) the annuity is not included in *A*'s gross estate because it expires at death; and, (3) sections 2036(a) and 2702 do not apply because there is no retained interest of *A* "in" the transferred property (only a promise by *B* to pay a cash annuity), and § 2704(a) simply doesn't extend to annuities.

   b. *The economics.* The private annuity really saves transfer taxes only if *A* dies before her actuarial life expectancy. Otherwise, the cumulative annuity payments received by *A* will equal (or exceed) the value of the property transferred by *A* plus the income thereon. Also, the annuity obligation may be quite onerous to *B* (who is also badly treated from an income tax point of view).

   c. *Points of vulnerability.* The IRS basically has three theories on which it can attempt to defeat the private annuity transaction, all of which are fact-specific:

      (1) Sham transaction. If *B* does not have the financial wherewithal to make the annuity payments (considering the property received by *B* from *A*), then *A*'s annuity promise might be treated as a sham (having a zero value), resulting in a gift by *A* of all or most of the property.

      (2) Annuity as retained income from property: The IRS may argue that the annuity promise of *B* is really a retained right of *A* to the income from the transferred property under § 2036(a)(1) (and possibly § 2702 as well). The court decisions in this area are not easy to reconcile. The IRS might have to show that: (1) the annuity obligation approximates the actual or expected income yield of the property, *and* (2) the annuity obligation is chargeable to the transferred property (as opposed to being a mere promise of B). Query if securing the annuity promise by a mortgage or lien on the transferred property by itself satisfies this second test. (Also

query if the first requirement is really appropriate.) *See* Ch.3, II.C.2.a.(4)., *supra,* for a more detailed discussion of transfers with retained annuity rights.

(3) Waiver of actuarial tables. The IRS might argue that *A*'s actual short life expectancy should be used, instead of the actuarial tables, in valuing *B*'s annuity promise. However, Reg. § 20.7520-3(b)(3) states that the tables *must* be used unless the measuring life (*A*) is "terminally ill," defined as as suffering from an incurable disease or condition such that there is at least a 50% likelihood of death within the year. However, if the measuring life outlives the transfer date by 18 months, then he or she will not be deemed to have been terminally ill, unless there is clear and convincing evidence to the contrary.

6

5. *Retained-interest-for-term-of-years transfers.* Herein is discussed a transfer of property in which an interest is retained for a fixed term of years.

a. *"Classic" GRIT.* The GRIT (grantor retained-income trust) involves a situation where the grantor creates an irrevocable trust under which the grantor is to receive the income for a fixed term of years, which term is expected to end shortly before the grantor's death. If the term for years in fact expires before the grantor's death, section 2036(a) is avoided, since that section requires that the income be retained for life or a period which does not in fact end before death (etc.). Since the lapse of a retained interest is not a "transfer" thereof, section 2035(a)(2) does not trigger § 2036(a)(1), even if the term for years expires within three years of the grantor's death. (Section 2704(a) does not cover this type of lapsing interest.) For gift tax purposes the grantor has made a completed gift of the remainder interest following the retained term of years.

(1) Factors affecting value of remainder. The higher the discount rate built into the applicable actuarial tables, and the longer the term of years, the lower is the value of the gifted remainder interest.

(2) Estate freeze result. The gift of the remainder interest is a variety of estate freeze, *i.e.,* subsequent appreciation is removed from the transfer tax base (so long as § 2036 is avoided) at a low gift tax cost. Moreover, if the actual income yield from the property is less than the yield built into the actuarial tables (which is very easy to arrange), the income coming back into the grantor's potential § 2033 gross estate is less that what the actuarial tables assumed in valuing the retained interest. However, use of the actuarial tables is limited to cases where the income right is not illusory, considering the trust instrument and the law of trusts. *See* Reg. § 20.7520-3(b)(2)(ii)(A).

b. *Impact of § 2702.* Section 2702, enacted largely in response to the GRIT, is applicable to transfers made after October 8, 1990.

(1) General rule. A GRIT is a retained-interest transfer subject to § 2702, so that the value of the retained interest is *not* subtracted for gift tax purposes, meaning that the entire property is subject to gift tax when the trust is created. Subsequent appreciation is removed from the transfer tax base if the grantor outlives the term of years. If that is not the case,

however, the trust is included in the grantor's gross estate, but the deemed § 2702 gift of the income interest is not removed from the cumulative tax base. Thus, the classic GRIT is now too risky tax-wise; there is little to gain and much to lose.

(2) GRATs and GRUTs. Section 2702 will not apply if the retained interest is in the form of a qualified annuity interest or qualified unitrust interest. ("GRAT" stands for "[qualified] grantor retained annuity trust" and "GRUT" stands for "[qualified] grantor retained unitrust.") The qualification rules are spelled out in Reg. § 25.2702-3. The idea of the annuity or unitrust format is to assure that the retained interest is accurately valued at the time of the gift.

(3) High investment return needed. Transfer taxes can be saved under the GRAT format if the actual investment return (net income and appreciation) on the property exceeds the income yield built into the actuarial tables: such excess investment return in effect is added to corpus and passes to the remainder free of transfer tax (assuming § 2036 does not apply). Of course, finding such an investment return is not always assured, and if the actual return falls below the income yield used in the tables, the amount of the gift will have been overstated. (The GRUT format has less upside potential or downside risk, since periodic distributions are keyed to the value of the trust assets as determined from year to year.)

> **Example 13:** *X* creates a GRAT with $100,000, retaining an annuity right of $10,000 for ten years (and *X* in fact outlives the ten-year period). If the actuarial tables assume an income yield (and discount rate) of 10%, the present value of the retained interest is $61,446, resulting in a gift of $38,554. Suppose the trust invests in $100,000 of bonds yielding 13% ($13,000 per year). The income yield exceeds the annuity obligation by $3,000 per year, which sums, invested at 13% compounded annually, add up to $81,639 after ten years. Thus, the remainder ends up with $181,639 after ten years, the present value of which (using 10% tables) would have been $70,030, but *X* was charged with a gift of only $38,554. Asset appreciation has the same effect as a high income yield

c. *Qualified Personal Residence Trusts (QPRTs).* Section 2702 does not apply if real property is transferred into a trust meeting certain stringent requirements, and the grantor is entitled to use the property as a personal residence for the term of years. "Personal residence" can include vacation homes. The qualification requirements are spelled out in Reg. § 25.2702-5. The QPRT is a classic "loophole." The grantor is treated for gift tax purposes as having retained an income interest that would augment the grantor's § 2033 gross estate, but in fact the grantor receives no income. The economic return is likely to include significant appreciation, which inures to the holder of the remainder interest free of transfer tax. It is true that the grantor, during the term of years, avoids housing expenses, but such expenses would have been avoided anyway if the transaction had not occurred (and there are no outstanding mortgages).

d. *Art works and unimproved land.* A retained interest in certain nondepreciable tangible property escapes § 2702, but the retained interest is valued under the willing-buyer, willing-seller test (instead of the actuarial tables). *See* Reg. § 25.2702-2(c).

6. *Spousal election wills.* Here (typically) a husband's will purports to bequeath both his *and his wife's* property to a trust, income to her for life, and giving her a limited special power of appointment by will, in default of which the remainder passes to their descendants. This arrangement commonly occurs in a community property setting, where spousal wealth is roughly equal.

Example 14: Assume that *W* acquiesces to this arrangement, in which case she has in effect transferred her own property to the trust, retaining the income for life and a limited power to alter the remainder, in consideration for receiving the right to the income from *H*'s property for her life. *W* has made a constructive transfer that avoids gift tax (including § 2702), because of the retained interest combined with an incomplete transfer of the remainder.

a. *Effect of consideration offset.* The portion of the trust transferred by the consenting spouse (*W*) will initially be included in her gross estate under §§ 2036(a)(1) and 2038 on account of the retained income interest and power to alter the remainder interest. The income interest in *H*'s property, valued under actuarial tables, has been held to be "consideration" for *W*'s constructive transfer in trust.

(1) Can the consideration be full and adequate? If the income interest in *H*'s property is worth more than the value of the remainder interest in *W*'s property, conceivably the consideration will be treated as being "full and adequate," resulting in full exclusion from *W*'s gross estate. However, the IRS takes the position that the consideration can only be "partial," since to be "full and adequate" the consideration must equal the full value of the property transferred by W, not just the remainder interest therein. Although earlier cases had upheld the IRS's position, more recent cases (not, however, involving spousal election wills) suggest that the consideration can, depending on the facts, be "full and adequate." *See* Ch.3, at II.C.6.c., *supra*.

(2) When will the consideration be full and adequate? Whether the consideration received by *W* (the income interest in *H*'s share) equals or exceeds the value of the remainder interest in W's property is a question of fact to be ascertained as of the time of W's transfer (which occurs at or shortly after H's death). In a community property situation, *H*'s share is likely to be smaller than *W*'s, because *H*'s share is reduced by administration expenses, debts, funeral expenses, and estate taxes (if any). (*H*'s estate does not obtain the marital deduction here on account of § 2056(b)(4).) At *H*'s death, *W*'s life expectancy is probably not great. (Statistically, the average widow outlives her husband by about 10 years.) The shorter her life expectancy, the lower is the value of the income-interest consideration received relative to the value of the remainder interest transferred. A low discount rate likewise reduces the value of income interests (the consideration) relative to remainders (the interest transferred). Thus, it would be fairly uncommon for the consideration to be full and adequate as a factual matter.

(3) Effect of partial consideration. If the consideration is "partial," the amount includable in *W*'s gross estate under §§ 2036 and 2038 is the

estate tax value of *W*'s property less the actuarial value of the income interest in *H*'s property as of *H*'s death.

    (4) *Actuarial gain.* As in the private annuity situation, if *W* dies before her actuarial life expectancy, the consideration offset will have been overvalued relative to what *W* actually received from *H*'s property to augment her § 2033 gross estate. This possibility is, however, not sufficient to render this device desirable, all things considered.

  b. *Caveats.* Aside from the possibility that the IRS will prevail on the "full and adequate consideration" issue, the likelihood that the consideration will not be full and adequate as a factual matter, and the possibility that *W* might outlive her actuarial life expectancy, there are other problems. Cumulatively, the various problems appear to have had the effect of rendering the spousal election will as being very rarely used.

    (1) Should the consideration "count" at all? There are three problems in treating the income interest in *H*'s property as "consideration" for *W*'s transfer. First, *W* might have received bequests from *H* even if the arrangement had not been entered into. Second, if *W* retains the power to alter the remainder (if within a limited class), it would seem that she has surrendered little more than the power to invade the corpus for her own benefit. Third, the consideration received by *W* did not come from the remainders, but from *H*, and it is unclear that *H*, being now dead, really gave up anything. Thus, the arrangement more closely resembles one of synchronized gratuitous transfers than a sale for consideration. However, there may be too many cases assuming that the consideration is "real" for the IRS to pursue any of these lines of attack.

    (2) *Income tax issues.* The income tax issues involved in spousal election wills are numerous but their resolution is either unclear or not favorable. Thus, under § 167(e), enacted after spousal election wills were publicized, *W*'s "purchased" income interest cannot be amortized if (as is likely) the remainder interest is held by a related party. It would seem that *H*'s estate, and possibly *W*, is engaged in a carve-out sale with no basis offset and no capital gain treatment. *See* § 1001(e).

    (3) *Professional responsibility issues.* An attorney advising both *H* and *W* to enter into this kind of arrangement would appear to be faced with a serious conflict of interest.

III. **CHARITABLE DEDUCTION PLANNING. Outright gift and estate transfers are fully deductible for gift and estate tax purposes and are not covered by the generation-skipping tax. The tax-avoidance "game" is here played with "split interest" charitable transfers, referring to transfers in which successive interests in the same property are transferred to charitable and noncharitable recipients.**

CHARITABLE DEDUCTION PLANNING

  A. **Split-Interest Trust Transfers.** No deduction is available with respect to a split-interest trust transfer unless the transfer takes one of the forms specified below which are required in order that the charitable interest qualify for the deduction. §§ 2055(e)(2) & 2522(c)(2). These rules are designed so that the charitable interest may be valued fairly accurately. If the charitable interest qualifies for the deduction, the amount of the deduction is determined under actuarial tables.

1. **Charitable remainder trusts.** Here the remainder interest in the trust passes to charity following one or more "lead" (initial) interests to noncharitable beneficiaries (including the grantor). Charitable remainder interests in trust are deductible *only* if they take the form of the charitable remainder annuity trust ("CRAT") or the charitable remainder unitrust ("CRUT"). The charitable remainder "income" trust does not qualify for any deduction at all!

    a. *Technical requirements of CRATs and CRUTs.* Strict compliance with the qualification rules, found in § 664(d) and the regulations thereunder (as well as revenue procedures and revenue rulings), is absolutely required. Failure to so comply results in total disallowance of the charitable deduction.

        (1) Charitable remainder unitrust ("CRUT"). Here the noncharitable "lead" interest (for one or more lives or terms of years) must be a "unitrust" interest, namely, the right to a fixed percentage (not less than 5%) of the corpus of the trust as valued annually. The trustee cannot distribute to the noncharitable beneficiary an amount greater than the specified unitrust amount.

            (a) Where income is less than unitrust amount. If the unitrust amount in any year is greater than the income amount, the trust may provide that the shortfall is to be made up out of the corpus then, later, or never; if the shortfall is never made up, the charity ultimately benefits at the expense of the noncharitable beneficiary.

            (b) Effect of high unitrust amount. If the unitrust amount exceeds the yield (income and appreciation) and corpus is invaded to make up the shortfall, the trust will shrink, and both the charitable and noncharitable beneficiaries will be losers. Thus, it would be unusual for the unitrust percentage rate to be set very high.

        (2) Charitable remainder annuity trust ("CRAT"). Here the noncharitable lead interest must take the form of an annuity (fixed dollar amount annually). The annuity obligation may well exceed the income yield, meaning that the noncharitable beneficiary will receives both income and corpus.

            (a) Effect of low economic return. If the annuity obligation exceeds the total economic yield (income and appreciation), the charitable interest depletes, but not the interest of the noncharitable beneficiary (at least not until the trust is fully depleted).

            (b) Setting the annuity amount. The annuity amount under a CRAT must be no less than 5% of the *initial* value of the corpus. The trustee is prohibited from distributing more than the specified annuity amount to the noncharitable beneficiary. The annuity amount should not be too high: the trust is disqualified if there is a greater than 5% actuarial chance that the *entire* trust will be paid to noncharitable beneficiaries before the charitable remainder takes effect. Rev. Rul. 77-374, 1972-2 C.B. 329. Also, the charitable remainder interest must be worth at least 10% of the initial corpus.

b. *Tax planning.* The aggressive estate planner might seek more than actual compliance with the qualification requirements (so as to obtain the deduction) but to "avoid" transfer taxes as well.

(1) Tax avoidance defined. Tax "avoidance" (legally) occurs in the charitable context where (1) the amount of the charitable deduction exceeds (in present value terms) the amount the charity actually receives *and* (2) the noncharitable beneficiaries (other than the grantor) receive more (in present value terms) than the actuarial value of their interests. If these two conditions are satisfied, the grantor will have manipulated the charitable deduction rules to pass wealth to a noncharitable beneficiary free of transfer tax. In effect, wealth will have shifted from the deductible charitable interest to the nondeductible noncharitable interest, held by a person who was the natural object of the grantor's bounty.

(2) Why lead interest can't be an income interest. The congressional purpose in requiring a CRAT or a CRUT can be gleaned by comparing the CRAT and the CRUT to a trust in which the noncharitable beneficiary had a right to *income* for life or a term of years. If an income-remainder trust were allowed to qualify for the charitable deduction, the grantor could beat the actuarial tables by funding the trust with property that produced income at a rate greater than the rate assumed by the actuarial tables; then, the nondeductible lead interest would be undervalued for transfer tax purposes (and the deductible remainder interest might be overvalued as well).

(3) Why lead interest must be an annuity or unitrust interest. Thanks to § 664, the noncharitable interest in a CRAT or a CRUT cannot be undervalued relative to the charitable remainder interest solely on account of the economic (income and appreciation) yield of the trust property.

(a) CRAT format. In the CRAT, if the property has a low yield (so that the annuity obligation consumes corpus), the charitable remainder will be shortchanged but the noncharitable interest will not have been undervalued in absolute terms; the depletion of the charitable remainder will have been simple economic waste.

(b) CRUT format. In the CRUT, the values of the charitable and noncharitable interests move in tandem. Thus, if the property has a yield greater than that assumed by the actuarial tables, *both* the noncharitable and charitable interests will have been undervalued; the charity will share in the overall economic gain.

(4) Life expectancies. The manner in which tax avoidance results under CRAT and CRUT differs as follows:

(a) CRAT format. Tax avoidance occurs under the CRAT format if: (1) the noncharitable interest is held by a person other than the grantor, (2) such interest is an interest "for life" (as opposed to being a term of years), (3) the noncharitable beneficiary outlives his or her life expectancy, (4) the annuity obligation exceeds the economic yield, *and* (5) the trust generates a reasonable yield in absolute terms. Ideally (from the tax standpoint), the trust would run dry at the very moment of the noncharitable beneficiary's long-delayed death, and the charity will get nothing (but there will have been no economic waste)!

    (b) CRUT format. In the CRUT format, if the noncharitable beneficiary outlives her actuarial life expectancy, the noncharitable interest will have been undervalued *relative* to the charitable interest at the time of transfer, but the charity will still end up getting the corpus. (If the unitrust percentage was set too high relative to the yield, both parties will have been economic losers.)

    Example 15: *X* creates an irrevocable trust with $1 million, providing an annuity to *B* (age 70) of $120,000 per year for life, remainder to the *Z* Charity. Assuming that the trust is a qualified CRAT and that the 10% actuarial tables are applicable, the value of the nondeductible annuity for *B* is $726,264, and the deductible remainder interest is worth $273,736. (The tables assume *B* has a life expectancy of about nine or ten years.) If *B* lives a little more than 18 more years, *B* will obtain all of the income *and* principal of the trust and the *Z* Charity will get nothing. The sum of $273,736 (in present value as of the creation of the trust) will have shifted from the charity to *B* free of transfer tax. Under the CRAT format, the lower the discount rate used in the actuarial tables, the greater the charitable remainder deduction and (therefore) the greater the opportunity for tax avoidance.

2. **Pooled-income funds.** Money or property is transferred to an "umbrella" trust for numerous transferors managed by the donee charity; the transferor can reserve an "income" interest in herself or another noncharitable beneficiary for life.

    a. *Termination of noncharitable interest.* When the noncharitable interest terminates, the donee charity withdraws from the trust that amount from which the beneficiary was receiving income.

    b. *Calculating value of charitable remainder deduction.* The value of the charitable remainder deduction is calculated on the basis of the fund's actual income yield, not the yield assumed by the actuarial tables: This rule has the effect of valuing the income interest as if it were an annuity. *See* § 642(c)(5).

    c. *When beneficiary outlives life expectancy.* Again taxes are avoided if the noncharitable beneficiary (if not the grantor) outlives his or her life expectancy.

3. **Charitable lead trusts.** In a charitable lead trust, amounts are paid to a charity for a period of years (usually a fixed term), with the remainder paid to a noncharitable beneficiary (other than the grantor).

a. *Qualification.* To obtain a gift or estate tax deduction for he charitable lead interest, such interest must be a charitable unitrust interest (here the trust is called a "CLUT") or a charitable annuity interest (the trust is a "CLAT"). These charitable lead interests are similar to the interests described above in the context of CRATs and CRUTs, except that there is no minimum payout requirement. No amounts can be paid to noncharitable beneficiaries so long as the charitable lead interest is running.

b. *Tax avoidance.* Tax avoidance will occur if the nondeductible remainder interest is undervalued relative to the deductible charitable interest, from the vantage of hindsight.

(1) Death of designated person. One technique is to key the term of the charitable lead interest to the death of a designated person. If the person dies before his or her life expectancy, the noncharitable remainder will have been (from the vantage of hindsight) undervalued relative to the value of the charitable lead interest.

(2) Actual yield in excess of high discount rate. Another tax avoidance possibility, in the case of CLATs only, occurs where there is a high discount rate in the applicable actuarial tables (which enlarges the value of the charitable lead interest) *and* the actual yield exceeds such rate. In fact, the charitable deduction can approach or equal 100% in the case of a CLAT of this type.

Example 16: *X* transfers $1 million into an irrevocable trust providing for an annuity of $117,500 per year to the *Y* Charity for 20 years, remainder to *C.* Under a 10% discount rate, the charitable deduction is 100% ($1 million), since the actuarial tables postulate complete depletion of the trust during the 20-year period on the assumption that the yield (income and appreciation) will also be 10%. However, if the actual yield is greater than 10%, the noncharitable remainder will actually receive something (how much depends on the actual yield in excess of 10%). In the context of a 100% charitable deduction, anything the noncharitable remainder actually receives is free of transfer tax. In this respect, the CLAT resembles the classic estate freeze: all post-transfer excess yield inures to the transferee (the remainder) tax free.

B. **Nontrust Split-Interest Transfers.** Nontrust split-interest transfers do not generate any gift or estate tax charitable deductions, except as follows (*see* §§ 2055(e)(2) and 2522(c)(2), referring to § 170(f)(3)(B)).

1. *Charitable remainder in home or farm.* Under § 170(f)(3)(B)(i), the charitable remainder interest is valued by using a low discount rate as applied to the property after reduction by expected depreciation to the date the remainder is expected to come into possession. *See* § 170(f)(4); Reg. § 1.170A-12. Transfer tax can be avoided if the holder of the life estate (if not the grantor) outlives her actuarial life expectancy.

2. *Concurrent interests.* Only certain kinds of concurrent interests in property can qualify for the charitable deduction if given to charity:

a. *Undivided interests.* An undivided portion of the donor's entire interest in the property, such as a tenacy in common, qualifies. § 170(f)(3)(B)(ii).

b. *Retained copyrights.* Also qualifying is a copyright in a retained art work or the work itself detached from the retained copyright. §§ 2055(e)(4) & 2522(c)(3).

c. *Conservation easements.* A concurrent interest that takes the form of a "qualified conservation contribution" as defined in § 170(h)(4) qualifies for the charitable deduction. § 170(f)(3)(B)(iii).

   (1) Property restriction. A conservation easement involves some restriction on property (usually granted to a governmental entity) that reduces the market value of the retained property and which benefits the public, such as a prohibition on development.

   (2) Value of donation. The value of the donation is computed with reference to the decrease in the private value of the property caused by the restriction. This technique is appealing where there is family recreational property, and the family members place a high subjective value on its recreational, scenic, and/or natural features: the donor may, in effect, get something (a charitable deduction) for nothing (promising to do what would have been done anyway, *i.e.,* declining to develop the property).

   (3) Amount includible in gross estate. *See* the discussion of § 2031(c) in Chapter 4, at II.B.2., *supra.*

d. *Retained mineral interests.* This category refers to a gift of real property as reduced by a "qualified mineral interest." *See* § 170(h)(6).

C. Direct Charitable Annuities. Direct charitable annuities involve money or property given outright to a charity, with the charity promising to pay an annuity to the donor for life. The charitable remainder trust qualification rules do not apply. The deduction is the excess of the transferred amount over the actuarial value of the annuity.

1. ***Analogous to private annuity.*** Since the donor receives the annuity, this situation is analogous to a private annuity, *supra,* except that here the premature death of the donor does not create any tax avoidance opportunity: although the donor's § 2033 gross estate will be less than predicted by the actuarial tables, the charitable deduction will also have been understated from the vantage of hindsight.

2. ***If donor outlives life expectancy.*** If the donor outlives his or her actuarial life expectancy, the charitable deduction will have been overstated, but the donor's § 2033 gross estate will have been augmented by a corresponding amount.

D. Miscellaneous Considerations:

1. ***Section 2702.*** Section 2702 does not apply to most of the *trust* transactions described above, even if the grantor retains an interest. *See* Reg. § 25.2702-

1(c)(3)-(5). A direct charitable annuity does not involve a retained interest that would trigger § 2702. A retained income or remainder interest in a residence or farm would run afoul of § 2702 unless taking the form of a qualified personal residence trust (QPRT).

2. *Generation-skipping tax.* The generation-skipping tax will come into play if any noncharitable distributees or donees are two or more generations below that of the grantor or donor. *See* Ch.5, at I.B.1., *supra.*

IV. **PLANNING TRANSFERS BETWEEN SPOUSES. The most important consideration in planning for interspousal transfers is the gift and estate tax marital deduction. The marital deduction, however, is significant only if the combined net wealth of the married couple exceeds the exemption equivalent of the Unified Transfer Tax Credit, which, for purposes of illustration, will be assumed to be $1 million.**

A. **Qualification Rules.** The nontax planning objectives for interspousal transfers interact with the tax planning objectives. This interaction cannot be comprehended without a grasp of the marital deduction qualification rules.

1. *"Terminable interest" rule.* The qualification rules are discussed at Ch.2, at X.B., and Ch.3, at IV.C.5., *supra.* Of particular importance is the "terminable interest" (disqualification) rule and its express and implied exceptions. Recall that a "terminable interest" is an interest in the transferee spouse that, *as of the date of transfer*, might fail or lapse (regardless of the remoteness or unlikelihood of the condition that would cause the interest to fail). A *nondeductible* terminable interest is a transfer in which a third party would take upon the failure of the terminable interest.

2. *List of qualifying transfers.* The following types of transfers qualify for the marital deduction:

   a. *Outright transfers.* Outright (*i.e.*, nontrust) transfers in fee simple absolute qualify. (However, even an outright transfer may not be deductible if the surviving spouse is under a binding obligation to transfer or bequeath the property to a third party. *See* § 2056(b)(4).)

   b. *Right to installment payments.* A property interest consisting of a right to periodic or installment payments qualifies for the marital deduction, provided that no interest in the property is obtained by a third party from the transferor spouse. Examples are bonds, notes, insurance policies, annuities (and life insurance settlement options), with no survivorship feature (no interest held by another party). In a few states, a "widow's allowance" awarded by a probate court qualifies under this rule.

   c. *Estate trusts.* An estate trust provides that the income is to be paid to the surviving spouse or accumulated, with remainder (upon the surviving spouse's death) to be paid to the surviving spouse's estate. The trustee must not be allowed to make distributions to any third parties. The entire amount transferred to trust qualifies for the marital deduction, which is also the case for power-of-appointment and QTIP trusts, *infra.*

d. *Power-of-appointment trust.* The trust must give the surviving spouse (1) the right to all of the income for life payable at least annually *and* (2) a general power of appointment (by deed or by will) exercisable "alone and in all events." A nontrust transfer, such as a legal life estate coupled with the requisite general power of appointment, can also qualify. The value of the entire trust transfer, not just the value of the income interest, qualifies.

e. *QTIP trust.* The requirements for a QTIP trust are:

(1) that the surviving spouse have the right to all of the income payable at least annually;

(2) distributions to third parties during the surviving spouse's lifetime must be prohibited; and

(3) the donor spouse, or the personal representative of the deceased spouse, must make a QTIP election by checking the appropriate box on the gift or estate tax return.

A nontrust transfer, such as a legal life estate or common-law dower, can also qualify under the QTIP rules. Again, the entire value of the transfer, not just the value of the income interest, qualifies.

f. *Marital-charitable trust.* For a marital-charitable trust, the surviving spouse must have the sole annuity or unitrust interest in a CRAT or a CRUT. The entire transfer is deductible.

g. *Spousal remainder trust.* Here the transferee spouse is given a vested remainder in fee simple following an (income) interest in a third party (perhaps a parent of the transferor). Here only the actuarial value of the remainder interest qualifies.

3. *Some basic pitfalls.* Traps to watch out for include:

a. *Conditional transfers.* Except as provided above, the transfer to the spouse must not be subject to any condition precedent or subsequent, such as a condition that the spouse survive the decedent by a certain period of time. Note, however, the exception found in § 2056(b)(3) (survival for six months, etc.).

b. *"Income" requirement.* In the power-of-appointment and QTIP trusts, the transferee spouse must have the right to all of the income payable at least annually. This right must not be made illusory, *e.g.,* by locking the trust into a nonincome-producing investment. *See* Reg. § 20.2056(b)-5(f).

c. *Contractual wills.* Contractual wills (under which the surviving spouse is prohibited from revoking a pre-existing will benefiting third parties, usually the children) appear to create an interest in the surviving spouse that resembles a life estate coupled with a general power of appointment (power to consume). However, most of the cases hold that qualification as a power-of-appointment trust is defeated because the power is not exercisable alone and in all events. A contractual will situation will also be disqualified under the QTIP rules if the surviving spouse can make gifts to third parties.

d. *Spousal election wills.* Spousal election wills are discussed at II.F.6., *supra.* Basically, the surviving spouse allows her property to be transferred into trust by the decedent spouse. The surviving spouse receives property (often an income interest) from the deceased spouse "on condition that" the surviving spouse transfer property (usually a remainder interest in her own property) to a third party. Even if the transfer avoids the terminable interest rule, the deduction is lost under § 2056(b)(4)(B), the theory being that no *net* value passes from the decedent spouse to the surviving spouse. (That is, the surviving spouse is really a conduit for a transfer from the decedent spouse to a third party.)

e. *Charging marital bequests with nondeductible items.* The marital deduction is reduced by any charges, etc., to be paid out of the marital transfer. § 2056(b)(4). If the charges are deductible under some other provision (such as deductible debts, etc.), there is no harm, since the reduction in the marital deduction is compensated for by the deduction for debts. However, if the charges are nondeductible, such as administration expenses deducted for income tax purposes and death taxes, the marital deduction is reduced without compensation.

(1) Tax payment clauses. Thus, one must carefully consider clauses in wills and trusts that relate to the payment of taxes, debts, administration expenses, etc. If the tax-payment clause states that all debts, taxes, etc., are to paid out of the residue, and the residue is a marital-deduction transfer, the marital deduction will be reduced, and a circular computation will be required. (The foregoing is also true with respect to the charitable deduction.)

(2) Reduce-to-zero formula clauses. A reduce-to-zero formula clause in a will or trust attempts to create a situation where aggregate marital deduction bequests exactly equal the taxable estate reduced by the exemption equivalent of the Unified Transfer Tax Credit (assumed for purposes of illustration to be $1 million) and possibly by other available credits. Alternatively, the formula can produce aggegate nondeductible transfers equal to the Unified Transfer Tax Credit (and possibly other credits.) The formula, to reach the correct outcome, must provide that the bequest under the clause be adjusted appropriately for (1) other qualifying marital-deduction (or nonmarital deduction) transfers and (2) amounts deductible otherwise than under the marital deduction.

Example 17: *H*'s gross estate is $4 million. Deductible debts are $300,000 and nondeductible payments are $200,000. There is a nonmarital bequest of $100,000 to John, and *H*'s tangible personal property and personal residence (worth $500,000) are specifically bequeathed to *W*. The formula is located in a "pecuniary" nonmarital bequest clause, with the residual bequest set up so as to qualify for the marital deduction. (There are no other estate-included transfers, and no credits are available other than the Unified Transfer Tax Credit.) The formula bequest (which does not qualify for the marital deduction) should be in the amount of the available Unified Transfer Tax Credit (assumed to be $1 million) *reduced* by other *nondeductible* amounts payable under under *other* clauses (or instruments) (= $100,000) and *increased* by *deductible* amounts payable out of *this* clause (= $300,000). The deductible and nondeductible debts, administration expenses , and taxes are to be paid out of the formula bequest. The formula produces an amount of $1.2 million under these facts. Of this amount, $300,000 goes to paying items that are deductible under § 2053, $200,000 goes to the payment of nondeductible items, and $700,000 passes to legatees in a manner that does not qualify for the marital deduction. Total nondeductible items under this clause total $900,000 and other nondeductible bequests (the bequest to John) are $100,000, for a total of $1 million. The remaining bequests (including the residuary bequest) all qualify for the marital deduction. They total $3 million. The taxable estate is $1 million, which produces a zero net estate tax after the Unified Transfer Tax Credit.

f. *Funding with "credit" assets.* The credits under §§ 2012 (pre-1977 gift taxes) and 2014 (foreign death taxes) are lost if the previously taxed property funds the marital bequest. Thus, the will or trust should prohibit funding of any marital transfer with such property (to the extent practicable).

B. Nontax Planning Objectives. The qualification rules provide a background for analyzing whatever nontax objectives pertain to the particular marital situation.

1. *Objectives listed.* The objectives are usually (1) to provide the surviving spouse with sufficient resources to maintain her accustomed standard of living and (2) to assure that the couple's wealth devolves reasonably intact to lower-generation family members. The latter objective implies the possibility of dead-hand control, *i.e.,* the first spouse to die might desire that the surviving spouse not transfer the first spouse's wealth to "outsiders," such as a second spouse or children of a prior marriage. Such dead-hand control can be obtained through a trust, pursuant to contractual wills, or under a spousal election will.

    a. *Trusts.* Trusts are frequently used in this context. The main point here is that there is little correlation between qualification for the marital deduction and the degree of enjoyment by the transferee spouse.

        (1) Marital trusts. A trust that qualifies for the marital deduction (hereinafter referred to as a "marital trust") may provide the transferee spouse with as "little" as the right to the income (QTIP trust) or the power of testamentary disposition ("estate trust" with power or direction to accumulate income). The QTIP trust is ideally suited to preventing the transferee trust from transferring the corpus to outsiders. The estate trust does not appear to be frequently used. Income can be accumulated in an estate trust, but accumulated income is subject (mostly) to the highest marginal income tax rates and will be subject to the surviving spouse's power of testamentary disposition (including the creditors of her estate). Of course, a marital trust can provide "more" than the minimum, as in a "power-of-appointment" trust.

        (2) Nonmarital ("by-pass") trusts. A trust that does not qualify for the marital deduction is often referred to as a "by-pass" trust or sometimes as

a "family trust." A by-pass trust can provide for children and various objects of the transferor's bounty. Alternatively, or in addition, the by-pass trust can provide all or any of the following benefits to the transferor's spouse *without* qualifying for the marital deduction *and without* having the trust be included in the transferee spouse's gross estate:

1) right to income (or possibility of receiving same according to trustee's discretion or standards);

2) possibility of receiving corpus according to trustee's discretion or standards;

3) "special" power of appointment over corpus by deed and/or will;

4) "five-and-five power" to withdraw corpus annually (*see* Ch.3, at II.F.5.b., *supra*); and

5) administrative powers over the trust.

However, *it is crucial that the transferee spouse not be given a "general" power of appointment over the by-pass trust* (other than a five-and-five power). Thus, the transferee spouse should not be made trustee or co-trustee if the trust provides for discretionary corpus distributions to the transferee spouse, nor should the transferee spouse be given the right, in effect, to demand corpus for herself.

b. *Contractual wills.* In smaller estates, contractual wills are sometimes used to combine spousal benefits with dead-hand control. The effect of valid contractual wills is to prevent the surviving spouse from revoking a pre-existing will (benefiting the couple's descendants). The reason contractual wills are usually confined to poorer couples is that (1) no trust expenses are involved, (2) such wills usually allow the surviving spouse to consume the couple's wealth (if not to transfer it to third parties), and (3) bequests under such wills usually do not qualify for the marital deduction, but qualification is not needed in this context.

c. *Spousal election wills.* A third device is the spousal election will, under which the first spouse to die purports to bequeath both his wealth and the surviving spouse's wealth (usually in trust, income to the surviving spouse for life, remainder to their descendants). *See* II.F.6., *supra.*

C. **Tax-Planning Objectives.** The basic idea here is to maximize the amount of wealth that can be passed on intact to lower generations. Because of the fact (*see* IV.B., *supra*) that there is no necessary correlation between deductibility and economic benefit for the transferee spouse, marital deduction tax planning is essentially a game. There are two basic scenarios for marital deduction planning, estate equalization and deferral of tax. (For purposes of discussion, it will be assumed that *H* will likely be the first spouse to die.)

1. ***Effect of qualifying marital deduction transfers.*** Recall that amounts that qualify for the deduction reduce the tax base of the transferor spouse but are likely to increase the tax base of the transferee spouse, since the marital

deduction qualification rules are designed to assure that the transfer is in a form that results in inclusion in the transferee spouse's transfer tax base. Of course the property will not actually appear in the transferee spouse's tax base to the extent that the latter consumes it, suffers economic waste, or effects tax-free gifts and support transfers. For couples potentially subject to transfer taxes, it is imperative to avoid making transfers that will appear in the tax base of both spouses, namely, nondeductible transfers that will appear in the transferee spouse's tax base (on account of a general power of appointment or remainder to the transferee spouse's estate).

2. **Estate splitting.** Under the progressive rate system of the unified estate and gift tax, the lowest aggregate tax is obtained if the married couple's total wealth is split evenly between the two spouses.

Example 18: If *H* has a taxable estate of $4 million and *W* has a taxable estate of $1 million, the net tax on *H*'s estate is $1,495,000 ($1,840,800 - $345,800) and the net tax on *W*'s estate is zero ($345,800 - $345,800). But if each of them has a taxable estate of $2.5 million, the aggregate tax is $1,360,000 [2 x ($1,025,800 - $345,800)]. This is a tax savings of $135,000, which is wholly attributable to the fact that marital deduction transfers move wealth from higher marginal rate brackets to lower marginal rate brackets.

a. *Small estates.* Each spouse is a separate taxpayer with his or her own unified transfer tax credit. Where the couple's aggregate wealth is less than $1 million, no marital deduction planning is necessary, since neither spouse will incur any tax. Either spouse can make marital deduction bequests to the other, or may decline to do so.

b. *Medium-sized estates.* At a minimum, it is desirable to fully use the unified transfer tax credit of both spouses. Also, the poorer spouse should not make marital deduction bequests to the wealthier spouse (other than de minimis bequests, such as of personal effects and furnishings), since the imbalance between the two taxable estates will be aggravated. If the combined estates of the couple are greater than $1 million, but not greater than $2 million, the wealthier spouse should consider make marital transfers in an amount that reduce his estate to $1 million or less and augment the poorer spouse's estate to a maximum of $1 million.

Example 19: *H* owns property with a net value of $800,000 and *W* owns property with a net value of 400,000. *H*'s will need not make any marital deduction transfers, but if he does make marital deduction transfers they should not exceed $600,000. By similar logic, *W* need not make any marital deduction transfers, but if she does they should not exceed $200,000.

c. *Large estates.* If the combined estates are greater than $2 million, the wealthier spouse should make marital deduction bequests to the poorer spouse in an amount that will equalize their taxable estates.

Example 20: *H* has $2 million and *W* $400,000. *H* should make marital deduction bequests of $800,000 to *W* (equalizing their estates at $1.2 million each), and *W* should not make any marital deduction bequests to *H*.

d. *Very large estates.* Once *both* estates are in the highest marginal rate brackets ($3 million and more), estate splitting does not save any taxes. However, if one estate exceeds $10 million and the other is less than $10 million (but more than $3 million), estate splitting mitigates the "surtax" imposed by § 2001(c)(2).

e. *Community property estates.* If the couple's wealth consists entirely of community property, estate splitting already exists, and neither spouse needs to make any marital deduction bequest to the other (although, in small or medium wealth situations, some marital deduction bequests might be made without harm).

3. **Tax deferral (credit-shelter approach).** The first spouse to die can totally avoid estate and gift tax by leaving *all of his property,* in excess of a net cumulative tax base of $1 million, to his spouse in a form that qualifies for the marital deduction. The nondeductible ("credit shelter") transfers and payments of $1 million avoid tax liability because of the unified transfer tax credit. (Other estate tax credits might increase the amount that can be passed on tax free in a nondeductible form.) The nonmarital transfers can (and, where taxes are an issue, should) be made in a form that will avoid inclusion in the transfer tax base of the surviving spouse, *i.e.,* they should benefit lower generations (children, grandchildren, etc.). *See* the discussion of "by-pass trusts," *supra.* The marital deduction transfers (in excess of the $1 million or so) are said to "defer" transfer tax by eliminating all tax liability for the first spouse to die while augmenting the potential tax base of the second spouse to die. The augmentation of the second spouse's estate will produce a greater net tax on the second spouse's death than the aggregate net taxes on both spouses that would be imposed under the estate-splitting scenario, *supra.* In short, deferral of tax through maximum use of the marital deduction produces a worse *tax* result than under estate splitting in gross dollar terms.

4. **Evaluating the alternatives.** Under estate splitting, the couple loses the use of the funds used to pay tax on the death of the first spouse. This is not the case under the deferral (credit-shelter) approach.

a. *Value of deferral.* Under the deferral scenario, the taxes saved on the first spouse's death can be invested so as to produce economic return (income and appreciation) by the time of the second spouse's death that exceeds the *incremental* taxes due on the second spouse's death by reason of following the deferral scenario. This insight appears to lead to the conclusion that the deferral scenario is actually preferable to estate splitting if the economic return on the taxes saved (the tax that would have been paid on he first spouse's death under the estate-splitting scenario) exceeds the *incremental* taxes under the deferral scenario (aggregate taxes under deferral less aggregate taxes under estate splitting).

b. *Value of early tax payment.* The foregoing analysis focuses only on the *net* loss due to tax payments. It must be kept in mind that the by-pass trust escapes tax on the death of the surviving spouse, and under estate splitting the by-pass trust, although incurring a tax on the death of the first spouse, will be larger than what it would be under a deferral scenario. It turns out that, under estate splitting, the projected increase (if any) in the *incremental* nonmarital share (nonmarital share under estate splitting less nonmarital share under deferral) can also be considered. The maximum increase is possible only if the by-pass trust is able to avoid making distributions to beneficiaries for current consumption *See* Example 21 below.

c. *Summary of considerations.* Whether deferral is ultimately better than estate splitting is, then, a function of:

(1) the taxes deferred (*i.e.,* the taxes that can be saved on first spouse's death under deferral);

(2) the period by which the second spouse is expected to outlive the first spouse;

(3) the likely return rate;

(4) the incremental taxes resulting from deferral;

(5) whether the by-pass trust can avoid making current distributions (at least until W's death); and

(6) whether the surviving spouse's estate will be further augmented or diminished by actions and events occurring before her death.

d. *Evaluating factors in advance.* These factors can be evaluated in advance (with the aid of computer software) with a view at arriving at a basic decision whether to pursue the estate-splitting or deferral scenarios. Off course, such an evaluation involves "guesstimates" of future conditions and events.

e. *Huge estates.* In very large estates, deferral begins to look better, since the potential advantage of estate splitting is diminished where both net estates are in (or near) the highest marginal rate brackets. On the other hand, it may be that in huge estates it is more feasible to avoid making distributions from the by-pass trust (and allowing the marital trust to appreciate).

f. *Proximate deaths.* Estate splitting is clearly best if *H* and *W* die within a very short time of each other. The will of the wealthier spouse can provide for an estate-splitting scheme to take effect if the poorer spouse survives him by not more than six months, but otherwise a deferral scheme is to take effect. (Recall that a purported marital bequest contingent on survival by more than six months fails to qualify.)

Example 21: Assume that *H* and *W* each own $2 million of net wealth. Assume also that *H* will die first, *W* will die unmarried 4 years later than *H,* that the value of the property is unchanged at all times, and that the discount rate is 10%.

If estate splitting is opted for, *H* will leave his entire estate in a nonmarital-deduction form (*e.g.,* by-pass trust), and the net estate tax on each of *H*'s estate and *W*'s estate will be $405,000 ($780,800 - $345,800), for an aggregate tax of $810,000.

If the deferral approach is opted for, *H* will leave $1 million in a nonmarital form and $1 million in a marital form, reducing his taxable estate to $1 million, which suffers a zero tax thanks to the unified transfer tax credit. *W*'s taxable estate (assuming no changes) will be $3 million ($2 million of her own + $1 million from *H*), producing an estate tax of $945,000 ($1,290,800 - $345,800). Although $945,000 is $135,000 more than $810,000, the $405,000 of taxes avoided on *H*'s death will yield more than $135,000 (in fact, $188,000) to the by-pass trust in 4 years (assuming a 10% after income-tax rate of return). (The lower the rate of return, the longer it will take to come out ahead in the marital share.)

The marital share, if in a QTIP (or power-of-appointment) trust, must produce income. It can be assumed that this income, generated at the after-income-tax rate of 10% per year, is consumed by *W*. It will also be assumed, for the sake of simplicity, that there is no appreciation in the marital share. The by-pass trust does not have to distribute income. It will be assumed that income is accumulated at the after-income-tax rate of 10% per year (but that there is no appreciation).

Under the estate-equalization scenario, the *incremental* by-pass trust is $595,000 million ($2 million less estate tax of $405,000 on *H*'s death payable out of the by-pass trust and less the $1 million that would be the by-pass trust under the deferral scenario). After 4 years, the income accumulated (at 10%) on this incremental $595,000 is $276,000.

In comparing the two approaches, appreciation in the first $1 million of the by-pass trust can be ignored, as can be the economic return on *W*'s own property, since these would presumably be the same under both approaches. Looking to the bottom line, under the deferral approach the next generation takes (if *W* dies at the end of year 4) a total of $3,243,000 [$1,188,000 by-pass trust ($1 million + $188,000 accumulation on $405,000 taxes saved) plus $2,055,000 from the marital trust and *W*'s own property ($3 million less $945,000 estate taxes on *W*'s estate)].

Under estate equalization, the next generation takes $3,466,000 [$1,871,000 in by-pass trust ($2 million less $405,000 taxes on *H*'s death plus $276,000 accumulation on $595,000) plus $1,595,000 from *W*'s own property ($2 million less $405,000 estate taxes on *W*'s death)].

Under these facts and assumptions, estate equalization produces the larger bottom line for the next generation.

5. ***If the poorer spouse dies first.*** All of the above examples assumed that the wealthier spouse died first. If the poorer spouse dies first, and the poorer spouse has net wealth of less than $1 million, the poorer spouse will have failed to fully use her unified credit. Also, estate splitting is not possible if the poorer spouse dies first.

   a. *Gifts.* The richer spouse can make gifts to the poorer spouse sufficient to bring the spouse's net wealth up to $1 million. More than that can be given if estate splitting is desired. If the wealthier spouse wants to prevent the poorer spouse from transferring the corpus of the gift outside of the immediate family, a QTIP trust can be used.

b. *Survivorship clauses:*

(1) In the wealthier spouse's will. The will (and other dispositive instruments) of the wealthier spouse should state that she is deemed *not* to survive the poorer spouse if their order of deaths cannot be determined. Such a provision is effective under state law and will trigger the marital-deduction transfers provided under the wealthier spouse's will (and other instruments).

(2) In the poorer spouse's will. Since estate equalization is preferable if the deaths occur in close proximity, any marital-deduction transfers in the poorer spouse's will (etc.) should be made contingent on the wealthier spouse surviving the poorer spouse by six months and not dying as a result of a common disaster in which both of them died. *See* § 2056(b)(3).

6. *Generation-skipping tax considerations.* Each spouse has a $1 million exemption equivalent (as indexed) under the generation-skipping tax.

a. *Review.* The by-pass trust might involve generation-skipping transfers (depending on the beneficiaries and ultimate distributees), with the grantor of such trust being the "transferor" for generation-skipping tax purposes. In a marital trust, the surviving spouse will be the "transferor" of such trust for generation-skipping tax purposes by virtue of the fact that the trust is included in the gross estate of the surviving spouse.

b. *The problem.* Under a deferral scenario, the by-pass trust will be equal to the exemption equivalent of the Unified Transfer Tax Credit. For decedents dying before the year 2006, the exemption equivalent is less than $1 million. *See* § 2010(c). The marital transfers will build up the wealth of the surviving spouse. Thus, the wealthier spouse (if dying before 2006) may fail to use his $ 1 million exemption-equivalent, while the surviving spouse may be the transferor of generation-skipping transfers that exceed the exemption-equivalent. This problem can exist even for decedents dying after 2005, because the GST exemption is indexed whereas the Unified Transfer Tax Credit is not.

c. *The solution.* The wealthier spouse can make herself the "transferor" of a QTIP-type marital transfer by making a "reverse QTIP election" for generation-skipping tax purposes. (A regular QTIP election can also be made for gift or estate tax purposes.) However, it is not possible to make a "partial" *reverse* QTIP election. Therefore, a three-trust scheme may be called for.

Example 22: *H* has $4 million of net wealth and *W* has $1 million. *H* dies in the year 2002, when the exemption equivalent of the Unified Transfer Tax Credit is $700,000. *H*'s dispositive instruments create a generation-skipping by-pass credit-shelter trust of $700,000, and the rest ($3.3 million) is left in two QTIP trusts which will (or might) involve generation-skipping transfers at or after *W*'s death. An estate tax QTIP election is made for both QTIP trusts, and a reverse QTIP election for GST purposes is made for the smaller of them, which is still large enough ($300,000 or more) so that, when combined with the by-pass trust, *H* will be the "transferor" of at least $1 million aggregate of generation-skipping transfers.

7. ***Formula clauses.*** The precise results obtainable by applying the considerations described above can be implemented, despite changes in wealth holdings over time, by the use of "formula clauses."

   a. *Types of formula bequests.* A formula clause is a clause in the controlling dispositive instrument (will or trust) that essentially describes the appropriate marital or nonmarital bequest in terms of the end-result desired to be obtained. The principal types:

      (1) Estate equalization formula. Here the clause leaves that amount of a *marital* bequest to the surviving spouse which will equalize the spouses' potential taxable estates as of the estate tax valuation date of the deceased spouse. *See Estate of Smith v. Com'r,* 66 T.C. 415 (1976), *aff'd per curiam,* 565 F.2d 455 (7th Cir.1977), *acq.,* Rev. Rul. 82-23, 1982-1 C.B. 139 (upholding clause under terminable interest rule).

      Example 23: The wealthier spouse's will would contain a clause with language to the following effect: "I leave to my spouse [in a bequest that qualifies for the federal estate tax marital deduction], if she survives me, that amount which, when added to other transfers included in my gross estate and which qualify for the marital deduction, would obtain for my estate a marital deduction which would result in the lowest aggregate federal estate tax in my estate and my spouse's estate on the assumption that my spouse died after me but on the date of my death and that my spouse's estate is valued on such date and in the same manner as my estate is valued."

      (2) Reduce-to-zero formula. This kind of clause leaves that amount of a *nonmarital* bequest that will produce a taxable estate that will yield a zero net estate tax after the Unified Transfer Tax Credit and perhaps other credits; the remaining bequests are all marital bequests.

      Example 24: Here the language would be along these lines, if it were contained in a bequest that qualified for the marital deduction: "I leave to my spouse [in a bequest that qualifies for the federal estate tax marital deduction], if she survives me, that amount which, when added to other transfers included in my gross estate and which qualify for the marital deduction, would obtain for my estate the maximum marital deduction that would reduce my taxable estate for federal estate tax purposes to the maximum amount which would produce a zero net federal estate tax after subtracting the Unified Transfer Tax Credit [and other enumerated credits]."

   b *Formula "control" of entire estate plan.* The formula must "control" the entire estate plan. The formula clause should be located in the decedent spouse's will or an inter vivos trust created by the decedent to which other probate and nonprobate assets are poured over.

   c. *Location of formula clause:*

      (1) Estate equalization scenario. In an estate-equalization scheme, the formula will be contained in a marital-deduction transfer, as in Example

23, since marital-deduction transfers are what can equalize the estates of the two spouses.

(2) Deferral scenario. In a deferral (reduce-to-zero) scheme, the formula can be contained in either a marital-deduction clause (such as a QTIP trust), as in Example 24, or in a nonmarital transfer clause (such as the by-pass trust), along the lines described in Example 17, *supra*.

d. *Adjustments in formula.* The basic estate equalization amount or the reduce-to-zero amount (the exemption equivalent of the Unified Transfer Tax Credit and other credits), as the case may be, must be adjusted to reflect transfers and payments outside of the formula clause so as to produce the correct end result.

(1) Marital formula clause. If the formula is contained in a marital deduction estate-included transfer, the formula must reduce the transfer under that clause by the estate tax value of other marital-deduction transfers, whether occurring under the same instrument or outside of said instrument. *See* Examples 23 and 24. (In theory, the bequest should be increased by any nondeductible payments to be made out of this marital transfer, such as estate taxes. However, the instrument can be drawn so that no such payments are to be made out of, or chargeable to, the bequest.)

(2) Nonmarital reduce-to-zero clause. In a nonmarital reduce-to-zero formula clause, the clause must reduce the amount of the bequest by the estate tax value of other estate-included transfers that do not qualify for the marital deduction, etc. Also, it must increase the amount by any amounts payable out of this transfer (such as estate debts) that are deductible for estate tax purposes (other than as a marital deduction). *See* Example 17, *supra*.

e. *Types of formula clause.* The formula clause can produce a "pecuniary bequest" or it can produce a fractional share of the "residue."

(1) Technical explanation. The amount produced under the pecuniary bequest type is the amount actually distributed to the formula-clause legatee, notwithstanding changes in the "estate" occurring between the estate tax valuation date and the distribution date. The fractional share type produces a fraction that, when multiplied by the residue, would produce the "correct" bequest *as of the estate tax valuation date*, but applying the fraction to the residue *as of the distribution date* will result in the formula-clause legatee sharing in the estate appreciation or depreciation occurring between the estate-tax-valuation and distribution dates.

Example 25: *H* dies with an estate worth $1.6 million at the estate tax valuation date and worth $2 million at whatever date the estate is distributed to the legatees. *H*'s will contains a reduce-to-zero formula, which produces a nonmarital amount of $1 million and a marital deduction of the remainder. Under the pecuniary bequest form, the nonmarital legatee (perhaps a by-pass trust) will receive $1 million and the marital-deduction distribution will be $1 million. Under the fractional-share approach, the fraction will be $1 million divided by $1.6 million (the estate tax value of the residue), and this fraction will be applied against the value of the residue on the distribution date ($2 million), resulting in a nonmarital distribution of $1.25 million and a marital distribution of $750,000. The marital deduction itself will be $600,000 in both cases, since the marital deduction is calculated as of the estate tax valuation date.

(2) Significance of the different approaches:

(a) Transfer tax. The marital deduction is the same either way. For transfer tax purposes it is desirable to reduce (relatively-speaking) the amount of the actual marital transfer, since the latter will augment the surviving spouse's potential gross estate, whereas the nonmarital transfer hopefully will not augment the surviving spouse's potential gross estate. In short, the estate planner must decide whether to place the formula in the marital or nonmarital clauses, and whether to adopt a pecuniary or fractional-share form, while trying to predict whether the estate will appreciate or depreciate after the estate tax valuation date.

Example 26: In Example 25, where the estate appreciates after the estate tax valuation date, the fractional share approach is preferable from a transfer-tax standpoint, since it decreases the amount actually disributed under the marital bequest and increases the nonmarital (by-pass) distribution, in both cases relative to what would occur under the pecuniary bequest form. An even better result here would have occurred if the formula language were in the marital clause and produced a pecuniary bequest: the marital transfer would have been frozen at $600,000 and $1.4 million would have passed under the nonmarital bequest.

(b) Income tax:

(i) Satisfaction in cash. Under state law, a pecuniary bequest must be distributed in cash, unless the governing instrument (or state law) provides that it can be satisfied in kind. Sales of estate or trust assets to produce cash will generate gains and losses to the estate or trust for income tax purposes.

(ii) Satisfaction in kind. Suppose the governing instrument or state law allows the pecuniary bequest to be satisfied in kind. Then, the personal representative or trustee can satisfy the pecuniary bequest with assets having an aggregate value equal to the pecuniary amount. The income tax law, nevertheless, *deems* such in-kind satisfaction to be a sale by the estate or trust, producing gain or loss equal to the difference between the basis and value of each asset on the distribution date. Rev. Rul. 68-392, 1968-2 C.B. 284. (Distributions of residual bequests, including fractional-share-of-residue bequests, are not deemed sales.)

f. *"Hybrid" formula clause.* Estate planners have developed the technique of designing a pecuniary (formula) clause that would avoid deemed sales under the income tax rules: the pecuniary bequest clause provides that it can be satisfied in-kind at "estate tax" (as opposed to distribution-date) values. Since estate tax values correspond to income-tax basis under § 1014 (except for rights to "income in respect of a decedent" and annuities under § 691), there would be no gain or loss to the estate or trust.

(1) IRS concern. The IRS was concerned that such a bequest, if a marital bequest, could be satisfied with those assets that had depreciated the most since the estate tax valuation date, producing the lowest possible augmentation of the surviving spouse's gross estate.

(2) Marital deduction requirements. In Rev. Proc. 64-19, 1964-1 C.B. 682, the IRS said the marital deduction would be disallowed unless the governing instrument (or state law) mandated either that the distributed assets under a marital-deduction hybrid formula bequest have an aggregate value at least equal to the pecuniary amount or that the distributed assets be fairly representative of the appreciation or depreciation in the estate as a whole. However, the personal representative or trustee cannot be allowed to chose between these two approaches.

(3) Extension to nonmarital formula clauses. A hybrid formula can be contained in a reduce-to-zero nonmarital (by-pass) bequest. Here the IRS would be concerned that the bequest would be funded with highly-appreciated assets, as the by-pass trust is not subject to estate tax at the surviving spouse's death. Accordingly, the IRS has extended Rev. Proc. 64-19 to hybrid nonmarital formula bequests. Rev.Rul. 90-3, 1990-1 C.B. 174.

D. **Post-Mortem Planning.** The marital deduction and/or augmentation of the surviving spouse's gross estate can be manipulated by various techniques subsequent to the transfer.

1. *Disclaimers.* A disclaimer is a refusal to accept a bequest or other gratuitous transfer such that the property passes as if the disclaimant predeceased the transferor. A disclaimer can be effected so as to increase or decrease the marital deduction (or the charitable deduction), depending on how the governing instrument is set up. A disclaimer does not involve a "transfer" or a "gift" for transfer tax purpose if it satisfies the qualification rules of § 2518 and the regulations thereunder. *See* Ch.2, at IV.D.3., *supra*. Note the rule under which a disclaimer is disqualified unless, as a result of the disclaimer, the property passes to a person other than the disclaimant, except in the case of the decedent's spouse. § 2518(b)(4).

Example 27: *H* leaves an estate equalization formula pecuniary bequest of $1.6 million to *W*, with the residue to a by-pass trust in which *W* is one of the income and corpus beneficiaries. *W* disclaims $600,000 of the pecuniary bequest, with the result that the $600,000 lapses and falls into the residue (the by-pass trust). The disclaimer is a qualified one even though *W* is also a beneficiary of the by-pass trust. Accordingly, the disclaimer by *W* is not a gift or transfer by *W*, and the marital deduction for *H*'s estate is reduced by $600,000. If the disclaimer were not qualified, *W* would be charged with a gift (and transfer) of $600,000, and the marital deduction would not be reduced.

2. ***Suppressing the value of the surviving spouse's gross estate.*** The goal is to decrease the surviving spouse's potential gross estate.

    a. *Consumables.* The will of the wealthier spouse should leave consumables outright to the surviving spouse. Consumables are items like clothing, furniture, automobiles, and other consumer items which can be expected to decrease in value. Artworks, jewelry, and collectibles, which are expected to appreciate, do not fall in this category. Other things being equal, they should be bequeathed in a nonmarital (or charitable) transfer.

    b. *Estate trusts.* Under the "estate trust" format, there is no "income" requirement. Therefore, such a trust might be funded with low-income nonappreciating property to suppress the surviving spouse's gross estate. However, this kind of investment essentially entails economic waste, so this option is feasible only if the family is "stuck" with some assets of this type, such as nonappreciating land or collectibles, exhausted mineral interests, or an interest in a closely held business the future success of which is highly uncertain after the death of the "key person."

    c. *Pecuniary marital bequests.* Although pecuniary marital bequests must be funded with assets worth the pecuniary amount as of the distribution date, assets can be chosen that will be expected to depreciate following the distribution date (such as consumables). In contrast, fractional-share residuary bequests must be funded with assets representing a cross-section of the estate as a whole, although appropriate governing-instrument language and astute judgment can create room for maneuver.

    d. *Special power of appointment by deed.* In a power-of-appointment trust, the surviving spouse can be given a special power of appointment by deed over corpus. If the general power is one by deed, the exercise of the special power entails a gift because it is a release of the general power to the extent of the amount exercised. The same result should occur if the general power is a testamentary one: (1) the partial release of the future general testamentary power is equivalent to a transfer of a remainder interest in the amount exercised under the special power; (2) such exercise is also a transfer of the surviving spouse's income interest in such amount; (3) the amounts transferred under (1) and (2) equal the amount exercised; but (4) only item (2) entails a present-interest transfer. *See* Ch.2, at IV.C., *supra.* (A special power by deed will disqualify a QTIP trust.)

    e. *Excluded gifts by surviving spouse.* The surviving spouse should be encouraged to make gifts to descendants within the various gift tax exclusions.

    f. *Exhaust marital trust first.* If the income from the marital trust is insufficient to provide for the surviving spouse's consumption and gift needs, the trustee should be empowered to invade the corpus of the marital trust for the surviving spouse. Moreover, the will or trust should make clear that the marital trust is to be exhausted before *any* corpus or income of the by-pass trust is to be distributed to the surviving spouse. (It goes without saying that the surviving spouse should not be a *mandatory* income or corpus beneficiary of the by-pass trust.)

g. *Annuitizing the marital transfer.* The ultimate estate tax avoidance is for the marital bequest to be an annuity that expires at the surviving spouse's death (with no interest therein payable to a third party or to the surviving spouse's estate), at least if the annuity payments will all be consumed or given away. Such an annuity is not disqualified under the terminable-interest rule unless acquired by the personal representative or trustee at the direction of the decedent. *See* § 2056(b)(1)(C). Thus, the decedent can simply bequeath such an annuity to the surviving spouse (or take out a joint-and-survivor annuity for the both of them) or else the surviving spouse (or personal representative or trustee) can simply acquire such an annuity on their own accord.

h. *Income in respect of a decedent (IRD):*

(1) What is IRD? The term "income in respect of a decedent" ("IRD") refers to to an item included in the decedent's gross estate but not included in the decedent's income prior to death (because not received by the cash-method taxpayer prior to death). § 691(a). Examples are accrued but unpaid salary and investment income and lump-sum employee death benefits. Survivor annuities are treated like IRD. § 691(c). Assets consisting of rights to IRD obtain a carry-over basis, rather than a § 1014 basis, and the recipient (estate, legatee, trust, or designated beneficiary) is subject to income tax on all income or gain.

(2) Candidate to fund marital bequest. Initially, an IRD right is an attractive candidate for funding a marital deduction bequest, because the payouts will likely be viewed as consumable income items. In addition, since IRD rights have a low or zero basis, and the owner of the IRD right is taxed on the income therefrom, the income tax burden thereon can further reduce the surviving spouse's potential estate.

(3) Section 691(c) deduction. The recipient of the right to the IRD obtains an income tax deduction under § 691(c) equal to the estate tax attributable to inclusion of the IRD right in the decedent's gross estate. The § 691(c) income tax deduction is lost if the right to the IRD is not subject to estate tax (because it passes to the surviving spouse and qualifies for the marital deduction).

(4) Discretionary funding of marital bequest with IRD item. Notwithstanding the foregoing, the Tax Court has held that the § 691(c) deduction is not lost where the the right to the IRD was not specifically bequeathed to the surviving spouse (or does not pass to her by way of a beneficiary designation), but rather was a general estate asset, and the estate personal representative exercised its discretion to fund the marital deduction with such right. *Estate of Kincaid v. Com'r*, 85 T.C. 25 (1985).

(5) Reduce-to-zero plan. Under a reduce-to-zero (deferral) plan, there will be no § 691(c) deduction anyway, since there will be no estate tax on the decedent spouse. In that case, IRD, may be a good candidate for funding the marital transfer.

V. **LIQUIDITY PLANNING. Since the government does not accept payment in kind, planning must consider how the tax is to be paid in cash.**

LIQUIDITY PLANNING

A. Flower Bonds. "Flower bonds" are low-interest U.S. government obligations that can be redeemed at par to pay estate taxes. Due to the low interest rate, which makes them a poor investment, these bonds can often be purchased at a substantial discount. (However, the discount lessens as the bonds move closer to maturity.) The difference between the purchase price and par value is pure economic gain to the estate. Flower bonds have not been issued for some time, so that it might be hard to purchase them.

Example 28: Under a durable power of attorney, *D*'s attorney purchases $400,000 par value of flower bonds on behalf of D for $260,000 just prior to *D*'s death. *D*'s estate tax liability is $420,000. *D*'s estate satisfies $400,000 of this liability by tendering the bonds for redemption to the U.S. government. (For estate tax purposes, the bonds are valued at $400,000, not their lower fair market value.) *D*'s estate has pure economic gain of $140,000 less any estate tax due to valuing the bonds at $400,000 rather than their fair market value.

B. Section 303 Redemptions. Under § 303, stock in closely-held corporations can be redeemed by the business (in exchange for cash), and the redemption will be treated as a "sale" (rather than a "dividend," with no basis offset) for income tax purposes. Since the basis of the stock will be determined under § 1014, there should be very little gain or loss in a § 303 redemption.

1. *Limitation.* The § 303 privilege only extends to that amount necessary to pay death taxes plus funeral and estate administration expenses.

2. *Qualification.* To qualify under § 303, the value of the stock must exceed 35% of the decedent's net gross estate.

    a. *Application of 35% rule.* For purposes of applying the 35% rule, any gifts (other than of qualifying stock) within three years of death will be disregarded. § 2035(c)(1)(A).

    b. *Section 302 alternative.* If § 303 is not available, the estate can take its chances under § 302, which is far more likely to produce "dividend" treatment.

C. Buy-Sell Agreements. The decedent may have entered into a buy-sell agreement with any party (including an entity), requiring the latter to purchase or redeem any given property (usually an interest in a closely held business) from the decedent's estate (or giving the estate a "put" option, etc.) for cash. (For a buy-sell agreement to fix the *value* of the property for estate tax purposes, the agreement must satisfy the requirements of § 2703, *see* II.C.5., *supra.*)

D. Insurance Trusts. Insurance proceeds and death benefits, being in the form of cash, are an obvious source of liquidity, and may be purchased or contracted for with just this purpose in mind.

1. *Loss of exclusion.* If the insurance proceeds (or death benefits) are not included in the gross estate (for example, they reside in an irrevocable trust), the exclusion will be lost, under § 2042(1), if the insurance proceeds (or death benefits) are *required* by the terms of the governing instrument to be used to pay obligations of the estate. *See* Rev. Rul. 77-157, 1977-1 C.B. 279.

2. *Avoiding loss of exclusion.* To avoid this problem, the governing instrument should "authorize" the trust to use the cash to purchase (nonliquid) estate assets and to lend money to the estate on reasonable terms.

E. **Deferral of Tax Payment.** If all else fails, deferral of the tax payment may be obtained in certain cases. *See* Ch.3, at VI.2., *supra.* If a § 303 redemption is used, deferral of tax payment under § 6166 is available only for any remaining death tax liability.

CHAPTER 6 - QUESTIONS, ANSWERS, AND TIPS

EXAM TIPS:

1. Answer the question asked. The question may ask for the probable transfer tax result of some arrangement, how some estate planning gambit is supposed to work, or whether some technique should be used. Professional responsibility issues may also be present, especially in husband-wife planning situations. Questions involving planning choices often raise issues of judgment and the weighing of risks and likely transaction costs.

2. Do not overlook §§ 2701-2704. Sections 2701-2704 were enacted only in 1990, so that there is little in the way of case law or rulings on these sections, and your casebook may not devote much attention to them. These sections operate as a kind of "anti-abuse overlay" on existing doctrine. That is, it is hard to understand these provisions without knowing the underlying doctrine, as well as the tax avoidance devices that these provisions are aimed at.

3. Do not overlook GST issues. If your course touches on income tax issues, do not neglect those either.

REVIEW QUESTIONS:

1. What is a GRAT, how is it supposed to work, and what are the optimum conditions for using it? (You could be asked a question like this about any tax-avoidance device, such as a "SCIN," a "CRAT," or whatever.)

ANSWER:

A grantor retained annuity trust (GRAT) involves an inter vivos transfer of property (say, $1 million) in trust, with an annuity payable to the grantor for a term of years, followed by a remainder to some family member. The idea is to avoid application of § 2702. Only a qualified retained annuity (or unitrust) interest avoids § 2702. If § 2702 were to apply, the retained annuity interest would be valued at zero, resulting in a gift of $1 million, none of which is excludible. By avoiding § 2702, the gift is the excess of $1 million over the actuarial value of the retained annuity interest. The greater the annuity payout and/or the higher the "applicable federal rate" (AFR) (the discount rate in the tables is 120% of the AFR), the greater the value of the annuity and the smaller the value of the gift of the remainder. Since the gift is of a future interest, there is no exclusion.

For estate tax purposes, this trust will be included in the grantor's gross estate if the grantor dies within the term of years. Otherwise the trust will not be included in the gross estate.

The question of how long the grantor will live is an element of risk. Unlike some tax-avoidance devices, here you do not want the grantor to die prematurely. But even if § 2036 applies, the result will not be any worse, overall, than if a GRAT had not been used. If § 2036 is avoided, then the GRAT operates as an estate freeze: a fixed $$ amount returns to the grantor's § 2033 estate, but all growth in the trust avoids estate or gift tax.

If the remainder is to persons two or more generations below the grantor (and assuming that § 2036 does not apply), the termination of the trust will produce a "taxable termination" type of generation-skipping transfer. (The creation of the trust would not be direct-skip transfer, since the grantor is a nonskip beneficiary.) In this case, the grantor must decide whether or not to allocate the GST exemption to this transfer (or hold it in reserve).

2. In a common-law state, Hector (age 45) has assets worth $3 million and his wife Shawna (age 42) has assets worth $600,000. There is nothing seriously wrong with this marriage.

   (a) What steps should be taken now in terms of marital deduction planning?

   (b) What should Hector's will provide for Shawna? What kind of "common disaster" language should be inserted in Hector's will?

   (c) What should Shawna's will provide for Hector? What kind of "common disaster language" should be inserted in Shawna's will?

ANSWER:

In (a), Shawna will lose part of her exemption equivalent (assume that it is $1 million) if she dies first with a taxable estate of $600,000 or less. Hector should make a gift of at least $400,000 to Shawna. If Hector is uncomfortable about this, the gift could take the form of a QTIP trust, so that Shawna will not be able to control its disposition.

In (b) and (c) the choice is between an "estate equalization" plan (lowest aggregate tax) and "reduce to zero" (no tax on first death) plan.

Under a reduce-to-zero plan, Hector should leave marital-deduction transfers to W such that nondeductible transfers equal the applicable exemption equivalent. Shawna's will would be similar for marital-deduction bequests to Hector. A reduce-to-zero plan is desirable only if there is a meaningful gap between the deaths of the two spouses. Thus, each will's marital-deduction bequests should be conditioned on the other spouse's surviving for six months. (A longer period would disqualify the bequests from the marital deduction under § 2056(b)(3).) If the other spouse does not survive the decedent by more than six months, the bequests should be of the estate equalization type.

Under an estate-equalization plan, Hector should leave Shawna marital-deduction bequests in that amount which, when added to Shawna's own assets, equals one-half of their aggregate taxable estates. (Such a clause means that Shawna's assets will have to be valued at Hector's death, and this results in added transaction costs.) If Shawna dies first, she (having the smaller estate) can't achieve estate equalization. The best she can do is to leave nothing to Hector in a marital deduction form.

If the couple prefers an estate-equalization plan in all events, Hector's will should leave the marital-deduction bequests "to Shawna if she survives me," and a add language to the effect that "if it cannot be determined which of Shawna or me shall survive the other, Shawna shall be deemed to have survived me." The idea is to obtain the desired estate splitting.

6

3. In which of the following "tax planning" techniques is it desirable (from the tax angle, of course) that the "measuring life" dies before his or actuarial life expectancy:

    (a) GRUT
    (b) CRAT
    (c) SCIN
    (d) Private annuity
    (e) Spousal remainder trust?

ANSWER:

Not in (a). In a grantor retained unitrust (for a term of years), it is essential that the grantor outlive the term of the retained unitrust interest.

Not in (b), which is a charitable remainder annuity trust. The idea is that the noncharitable "lead" interest should be undervlaued, and this occurs if the holder of the lead interest (if not the grantor) outlives his or her life expectancy.

Yes in (c), which is a self-cancelling installment note. The idea is that these notes (which are consideration for gift tax purposes) be over-valued, which happens if the donor-noteholder dies prematurely (so that less comes into his or her § 2033 estate).

Yes in (d). Same basic idea as (c). It's advantageous that "consideration in money or money's worth" be overvalued for estate and gift tax purposes relative to what actually comes back into the transferor's § 2033 gross estate.

Not in (e), which is a trust to a nonspouse (perhaps a parent) for life, vested remainder to spouse. If the non-spousal lead interest outlives his or her life expectancy, the present-value of the deductible marital remainder interest will have been overstated, which is good.

4. What advantages inhere in a limited partnership as an estate-freezing vehicle, as opposed to a corporation?

ANSWER:

The idea is to maximize discounts for minority interests and lack of marketability. Restrictions on liquidation of the limited partnership entity imposed by state-limited partnership law depress value, whereas equivalent contractual restrictions would be disregarded under § 2704(b).

A partnership cannot run afoul of § 2036(b), which only comes into play if a donor retains voting rights in transferred "stock" (of a corporation). In a limited partnership, a person can retain management control without triggering § 2036(b). (On the other hand, control entials a valuation premium.)

A nontax advantage is that a judgment creditor of a limited partner acquires only a "charging interest," not the partnership interest itself, so that there is protection against creditors and outsiders somewhat akin to a "spendthrift" trust.

APPENDIX

EXAM PREPARATION

Introduction. Hopefully, you have picked up some exam-taking skills by this stage of your law school career. General hints on exam taking in taxation subjects are set forth at EP-1 through EP-3 of the *Casenote Law Outline: Federal Income Taxation.* Here are some that are particularly pertinent to the subject of this outline.

1. Answer the question asked. This is often overlooked. Students tend to think that every question is "Give me the law on this topic." But the question may take such forms as "What would you advise the client?" or "How should you (as a lawyer) proceed?" Questions phrased in such a manner may raise procedural and/or professional responsibility issues, or call on you to evaluate the benefits and risks of a certain course of action. (In estates practice, taking unnecessary risks is a no-no, since litigation costs are themselves a kind of "tax" on the estate.) Planning questions demand that you weigh alternatives and exercise judgment.

2. Work the facts into the answer. Most instructors don't want a section of a treatise or outline thrown back at them. The practice of law is not a memory exercise. The answer should discuss the facts given in terms of the applicable law and practice. My favorite example of where this is not done involves a question on my Wills & Trusts exam dealing with investment powers and duties. The question usually states that *T* dies leaving three or four described items of property to a trust. At least half of the answers merely describe the Prudent Person Rule and maybe the duty to diversify, without any discussion at all of the assets described in the question! (Also, a majority of the answers state what the trustee can legally get away with at a minimum, but the question is usually what course of action the trustee *should* take, which implies far more than the minimum.) By the way, don't assume facts that are not given, unless you need to supply them (as alternative assumptions) in order to proceed to a conclusion. By answering questions that are not posed, you are simply wasting time (and annoying the grader by showing off).

3. Be specific and definite. Avoid generalities. Use numbers, where appropriate. Cite Code and Regulation sections, where applicable; citing them is a lot more efficient than paraphrasing them (and don't cite a case for a rule of statutory or regulatory law). Indicate crucial words and phrases in statutes, regulations, documents, etc. Don't use "may" or "might" unless the law is really unclear (which is rarely the case in the tax area). Show that you understand what issues are crucial. If an election is available, say so and describe the consequences of alternative courses of action.

PRACTICE EXAM QUESTIONS

Introduction. It will be assumed that you have access to the Code and Regulations. It will also be assumed that the applicable actuarial tables are those that presuppose a 10% discount rate and rate of return. Assume that community property is not involved, unless indicated to the contrary. These questions may be more difficult, complex, or involved than you would get on a real exam, but it is better to err on the side of over-preparation. *The suggested answers appear at the end of this section.*

QUESTION 1: *T* has just died, survived by his wife *W*, and your task is to compute *T*'s net gift and estate tax liability as best you can, showing all steps in your answer, on the basis of the following facts:

In 1978, *T,* who was then unmarried, made a gift of $50,000 worth of securities to a child *C.*

In 1982, *T,* who was courting *W,* created an irrevocable trust with securities worth $1 million, income to *T* for life (*T* was then 82 years old), remainder to *W* if living and married to *T* at *T*'s death, but if *W* is not then living the remainder goes to child *E.*

In 1983, *T,* who had by then married *W,* purchases term life insurance on his own life, face amount $500,000, naming *W* as beneficiary.

In 1985, *T* buys a home in Maine for $100,000; title is held by *T* and *W* as joint tenants with right of survivorship.

In 1988, *T* creates a revocable trust funded with securities worth $200,000. During *T*'s lifetime, the income and corpus are payable to *T* on *T*'s demand. On *T*'s death, the trustee is to pay income and/or corpus to or among *T*'s children and the issue of any of *T*'s deceased children as the trustee determines for their support and comfort; after 20 years the trust terminates and is to be distributed to *T*'s then living issue, per stirpes, or if none to Harvard University.

In 1991, *T* makes a gift of the life insurance policy to his child *D*; the gift tax value of the policy (interpolated terminal reserve, probably zero, plus unexpired premium for the year) is $7,000. *D* thereupon changes the beneficiary to herself.

In 1992, *T* releases his power to revoke the 1988 trust, then worth $400,000, including the power to demand income and corpus.

In 1993, *T* dies. The 1982 revocable trust is then worth $500,000. The 1984 irrevocable trust is then worth $1.2 million. The Maine home is worth $200,000. The assets in *T*'s probate estate are worth $2 million.

T's will is as follows:

Debts ($100,000), administration expenses, and taxes are to be paid out of the residue.

The residence and tangible personal property (worth $300,000) are bequeathed outright to *W.*

A testamentary trust is created with $500,000, naming *W* as trustee, income to *C* for life (*C* is then age 55), remainder to the Nelson Gallery of Art in Kansas City.

Another testamentary trust is created with $1 million, naming the *X* Bank as trustee, income to *W* for life (payable at least annually), giving *W* the power during her lifetime to appoint corpus to or among *T*'s descendants from time to time, and on *T*'s death the trust is to be continued for *T*'s living issue for 20 years, etc.

The residue passes into a third testamentary trust, naming the *X* Bank and *W* as co-trustees, income and/or corpus to or among *T*'s issue and *W* from time to time; on *W*'s death, remainder to *T*'s living issue.

Administration expenses are $200,000.

There is a state "pick up" ("piggy-back") estate tax equal to the maximum available federal estate credit for state death taxes.

QUESTION 2: Analyze the following transfer for estate, gift, and generation-skipping tax purposes:

G, widowed, creates an irrevocable inter vivos trust, naming herself as trustee, income and/or corpus to or among *G*'s issue from time to time for their support and comfort as determined by *G,* with any undistributed income being added to corpus; on *G*'s death the trust is to terminate and be distributed to *G*'s then living issue. Throughout, *G* has two unmarried daughters, one of whom survives *G.*

QUESTION 3: Analyze the following transfer for estate, gift and generation skipping tax purposes:

X creates an irrevocable inter vivos trust, naming his 22-year-old daughter D and his sister S as co-trustees, income to X or accumulated in the trustees' sole discretion; upon X's death, income to D for life, with the trustees having the power to pay corpus to D for her support and comfort; on D's death, the trust to terminate and the remainder distributed to or among such of D's issue as D appoints by her will, and in default of such appointment to X's living issue (but if none to Duke University). Income is sometimes distributed to X; up until X's death, about 40% of the income is distributed to X. After X's death, no corpus is distributed to D; S survives D. There is no appointment under D's will; all of the property passes to the children of X's child C, who predeceased D.

QUESTION 4: Can an employee death benefit be structured so as to avoid being subject to both the estate and gift taxes?

QUESTION 5: What is the purpose of an irrevocable insurance trust, and how should it be set up?

QUESTION 6: W's will has the following provisions: (1) "If my husband survives me by six months, I leave an amount equal to one-half of my gross estate to the X Bank in trust, income to my husband for life, then to such persons, including my husband's estate, as my husband shall appoint by will, but if no such appointment then at my husband's death to my then surviving issue per stirpes, but if none to the American Cancer Society, it being my intent that this bequest shall qualify for the federal estate tax marital deduction. My executor shall satisfy this bequest in cash or in kind, but if satisfied in kind this bequest shall be satisfied with assets at their value for federal estate tax purposes." (2) "I leave the residue of my estate to the X Bank to be held in trust, income to my husband for life, with the trustee being authorized to distribute corpus to my husband in its sole discretion, remainder at my husband's death to my then living issue per stirpes, but if none to the American Cancer Society." At W's death on January 1, 1993, W's net estate was worth $2 million and H's then-potential net estate was worth $500,000. Amounts deductible to W's estate under §§ 2053 and 2054 total $400,000. H, who was in mediocre health already, was devastated by W's death and went into a decline, finally passing away on September 4, 1993.

(1)   Comment on the tax aspects of this estate plan as it is drafted.

(2)   If the plan is defective from the tax point of view, can anything be done about it after W's death?

QUESTION 7: The following questions are short-answer or "modified" true-false.

A.   Pursuant to a separation agreement incorporated into a divorce decree, H is required to create a trust, providing an annuity to W for life, then to H if living, but if not to their children. Is this transfer subject to tax?

B.   X lends $40,000 to her nephew Y at 4% interest, repayable in 15 years, so that Y may attend college. X intends to enforce the note. Are there any transfer tax consequences?

C.   D can avoid gift tax by giving $40,000 cash to E on condition that E use the money exclusively for college tuition and fees.

D. *A* creates a trust in which *B* is given a general power of appointment by will. For the five-year period prior to *B*'s death, *B* is an adjudicated incompetent. The trust is not included in *B*'s gross estate.

E. *H* and *W* own 90% of the stock of *X* Corp., as of *H*'s death, as community property, of which *H* is the sole manager. *H*'s estate can obtain a minority interest discount.

F. *D* can remove voting preferred stock in a controlled closely held corporation from her gross estate by making a gift of it to *E*, retaining the right to vote the stock.

G. *H* purchases an annuity that provides equal payments to *H* and *W* for their joint lives, and on *H*'s death provides a payment to the survivor for life. *H* dies first. The value of the annuity qualifies for the estate tax marital deduction.

H. *H*'s will bequeaths all of the community property bequeathed by *H* and *W* into a testamentary trust, income to *W* for life, remainder to children, etc. *W* acquiesces in this transfer. As of *H*'s death, the value of the income interest in *H*'s half of the community property is slightly greater than the value of the remainder interest in *W*'s half of the community property. Assuming that nothing qualifies for the marital deduction in *H*'s estate, no part of the trust is included in *W*'s gross estate.

I. In 1988, *A* purchases Blackacre and puts it in the name of *A* and *B* as joint tenants with right of survivorship. In 1994 *A* dies.

   (1) Half of Blackacre is included in *A*'s gross estate.

   (2) If *B* disclaims within nine months of *A*'s death, *B*'s disclaimer does not qualify under § 2518 since it was made more than nine months after *B*'s interest was created.

J. If *T*, owning 80% of the stock of *X* Corporation, bequeaths half of her shares to *A* and half to *B*, *T*'s estate is entitled to claim minority interest discounts on each bequest.

K. Each of *A* and *B* simultaneously create trusts with $1 million, income to the other for life, remainder to *C*.

   (1) Neither trust is included in *A*'s or *B*'s gross estate, since neither has retained any interest in the property transferred.

   (2) The income interest received in the trust created by the other is consideration in money or money's worth.

L. At the date of *T*'s death her gross estate is worth $1 million. On the alternate valuation date, it is worth $1.2 million. *D*'s personal representative can elect the alternate valuation date in order to obtain a higher basis for income tax purposes in the estate-included assets.

M. *D* transfers Blackacre (worth $1 million) to *E* in exchange for *E*'s promise to pay $70,000 per year to *D*. Blackacre is included in *D*'s gross estate under § 2036(a)(1).

N. *D* creates a trust, naming herself as trustee, income to or among *D*'s and the remainder goes to *R*. This trust is fully complete for gift tax children in the trustee's discretion; on *D*'s death the trust is to terminate purposes.

O.   *F* owns property worth $1 million, $400,000 of which would be "qualified real property" under § 2032A(b)(1) except for failure to comply with the 50% test. Assuming no mortgages or debts, if *F* makes gifts of $250,000 of nonqualifying assets, qualification under § 2032A can be assured.

SUGGESTED ANSWERS TO PRACTICE EXAM QUESTIONS

Outline of answer to QUESTION 1:

The 1978 gift of $50,000 is reduced by the $10,000 exclusion. The gift tax on $40,000 is $8,200, and $8,200 of the § 2505 credit is used, reducing the tax to zero.

The 1982 trust was created before the enactment of § 2702, which therefore does not apply. The retained interest is worth $402,950, using the 10% actuarial tables. (We'll round it off to $400,000 to ease the computations.) There is no indication that *W* gave consideration in money or money's worth for the remainder interest. The remainder to *W* does not qualify for the marital deduction, because it is a nondeductible terminable interest: it is contingent on outliving *T* (and upon failure it would pass to a third party). (If the remainder to *W* were vested, it would qualify for the marital deduction.) So, *H* has made a gift of a remainder interest worth $600,000. There is no $10,000 exclusion for gifts of future interests. The gift tax on the cumulative tax base of $640,000 ($40,000 + $600,000) is $207,600, which is reduced by $8,200, the gift tax (before credit) on $40,000. From the resulting gift tax of $199,400, the unused credit of $184,600 is subtracted ($192,800 - $8,200). The net gift tax is $14,800. (The shortcut method is to multiply $40,000, the tax base above the exemption equivalent of $600,000, by the marginal rate of 0.37.)

The 1983 purchase of life insurance is not a gift, since *T* could have changed the beneficiary, etc.

The 1985 purchase of the Maine home produces a gift to *W* of half ($50,000), if the joint tenancy is severable. Whatever the value of the gift to *W,* it is reduced to zero by the marital deduction. *See* § 2523(d) (interest in joint tenancy not a terminable interest).

The 1988 trust does not involve a gift, since revocability renders the transfer "incomplete."

The 1991 gift of the life insurance policy is reduced to zero by the § 2503(b) exclusion. Outright gifts of life insurance policies come under the "contract right" rule, meaning the gifts are of present interests (the right to current insurance protection).

The 1992 release of the retained powers in the revocable trust creates a gift of $400,000. Assume gift splitting with *W* under § 2513, so that *H* and *W* are each deemed to make a gift of $200,000. No exclusion is available because no present interests exist. No charitable deduction is available because there is not a vested remainder following a qualified annuity or unitrust interest. The tax on the cumulative gift tax base of $840,000 ($40,000 + $600,000 + $200,000) is $283,400. Subtract the before-credit gift tax on the prior taxable gifts of $640,000 = $207,600. That leaves a gift tax of $75,800 on *T. T* has no credit left. (*W* is probably still within the credit.)

In 1993, at the date of *T*'s death, the gross estate is as follows:

- $2 million probate estate. § 2033.
- $1.2 million then value of 1982 irrevocable trust. § 2036(a)(1) (retained income for life).
- $500,000 insurance policy. Gift within three years of death. § 2035(d)(2), invoking § 2042(2). Note also last sentence of § 2035(b). Amount includable is proceeds.
- $500,000 then value of revocable trust. § 2038(a)(2) and § 2035(d)(2) (relinquishment of power within three years of death). Gift splitting has no effect on the amount includable under § 2038: *T* was the transferor of the entire trust.
- $100,000. Half of inter-spousal joint tenancy. § 2040(b).
- $75,800. Gift tax on gifts within three years of death. § 2035(c).

TOTAL GROSS ESTATE = $4,375,800.

Deductions are as follows:

- $100,000 debts.
- $200,000 administration expenses, if not deducted for income tax purposes. *See* § 642(g). If the taxable estate would otherwise be $800,000 or more, these should be deducted for estate tax purposes, since the estate tax lowest marginal rate of 37% is greater than the highest income tax rate.
- The remainder interest in the first testamentary trust under the will does not qualify for the charitable deduction. An income interest is not a qualifying charitable annuity or unitrust interest.

- Marital deduction:

    - The life insurance would have qualified had not *D* changed the beneficiary to herself. The proceeds don't "pass" to *W* from *T*.
    - The $1.2 million trust included under § 2036 qualifies in full, since (at *T*'s death) the remainder goes to *W* immediately, the contingencies having dropped off; hence, the property passes to *W* and it is no longer a terminable interest.
    - The house in Maine passes to *W* by right of survivorship. The deduction for this item is $100,000, the amount included in *T*'s gross estate.
    - $300,000 specific bequests to *W* qualify.
    - The second testamentary trust looks like a QTIP trust, but it fails to qualify due to *W*'s power to appoint corpus to third parties during her lifetime.
    - The third testamentary trust fails to qualify. Although *W* has a general power of appointment (co-trustee with nonadverse party having power to pay corpus to herself), it is not exercisable "alone and in all events," nor does *W* have an income interest.

Total marital deduction = $1,600,000

TOTAL DEDUCTIONS = $1,900,000.

THE TAXABLE ESTATE = $2,475,800.

The total death tax calculation is completed as follows:

- Adjusted taxable gifts (post-1976 taxable gifts *not* included in the gross estate) are $440,000 ($40,000 + $400,000). The 1980 gift of $600,000 is not an adjusted taxable gift because the remainder was included in *H*'s gross estate under § 2036.
- The cumulative tax base is $2,915,800. The tax on this sum is $1,233,700.
- Subtract actual gift taxes paid (after credit) of $90,600 ($14,800 + $75,800).
- Subtract the full credit of $192,800.
- The maximum § 2011 credit is $136,864 (the adjusted taxable estate is $2,475,800 - $60,000 = $2,415,800).

The net federal estate tax is $813,436, and the state estate tax is $136,864, for a grand death tax total of $950,300.

If the question had asked you to criticize T's estate plan, there would be several errors to discuss.

First, the remainder to *W* in the 1982 trust should have been vested; in that case, there would have been no gift and no gift tax. Even though the 1982 gift was included in the gross estate, it is better not to have to pay a gift tax up front unless an "estate freeze" transfer is involved. A better plan would have been to make this a revocable trust; if *T* and *W* became

EP

divorced, *T* could have amended the trust so as to remove *W* as the remainder.

Second, there was no need to make a gift of the life insurance to *D,* since the proceeds would have qualified for the estate tax marital deduction. If *T* really wanted *D* to have it, *T* should have made the gift to *D* earlier (outside of the three-year period prior to death) or have arranged for *D* to take out the policy directly.

The first testamentary trust was botched. The noncharitable lead interest should have been in the form of a qualified annuity or unitrust interest.

The second testamentary trust should not have given *W* the special power of appointment. In that case, so much of the value of the trust for which *T*'s executor made the QTIP election would have qualified for the marital deduction.

In the third testamentary trust, *W* should not have been made a co-trustee with power to pay corpus to herself. It is utter disaster to have a trust not qualify for the marital deduction but be includable in the surviving spouse's gross estate. *W*'s resigning as co-trustee would not help; that would be a "release" of a general power, which is a deemed exercise under § 2514, which would have resulted in a gift by *W* of the whole trust. *W* should disclaim the trusteeship (not accept it) immediately. Check the partial-disclaimer regulations under § 2518 to see if *W* would have to disclaim her corpus interest also. Better, *W* should not have been made co-trustee in the first place. Alternatively, *W* could be co-trustee under "standards" relating to support, maintenance, health, and/or education.

The size of the marital deduction could be discussed. We don't know *W*'s wealth holdings. Probably a formula clause should have been used.

Outline of answer to QUESTION 2 (material in brackets discusses alternative versions of the question; the student in answering an exam question should not add such variant answers):

1.   *Gift tax*

   a.   *Nature of G's transfer:* *G* has made a transfer with retained power over income and corpus in her capacity as trustee. Is the transfer incomplete on the ground that *G* has retained the power to alter beneficial enjoyment by shifting distributions among her issue or withholding distributions? No, because *G*'s power is limited by a "reasonably definite and ascertainable standard." *See* Reg. § 25.2511-2(g). So, the transfer is complete for gift tax purposes. [If there were no standards, the transfer would be incomplete.]

   b.   *Implied reversion:* *G* has retained an implied reversion, since it is possible that *G* might outlive her issue. The actuarial computation of this reversion is far too complex to perform in an exam. That is not important, however, since § 2702 applies, this being a retained-interest transfer. Therefore, the retained interest is not subtracted for gift tax purposes. [If there were no standards, § 2702 would not apply because the transfer of all non-retained interests would have been incomplete.]

   c.   *No present interest exclusion:* There is no present interest exclusion, since neither beneficiary has an interest assured of taking effect immediately that is capable of actuarial valuation.

2.   *Estate tax*

   a.   *Does G have the power to "alter" or to affect the beneficial enjoyment of income under § 2038 or § 2036(a)(2)?:* No, under case law, because of the reasonably definite and ascertainable standards. Also, mere administrative powers do not fall within these sections. [Without the standards, both sections would apply; § 2036(a)(2) would control, resulting in inclusion of the entire property in *G*'s gross estate.]

b. *Section 2037 issue:* Even though *G*'s surviving daughter takes the remainder, *G* still possessed, at the moment just prior to death, an implied reversion (the possibility that she might die without issue), and this raises a § 2037 issue. Since this reversion cannot be valued in an exam setting, alternative assumptions must be made. If the reversion is worth less than 5% at the moment just prior to *G*'s death, § 2037 would not apply. If the reversion is worth more than 5%, then § 2037 applies if the survivorship requirement is met. It *is* met, because whether the remainder takes is contingent on whether *G* outlives her issue. In other words, *G*'s death was a necessary (if not sufficient condition) for the remainders to take. Also, no remainder can take until *G*'s death regardless. Since, at *G*'s death, no noncontingent interests remain outstanding, the entire trust would be included in *G*'s gross estate at its value on the estate tax valuation date. [If *G* had outlived all of her issue, the property would have reverted to *G* (*G*'s estate) on *G*'s death, and would have been included in full under § 2033.]

c. *Effect on cumulative tax base:* If § 2037 does not apply, the completed gift is an adjusted taxable gift that figures in the cumulative tax base at estate tax computation time. If § 2037 does apply, is any of the gift tax value removed from the adjusted taxable gifts total? Only twice-taxed interests are so removed. The remainder was taxed twice. *G*'s executor would argue that the actuarial value at the time of gift of the remainder interest should be excluded from the adjusted taxable gifts total. The government might argue that this interest was not capable of valuation at the time of gift, since *G* as trustee might have paid all of the corpus by the time of her own death, leaving no remainder at all. There is authority from analagous areas (*e.g.,* under § 2013) that would support this position. Was the reversion taxed twice? Not really; it had a value of zero at *G*'s death. Thus, it is possible, but not certain, this transfer would be subject to both estate and gift tax in full.

d. *Generation-skipping tax:* The remainder is a non-skip person, so there is no generation-skipping transfer. [If the remainder passed to a grandchild; there would have been a taxable termination as of *G*'s death. In fact, since § 2037 applies, it might actually be a direct-skip transfer at *G*'s death, since a transfer subject to both gift and estate tax is deemed to occur at the later date.]

Outline of answer to QUESTION 3 (material in brackets discusses alternative versions of the question; the student in answering an exam question should not add such variant answers):

There are two possible transferors here, *X* and *D*; the latter has one or powers of appointment.

As to *X*:

1. ***Gift tax:*** *X* has made a completed gift of the remainder interest. Has *X* retained an income interest? Under *Robinette,* the grantor has the burden of proving the value of any retained interest for gift tax purposes. Here, the trustee has discretion to pay income to *X*; hence, *X* has not retained any interest of ascertainable value. The fact that the trustees are close relatives of *X* (who may accede to *X*'s wishes) is disregarded; trustees are assumed to act like trustees. However, if under the law of trusts (creditor's rights) *X*'s creditors can reach the income interest, then *X* has retained the income interest by operation of law. Would this kind of retained interest fall under § 2702? The regulations seem, oddly, to say no, although the

regulations may be construed not to apply where the grantor's creditors can reach the income interest (since the creditors claims would then supersede and render moot the trustees' discretion). So the transfer is probably wholly complete.

2. ***Estate tax:*** Taking the trust at face value, X has not "retained" the income interest, due to the trustees' discretion. The fact that 40% of the income was in fact paid to X, sporadically, is also disregarded. The distributions were pursuant to the exercise of the trustees' discretion, not X's rights under the trust. [The answer might be different if all of the income had been paid to X; that might have constituted circumstantial evidence of an agreement or understanding between X and the trustees that would have satisfied the "retention" requirement.] However, if X's creditors could have reached the income, then X retained the income interest by operation of law, and the trust would be included under § 2036(a)(1) at its value on the estate tax valuation date.

3. ***Cumulative transfer tax base:*** If the trust is not included in the gross estate, that which is taxable is an "adjusted taxable gift." If the trust is included in X's gross estate, the gift tax value of the remainder interest is removed from the "adjusted taxable gifts" figure, since the remainder was subject to both gift and estate tax. If the income interest was subject to gift tax by reason of § 2702, the gift tax value of such income interest is included in "adjusted taxable gifts," since the income interest was not taxed twice.

4. ***Generation-skipping tax:*** Since there are non-skip persons (D) who will be possible distributees, neither the creation of the trust nor X's death involves a direct-skip transfer. *See* below for D's death.

As to D:

1. ***Gift tax:*** D has a general power of appointment over corpus, for the reasons explained shortly. Since there is no exercise, release, or lapse of such power (prior to D's death), there is no gift tax exposure. [If corpus had been distributed to D, there would still be no gift; you cannot make a gift to yourself.]

2. ***Estate tax:*** D's power by will to appoint to his issue is not a general power; D cannot appoint to her estate or its creditors. D's power as co-trustee with S to distribute corpus to D is a potential general power. The "standards" exception does not apply because "comfort" is broader than the "health, education, support, or maintenance" listed in § 2041(b)(1)(A). S does not have any interest in the trust, so S cannot be an adverse party. Hence, D has a general power by deed, even though the power is held jointly with S. The trust is included in D's gross estate, since D possessed the general power at death; the fact that it was never exercised is irrelevant. The amount includable is the value of the trust on D's death or alternate valuation date (if elected). There was no gift, so no adjusted taxable gifts issue exists.

3. ***Generation-skipping tax:*** When the trust terminates, the remainder passes to X's grandchildren. This would be a taxable termination; however, D's general power of appointment (resulting in inclusion in D's gross estate) causes D, not X, to be the "transferor." That means that the remainders are non-skip persons. Hence, there is no generation-skipping transfer in this problem.

[*See* the examples in the portions of the gift and estate tax chapters (Chapters 2 and 3, respectively) dealing with powers of appointment for more on that topic.]

Suggested answer to QUESTION 4:

Yes. Under the estate tax, there are two ways to avoid § 2039. The first is to avoid the retained payments requirement. The plan or plans can be set up so that the employee is not receiving any pension, or has no right to one or more future payments, at death. In order to accomplish this, one must forego all retirement benefits (other than salary and consulting fees) under the employment relationship (including disability benefits that commence at retirement age). Alternatively, one could have a retirement benefit payable in a lump sum which is in fact paid to the employee prior to death. The second way is not to have any contractual right to a death benefit prior to or at the employee's death. This is feasible where the employee can pass control of the entity to the natural object of his bounty; the latter can then prevail upon the board of directors (etc.) to spontaneously pay a death benefit to herself. Here, the employee never made a transfer during life or at death; the beneficiary essentially makes a gift to herself (loots the treasury). (The other equity holders may also be making gifts to the looter.)

Assuming § 2039 does not apply, one also must avoid §§ 2036-2038. If there is no binding agreement to pay a death benefit, there is no "transfer" under any of those sections. If there is no right to a pension or other payments before death, or if all payments have already been collected before death, § 2036 will not apply. To avoid § 2037, the employee's estate must not be a primary or contingent beneficiary of the death benefit (or the contingency must be worth less than 5% as of the moment just prior to the employee's death). To avoid § 2038, the employee must not have possessed the power to change the beneficiary within three years of death.

The best way to avoid gift tax is for the death benefit to be nonfunded (*i.e.*, a mere contract right) and subject to various contingencies of forfeiture affecting value. The gift is complete when the contract is entered into; the contingencies render the then-value of the future gift speculative and of a zero or minimal value. The IRS may try to impose the open-gift doctrine (postpone the gift until the contingencies lapse), but the only court decision on point has rejected this approach.

Suggested answer to QUESTION 5:

An irrevocable insurance trust can provide liquidity to pay debts, expenses, and taxes, and may also avoid transfer taxes.

The trust must be irrevocable so that the proceeds will not be included in the insured's gross estate under § 2038 or § 2042(2). It is also desirable to avoid risk of inclusion under § 2035(d)(2); therefore, the policy must not be transferred to the trust within three years of the insured's death. If the insured already owns the policy and makes a gift of it to the trust, this may involve a bit of luck. Risk might be avoided by having the trust purchase the policy (assuming that an insurance company will sell a policy to a trust). The mere fact that the insured cooperates in the acquisition of the policy by the trust (by filling out forms and taking a physical) should not render the insured as the transferor of the policy. Also, the payment of premiums on a policy owned by the trust does not constitute the insured as the transferor of the policy.

The gift tax value of the policy is usually lower than the estate tax value, especially for term insurance. If the trust purchases the policy, there is no gift at all, except for the amounts given to the trust by the grantor-insured to purchase the policy, pay the premiums, or to fund the premium payments by the trust. Any gift transfers by the grantor-insured will not normally qualify for the present interest exclusion, since the trust beneficiaries have future interests with respect to the policy. The exclusions can be obtained, nevertheless, by giving the beneficiaries "*Crummey* powers." *See* Ch.5, at I.C.3.b., of the main outline, *supra*.

The policy should not be pledged to secure the grantor-insured's debts, or else § 2042(1) will cause inclusion of the proceeds to the extent used to satisfy such debts. Similarly, the trustee should not be required to pay the insured's debts, death taxes, etc. The trust should authorize the trustee to purchase (nonliquid) assets of the estate and to lend money to the estate on reasonable terms, to provide liquidity to the estate.

If the ultimate beneficiaries are grandchildren of the grantor-insured, generation-skipping transfers will occur, but the $1 million exemption-equivalent may shield such transfers from tax.

[Answers to other possible questions about specific tax-avoidance devices, including the marital deduction and split-interest charitable transfers, can best be gleaned by studying Chapter 5 of the outline.]

Formal outline of answer to QUESTION 6:

I. PRE-DEATH TAX PLANNING AND EXECUTION

A. Marital Trust

1. *Survivorship clause:* There is nothing technically wrong with conditioning the marital bequest on the spouse surviving for six months (but no more than that!). However, the survivorship clause shows bad judgment. If *H* outlives *W* at all, *W*'s estate wants the marital deduction, even if *H* doesn't live to enjoy it. Instead, there should be a clause that says, "If it cannot be determined which of my husband or myself died first, my husband shall be deemed to have survived me."

2. *Qualification:* The trust should have said that the income was to be payable to the husband at least annually. This defect may be cured under the last phrase stating the intent to qualify, or perhaps under state law, but omission of the "payable at least annually" might still result in costly litigation. [If the question also contains a clause describing trust investment powers, be sure that the trustee is not authorized to retain or invest in nonproductive assets, etc. Also, the power of appointment must be unconditional, *i.e.,* exercisable alone and in all events.]

3. *Power-of-appointment trust:* Subject to the above, this bequest qualifies for the marital deduction. However, it might have been better to use a QTIP trust. The latter is more flexible in that a partial QTIP election can be made, in case (as here) the marital deduction is too large.

4. *The formula:* There is nothing wrong with using a formula as such. As it turns out, the marital deduction is too large ($1 million), overloading *H*'s potential estate. The marital bequest would have been reduced if the bequest had been "one-half of my gross estate as reduced by items deductible under §§ 2053 and 2054." The conventional approach would have been a reduce-to-zero formula, resulting in a marital deduction of $1.4 million. But if interest rates are low and *H* was not expected to outlive *W* by much, an estate equalization formula, taking *H*'s net wealth into account, would have been appropriate.

5. *Funding in kind:* Requiring funding at estate tax values, rather than distribution-date values, avoids having income tax gain or loss, but, as the clause stands, it runs afoul of Rev. Proc. 64-19 (p. 3-68, *supra*). The clause should say either that the assets should have distribution-date values equal to the formula amount or that the assets be fairly representative of appreciation and depreciation in the estate between the date of *W*'s death and the

distribution date. State law may bail the clause out on this one too. Even if the clause fails under Rev. Proc. 64-19, it is not clear that the clause is disqualified, since there is no case or regulation on point, but the clause as drafted is risky and could well breed costly litigation.

B.   **Residual By-Pass Trust**

1.   *QTIP trust?* This looks like a QTIP trust. Again there is a problem in that there is no "payable at least annually" language. Normally, you would not want the QTIP election to be made, as this would vastly overload *H*'s potential estate and waste *W*'s § 2010 credit. But if the first trust fails to qualify for the marital deduction, then here it would come in handy, fortuitously, for this trust to qualify as a QTIP trust.

2.   *Distribution scheme:* The marital trust should be used up for *H*'s benefit before the by-pass trust is used at all, since normally the by-pass trust avoids inclusion in the surviving spouse's gross estate. *H* should not have been made a mandatory income beneficiary, and the power to invade corpus should have been placed in the first trust, which clearly will be included in *H*'s gross estate due to the general power of appointment.

II.   **POST-MORTEM TAX PLANNING: Since *H* and *W* died close together, the aim is to equalize their taxable estates. Various alternative scenarios must be considered:**

A.   **First Trust Qualifies for Marital Deduction:** Here, *H* (or his executor) should disclaim an appropriate fraction of the first trust in compliance with § 2518 so as to cut down on the marital deduction. If disclaimed amounts fall into the residue, the disclaimer is not disqualified just because *H* is a beneficiary of the residuary trust. No QTIP election should be made with respect to the second trust, assuming it qualifies.

B.   **Second Trust Only Qualifies as a QTIP Trust:** Make a partial Q T I P election for the second trust in an appropriate amount.

C.   **Neither Trust Qualifies for the Marital Deduction:** It might be possible for *all* beneficiaries of the second trust (and maybe the first trust also) to effect § 2518 disclaimers with the aim of having the "right" amount pass to *H* by intestacy. This move would probably entail the appointment of guardians *ad litem* to represent unborn and unascertained issue.

Suggested answers to QUESTION 7, parts A through O:

A.   **Probably not.** This transfer is exempt from gift tax under § 2516. If *H* outlives *W*, the property will appear in *H*'s § 2033 gross estate; if not, the reversion has a value of zero under § 2033, but § 2037 would apply if the reversion was worth more than 5% as of the moment just prior to *H*'s death. Although § 2516 does not literally extend to the estate tax, and although § 2043(b) does not incorporate § 2516 for this purpose, the better-reasoned result is that the estate and gift taxes are to be construed in para materia, *i.e.*, what cannot be a "transfer" for gift tax purposes cannot be a transfer for estate tax purposes.

B.   **Of course there are.** Under § 7872(a) and (d)(2), X makes a gift to Y, in the year the loan is made, in an amount equal to the excess of $40,000 over the present value of Y's interest-plus-principal obligation, using the applicable federal rate discounted semi-annually.

C.   **False.** The § 2503(e) exclusion requires a direct payment by the donor to the institution.

D.   **False.** The transfer taxes usually ignore incompetency; B is still considered to possess the power at death.

E.   **True.** H is treated as owning a 45% interest, even though the "community might be thought of as an entity managed solely by H, and even if H and W acted harmoniously at all times.

F.   **False.** *See* § 2036(b). [If the question had dealt with a gift of *common* stock in a closely held corporation, you would need to apply § 2701, which might result in enhanced gift tax.]

G.   **True.** This is a deductible terminable interest: no third party gets anything on W's death. [If W died first, the answer would be "false": since H purchased the annuity, W is not the "transferor" under § 2039, nor is anything included in W's gross estate under § 2033; the marital deduction presupposes inclusion of the item in the decedent's gross estate.]

H.   **False.** This is a spouse's election will. W has made a constructive transfer of her half of the community property to a trust, retaining an income interest therein. (By the way, § 2702 applies for gift tax purposes.) The transfer is included in W's gross estate under § 2036, unless the transfer was made by W for "full and adequate consideration in money or money's worth." Even though that appears to be the case, the courts have held that the consideration supplied by H is not "full and adequate" unless it equals or exceeds the full value of W's share of the community property (not just the value of the remainder therein).

I.   (1)   **False.** If A and B are not married, all of it is includable in A's gross estate. § 2040(a).

       (2)   **The disclaimer is valid.** Court decisions hold that the nine-month period in the case of joint tenancies runs from the date interest vests (A's death). [In the case of trusts, the period runs from when the interest is created (even for contingent interests), not when the interest vests.]

J.   **False.** Although valuation generally looks to the future, the courts hold that a minority interest discount is not obtained where the minority interest is created in the act of transfer.

K.   (1)   **False.** The reciprocal trust doctrine applies. A is the deemed transferor of the trust created by B, and vice versa, so that § 2036(a)(1) applies. [It is unclear, however, if § 2702 would be deemed to apply for gift tax purposes.]

       (2)   **True, for gift tax purposes,** since only the net gift is subject to tax.

           False, for estate tax purposes, since the received income interest is the very element that triggers § 2036(a)(1).

L.   **False.** The election can be made only if it would reduce the taxable estate and estate taxes.

M.   **False.** This is a private annuity. *D* has not retained the income "from" the transferred property. [There would be a gift for gift tax purposes equal to $1 million less the actuarial value of *E*'s annuity promise.]

N.   **True.** Normally, a retained power over an interest (here, the income interest) render that interest incomplete. However, § 2702 applies here, so that the income interest is not subtracted from the amount of the gift. Although § 2702 appears to require a retained "interest," the regulations state that a retained interest exists where there is a retained power to alter, amend, or revoke an interest. (Section 2702 does not apply, however, where *all* nonretained interests are incomplete.) [This transfer is also included in *D*'s gross estate under § 2036(a)(2).]

O.   **False.** If *F* dies within three years of making the gifts, the gifts will be disregarded in applying the 50% test. § 2035(d)(3)(B).

EP

GLOSSARY

GLOSSARY

This glossary explains terms and abbreviations (including doctrines and rules named after cases and Code section numbers) commonly used in tax discourse, including selected business, financial, policy, and accounting terms, even though (in some cases) the term is not used or emphasized in this Outline. The definitions are general and concise rather than detailed and exhaustive. Items are omitted which are very obvious "return," "taxable income"), self-evident ("child care credit," "medical expense"), or too broad in scope ("gross income"). Items referred to by Code section numbers (*e.g.*, "§ 1231 gain") are found under "Section." See also the Index, *infra*, for a more exhaustive and logical arrangement of headings as it specifically relates to this Outline.

A

Accelerated Depreciation Any depreciation method that produces greater deductions in the earlier years than would occur under straight-line, unit-of-production, or income-forecast depreciation, all *infra*. See Declining Balance, *infra*.

Accrual Method Method of tax accounting in which gross income and expense items are included and deducted when the right or obligation to receive or pay future cash becomes fixed. *See* All-the-Events Test and Economic Performance, *infra*.

ACRS Accelerated Cost Recovery System of depreciation described in § 168.

Actuarial Tables Tables with built-in assumptions as to rate of return, discount rate, and life expectancies used to value annuities, life estates, terms of years, remainders, and reversions. "Actuarial risk" refers to the statistical chances of death within a certain period of time. "Actuarial life expectancy" refers to the life expectancy of a person (at any age) based on population statistics.

Adjusted Basis Original basis increased by cost of improvements and reduced by depreciation and loss deductions, and so forth.

Adjusted Gross Income (AGI) Gross income reduced by the deductions listed in § 62. Contrast Itemized Deductions, § 151 Deductions, and Standard Deduction.

All-the-Events Test The basic test for accruing income and expense items for Accrual Method taxpayers: an item is accrued when all the events have occurred which fix the right or obligation to receive or pay future cash, etc. *See also* Economic Performance Test.

Allow(able) Permit(ted) to be deducted. "Allowance" refers to depreciation allowed to be deducted. "Allowable" is sometimes used interchangeably with "deductible."

Alternative Depreciation System Straight-line depreciation under § 168(g) for AMT purposes, for Listed Property, and in certain other cases.

Amortization Straight-line depreciation required for depreciable intangible assets.

Amount Realized Cash plus fair market value (or, if on Accrual Method, face amount) of property received in Sale or Exchange, for purposes of computing Gain or Loss.

AMT Alternative Minimum Tax. Additional (alternative) income tax.

Applicable Federal Rate Interest rates on federal obligations, published periodically in the *I.R.B.,* used to impute interest (or principal) on debt obligations paying interest at lower rates, or to value certain items for tax purposes.

Arbitrage In general, making short-swing profits by buying and selling in different markets, such as buying gold in London and selling it in Zurich, or a municipality issuing exempt bonds (with low interest costs) and investing the proceeds in higher-yield corporate bonds (the interest from which is not taxable because a municipality is a tax-free entity). "Tax arbitrage" refers to making money from the differing tax treatment of the same dollars as they come in and go out. An example would be borrowing money at 10% interest to make an investment returning

10%, where the interest is fully deductible but the income is tax-favored (through deferral or other tax benefits attaching to the investment, such as Accelerated Depreciation).

***Arrowsmith* Doctrine** Holds that (deductible) repayment of previously includable amount has same Character (*infra*) as includable amount, in order to prevent "double" tax benefits from same dollars.

At-Risk Rules (or Amount) Anti-tax-shelter rules, found in § 465, which defer net tax losses from an activity where such losses exceed the "at-risk amount" of the taxpayer at the end of the year.

B

Below-Interest Loan Loan in which Stated Interest rate is below the Applicable Federal Rate.

Beyond-the-Taxable-Year Test Test that holds that a capital expenditure is an expenditure that has value beyond the taxable year in which the expenditure is made. *Compare* the Twelve-Month Rule, *infra*.

Blue Book Refers to publication of Joint Committee staff providing detailed technical explanation of the latest tax act. Sometimes treated as "authority" and "legislative history."

Boot Money or "other property" thrown in to equalize the amounts (values) exchanged in a tax-free exchange. *Compare* Nonrecognition Property, *infra*.

Business-Purpose Doctrine Certain transactions or deductions are not recognized or allowed for tax purposes unless there is a business purpose to the transaction or expense.

C

C Corporation Corporation which is a separate taxable entity, subject to the § 11 tax. *Compare* S Corporation, *infra*.

Capital 1. In tax, is often used synonymously with Basis. *See* Capital Recovery below. 2. In accounting, refers to an account that represents the equity (ownership) interests of the owners,

i.e., the amounts they would obtain if the business were liquidated.

Capital Asset Asset, defined in § 1221, the sale or exchange of which produces Capital Gain or Loss.

Capital Expenditure Expenditure which is not deductible currently (because it does not produce a decrease in wealth) but which creates, or adds to, basis. *See* Beyond-the-Taxable-Year Rule, Improvement, and Twelve-Months Rule.

Capital Gain and Loss Gain or loss from the "Sale or Exchange" of a "Capital Asset" as defined in § 1221. *Contrast* Ordinary Gain & Loss. *See also* Section 1231 Gains & Losses.

Capital Recovery Refers to method or methods of converting Basis into deductions or offsets. Depreciation, Amortization, and (cost) Depletion are methods of capital recovery as are methods that distinguish between "income" and "principal" (Basis) of financial investments.

Capitalization Treating, or being required to treat something, as a Capital Expenditure and creating or adding to basis. Sometimes used outside of tax to refer to valuation technique applying formula to future expected earnings from asset, as in "capitalization of future earnings" valuation.

Carve-Out Transaction in which property is divided into "temporal" segments, such as life estate and remainder, with the taxpayer retaining one interest (usually a reversion) and disposing of the other (usually a term interest).

Cash Equivalent Something treated as cash for Cash-Method taxpayers, such as checks and credit card transactions and (on the income side only) certain notes.

Cash Method Method of tax accounting in which gross income and expense items are included and deducted when received or paid in cash.

Character Refers to quality of gain, loss, income, etc., as Capital Gain or Loss, Section 1231 Gain or Loss, Ordinary Gain or Loss, tax-free income, foreign-source income, and so on.

G

Claim-of-Right Doctrine Doctrine under which amounts received are included in income (of a cash or accrual taxpayer) even though there is a contingent possibility of repayment. Applies whether or not the income was received lawfully. Any repayment gives rise to a deduction/credit issue in the year of repayment.

Class Life Useful Life of depreciable asset category according to Revenue Procedures, which determines the Recovery Period for § 168 depreciation.

***Clifford* Trust** See Grantor Trust, *infra*.

Closed Transaction Transaction reckoned for tax purposes in the current year as and when tax-significant events occur, as opposed to being deferred or treated as an Open Transaction.

Closing Inventory See Cost of Goods Sold, FIFO, and LIFO.

Collection Gain Gain (or loss) that occurs when a note, claim, or debt is satisfied, and the Basis does not equal the Amount Realized. Is not Capital Gain or Loss unless some provision (such as § 1271) deems it to be so.

Constructive Receipt Doctrine requiring Cash Method taxpayers to include in income items they haven't actually received, but which they have both the right and power to obtain. "One cannot turn his back on income."

Consumption Tax Tax system in which personal consumption is taxed indirectly by first adding up potential consumption for the year (wages, borrowed funds, gross receipt from business and sales of property) and then subtracting all business and investment expenditures, including loan principal and interest.

Contract Price For Installment Method reporting, it means the total payments to be received by the seller, unreduced by selling commissions but excluding mortgages assumed or taken subject to (except to the extent such mortgages exceed basis plus selling commissions at the time of sale).

Contribution to Capital Refers to situation where an owner (*e.g.,* shareholder) or third party transfers money or property to a business

without taking back additional stock or any additional ownership percentage.

***Corn Products* Doctrine** Judicial doctrine under which gains and losses from property which is closely related to inventory are treated as "Ordinary" Gains and Losses even though they fit definition of Capital Gains & Losses.

Cost of Goods Sold The "mass basis" of disposed-of inventory set off against gross receipts from the sale thereof in arriving at Gross Income From Business. Cost of Goods Sold for a year is Opening Inventory plus purchases for the Year less Closing Inventory, usually figured at cost. *See also* Lower-of-Cost-or-Market Rule, FIFO, and LIFO.

***Crane* Rule** Acquisition indebtedness, whether Recourse or Nonrecourse, is included in Basis so long as value of property equals or exceeds such indebtedness at the time of acquisition. Also, indebtedness secured by property is included in Amount Realized when the property is disposed of, regardless of whether the acquiring party assumes or takes subject to the liability or whether the debt is Recourse or Nonrecourse.

Credit 1. An amount which reduces tax liability. A "refundable credit" can generate a tax refund, whereas a "nonrefundable credit" cannot. 2. Accounting entry made on "right side" of Asset account (meaning reduction in asset account or addition to negative asset account) or of Claims account (meaning increase in Liability or Capital account). Opposite is Debit (or "charge").

Cut-Down Rule Rule found in § 170(e) which reduces amount of charitable contribution deduction with respect to appreciated property by amount of gain which would have been realized if the property were sold at the time of contribution.

D

Dealer In tax jargon, a party who owns "property primarily held for sale to customers in the ordinary course of trade or business," which property is an exception to the definition of Capital Asset. *See* § 1221(1) (containing the "dealer exception" to the capital gains definition). Usually applied in real estate setting.

Debit Accounting entry made on "left side" of Asset account (meaning increase in asset account) or of Claims account (meaning reduction in Liability or Capital account). Synonym is "charge." Opposite is Credit.

Declining Balance 1. Method of depreciation in which fixed depreciation rate is applied against Basis *as reduced by* prior depreciation deductions. If rate is greater than 1.0 (100%), is an Accelerated (method of) Depreciation. 2. Method of amortizing debt instruments and financial instruments in which any payment or distribution comes "first" out of earned income (interest) and the rest comes out of principal (as recovery of Basis), so that earned income (interest) for next period is figured on reduced principal base.

Deduction Subtraction (from gross income) in arriving at taxable income (the tax base).

Deficiency Refers to amount of tax taxpayer owes, or is claimed to owe, the IRS.

Depletion *Cost* depletion is a method of recovering basis in an interest in natural resources akin to the Unit-of-Production Method of Depreciation. *Percentage* depletion is a deduction equal to a specified percentage of net gross income from a mineral interest, subject to a limitation.

Depreciation Stream of annual deductions generated by the taxpayer's basis in a business or investment asset having an ascertainable useful life.

Direct Tax No legal definition exists, but a head tax or poll tax is certainly direct, a property tax is probably direct, and an income tax was held to be direct in an 1895 case that has been heavily criticized.

Discount Situation where bond or debt obligation has fair market value below "face amount." *See also* Market Discount and OID.

Discount Rate Rate used to reduce future sum(s) to present value for valuation purposes.

Distribution Deduction *See* DNI, *infra*.

Dividend 1. In tax, corporate distribution to shareholder treated as gross income under §§ 301(c) & 316 by reason of corporate E & P. 2.

In insurance lingo, reduction of current premium charged by "mutual" insurance company warranted by more favorable evaluation of actuarial risk.

DNI (Distributable Net Income) The "Distribution Deduction" of a trust or estate, as well as the income reportable by distributees, is (initially) the lesser of (a) distributions or (b) DNI, both for the current year. DNI, as defined in § 643(a), is trust or estate gross income (but usually excluding capital gains yet including Section 103 Interest) less expenses.

E

E & P (Earnings & Profits) E & P, roughly speaking, is net profit (after income taxes and prior dividend distributions) in the accounting (rather than income tax) sense. *See* Dividend.

Economic Benefit Doctrine Holds that, if income is set aside in a trust, escrow, or other account for future payment to the taxpayer, the taxpayer, even though on the Cash Method, has income currently (not when received), provided that the taxpayer's rights are vested, the account (etc.) earns interest for the taxpayer, and the transferor's creditor's can't reach the account (etc.).

Economic Interest Doctrine A party is entitled to take Depletion deductions if the party has an "economic" (as distinct from a "property") interest in natural resources. A right to royalties contingent on production or sales qualifies as an economic interest.

Economic Performance Test Deductions of an Accrual-Method taxpayer accrue upon the *later* to occur of satisfaction of the Economic Performance Test (as set forth in § 461(h)) or the All-the-Events Test.

Effective Rate 1. The tax divided by the tax base. 2. In tax policy discourse, the extent to which a given taxpayer (or class thereof) actually bears the burden of taxes nominally imposed upon it.

Endowment (Policy) *See* Maturity.

Equity 1. In tax policy, refers to fairness, as in "horizontal equity" (persons in the same position should pay the same tax") or "vertical equity" (persons in different positions should pay differing taxes"). 2. Ownership interest which is not Debt. 3. For mortgaged asset, the excess of value over the mortgage indebtedness.

Exclusion Ratio Technique, specified under § 72(b), of distinguishing excludible basis recovery from includable income with respect to an Annuity after the annuity starting date.

Exempt Trust A trust, exempt from tax under § 501(a), which is the Funding vehicle for a Qualified Plan.

Exemption Colloquial term usually used to refer to a Deduction not keyed to actual expenditures, such as (mainly) the Section 151 Deductions ("personal and dependency exemptions").

Expense Expenditure which is not a Capital Expenditure. Roughly, an expense is an outlay whose benefits or value to the taxpayer expire instantly or within the taxable year (or within 12 months). The verb "to expense" means to take as an expense rather than to Capitalize the outlay.

Estate Taxable entity that arises when person dies and terminates when probate estate is wound up. Taxed like trusts.

F

FIFO Method of accounting for mass basis of inventories (Cost of Goods Sold) in which earliest acquired goods are deemed to be the first ones sold and disposed of.

Floor Any rule that disallows deductions "from the bottom."

Funded (Plan, Trust) A (deferred compensation) plan is "funded" if money or property is paid into it. A *non*funded plan is simply a contractual promise to pay in the future.

G

Gain Refers to situation where Amount Realized exceeds Basis of asset.

Grandfather Clause Provision of law that

exempts transactions entered into before date of enactment (etc.).

Grantor Trust *Inter vivos* trust, the net income from which is attributed to the grantor under §§ 671-677 because of grantor's (or spouse's) retained power, interest, right, or control. Sometimes referred to as a "*Clifford* Trust."

Gross Income From Business Means gross income from the sale and disposition of inventories: gross receipts minus Cost of Goods Sold. *See* FIFO and LIFO.

Gross Profit For Installment Method reporting, is Selling Price less Basis (increased by selling expenses).

H

Haig-Simons Income Conceptual definition of "income" offered as a norm for tax policy: net increase in wealth (realized and unrealized) plus personal consumption, both for the taxable period (year).

Half-Year Convention Assumption in § 168 depreciation method for tangible personal property that deems property to have been in service for one-half of the first and last years of service. The convention is factored into the depreciation schedules published by the IRS.

Hobby Loss Rules *See* Not-for-Profit Activity, *infra.*

Holding Period Length of time Capital Asset is held (or deemed held) by taxpayer up to sale or exchange to determine if Capital Gain or Loss is "long-term" or "short term." *See* § 1223.

IDCs "Intangible drilling (and development) costs" allowed to be expensed under § 263(c).

I

Improvement Expenditure on existing asset that is capital expenditure, increasing basis.

Imputed (interest, etc.) Refers to any tax rule under which interest (etc.) is required to be included or deducted even though the transaction does not identify it as interest (etc.).

Incentive Stock Options Options receiving favorable tax treatment to employee under § 421, rather than being taxed under § 83.

Income Averaging Tax computational device that treats "extraordinary" tax base amount (excess of current taxable income over average taxable income of a specified base period) as having been received piecemeal over several prior years, in order to mitigate the "bunching effect" of having such extraordinary amount being subjected to abnormally high Marginal Rates.

Income in Respect of a Decedent *See* IRD, *infra.*

Income-Forecast Method A method of depreciation (common for copyrights and other entertainment property) under which the annual deduction is the Basis times a fraction, the numerator of which is the current income and the denominator of which is total income expected over the life of that asset.

Income-Splitting Trying to allocate net income equally between two taxpayers, as essentially occurs with community-property income and under the joint return rate schedule.

Income Tax Technically, a tax with a tax base keyed to net changes in wealth plus personal consumption, as opposed to personal consumption only.

Inconsistent-Events Test Describes the inclusionary side of the Tax Benefit Rule: a prior deduction, although correct when made, must be taken into current gross income if an event occurs currently that is inconsistent with taking the prior deduction.

Indexing Refers to fact that certain fixed dollar amounts in the Code are adjusted for inflation. In theory, Basis (and other tax attributes relating to a prior year) could be indexed also, but the tax law has not yet moved in this direction.

Indirect Tax A tax which is not a Direct Tax. Includes excises and wealth transfer taxes of all types. No constitutional bar to an indirect tax as such.

Installment Method Method of reporting an installment sale under § 453 under which the gain (but not loss) is pro-rated over two or more taxable years in proportion to the payments received in any year.

Inventories Goods sold in ordinary course of business. *See* Gross Income from Business, Cost of Goods Sold, Closing Inventory, FIFO, and LIFO.

Investment Income-producing venture or activity that is not Business (and not personal consumption).

IRA Individual Retirement Account, a kind of tax-favored savings account in which new investment is deductible (up to an annual limitation) and the annual earnings on which are tax free.

IRD Income In Respect of Decedent, meaning income earned by a taxpayer before death but not received in cash until after death, included by the recipient (not on the decedent's final return).

Itemized Deduction Any deduction of the taxpayer other than a Section 62 Deduction, a Section 151 Deduction, or the Standard Deduction.

J

Joint Committee Joint Tax Committee of Congress, notable because it has a paid staff of tax experts and economists who do technical, drafting, and policy work in the tax area.

K

Keough Plan Qualified Plan for self-employed individual.

L

LIFO Inventories Mass basis for inventories computed on a last-in, first-out basis, meaning that the goods disposed of during the year are deemed to have been the most recently acquired.

Like-Kind Exchange An exchange of "like-kind" properties that qualifies for tax-free (deferral) treatment under § 1031. *See also* Boot.

G

Liquidation Where an entity terminates and distributes its assets to its owners (and creditors), with the ownership interests legally disappearing.

Listed Property Property described in § 280F which is restricted as to depreciability or depreciation methods and amounts.

Loss Situation where Amount Realized (if any) exceeds the Basis upon the sale or other disposition of an asset. Also refers to fact of "Sustained" decline in value of asset (not disposed of) which gives rise to a deduction. There is also said to be a loss in a year where deductions exceed gross income. *See also* NOL.

Lower-of-Cost-or-Market Rule Taxpayers on the FIFO method can figure (the basis of) inventories (Cost of Goods Sold) at the lower of cost or market value, as opposed to cost only.

M

Marginal Rate Tax rate applicable to a given tax Bracket. Usually refers to tax rate applicable to "last" dollar of taxable income.

Market Discount Discount which is not OID, *see infra.*

Marriage Penalty Refers to fact that married couple filing jointly pays greater tax than aggregate tax of two unmarried persons with same combined taxable incomes as married couple, at least where the taxable incomes of the unmarried persons are not grossly unequal.

Matching Principle In accounting, refers to the metaprinciple under which accounting rules are designed to "match" expenditures with the revenues they produce and vice versa.

Maturity (of investment) A debt obligation matures when the principal is repayable in full. A life insurance policy matures at the earlier to occur of the insured's death or (in the case of Ordinary Life Insurance) when it becomes "fully endowed" (*i.e.*, the cash surrender value equals the face amount).

Mid-Month Convention Assumption in § 168 depreciation for real property that deems property to have been in service since, or up to, the middle of the first and last months of service. Worked into the depreciation tables published by the IRS.

Mitigation Provisions Refers to §§ 1311-1314, which allow for the correction of errors otherwise barred by the statute of limitations in certain cases where a party is taking an inconsistent position in both the barred and current years.

Moline Properties Doctrine Doctrine that holds that corporate net income will *not* be attributed to controlling shareholder by reason of shareholder's control.

N

National Carbide Doctrine Doctrine that holds that corporation will generally not be treated as "agent" of shareholders for income-attribution purposes, but that recognizes that a bona fide agency-principal arrangement existing in fact will be recognized for such purposes.

Necessary Expense "Necessary" in § 162 and cognate provisions means "appropriate or helpful in the taxpayer's judgment."

Net Worth Accounting term that means "assets less liabilities" or (the same thing) "Capital plus, if kept separately, retained earnings."

Ninety-Day Letter Letter that proposes a deficiency and gives the taxpayer 90 days to petition the Tax Court in order to contest the deficiency without paying it.

NOL Net operating loss, which for an individual is the excess of net business losses over non-business net income (with adjustments). For an entity, it is simply net loss. Can be carried over to other taxable years (in prescribed order) and deducted then, until used up (or time runs out). *See* § 172.

Nonqualified Plan A deferred compensation arrangement which is not a Qualified Plan. Can be funded or nonfunded.

Nonrecognition (Property, Rule) Property received in an exchange which qualifies the exchange for tax-free treatment, such as "like kind" property under § 1031. *Compare* Boot. A nonrecognition rule is one that provides tax-free treatment to a gain, loss, or other item that would otherwise be Recognized.

Nonrecourse Debt Debt which the debtor is not personally liable for. The creditor possibly "has recourse" against the property (if securing the debt) but not against the debtor for any deficiency.

Not-for-Profit Activity Activity subject to the deduction-disallowance rule of § 183.

O

Open Transaction Transaction (such as loan) held open (*i.e.*, not currently included or deducted) beyond the taxable year in which relevant facts occur in order to await future relevant events. An example is the way certain contingent payment sales are treated (if not reported on the Installment Method).

Opening Inventory Same as Closing Inventory for Prior Year.

Operating Foundation A Private "operating" Foundation as defined in § 4942(j)(3), which is somewhat more favorably treated than a plain-vanilla Private Foundation.

OID Original Issue Discount, *i.e.*, discount which exists at moment debt obligations are first issued, meaning that issuer borrows (receives) less "principal" than is obligated to repay. *See also* Imputed Interest.

Ordinary Gain and Loss Gain or Loss which is not Capital Gain or Loss or Section 1231 Gain or Loss.

Ordinary Expense An expense is "ordinary" under § 162 and cognate provisions if it falls within accepted business practices. It need not be regular or recurring.

Ordinary Life Insurance Life insurance with a reserve (cash surrender value), usually requiring level premium payments. *See also* Maturity.

Origin Test A test for determining whether expense is "business," "investment," or "personal," by looking at the origin of the transaction

giving rise to the expense. *See also* Principal Purpose Test.

Original Issue Discount *See* OID, *supra.*

Overnight Rule Rule under which meals (and lodging) connected with business (or investment) "travel" can be deducted only if taxpayer spends the night away from her home base area. Sometimes known as the "sleep or rest" rule.

P

Passive Activity Loss (PAL) Rules Rules found in § 469 deferring net losses from "passive activities" until future years.

Percentage-of-Completion Method Method of reporting income from long-term contracts in proportion to expenses, as they are incurred (*i.e.*, prior to completion), as required by § 460.

Personal Consumption Property Property held or used for the taxpayer's personal consumption. Not to be confused with "personal property" (as distinct from "real property").

Personal Holding Company (PHC) Generally, corporation owned by a few stockholders that holds investment portfolio, rather than carrying on a business. Can be subject to penalty tax under § 541 unless it pays dividends currently.

Portfolio Income Income from certain passive investments (such as interest and dividends) which is *not* treated as "passive activity income" for purposes of the Passive Activity Rules.

Premium Excess of value of debt obligation over its "face amount."

Pre-Opening Doctrine *See* Start-Up Expenditures.

Prepaid Expense Expense paid before the taxpayer receives goods or services. Usually required to be Capitalized, even by cash-method taxpayer.

Prepaid Income Income received in cash be-

G

fore it is earned by performing services of delivering goods. Must usually be included in income when received even by accrual-method taxpayer.

Principal Portion(s) of debt obligation which are not "interest."

Principal-Agent Rule Rule under which income is attributed to the principal and not to the agent, even though the agent does the actual work to earn the income.

Principal Purpose Test A common test for determining whether expense or loss is "business," "investment," or "personal." *See also* Origin Test.

Private Foundation Section 501(c)(3) Organization as defined in § 509, contributions to which are less favored in certain respects compared to contributions to other types of Section 501(c) Organization.

Production Payment Right to income from interest in natural resources until sum certain (with interest) is paid out. *See* § 636.

Public Charity Section 501(c)(3) Organization listed in § 170(b)(1)(A)(i) through (vi).

Q

Qualified Plan Funded deferred compensation plan that "qualifies" under §§ 401 *et seq.* and receives favorable tax treatment.

R

Rabbi Trust Nonqualified deferred compensation trust that avoids the Economic Benefit Doctrine (and hence achieves deferral of income for employees) by virtue of being reachable by the employer's creditors.

Realization General principle under which Gains and Losses are deemed to "exist" for income tax purposes only when "realized," referring to some event which marks the taxpayer's change of status with respect to the asset, principally as the result of sale, exchange, or disposition. A "deemed realization rule" is one wherein the tax law treats a nonrealization event as a realization event "Unrealized" gain (appreciation) or loss (depreciation) refers to changes in value, without more. *Compare* Recognition.

Recapture Tax term referring to any rule that imposes a tax result in the current year because of some event in the current year that is inconsistent with the original (but then correct) tax treatment. "Recapture gain" usually means a rule that converts Capital or Section 1231 Gain into Ordinary Gain. *See* Section 1245 (or 1250) Gain. *See also* Inconsistent Events Test.

Recognition Refers to situation where "realized" gain or loss is taken into account (included, deducted) for income tax purposes.

Recourse Debt Debt on which the taxpayer is personally liable to pay any deficiency if the value on foreclosure is less than the outstanding debt.

Recovery 1. In the Tax-Benefit Rule situation, refers to receipt of amount that was previously paid (and deducted). 2. Refers to deducting basis through depreciation (etc.) deductions and offsets, as in "basis Recovery" or "recovery of Capital."

Recovery (Property, Period) "Recovery property" is tangible property subject to depreciation under § 168. "Recovery period" is the Useful Life of such property based on Class Life.

Redemption Refers to situation where debt or equity instrument is surrendered to the issuer (and is then canceled or becomes extinguished), usually for consideration. Technically, a bond is "redeemed" at maturity.

Repair Expenditure on existing asset which is an expense.

Reserve 1. In accounting, a method under which there is an accrued current expense deduction for future estimated or contingent expenses, liabilities, or losses, often based on statistical projections. 2. Cash surrender value and related "savings" features of Ordinary Life Insurance policy.

Restricted Property Property (usually stock) subject to substantial risk of forfeiture for purposes of § 83 and "nontransferable" because forfeiture conditions are endorsed on the stock certificate.

Return of Capital Synonymous with Recovery (of Capital) *supra*. The "return-of-capital method" is sometimes used to refer to situations where gain is reported according to an Open-Transaction approach permitted for certain contingent-payment sales (not reported on the Installment Method): receipts are applied first against basis, and only when basis is exhausted is any gain deemed to be realized.

Rollover Act of taking the proceeds of sale, redemption, Qualified Plan, or IRA lump-sum distribution, etc., and reinvesting the same within a short period of time.

Rule of 72 Shorthand method of figuring when a principal sum will double: divide 72 by the annual interest rate (expressed as a whole number). For example, if a sum is invested at a 10% rate compounded annually, it will take about 7.2 years to double.

Rule of 78s Method of computing interest (on installment sales and loans) used by merchants and finance companies, but generally disregarded for tax purposes.

S

S Corporation Corporation electing to be taxed in way similar to partnership.

Sale or Exchange Requirement Prerequisite for Capital Gain & Loss treatment. Requires: (1) complete disposition of property or interest therein, (2) receipt of cash or property back, and (3) survival of disposed-of asset. Many Code provisions deem this requirement to be satisfied in situations where it would otherwise not be satisfied. *Compare* Carve-Out, *supra*.

Secretary The Secretary of the Treasury and subordinates, such as the Commissioner of the IRS.

Section 38 Property Depreciable tangible personal property, plus some exotic categories of real property, as defined in § 48.

Section 83(b) Election Election by taxpayer to have property (received for services) included

now rather than have inclusion deferred under § 83(a).

Section 401(k) Plan A kind of simplified Qualified Plan in which the employee can elect to take cash wages or have them contributed to the plan up to certain modest limits.

Section 446(b) Authority Authority of the IRS, limited by tax accounting rules, to require taxpayer to use accounting method that more clearly reflects income.

Section 501(c) Organization Tax-exempt organization, contributions to which are deductible, operated for charitable, educational, scientific, religious, medical, or certain other purposes. Term "charitable organization" is shorthand for § 501(c)(3) organization.

Section 691(c) Deduction Income tax deduction for estate tax attributable of inclusion of (right to receive) IRD in the gross estate of the person who earned the IRD.

Section 1231 Gains and Losses Gains and losses that go into § 1231 and come out all as Capital or Ordinary.

Section 1244 Stock Stock the worthlessness of which produces an Ordinary Loss, overriding § 165(g).

Section 1245 (or 1250) Gain Gain treated as Ordinary Gain because attributable to prior depreciation (or, in the case of § 1250, "excess" depreciation) deductions. These are examples of Recapture rules. In some instances, they override Nonrecognition rules.

Selling Price For Installment Method purposes, it means the total amount realized (reduced by selling commissions) for purposes of computing Gross Profit.

Separate Asset Test Test, adopted by some courts, that holds that a requirement for a capital expenditure (other than an Improvement, *supra*) is that there be created a separate and identifiable asset.

Settlement Options When insurance policy matures, refers to beneficiaries' possible election to take proceeds in various ways, such as

G

(1) in a lump sum, (2) as an Annuity, or (3) providing for delayed payment of the lump sum with periodic interest payments in the meantime.

Sham Transaction A transaction that didn't really occur, although it might exist on paper, and therefore is disregarded for tax purposes. Also refers to complex transactions in which there is a circular flow of cash that has no net effect on the taxpayer's wealth.

Singles Penalty Refers to fact that unmarried person pays greater tax than married couple with the same aggregate taxable income as the unmarried person.

Sleep or Rest Rule *See* Overnight Rule, *supra.*

Standard Deduction Fixed amount deduction, keyed to filing status, Indexed, and supplemented if blind or over 65. Cannot be taken in addition to the Itemized Deductions.

Start-Up Expenditures Outlays relating to a business prior to commencement of business operations that must be capitalized and amortized under § 195. Sometimes referred to as "pre-opening expenses."

Step Transaction Doctrine in aid of factual characterization under which intermediate steps in a transaction are ignored in favor of the "before and after."

Stripped Bond Bond with interest coupons attached; either the bond or the coupons are sold or assigned. *See* § 1286.

Subchapter (C, J, K, S) Subchapters of the Code dealing respectively with C Corporations (& shareholders), trusts and estates (& beneficiaries) (J), partnerships & partners (K), and S Corporations (& shareholders).

Substance-Over-Form Doctrine Refers to situations where tax outcome depends upon economic substance of transaction rather than its contractual form.

Sum-of-the-Years-Digits Method Type of Accelerated Depreciation in accounting. No longer used in tax.

Sustain (a Loss) A loss is sustained ("realized") for tax purposes only when it is fixed and final.

T

T & E "Travel and entertainment" (expenses).

Tax Benefit Rule Rule under which deduction is not disallowed just because recovery of expense might occur in the future, but if recovery does occur, it is *prima facie* gross income, except to the extent that it failed to reduce taxable income (or tax liability). See § 111. *See also* Inconsistent Events Test.

Tax Cost Rule under which basis of property included in gross income equals its fair market value on receipt.

Tax Detriment Rule Set of rules under which deduction for repayment in Claim-of-Right Doctrine situation is reduced or wiped out where earlier inclusion was not fully taxed. *See also Arrowsmith* Doctrine.

Tax Expenditure Tax policy concept under which (roughly speaking) any tax rule not conforming to the Haig-Simons definition of income, *supra,* should be, analyzed in the federal budget to determine the revenues foregone (*i.e.,* as if the provision in question were like a government subsidy for the activity the tax provision is intended to benefit).

Tax Float Describes situation in which "correct" tax treatment of one party to a transaction does not mirror that of another party to the transaction, resulting in an opportunity for both parties to save money at the expense of the government.

Tax Home Taxpayer's "home" for purposes of deducting "away from home" travel expenses. May be business headquarters rather than personal residence.

Tax Preference Item Deduction from the income tax which is "added back" in figuring the AMT tax base.

Tax Shelter Investment or activity in which net tax losses (resulting from, *e.g.,* interest, accelerated depreciation, and expense deductions), typically generated by Nonrecourse Debt, are available to offset ("shelter") other income of the taxpayer.

Temporary vs. Indefinite Test Travel (including meal and lodging) expenses air, deductible if the taxpayer's stay away from home is "temporary" rather than "indefinite."

Term Insurance Life insurance with no "reserve" (cash surrender value); thus, it is nothing more than a "betting (actuarial) pool."

Term Loan Loan which has a fixed maturity date, as compared to a demand loan.

Trader A party who buys and sells items (securities, etc.) on her own account through the market, hoping to profit from short-term swings in value.

Transitional Rule Statutory rule that phases-in or phases-out some new tax treatment. Sometimes used to refer to Grandfather Clause.

***Tufts* Rule** In situation where property subject to a *Nonrecourse* debt is sold, disposed of, or foreclosed upon, rule under which the Amount Realized includes the full amount of the debt (where that is greater than the then value of the property).

Twelve-Months Rule Rule, adopted by some courts, that holds that Capital Expenditure *(supra)* is expenditure that creates value that lasts more than 12 months from date of expenditure. *Compare* Beyond-the-Taxable-Year Rule *supra*.

U

UBIT Tax on "unrelated business income" of exempt organization, including Section 501(c)(3) Organization.

Uniform Capitalization Rules Rules for Capitalization found in § 263A.

Unit-of-Production Method Method of Depreciation in which annual depreciation is Basis multiplied by a fraction, the numerator of which is units produced by the asset during the current year and the denominator of which is the units expected to be produced over the entire life of the

asset.

V

VAT Value-Added Tax. Roughly, excise tax, levied at each level of trade, on difference between selling price and what taxpayer paid for item.

W

Wage Tax Alternative version of Consumption Tax under which Capital Expenditures are not deducted but all business and investment returns (income, gains) are entirely tax-free.

Whipsaw Situation where parties to a transaction take inconsistent positions in reporting it for tax purposes.

Willing-Buyer Willing-Seller Test Tax test for determining fair market value. Assumes neither party is under any constraints and that hypothetical sale would take place in the "retail" market.

Wraparound Sale Sale in which price paid by buyer, including installment notes, equals full value of property, *i.e.,* the buyer neither assumes nor takes subject to any mortgages of the seller. The idea is that the sales proceeds will be used by the seller to pay off whatever mortgages exist on the property.

Write Off As verb, is colloquial term for "deduct." Sometimes synonymous with the verb "Expense." Noun "write-off" means deduction.

Z

Zero Out Reduce taxable income (or tax liability) to zero.

TABLES OF AUTHORITIES

TABLE OF CASES CITED IN THE MAIN OUTLINE

TABLE OF INTERNAL REVENUE CODE SECTIONS

TA

TA

TA

TA

TABLE OF TREASURY REGULATIONS

TA

TABLE OF REVENUE RULINGS

TA

TA

ESTATE & GIFT TAX Casenote Law Outline Cross-Reference Chart	Bittker, Clark & McCouch 7th Ed. 1996	Bloom, Boyle, Gaubatz & Solomon 2nd Ed. 1998	Campfield, Dickinson & Turnier 21st Ed. 1999	Dodge 1st Ed. 1988	MacDaniel, Repetti & Caron 4th Ed. 1999
CHAPTER 1: Overview of the Federal Taxes on the Transfer of Wealth					
I. Nature of the Federal Transfer Taxes	19-21, 21-22, 28-29	11-23, 24, 26, 34	2-28, 257-264, 694-696	6-18, 59, 163, 223	1-12, 58-62, 696-722
II. Purposes and Effects	1-19, 559-560	9-11, 21, 609, 619, 632-639	2-3, 16, 24	19-30, 57, 246	44-48
III. Constitutionality	40-43, 221, 224, 282-286, 336-348	11-12, 14, 16	2, 24	57-58, 119-120	51, 49-50, 55-57
IV. History and Overview	1-18, 19	3, 7, 8-9, 24, 26, 30-34	2-3, 28, 257, 694	1-5, 16-47, 54-59, 107-109, 145-146, 153-154, 223-234	2-12, 58-60, 60-62, 696-703, 722
V. Jurisdiction to Tax	---	16, 24, 26, 30, 34, 36	29, 30, 150	59, 158	23-25
VI. Relationship to State Law	10, 29-39, 40, 552-553, 544	16	10-12, 15	144, 155-156, 242, 599	75-92, 91
VII. Relationship to Income Tax	13-14, 44, 57, 67-68, 118, 134, 150, 314, 434, 629-630	32-40, 36, 40-42	23, 31, 325, 367, 373	42-43, 92, 137-138, 246, 366-374, 370	18-19, 26-35, 717-718
CHAPTER 2: Gift Tax					
I. Federal Gift Tax Jurisdiction	---	11, 21, 24, 36	151-153	---	23-25, 49-57
II. Scope of Gift Tax	47-48, 49-88	155, 156-176	7, 28-29	179, 183, 215-219	70-74, 128-184
III. Identifying the Donor	125-133, 150-153, 155-157	209-210, 211, 213	32, 35, 46, 49, 56-59	200-201	58-60
IV. What Is a Transfer?	98-124, 78, 98-100, 104-110, 125, 235-237, 240-241	167-174, 177, 195, 197, 209	66, 67-78, 79, 80-82, 83-85, 86-95	164-167, 173-174, 533-535	129-146
V. Completed Gifts (Transfers Subject to Related Powers)	98, 104, 110, 119	155-176, 339-341, 367	7, 8, 10, 67-78, 1043, 1049, 1067	182-183, 188-191	147-169

Please visit **www.casenotes.com** for the latest version of the cross-reference chart.

Please visit **www.casenotes.com** for the latest version of the cross-reference chart.

ESTATE & GIFT TAX Casenote Law Outline Cross-Reference Chart	Bittker, Clark & McCouch 7th Ed. 1996	Bloom, Boyle, Gaubatz & Solomon 2nd Ed. 1998	Campfield, Dickinson & Turnier 21st Ed. 1999	Dodge 1st Ed. 1988	MacDaniel, Repetti & Caron 4th Ed. 1999
VI. Valuation of Gifts	48-58, 57-67, 79-88, 573-574	67-88, 209, 211, 213-214	32-58, 59-65	163, 211, 216, 218-219	58-60
VII. Retained-Interest Transfers	28, 124	300, 304, 310	67, 68-70, 71, 77	182-192	307, 318-323, 326-327
VIII. The Annual Exclusion	157-184	177, 178-183	108, 110-144, 145-147	206, 626-627	70
IX. Charitable Deduction	490, 465-490	215	150-151	172, 211, 609	544-574
X. Marital Deduction	490-550	216, 217	148-150	211-212, 219	683-684
XI. Gift Tax Computation	22-24, 28	24, 155-218	10-11, 153-155	179, 183, 215-219	58-60
XII. Gift Tax Procedure	643	24, 30	7, 151-155	218-221	26-43
CHAPTER 3: Estate Tax					
I. Estate Tax Jurisdiction of the United States	---	14-15, 63, 145, 153-154	257-264, 282, 289, 342, 405-408, 468	---	23-25, 60-62
II. Gross Estate	185-204	51, 52-57, 58	431-432, 434-443	59, 132	60, 94, 108-114
III. Valuation	25, 205-218, 574-577	67, 71-83, 84-87	525-536, 539-551	632-637	60-62, 809-829
IV. Deductions	437-558	90, 91, 90-98, 99, 100-135, 136, 145	552-559, 561-586, 588-672	132, 136-137, 140-142, 590-598	60-62, 503, 544
V. Tax Computation and Credits	22-24, 25, 573, 574-594	145, 146, 149, 152-153	675, 679-682, 684-686, 691	153-158, 184, 202-221, 569, 598-599, 623-624, 647	60-62
VI. Procedure and Practice	627-642	3, 14-15, 26, 30, 36, 63, 145, 153-154	678-680, 684, 685, 686	159-162, 220-221	27-29, 833-837
CHAPTER 4: Valuation					
I. The Willing-Buyer, Willing-Seller Test	573, 574	78-81	156, 158-162, 165-174	124, 637-644	779-781, 798-799, 800-803

CR

ESTATE & GIFT TAX Casenote Law Outline Cross-Reference Chart	Bittker, Clark & McCouch 7th Ed. 1996	Bloom, Boyle, Gaubatz & Solomon 2nd Ed. 1998	Campfield, Dickinson & Turnier 21st Ed. 1999	Dodge 1st Ed. 1988	MacDaniel, Repetti & Caron 4th Ed. 1999
II. Special Estate Valuation Rules	25-26, 63-65, 578-582, 621, 623-624	26, 67-87, 86	524, 529-536, 539-551	122-123, 127, 234-235, 632-637	60-62, 779-804, 809-829
III. Special Gift Tax Valuation Rules	68-73, 585-590	209-214	32-58, 59-65	192, 204, 205-206	58-60
IV. Special Generation-Skipping Tax Valuation Rules	507-568, 565, 566	232, 233-235	224-240, 690-700, 694	234-235	708-710
CHAPTER 5: The Generation-Skipping Tax					
I. Overview	28-29	7, 34-36, 221	694, 696-700	223-225	696-722
II. Generation-Skipping Transfers Defined	501, 104-110, 119-125, 235-246	34-36, 223-236, 237	696	225, 233, 240, 574-575	702-705, 706-708
III. The Tax Base	13, 44-46, 246, 432, 571	237, 238, 239-241	696, 698, 699	228-229, 231-232	708-711, 722
IV. The Tax Rate	22, 545-546, 567	34-36, 223	698, 699	224	712-716, 722
V. Credits and Miscellany	109, 554-557, 571	36, 236	697, 699, 700-701	242	717-718, 719-722
CHAPTER 6: Estate Planning Devices					
I. Inter Vivos Transfers	78, 98-110, 119-125	317-329, 331-337, 340-350, 359-379	431, 432-443	620-625, 626-629	429-443, 718, 908-918
II. Techniques Aimed to Freeze or Depress Value	585, 590-601	155, 381, 415, 421	224, 224-230, 233, 234-238	632, 633-648	809-829
III. Charitable Deduction Planning	465-490	136-144, 215	150-151, 561-586	609-612, 612-619	544-549, 556-570
IV. Planning Transfers Between Spouses	491-492, 495-502, 510-539, 542-550	56, 99-100, 216-217, 426, 482, 486, 435	588, 590-595, 595-623, 640-674	566-608	596-694
V. Liquidity Planning	602, 603-615, 617-620	36, 381-412, 415-435	106, 151-155, 675, 679-682, 684-686, 691	109-110, 140, 159-162, 261, 358, 562, 637-644	833-838, 844, 850-853

Please visit www.casenotes.com for the latest version of the cross-reference chart.

INDEX

Doctrinal points are found under the Estate Tax, Generation-Skipping Tax, and Gift Tax headings. Estate-planning devices, transactions, and miscellaneous terms are found as separate headings.

ID

ID

ID

ID

the Ultimate Outline

➤ **RENOWNED AUTHORS:** Every **Casenote Law Outline** is written by highly respected, nationally recognized professors.

➤ **KEYED TO CASENOTE LEGAL BRIEF BOOKS:** In most cases, **Casenote Law Outlines** work in conjunction with the **Casenote Legal Briefs** so that you can see how each case in your textbook relates to the entire subject area. In addition, **Casenote Law Outlines** are cross-referenced to most major casebooks.

➤ **FREE SUPPLEMENT SERVICE:** As part of being the most up-to-date legal outline on the market, whenever a new supplement is published, the corresponding outline can be updated for free using the supplement request form found in this book.

ADMINISTRATIVE LAW (1999) $21.95
　Charles H. Koch, Jr., Dudley W. Woodbridge Professor of Law, College of William and Mary
　Sidney A. Shapiro, John M. Rounds Professor of Law, University of Kansas

CIVIL PROCEDURE (1999) $22.95
　John B. Oakley, Professor of Law, University of California, Davis School of Law
　Rex R. Perschbacher, Dean of University of California, Davis School of Law

COMMERCIAL LAW (see SALES ● SECURED TRANSACTIONS ● NEGOTIABLE INSTRUMENTS & PAYMENT SYSTEMS)

CONFLICT OF LAWS (1996) $21.95
　Luther L. McDougal, III, W.R. Irby Professor of Law, Tulane University
　Robert L. Felix, James P. Mozingo, III, Professor of Law, University of South Carolina

CONSTITUTIONAL LAW (1997) $24.95
　Gary Goodpaster, Professor of Law, University of California, Davis School of Law

CONTRACTS (1999) $21.95
　Daniel Wm. Fessler, Professor of Law, University of California, Davis School of Law

CORPORATIONS (2000) $24.95
　Lewis D. Solomon, Arthur Selwin Miller Research Professor of Law, George Washington University
　Daniel Wm. Fessler, Professor of Law, University of California, Davis School of Law
　Arthur E. Wilmarth, Jr., Associate Professor of Law, George Washington University

CRIMINAL LAW (1999) $21.95
　Joshua Dressler, Professor of Law, McGeorge School of Law

CRIMINAL PROCEDURE (1999) $20.95
　Joshua Dressler, Professor of Law, McGeorge School of Law

ESTATE & GIFT TAX (2000) $21.95
　Joseph M. Dodge, W.H. Francis Professor of Law, University of Texas at Austin

EVIDENCE (1996) $23.95
　Kenneth Graham, Jr., Professor of Law, University of California, Los Angeles

FEDERAL COURTS (1997) $22.95
　Howard P. Fink, Isadore and Ida Topper Professor of Law, Ohio State University
　Linda S. Mullenix, Bernard J. Ward Centennial Professor of Law, University of Texas

FEDERAL INCOME TAXATION (1998) $22.95
　Joseph M. Dodge, W.H. Francis Professor of Law, University of Texas at Austin

LEGAL RESEARCH (1996) $21.95
　Nancy L. Schultz, Professor of Law, Chapman University
　Louis J. Sirico, Jr., Professor of Law, Villanova University

NEGOTIABLE INSTRUMENTS & PAYMENT SYSTEMS (1995) $22.95
　Donald B. King, Professor of Law, Saint Louis University
　Peter Winship, James Cleo Thompson, Sr. Trustee Professor, SMU

PROPERTY (1999) $22.95
　Sheldon F. Kurtz, Percy Bordwell Professor of Law, University of Iowa
　Patricia Cain, Professor of Law, University of Iowa

SALES (2000) $21.95
　Robert E. Scott, Dean and Lewis F. Powell, Jr. Professor of Law, University of Virginia
　Donald B. King, Professor of Law, Saint Louis University

SECURED TRANSACTIONS (1995 w/ '96 supp.) $20.95
　Donald B. King, Professor of Law, Saint Louis University

TORTS (1999) $22.95
　George C. Christie, James B. Duke Professor of Law, Duke University
　Jerry J. Phillips, W.P. Toms Professor of Law, University of Tennessee

WILLS, TRUSTS, & ESTATES (1996) $22.95
　William M. McGovern, Professor of Law, University of California, Los Angeles

CASENOTE LEGAL BRIEFS

PRICE LIST — EFFECTIVE JULY 1, 2000 ● *PRICES SUBJECT TO CHANGE WITHOUT NOTICE*

Ref. No.	Course	Adaptable to Courses Utilizing	Retail Price
1265	ADMINISTRATIVE LAW	ASIMOW, BONFIELD & LEVIN	21.00
1263	ADMINISTRATIVE LAW	BREYER, STEWART & SUNSTEIN	22.00
1266	ADMINISTRATIVE LAW	CASS, DIVER & BEERMAN	20.00
1260	ADMINISTRATIVE LAW	GELLHORN, B., S., R. & F.	20.00
1268	ADMINISTRATIVE LAW	FUNK, SHAPIRO & WEAVER	22.00
1264	ADMINISTRATIVE LAW	MASHAW, MERRILL & SHANE	21.50
1267	ADMINISTRATIVE LAW	REESE	20.00
1262	ADMINISTRATIVE LAW	SCHWARTZ	21.00
1350	AGENCY & PARTNERSHIP (ENT.ORG)	CONARD, KNAUSS & SIEGEL	24.00
1351	AGENCY & PARTNERSHIP	HYNES	24.00
1281	ANTITRUST (TRADE REGULATION)	HANDLER, P., G. & W.	20.50
1283	ANTITRUST	SULLIVAN & HOVENKAMP	21.00
1611	BANKING LAW	MACEY & MILLER	20.00
1305	BANKRUPTCY	JORDAN, WARREN & BUSSELL	20.00
1058	BUSINESS ASSOCIATIONS (CORPORATIONS)	KLEIN, RAMSEYER & BAINBRIDGE	24.00
1059	BUSINESS ORGANIZATIONS (CORPORATIONS)	SODERQUIST, S., C., & S.	24.00
1040	CIVIL PROCEDURE	COUND, F., M. & S	21.00
1043	CIVIL PROCEDURE	FIELD, KAPLAN & CLERMONT	23.00
1049	CIVIL PROCEDURE	FREER & PERDUE	19.00
1041	CIVIL PROCEDURE	HAZARD, TAIT & FLETCHER	22.00
1047	CIVIL PROCEDURE	MARCUS, REDISH & SHERMAN	22.00
1044	CIVIL PROCEDURE	ROSENBERG, S. & D.	23.00
1046	CIVIL PROCEDURE	YEAZELL	20.00
1311	COMM'L LAW	FARNSWORTH, H., R., H. & M.	22.00
1312	COMM'L LAW	JORDAN, WARREN & WALT	22.00
1310	COMM'L LAW (SALES/SEC.TR./PAY.LAW [Sys.])	SPEIDEL, SUMMERS & WHITE	24.00
1313	COMM'L LAW (SALES/SEC.TR./PAY.LAW)	WHALEY	23.00
1314	COMMERCIAL TRANSACTIONS	LOPUKI, W., K. & M.	22.00
1320	COMMUNITY PROPERTY	BIRD	20.50
1630	COMPARATIVE LAW	SCHLESINGER, B., D., H.& W.	19.00
1048	COMPLEX LITIGATION	MARCUS & SHERMAN	20.00
1072	CONFLICTS	BRILMAYER	20.00
1071	CONFLICTS	CRAMTON, C. K., & K.	20.00
1070	CONFLICTS	HAY, WEINTRAUB & BORCHER	23.00
1073	CONFLICTS	SYMEONIDES, P., & M.	23.00
1086	CONSTITUTIONAL LAW	BREST, LEVINSON, B.& A.	21.00
1082	CONSTITUTIONAL LAW	COHEN & VARAT	24.00
1088	CONSTITUTIONAL LAW	FARBER, ESKRIDGE & FRICKEY	21.00
1080	CONSTITUTIONAL LAW	GUNTHER & SULLIVAN	21.00
1081	CONSTITUTIONAL LAW	LOCKHART, K., C., S. & F.	21.00
1085	CONSTITUTIONAL LAW	ROTUNDA	23.00
1089	CONSTITUTIONAL LAW (FIRST AMENDMENT)	SHIFFRIN & CHOPER	18.00
1087	CONSTITUTIONAL LAW	STONE, S., S. & T.	22.00
1103	CONTRACTS	BARNETT	24.00
1102	CONTRACTS	BURTON	23.00
1017	CONTRACTS	CALAMARI, PERILLO & BENDER	26.00
1101	CONTRACTS	CRANDALL & WHALEY	23.00
1014	CONTRACTS	DAWSON, HARVEY & H.	22.00
1010	CONTRACTS	FARNSWORTH & YOUNG	20.00
1011	CONTRACTS	FULLER & EISENBERG	24.00
1013	CONTRACTS	KESSLER, GILMORE & KRONMAN	26.00
1016	CONTRACTS	KNAPP & CRYSTAL	23.50
1012	CONTRACTS	MURPHY & SPEIDEL	25.00
1015	CONTRACTS	ROSETT	24.00
1019	CONTRACTS	VERNON	23.00
1502	COPYRIGHT	GOLDSTEIN	21.00
1504	COPYRIGHT	JOYCE, PETRY, L. & J.	20.00
1501	COPYRIGHT	NIMMER, M., M. & N.	22.50
1218	CORPORATE TAXATION	LIND, S. L. & R	17.00
1050	CORPORATIONS	CARY & EISENBERG	22.00
1054	CORPORATIONS	CHOPER, COFFEE, & GILSON	24.50
1350	CORPORATIONS (ENTERPRISE ORG.)	CONARD, KNAUSS & SIEGEL	24.00
1053	CORPORATIONS	HAMILTON	22.00
1058	CORPORATIONS (BUSINESS ASSOCIATIONS)	KLEIN, RAMSEYER & BAINBRIDGE	24.00
1057	CORPORATIONS	O'KELLEY & THOMPSON	21.00
1059	CORPORATIONS (BUSINESS ORG.)	SODERQUIST, S., C.& S.	24.00
1056	CORPORATIONS	SOLOMON, S., B. & W.	22.00
1052	CORPORATIONS	VAGTS	21.00
1300	CREDITOR'S RIGHTS (DEBTOR-CREDITOR)	RIESENFELD	24.00
1550	CRIMINAL JUSTICE	WEINREB	21.00
1029	CRIMINAL LAW	BONNIE, C., J. & L.	20.00
1020	CRIMINAL LAW	BOYCE & PERKINS	25.00
1028	CRIMINAL LAW	DRESSLER	24.00
1027	CRIMINAL LAW	JOHNSON	22.00
1021	CRIMINAL LAW	KADISH & SCHULHOFER	22.00
1026	CRIMINAL LAW	KAPLAN, WEISBERG & BINDER	21.00
1205	CRIMINAL PROCEDURE	ALLEN, KUHNS & STUNTZ	20.00
1206	CRIMINAL PROCEDURE	DRESSLER & THOMAS	25.00
1202	CRIMINAL PROCEDURE	HADDAD, Z., S. & B.	23.00
1200	CRIMINAL PROCEDURE	KAMISAR, LAFAVE & ISRAEL	22.00
1204	CRIMINAL PROCEDURE	SALTZBURG & CAPRA	20.00
1300	DEBTOR-CREDITOR (CREDITORS RIGHTS)	RIESENFELD	24.00
1304	DEBTOR-CREDITOR	WARREN & WESTBROOK	22.00
1224	DECEDENTS ESTATES (TRUSTS)	RITCHIE, A, & E.(DOBRIS/STERK).	24.00
1222	DECEDENTS ESTATES	SCOLES, HALBACH, L. & R.	24.50
	DOMESTIC RELATIONS *(see FAMILY LAW)*		
3000	EDUCATION LAW (COURSE OUTLINE)	AQUILA & PETZKE	28.50
1670	EMPLOYMENT DISCRIMINATION	FRIEDMAN & STRICKLER	20.00
1671	EMPLOYMENT DISCRIMINATION	ZIMMER, SULLIVAN, R. & C.	21.00
1660	EMPLOYMENT LAW	ROTHSTEIN, KNAPP & LIEBMAN	22.50
1342	ENVIRONMENTAL LAW	ANDERSON, MANDELKER & T.	19.00
1341	ENVIRONMENTAL LAW	FINDLEY & FARBER	21.00
1345	ENVIRONMENTAL LAW	MENELL & STEWART	20.00
1344	ENVIRONMENTAL LAW	PERCIVAL, MILLER, S. & L.	21.00
1343	ENVIRONMENTAL LAW	PLATER, A., G. & G.	20.00
1217	ESTATE & GIFT TAXATION	BITTKER, CLARK & McCOUCH	18.00

Ref. No.	Course	Adaptable to Courses Utilizing	Retail Price
	ETHICS *(see PROFESSIONAL RESPONSIBILITY)*		
1063	EVIDENCE	LEMPERT, GROSS & LIEBMAN	TBA
1066	EVIDENCE	MUELLER & KIRKPATRICK	20.00
1064	EVIDENCE	STRONG, BROUN & M.	25.50
1062	EVIDENCE	WELLBORN	25.00
1061	EVIDENCE	WALTZ & PARK	21.00
1060	EVIDENCE	WEINSTEIN, M., A. & B.	25.50
1244	FAMILY LAW (DOMESTIC RELATIONS)	AREEN	25.00
1242	FAMILY LAW (DOMESTIC RELATIONS)	CLARK & ESTIN	22.00
1245	FAMILY LAW (DOMESTIC RELATIONS)	ELLMAN, KURTZ & BARTLETT	23.00
1246	FAMILY LAW (DOMESTIC RELATIONS)	HARRIS, T. & W.	22.00
1243	FAMILY LAW (DOMESTIC RELATIONS)	KRAUSE, O., E. & G.	27.00
1240	FAMILY LAW (DOMESTIC RELATIONS)	WADLINGTON & O'BRIEN	23.00
1247	FAMILY LAW (DOMESTIC RELATIONS)	WEISBERG & APPLETON	22.00
1360	FEDERAL COURTS	FALLON, M. & S. (HART & W.)	22.00
1360	FEDERAL COURTS	HART & WECHSLER (FALLON)	22.00
1363	FEDERAL COURTS	LOW & JEFFRIES	19.00
1361	FEDERAL COURTS	McCORMICK, C. & W.	23.00
1364	FEDERAL COURTS	REDISH & SHERRY	20.00
1690	FEDERAL INDIAN LAW	GETCHES, W. & W.	23.00
1089	FIRST AMENDMENT (CONSTITUTIONAL LAW)	SHIFFRIN & CHOPER	18.00
1700	GENDER AND LAW (SEX DISCRIMINATION)	BARTLETT & HARRIS	22.00
1510	GRATUITOUS TRANSFERS	CLARK, L., M., A., & M.	21.00
1651	HEALTH CARE LAW	CURRAN, H., B. & O.	24.00
1650	HEALTH LAW	FURROW, J., J. & S.	20.50
1640	IMMIGRATION LAW	ALEINIKOFF, MARTIN & M.	19.00
1641	IMMIGRATION LAW	LEGOMSKY	22.00
1690	INDIAN LAW	GETCHES, W. & W.	23.00
1373	INSURANCE LAW	ABRAHAM	23.00
1371	INSURANCE LAW	KEETON	24.00
1370	INSURANCE LAW	YOUNG & HOLMES	20.00
1503	INTELLECTUAL PROPERTY	MERGES, M.& J.	22.00
1394	INTERNATIONAL BUSINESS TRANSACTIONS	FOLSOM, GORDON & SPANOGLE	18.00
1393	INTERNATIONAL LAW	CARTER & TRIMBLE	19.00
1392	INTERNATIONAL LAW	HENKIN, P., S. & S.	20.00
1390	INTERNATIONAL LAW	OLIVER, F., B., S. & W.	25.00
1331	LABOR LAW	COX, BOK, GORMAN & FINKIN	22.00
1471	LAND FINANCE (REAL ESTATE TRANS.)	BERGER & JOHNSTONE	21.00
1620	LAND FINANCE (REAL ESTATE TRANS.)	NELSON & WHITMAN	21.00
1452	LAND USE	CALLIES, FREILICH & ROBERTS	20.00
1421	LEGISLATION	ESKRIDGE, FRICKEY & GARRETT	18.00
1480	MASS MEDIA	FRANKLIN & ANDERSON	18.00
1312	NEGOTIABLE INSTRUMENTS (COMM. LAW)	JORDAN, WARREN & WALT	22.00
1541	OIL & GAS	KUNTZ, L., A., S. & P.	21.00
1540	OIL & GAS	MAXWELL, WILLIAMS, M. & K.	21.00
1561	PATENT LAW	ADELMAN, R., T. & W.	25.00
1560	PATENT LAW	FRANCIS & COLLINS	26.00
1310	PAYMENT LAW [SYST.][COMM. LAW]	SPEIDEL, SUMMERS & WHITE	25.00
1313	PAYMENT LAW (COMM.LAW / NEG. INST.)	WHALEY	23.00
1431	PRODUCTS LIABILITY	OWEN, MONTGOMERY & K.	25.00
1091	PROF. RESPONSIBILITY (ETHICS)	GILLERS	16.00
1093	PROF. RESPONSIBILITY (ETHICS)	HAZARD, KONIAK, & CRAMTON	21.00
1092	PROF. RESPONSIBILITY (ETHICS)	MORGAN & ROTUNDA	16.00
1094	PROF. RESPONSIBILITY (ETHICS)	SCHWARTZ, W. & P.	16.00
1030	PROPERTY	CASNER & LEACH -(by F., K. & V.	24.00
1031	PROPERTY	CRIBBET, J., F. & S.	24.50
1037	PROPERTY	DONAHUE, KAUPER & MARTIN	21.00
1035	PROPERTY	DUKEMINIER & KRIER	20.00
1034	PROPERTY	HAAR & LIEBMAN	23.50
1036	PROPERTY	KURTZ & HOVENKAMP	21.00
1033	PROPERTY	NELSON, STOEBUCK, & W.	23.50
1032	PROPERTY	RABIN & KWALL	23.00
1038	PROPERTY	SINGER	21.50
1621	REAL ESTATE TRANSACTIONS	GOLDSTEIN & KORNGOLD	21.00
1471	REAL ESTATE TRANS. & FIN. (LAND FINANCE)	BERGER & JOHNSTONE	21.00
1620	REAL ESTATE TRANSFER & FINANCE	NELSON & WHITMAN	21.00
1254	REMEDIES (EQUITY)	LAYCOCK	23.00
1253	REMEDIES (EQUITY)	LEAVELL, L., N. & K-F.	24.00
1252	REMEDIES (EQUITY)	RE & RE	26.00
1255	REMEDIES (EQUITY)	SHOBEN & TABB	25.50
1250	REMEDIES (EQUITY)	RENDLEMAN	28.00
1310	SALES (COMM. LAW)	SPEIDEL, SUMMERS & WHITE	25.00
1313	SALES (COMM. LAW)	WHALEY	23.00
1312	SECURED TRANS. (COMMERICIAL LAW)	JORDAN, WARREN & WALT	22.00
1310	SECURED TRANS.	SPEIDEL, SUMMERS & WHITE	25.00
1313	SECURED TRANS. (COMMERCIAL LAW)	WHALEY	23.00
1272	SECURITIES REGULATION	COX, HILLMAN, LANGEVOORT	21.00
1270	SECURITIES REGULATION	JENNINGS, M., C. & S.	21.00
1680	SPORTS LAW	WEILER & ROBERTS	20.50
1217	TAXATION (ESTATE & GIFT)	BITTKER, CLARK & McCOUCH	18.00
1219	TAXATION (INDIV. INCOME)	BURKE & FRIEL	22.00
1212	TAXATION (FEDERAL INCOME)	FREELAND, L., S. & L.	21.00
1211	TAXATION (FEDERAL INCOME)	GRAETZ & SCHENK	20.00
1210	TAXATION (FEDERAL INCOME)	KLEIN, BANKMAN & SHAVIRO	21.00
1218	TAXATION (CORPORATE)	LIND, S., L. & R.	17.00
1006	TORTS	DOBBS	22.00
1003	TORTS	EPSTEIN	23.50
1004	TORTS	FRANKLIN & RABIN	20.50
1001	TORTS	HENDERSON, P. & S.	23.50
1000	TORTS	PROSSER, W., S., K. & P.	25.00
1005	TORTS	SHULMAN, JAMES & GRAY	25.00
1281	TRADE REGULATION (ANTITRUST)	HANDLER, P., G. & W.	20.50
1410	U.C.C.	EPSTEIN, MARTIN, H. & N.	18.00
1510	WILLS/TRUSTS (GRATUITOUS TRANSFER)	CLARK, L., M., A., & M.	21.00
1223	WILLS, TRUSTS & ESTATES	DUKEMINIER & JOHANSON	22.00
1220	WILLS	MECHEM & ATKINSON	23.00

CASENOTES PUBLISHING CO. INC. ● 1640 FIFTH STREET, SUITE 208 ● SANTA MONICA, CA 90401 ● (310) 395-6500

E-Mail Address - info@casenotes.com
Website - www: http://www.casenotes.com